Table 2. THE MOST IMPORTANT RADICALS
(arranged by position within the character)

HEN (left)	亻 9	氵 15	口 30	土 32	女 38	弓 57	彳 60
	忄 61	扌 64	方 70	日 72	木 75	礻 85	火 86
	牛 93	犭 94	王 96	目 109	矢 111	石 112	礻 113
	禾 115	米 119	糸 120	月 130	舟 137	衤 145	言 149
	貝 154	車 159	金 167	阝 170	馬 187		
TSUKURI (right)	刂 18	力 19	卩 26	彡 59	攵 66	斤 69	欠 76
	殳 79	阝 163	隹 172	頁 181			
KANMURI (top)	亠 8	八 12	冖 14	宀 40	癶 105	穴 116	竹 118
	罒 122	耂 125	艹 140	雨 173			
ASHI (bottom)	儿 10	心 61	灬 86	皿 108	貝 154		
KAMAE (enclosure)	冂 13	匸 22	囗 31	戈 62	行 144	門 169	
TARE (upper left border)	厂 27	尸 44	广 53	疒 104			
NYŌ (lower left border)	廴 54	走 156	辶 162				

KANJI AND KANA

KANJI & KANA

A HANDBOOK AND DICTIONARY
OF THE JAPANESE WRITING SYSTEM

by Wolfgang Hadamitzky and Mark Spahn

CHARLES E. TUTTLE COMPANY
Rutland · Vermont : Tokyo · Japan

German-language edition published
in 1979 by Verlag Enderle GmbH, Tokyo
in 1980 by Langenscheidt KG, Berlin and Munich

Published by the Charles E. Tuttle Company, Inc.
of Rutland, Vermont and Tokyo, Japan
with editorial offices at
Suido 1-chome, 2–6, Bunkyo-ku, Tokyo

Copyright in Japan, 1981
by Charles E. Tuttle Co., Inc.

Library of Congress Catalog Card No. 81–50106
International Standard Book No. 0–8048 1373–6

First printing, 1981
Thirteenth printing, 1989

Printed in Japan

TABLE OF CONTENTS

LIST OF TABLES

PREFACE

The aim of this book is to present a systematic and comprehensive introduction to the modern Japanese writing system. It is intended primarily as a textbook, to be used in conjunction with the three accompanying writing-practice manuals, for those who wish to acquire in the shortest possible time a practical working knowledge of the written language, either active or passive. But it serves equally as a concise dictionary of Japanese writing: its indexes and tables allow the reader to look up any of the 2,000 or so characters and written symbols which are dealt with.

In addition, the introductory chapters will be of use to linguists, travelers, devotees of Japanese art and culture, and others who desire only to familiarize themselves with the basics or certain aspects of the writing system.

The first part of this text deals with transliteration; the *kana* syllabaries; punctuation; and the origin, form, reading, writing, and dictionary arrangement of *kanji*. The bulk of the book consists of a list of the 1,900 basic *kanji* which the Japanese Language Council (Kokugo Shingikai), organized by the Ministry of Education, recommended for general use on January 21, 1977. The order of presentation is based on pedagogical principles, proceeding from the simplest and most often used characters to those which are more complex and occur less frequently. Within this general framework, characters which are graphically similar and easily confused are presented together in order to call attention to their similarities and differences in form, reading, and meaning.

Each character is presented along with its stroke order, readings, meanings, and a brief list of its most important compounds, consisting exclusively of characters which have already been introduced and are therefore already familiar, with a cross-reference number to the main entry for each.

Associated with the 1,900 characters are 4,032 readings, some 2,000 of which represent independent words. Approximately 9,000 compounds are given to show how the characters are used in combination. In all, the Kanji List contains a basic vocabulary of about 11,000 words.

For easy reference, the 1,900 characters are listed in three indexes at the end of the book, arranged respectively according to radicals, stroke count, and readings.

In 1981, while this book was in the making, the Japanese Language Council recommended a new list of 1,945 characters called Jōyō Kanji (Characters for Daily Use). This consists of the 1,900 characters in the 1977 proposal—and hence in this book's Kanji List—plus an additional 45. To bring the book fully up to date, these 45 characters have been added as a special Supplement, with separate indexes. The Kanji List and the Supplement thus encompass all 1,945 Jōyō Kanji.

With the simultaneous use of a Japanese language text in an intensive course of study, the student should be able to master all the characters with their most important meanings, readings, and compounds in about two years. He will then be able to read Japanese newspapers and other texts which adhere to the list of characters prescribed by the government, without the time-consuming chore of looking up characters. (This, however, does not apply to proper names, which frequently have exceptional readings or employ rather uncommon characters.)

The authors hope that this work, by making possible direct access to written sources, will provide a solid basis for a more than superficial treatment of the language and culture of Japan. For it is primarily the barriers of the spoken and written language that hinder the foreigner in his understanding of a country which deserves our interest for more reasons than its economic and political importance alone.

The authors wish to thank Teisuke Higuchi, who wrote the characters in the Kanji List; Yuriko Yamada, who did the calligraphy on the title page; Hiroko Kikuchi, who proofread the Japanese portions of the manuscript and assisted in the preparation of the indexes; Volker Hartmann, who provided valuable encouragement in the preparation of the manuscript; and the Charles E. Tuttle Company and its editorial staff.

We are much indebted to the following works, to which reference was made in the course of writing this book:

Alfonso, Anthony: *The Japanese Writing System,* Sophia University, Tokyo, 1972

Arahari, Kazuko: *Hyōki: Kyōshi-yō Nihongo Kyōiku Handobukku 2,* Japan Foundation, Tokyo, 1975

Atarashii Kokugo Hyōki Handobukku, Sanseidō, Tokyo, 1977

Crowley, Dale P.: *Manual for Reading Japanese,* The University Press of Hawaii, Honolulu, 1972

Emori, Kenji: *Tōyō Kanji no Hitsujun,* Nihon Shūji Fukyū Kyōkai, Tokyo, 1970

Gaikokujin no Tame no Kanji Jiten, Agency for Cultural Affairs, Tokyo, 2nd ed. 1973

Jorden, Eleanor Harz, and Chaplin, Hamako Itō: *Reading Japanese,* Yale University Press, New Haven, 1976; Tuttle, Tokyo, 1977

Kawashima, Yutaka: *Shōgakusei no Tame no Kanji o Oboeru Jiten,* Ōbunsha, Tokyo, 1975

Kindaichi, Kyōsuke, ed.: *Shin-Meikai Kokugo Jiten,* Sanseidō, Tokyo, 1972

Kotoba no Shirube, Gakkō Tosho, Tokyo, 1971

Lewin, Bruno: *Abriss der japanischen Grammatik,* Harrassowitz, Wiesbaden, 1959

Masuda, Koh, ed.: *New Japanese–English Dictionary,* Kenkyūsha, Tokyo, 4th ed. 1974

Ministry of Education, ed.: *Hitsujun Shidō no Tebiki,* Hakubundō, Tokyo, 1958

Naganuma, Naoe: *Characters for Daily Use and Personal Names,* Chōfūsha, Tokyo, 1972

Nelson, Andrew Nathaniel: *The Modern Reader's Japanese–English Character Dictionary,* Tuttle, Rutland and Tokyo, 2nd rev. ed. 1974

Nishio, Minoru; Iwabuchi, Etsutarō; and Mizutani, Shizuo: *Iwanami Kokugo Jiten,* Iwanami Shoten, Tokyo, 1971

Okutsu, Hikoshige: *Wa–Doku Jiten,* Hakusuisha, Tokyo, 1959

O'Neill, Patrick G.: *Essential Kanji,* Weatherhill, New York and Tokyo, 1973

PREFACE

Pye, Michael: *The Study of Kanji,* Hokuseidō Press, Tokyo, 1971
Sakade, Florence, ed.: *A Guide to Reading & Writing Kanji,* Tuttle, Rutland and Tokyo, rev. ed. 1961
Satō, Kiyoji; Katō, Akihiko; and Hida, Yoshifumi: *Tōyō Kanji Hyōki Jiten,* Ōfūsha, Tokyo, 1975
Shin-Kanjihyō Shian, Kokugo Shingikai, Tokyo, 1977
Shinmura, Izuru: *Kōjien,* Iwanami Shoten, Tokyo, 1969
Shiraishi, Daiji, ed.: *Tōyō Kanjihyō; Kaitei Tōyō Kanji On-Kunhyō; Gendai Kanazukai; Kaitei Okurigana no Tsukekata,* Ōkurashō Insatsukyoku, 1974
Takatsuka, Chikudō: *Kakikata Jiten,* Nobarasha, Tokyo, 1974
Tōdō, Akiyasu: *Kanji Gogen Jiten,* Gakutosha, Tokyo, 1965
Zahl, Karl F.: *Japanische Schriftlehre,* privately published, Tokyo, 1973

———— 1. INTRODUCTION ————

Written Japanese consists of a mixture of several types of symbols, each with its own function:

■ *Kanji*
These pictographic-ideographic characters, adopted from the Chinese language, are used for conceptual words (mainly substantives, verbs, and adjectives) and indigenous names.

■ *Kana*
These phonetic symbols were developed in Japan. Each symbol represents the sound of one syllable. Kana are divided into two groups (syllabaries):
1. *Hiragana* are used to write the inflectional endings of the conceptual words written in kanji, as well as all types of native words not written in kanji.
2. *Katakana* are used chiefly for words of foreign origin.

Besides these, one often finds in Japanese texts roman letters and arabic numerals; for example, the name of the semigovernmental radio and television broadcasting corporation, Nippon Hōsō Kyōkai, is abbreviated NHK (the letters are pronounced as in English), and in horizontal writing, the use of arabic numerals rather than the corresponding kanji is usual.

There has never existed an independent, purely Japanese system of writing. Around the seventh century the attempt was first made to use Chinese characters to note down Japanese speech. In the ninth century the Japanese simplified the complex Chinese ideographs into what are now the kana. Each of the two kana syllabaries allows one to represent any syllable occurring in the Japanese language, so that it is quite possible to write exclusively in kana (and in fact telegrams and computer printouts are written in kana alone). In practice, however, this would hamper communication due to the large number of words pronounced alike but different in meaning (homophones), which are distinguished from one another by the use of different kanji. The same problem of ambiguity holds for romanized Japanese, which otherwise presents no problems.

Japanese today is written either in vertical columns proceeding from right to left or in horizontal lines which are read from left to right. The traditional vertical style is seen mostly in literary works. The horizontal European style, recommended by the Ministry of Education, is found more in technical literature and works dealing with the natural sciences. Newspapers use both styles: most articles are written vertically, head-lines and advertisements appear in both styles, and radio and television program listings are given horizontally.

Letters and other handwritten Japanese may be written vertically or horizontally. The type of manuscript paper *(genkō yōshi)* commonly used in Japan contains either 200 or 400 squares per page, usually arranged in vertical columns. Each written symbol, including the punctuation marks, takes up a full space. For writing practice it is recommended that the beginner use either *genkō yōshi* or the practice manuals which accompany this text.

Whether handwritten or printed, the individual characters are written separately one after another; the characters of a single word are not strung together, nor are any blank spaces left between words. There is no distinction analogous to that between capital and lowercase letters. Hence the conventions governing the use of kanji and kana for various types of words aid the reader in determining where one word ends and the next begins.

As with roman letters, there are a few differences between the printed and handwritten forms, and these differences sometimes make character recognition difficult for the beginner. In order to familiarize the student with these differences, each of the 1,900 kanji presented in the Kanji List and in the practice manuals appears three ways: in brush form, in pen form, and in printed form. Within the printed form there are various typefaces, but the differences between them are usually insignificant.

In handwriting (with brush or pen) three styles are distinguished:

1. The standard style *(kaisho)*, which is taught as the norm in elementary school and which is practically identical to the printed form. All the handwritten characters in the Kanji List are given in the standard style.
2. The semicursive style *(gyōsho)*, a simplification of the standard style which allows one to write more flowingly and rapidly.
3. The cursive style or "grass hand" *(sōsho)*, which is a kind of calligraphic shorthand resulting from extreme simplification according to esthetic standards.

| KAISHO | GYŌSHO | SŌSHO |

In addition, several frequently used characters are sometimes written in greatly simplified forms which are not officially recognized; for example, the character 曜 is sometimes simplified to 旺 and 第 to 㐧. And let it be noted in passing that there is also a Japanese shorthand intended for purely practical rather than artistic purposes. The typewriter does not lend itself to the writing of Japanese; it is much faster to write out a business letter or manuscript by hand than to manipulate a Japanese typewriter with its over two thousand pieces of type.

2. ROMANIZATION

The transliteration of Japanese words and texts into roman letters presents no problems; the Japanese language can easily be transliterated by using only 22 roman letters and 2 simple diacritical marks.

Why then have the Japanese not adopted such an alphabet to replace a system of writing which even they find difficult? The answer lies in the large number of homophones, especially in the written language: even in context it is frequently impossible to uniquely determine the sense of a word without knowing the characters it is written with. Other rational as well as more emotional considerations, including a certain inertia, make it very unlikely that the Japanese writing system will undergo a thorough overhaul anytime soon.

In 1952 the Japanese government issued recommendations for the transliteration of Japanese into roman letters. Table 3 on pages 16 and 17 summarizes the two recommended systems of romanization, the *kunrei-shiki rōmaji* system and the Hepburn system, which differ only slightly and are both in use today. Where the two systems differ, the table gives both romanizations, in the form: Hepburn/*kunrei-shiki*. Parentheses enclose romanizations that apply only when the kana are used as grammatical particles.

■ The kunrei-shiki rōmaji system

This system is patterned after the Fifty-Sounds Table *(gojū-on zu),* the five-by-ten grid in which each kana syllabary is conventionally arranged (although the layout contains several blank spaces, and diacritical marks are not shown). In the *kunrei-shiki* the initial consonant sound of all five syllables in each row is represented uniformly with the same roman letter, despite any phonetic variation associated with different final vowel sounds. The government introduced the *kunrei-shiki* for official use in 1937, in a form which differs only slightly from that used today.

■ The Hebon-shiki rōmaji or Hepburn system

This system is similar to the *kunrei-shiki,* except that the consonant sounds in the same row are not represented uniformly with the same letter. The Hebon-shiki was developed by a commission of Japanese and foreign scholars in 1885 and was widely disseminated a year later through its use in a Japanese–English dictionary compiled by the American missionary and philologist James Curtis Hepburn (in Japanese: Hebon). In the Hepburn system the consonant sounds are spelled as in English, and the vowel sounds as in Italian.

Although the *kunrei-shiki* has a more systematic one-to-one relationship with actual Japanese orthography, the much more widely known Hebon-shiki is better suited to texts intended for foreigners. "Fuji," the name of Japan's sacred mountain, is written *Huzi* in the *kunrei-shiki* and *Fuji* in the Hepburn system. As illustrated by this example, the Hepburn system allows an English speaker to approximate the original Japanese pronunciation without the need to remember any unfamiliar pronunciation rules, and is therefore less likely to lead the student into mispronunciations. For these reasons the Hepburn system has been adopted for all transliterations in this book.

The following additional transliteration rules are taken from official recommendations. The examples as well as the remarks in parentheses have been added. (For an explanation of the corresponding kana orthography, see Orthography, page 30.)

1. The end-of-syllable sound ん is always written *n* (even when it appears before the labials *b, p,* or *m* and is phonetically assimilated to *m*: *konban, kanpai, kanmuri*).
2. When the end-of-syllable sound *n* is followed by a vowel or *y*, an apostrophe ['] is inserted to indicate that *n* should not be slurred together with the following syllable: *man'ichi, kon'yaku.*
3. Assimilated, or "stretched," sounds *(soku-on)* are represented (as in Italian) by double consonants: *mikka, massugu, hatten, kippu; sh* becomes *ssh, ch* becomes *tch,* and *ts* becomes *tts: ressha, botchan, mittsu.*
4. Long (double) vowels are marked with a circumflex [^] (this does not correspond to the kana orthography), and if a long vowel is capitalized it may be doubled instead. (In practice the simpler macron [‾] has become prevalent: *mā, yūjin, dōzo.* The long *i* is indicated by double *i: oniisan.* The long *e* is indicated in words of Chinese origin by writing *ei: meishi;* and in words of Japanese origin by a macron: *onēsan.* In foreign words and names written in katakana, the long *i* and *e* are written with a macron if they are represented in katakana by a lengthening stroke [—]: ビール *bīru,* メートル *mētoru,* ベートーベン *Bētōben;* but the long *e* vowel is written *ei* if it is represented by successive katakana instead of a lengthening stroke: スペイン *Supein,* エイト *eito.*)
5. For the representation of certain sounds there are no binding rules. (Short, suddenly broken-off vowels at the ends of words or syllables—

Table 3. TRANSLITERATION

The Fifty-Sounds Table (within darker lines) and supplementary tables, with				
	あア a	いイ i	うウ u	えエ e	おオ o
k	かカ ka	きキ ki	くク ku	けケ ke	こコ ko
s	さサ sa	しシ shi/si	すス su	せセ se	そソ so
t	たタ ta	ちチ chi/ti	つツ tsu/tu	てテ te	とト to
n	なナ na	にニ ni	ぬヌ nu	ねネ ne	のノ no
h	はハ ha(wa)	ひヒ hi	ふフ fu/hu	へヘ he(e)	ほホ ho
m	まマ ma	みミ mi	むム mu	めメ me	もモ mo
y	やヤ ya		ゆユ yu		よヨ yo
r	らラ ra	りリ ri	るル ru	れレ re	ろロ ro
w	わワ wa	—	—	—	をヲ o
					んン n
g	がガ ga	ぎギ gi	ぐグ gu	げゲ ge	ごゴ go
z	ざザ za	じジ ji/zi	ずズ zu	ぜゼ ze	ぞゾ zo
d	だダ da	ぢヂ ji/zi	づヅ zu	でデ de	どド do
b	ばバ ba	びビ bi	ぶブ bu	べベ be	ぼボ bo
p	ぱパ pa	ぴピ pi	ぷプ pu	ぺペ pe	ぽポ po
	a	i	u	e	o

きゃキャ kya	きゅキュ kyu	きょキョ kyo
しゃシャ sha/sya	しゅシュ shu/syu	しょショ sho/syo
ちゃチャ cha/tya	ちゅチュ chu/tyu	ちょチョ cho/tyo
にゃニャ nya	にゅニュ nyu	にょニョ nyo
ひゃヒャ hya	ひゅヒュ hyu	ひょヒョ hyo
みゃミャ mya	みゅミュ myu	みょミョ myo
—	—	—
りゃリャ rya	りゅリュ ryu	りょリョ ryo
—		—

ぎゃギャ gya	ぎゅギュ gyu	ぎょギョ gyo
じゃジャ ja/zya	じゅジュ ju/zyu	じょジョ jo/zyo
—	—	—
びゃビャ bya	びゅビュ byu	びょビョ byo
ぴゃピャ pya	ぴゅピュ pyu	ぴょピョ pyo
ya	yu	yo

hiragana to the left and katakana to the right above each transliteration

— 17 —

glottal stops, or *soku-on*—are denoted in this book by adding an apostrophe: *a', are', ji'*.)

6. Proper names and the first word of every sentence are capitalized. The capitalization of substantives is optional: *Ogenki desu ka? Nippon, Tōkyō, Tanaka, Genji Monogatari, jūdō* or *Jūdō*.

A close examination of Table 3 and these six rules shows that the transliteration system is based partly on the Japanese syllabary and partly on phonetic considerations.

The only real problem in romanizing Japanese text, in which there are no spaces between words, is in deciding where one word ends and the next begins. There are no universal rules for this, but, as a basic principle, components which are perceived to be independent units are written separately: *Hon o sagashite iru n desu*. Hyphenation is used for various suffixes and other word units that one does not want to run together but does not want to write separately either: *Tōkyō-to, Minato-ku, Endō-san*. For readability, long compounds are broken up into smaller units: *Nihon Shoki, kaigai ryokō, minshu shugi*.

——————— 3. THE KANA ———————

ORIGIN

The characters in Chinese texts brought into Japan via Korea, beginning in the fourth century, gradually came to be adopted by the Japanese for the writing of their own language, for which there was no native system of writing. The Chinese characters were used phonetically to represent similar-sounding Japanese syllables; the meanings of the characters were ignored. In this way one could represent phonetically any Japanese word. But since each Chinese character corresponded to only one syllable, in order to write a single multisyllabic Japanese word one had to employ several kanji, which frequently consist of a large number of strokes. To simplify this bothersome process, instead of the full angular style *(kaisho)* of the kanji a cursive, simplified, derivative style *(sōsho)* was used. In addition, the flowing and expressive lines of the *sōsho* style were felt to be better suited to literary notation. Toward the end of the Nara period (710–94) and during the Heian period (794–1185) these symbols underwent a further simplification, in which esthetic considerations played a part, resulting in a stock of linguistic symbols which was extensive enough to encompass the entire sound system of the Japanese language. This was the decisive step in the formation of a purely phonetic system of representing syllables. These simple syllable-symbols, today known as hiragana, were formerly referred to as *onna-de,* "ladies' hand," since they were first used, in letters and literary writing, by women of the Heian period, who were ignorant of the exclusively male domain of Chinese learning and literature and the use of Chinese characters. But the hiragana gradually came to prevail as a standard syllabary.

The katakana symbols were developed only a little later than the hiragana. While listening to lectures on the classics of Buddhism, students wrote in their texts notations on the pronunciations or meanings of unfamiliar characters, and sometimes wrote commentaries between the lines of certain passages. This practice required some sort of phonetic shorthand, and this need led to the development of a new script based on Chinese characters. Like hiragana, each katakana was developed from a Chinese character corresponding to a particular syllable and was thenceforth used purely phonetically to represent that syllable. But unlike hiragana, which are cursive simplifications of entire kanji, the more angular katakana were made by taking a single component of a kanji in *kaisho* style. In a few cases (チ, ハ, ミ) the katakana is only a slight alteration of a simple kanji. Since katakana were closely associated with science and learning, this angular syllabary was for a long time used only by men. (Tables 4 and 5 on pages 20 and 21 show the kanji from which each kana was derived.)

The shapes of the hiragana and katakana in use today were laid down in the year 1900 in a decree for elementary schools. Two obsolete hiragana (ゐ *wi,* ゑ *we*) and the corresponding katakana (ヰ *wi,* ヱ *we*) were dropped as part of orthographic reforms made shortly after World War II. As a result, today there are 46 officially recognized symbols in each syllabary.

Table 4. HIRAGANA DERIVATIONS

あ	安	い	以	う	宇	え	衣	お	於
か	加	き	幾	く	久	け	計	こ	己
さ	左	し	之	す	寸	せ	世	そ	曽
た	太	ち	知	つ	川	て	天	と	止
な	奈	に	仁	ぬ	奴	ね	祢	の	乃
は	波	ひ	比	ふ	不	へ	部	ほ	保
ま	末	み	美	む	武	め	女	も	毛
や	也			ゆ	由			よ	与
ら	良	り	利	る	留	れ	礼	ろ	呂
わ	和							を	遠
ん	尤								

Table 5. KATAKANA DERIVATIONS

ア阿	イ伊	ウ宇	エ江	オ於
カ加	キ幾	ク久	ケ介	コ己
サ散	シ之	ス須	セ世	ソ曽
タ多	チ千	ツ川	テ天	ト止
ナ奈	ニ仁	ヌ奴	ネ祢	ノ乃
ハ八	ヒ比	フ不	ヘ部	ホ保
マ末	ミ三	ム牟	メ女	モ毛
ヤ也		ユ由		ヨ與
ラ良	リ利	ル流	レ礼	ロ呂
ワ和				ヲ乎
ン尓				

ORDER

The order of arrangement of the sounds of Japanese, shown in Table 3 on pages 16 and 17, has a history of one thousand years of development. Around the year 1000, people began to arrange systematically, according to their sounds, the kana which had been in use since the beginning of the Heian period. The result is the *gojū-on zu,* the "Fifty-Sounds Table," which forms an "alphabet" for the Japanese language. The *gojū-on zu* is shown within the heavy dark lines in Table 3 on page 16. The table is read from left to right across each row, starting with the top row; its order is therefore *a, i, u, e, o; ka, ki, ku, ke, ko. . . .* The ten horizontal rows are arranged according to the initial (consonant) sound of the syllables, and the five vertical columns are arranged according to the final (vowel) sound of the syllables. This systematic ordering makes the table easy to memorize.

The *gojū-on zu* can be written in either hiragana or katakana. Although the symbols composing the two systems are different, the systems represent the same sounds and arrange them in the same order.

Linguistic changes over the centuries caused some sounds to fall into disuse. Thus, the number of kana in the Fifty-Sounds Table in use today has decreased to 45 (46 if ん/ン *n* is counted). At the same time, new sounds became part of the language, requiring new symbols or diacritical marks, or an extended usage of the old symbols.

Strictly speaking, the end-of-syllable *n* is not part of the *gojū-on zu,* since this sound did not occur in the Japanese language until after the kana syllabaries had been constructed. Today, however, *n* is included at the end of the *gojū-on zu.* Similarly, the designation of the "muddied," that is, voiced, sounds *g, z, d,* and *b (daku-on)* by a *daku-ten* or *nigori-ten* [゛], and the representation of the "half-muddied" sound *p* (*handaku-on*) by a *handaku-ten* or *maru* [°] did not come until later. The same is true of the "twisted" sounds (*yō-on*: consonant + *y* + *a, u,* or *o*) and the assimilated sounds (*soku-on:* unvoiced long [double] consonant, or glottal stop), which did not appear until about the middle of the Heian period. There are no special diacritical marks for *yō-on* or *soku-on;* instead, as shown in the examples below, they are written with two kana, the second of which is written smaller. As seen in the example of きゃっか *kyakka,* the one-syllable combination of *yō-on* + *soku-on* (きゃっ *kya'*) is written with three kana, the final two of which are written small.

SOKU-ON	SOKU-ON	YŌ-ON	SOKU-ON AND YŌ-ON
あっ	あっか	きゃ	あっきゃ
アッ	アッカ	キャ	アッキャ
a'	*akka*	*kya*	*akkya*
かっ	かっか		きゃっか
カッ	カッカ		キャッカ
ka'	*kakka*		*kyakka*

Japanese dictionaries, encyclopedias, and other reference works whose entries must appear in a definite order are "alphabetized" in the order (called *a-i-u-e-o jun* or *gojū-on jun*) of the *gojū-on zu*.

In determining dictionary order, no distinction is made between whether a kana is written with a diacritical mark or not, whether a kana is written large or small, or whether it is hiragana or katakana, except when one of these distinctions must be used to differentiate between two otherwise identical words. This corresponds to the roman-letter alphabetization convention which dictates that a capital letter is treated like its lowercase counterpart, except where capitalization is the only feature that distinguishes the spelling of two words (like "china" and "China"). In these cases the rule is that the lowercase word comes first. In Japanese dictionary order the situation is more complex. The "same" kana may have as many as six versions; for example, は、ハ、ば、バ、ぱ、and パ are considered the same for purposes of dictionary order except in otherwise identical words.

Different reference books use different rules to govern this aspect of dictionary order. These are usually explained in detail in an introductory section of the reference book and should be consulted by the user. Below is a typical set of such rules:

1. A shorter word precedes a longer word beginning with the same kana (as "china" comes before "chinaware" in English-language dictionaries): あぶら before あぶらかす. (Virtually all reference books follow this convention.)

2. A character with no diacritical mark precedes its counterpart with a *daku-ten* or *handaku-ten,* and a character with a *daku-ten* precedes its counterpart with a *handaku-ten:* は り , then ば り , then ぱ リ . (Another virtually universal rule.)
3. A kana written large precedes its counterpart written small (this applies mostly to *soku-on* with a small っ and *yō-on* with a small ゃ , ゅ , or ょ): か つ て before か っ て, and い し や before い し ゃ .
4. A hiragana precedes its katakana counterpart: これ ら before コレラ .

In cases of conflict between these rules, Rule 1 takes precedence over Rule 2, Rule 2 over Rule 3, and Rule 3 over Rule 4. A few examples will help to make this clear. Because Rule 1 takes precedence over Rule 2: ば り き before は り き っ て.

Rule 1 over Rule 3: ち ょ	before ち よ が み
Rule 1 over Rule 4: カ ッ パ	before か っ ぱ つ
Rule 2 over Rule 3: は っ き	before は つ ぎ
Rule 2 over Rule 4: キ ス	before き ず
Rule 3 over Rule 4: ア ツ シ	before あ っ し

In Japanese dictionary order, there is also the issue of how to handle the mark — (called *chō-on kigō* or simply *bō*), which is used in foreign-derived words written in katakana to show the lengthening of the preceding vowel sound. Some dictionaries simply ignore it, as a hyphen would be ignored in English-language alphabetization. Others take it to represent the katakana for the preceding vowel sound, so that for example ウ ー リ ー "wooly" is ordered as if it were written ウ ウ リ イ . This latter convention is the one we adopt here.

Table 6 below presents further examples of the order in which words written in kana are arranged in dictionaries and the like. In order to use Japanese reference works with assurance, mastery of this ordering is essential. First read down the left-hand column, then down the middle column, then down the right-hand column.

In addition to the *gojū-on zu,* the hiragana may be ordered according to the *iroha* arrangement, which is presented in Table 7 on page 26.

Table 6. EXAMPLE OF DICTIONARY ORDER

あ	あいかぎ	あいぎん
ア	あいき	あいく
ああ	あいぎ	………
アー	あいきどう	あち
アート	あいきゃく	あつ
ああら	アイキュー	あつ
あい	あいきょう	あつい
あいか	あいぎょう	あつか
あいが	あいきわ	あっか
あいがえし	あいきん	あつかい

While both systems developed during the Heian period, the *iroha* is falling into disuse in this century. The *iroha* arranges all the hiragana in the form of a Buddhist poem, and is at present principally used as a scheme for labeling things in sequence (for example, playing cards or the rows of seats in a theater).

Table 7. THE IROHA

い *i*	ろ *ro*	は *ha*	に *ni*	ほ *ho*	へ *he*	と *to*
ち *chi*	り *ri*	ぬ *nu*	る *ru*	を *wo*		
わ *wa*	か *ka*	よ *yo*	た *ta*	れ *re*	そ *so*	
つ *tsu*	ね *ne*	な *na*	ら *ra*	む *mu*		
う *u*	ゐ *wi*	の *no*	お *o*	く *ku*	や *ya*	ま *ma*
け *ke*	ふ *fu*	こ *ko*	え *e*	て *te*		
あ *a*	さ *sa*	き *ki*	ゆ *yu*	め *me*	み *mi*	し *shi*
ゑ *we*	ひ *hi*	も *mo*	せ *se*	す *su*		

Note: This table includes the two obsolete hiragana ゐ *wi* and ゑ *we* (see page 19), as well as the obsolete reading *wo* for を.

WRITING

The best first step toward mastery of the Japanese writing system is to begin with the kana, for these reasons:

1. They are limited in number (46 per syllabary).
2. They are simple in form (one to four strokes each).
3. There is a one-to-one correspondence between sound and symbol (with a few exceptions; see page 33, Rule 10).
4. Each syllabary encompasses all the sounds of the Japanese language, so that any text can be written down in kana.

It is debatable which syllabary ought to be learned first. With katakana the beginner can write many familiar words, derived from English for the most part. But the hiragana occur far more frequently.

For a rapid mastery of written Japanese (even if only passive) the following recommendations are offered:

1. Break down the syllabaries into small learning units. For example, learn the kana five at a time, beginning with one row of Table 8 or 9 on pages 28 and 29.
2. Memorize the sound sequence (*a–i–u–e–o, ka–ki–ku–ke–ko,* etc.) by pronouncing the kana aloud.
3. Write the kana until the strokes can be written in the correct sequence, direction, and relative size without glancing at the model.
4. After one row has been learned, review all the preceding rows.
5. After the tables have been learned, practice the kana by copying texts written in kana, transliterating texts written in *rōmaji,* and taking dictation.

The following two principles govern the sequence and direction of writing the strokes of kana (as well as kanji):

1. From top to bottom
2. From left to right

Table 8. WRITING HIRAGANA

あ	い	う	え	お
か	き	く	け	こ
さ	し	す	せ	そ
た	ち	つ	て	と
な	に	ぬ	ね	の
は	ひ	ふ	へ	ほ
ま	み	む	め	も
や		ゆ		よ
ら	り	る	れ	ろ
わ				を
ん				

Table 9. WRITING KATAKANA

ア	イ	ウ	エ	オ
カ	キ	ク	ケ	コ
サ	シ	ス	セ	ソ
タ	チ	ツ	テ	ト
ナ	ニ	ヌ	ネ	ノ
ハ	ヒ	フ	ヘ	ホ
マ	ミ	ム	メ	モ
ヤ		ユ		ヨ
ラ	リ	ル	レ	ロ
ワ				ヲ
ン				

In the writing tables, the small numbers at the beginning of each stroke indicate the direction in which it is written, the sequence of the strokes, and the number of strokes which compose the kana.

Japanese is normally written not on lines, but rather in a printed (or at least imaginary) grid of squares or rectangles. In practicing writing, foreigners would be well advised to use, right from the beginning, either the printed manuscript paper which Japanese use, or the practice manuals which accompany this textbook.

ORTHOGRAPHY

Modern kana orthography *(gendai kanazukai)* reflects pronunciation closely. This section explains, with examples, the most important orthographic rules.

1. In hiragana, the long vowels *(chō-on)* *ā, ii,* and *ū* are represented by adding あ, い, or う to a hiragana containing the same vowel sound:

ああ	*ā*	Ah! Oh!
おかあさん	*okāsan*	mother
いいえ	*iie*	no
おにいさん	*oniisan*	elder brother
ゆうがた	*yūgata*	evening
すうがく	*sūgaku*	mathematics

2. In hiragana, the vowel *ē,* which occurs in words of Japanese origin, is written by adding え to a hiragana containing the *e* vowel sound:

ねえ	*nē*	indeed, right?
おねえさん	*onēsan*	elder sister

The identically pronounced long vowel *ei,* which occurs in words of Chinese origin, is written by adding い to a hiragana containing the *e* vowel sound:

| ていねい | *teinei* | polite |
| きれい | *kirei* | pretty |

3. The hiragana *ō* is normally represented by adding う to a hiragana containing the *o* sound:

| どうぞ | *dōzo* | please |
| おはよう | *ohayō* | Good morning. |

In some cases, however, お is used instead of う :

おおい (多い)	*ōi*	numerous
おおきい (大きい)	*ōkii*	big
オオカミ	*ōkami*	wolf
おおやけ (公)	*ōyake*	public, official
こおり (氷)	*kōri*	ice
とお (十)	*tō*	ten
とおい (遠い)	*tōi*	far
とおる (通る)	*tōru*	go along/through, pass
ほのお (炎)	*honō*	flame
もよおす (催す)	*moyōsu*	sponsor

The student need not concern himself too long with these historically based exceptions, since these words are usually written with kanji in such a way (shown in the parentheses) that the problem does not arise.

4. In the transliteration of foreign words into katakana, long vowels are represented with a lengthening stroke:

コーヒー	*kōhī*	coffee
ビール	*bīru*	beer
ボール	*bōru*	ball
ダンサー	*dansā*	dancer
エスカレーター	*esukarētā*	escalator

Exceptions:

エイト	*eito*	eight
スペイン	*Supein*	Spain

5. The voiced sounds *(daku-on)* g, z, d, and b are denoted by placing a pair of short diagonal strokes *(daku-ten)* on the upper right corner of the kana for the corresponding unvoiced sound. The p sounds *(handaku-on)* are denoted by adding a small circle *(handaku-ten)* on the upper right corner of the corresponding kana from the *ha* row of the *gojū-on zu* (given on page 16):

が ガ	ざ ザ	だ ダ	ば バ	ぱ パ
ga	*za*	*da*	*ba*	*pa*

6. The "twisted" sounds *(yō-on)* are denoted by two kana, which coalesce phonetically into a single syllable. The first one is selected from the *i* column and the second from the *ya* row of the *gojū-on zu*. The second kana, which is written smaller, is positioned toward the lower part of its space when the text is written horizontally, and toward the right side of its space when the text is written vertically:

kya	きゃ	キャ	きゃ	キャ
gya	ぎゃ	ギャ	ぎゃ	ギャ

7. Assimilated sounds *(soku-on)*, i.e., those sounds which are represented in romanization by double consonants, are denoted by a small つ/ッ before the consonant sound:

れっしゃ	*ressha*	train
じっぷん	*jippun*	10 minutes
ロケット	*roketto*	rocket
ちょっと	*chotto*	a little

8. Short, broken-off vowels at the ends of words or syllables (final glottal stops, or *soku-on*) are also denoted by a small っ/ッ:

あっ	*a'*	Oh!
きゃっ	*kya'*	Eek!
ジッ	*ji'*	(a Chinese reading, used in compounds, of the kanji for "ten")

9. The sounds *ji* and *zu* are usually written じ/ジ and ず/ズ:

ま<u>じ</u>め	*majime*	serious, sober
ま<u>ず</u>い	*mazui*	bad-tasting
ラ<u>ジ</u>オ	*rajio*	radio
<u>ジ</u>ャ<u>ズ</u>	*jazu*	jazz

But ち and づ are used
(a) when the preceding syllable (of the same word) consists of the same character without the *daku-ten:*

つ<u>づ</u>り	*tsuzuri*	syllable, spelling
つ<u>づ</u>く	*tsuzuku*	continue
<u>ちぢ</u>む	*chijimu*	shrink

(b) when the syllables ち and つ are voiced in compound words:

かな<u>づ</u>かい (かな＋つかい)	*kanazukai*	kana orthography
き<u>づ</u>かれ (き＋つかれ)	*kizukare*	mental fatigue
はな<u>ぢ</u> (はな＋ち)	*hanaji*	nosebleed

10. The syllables *e, o,* and *wa* are written え/エ, お/オ, and わ/ワ when part of a word:

いい<u>え</u>	*iie*	no
な<u>お</u>	*nao*	further, still
<u>わ</u>たし	*watashi*	I, me

エネルギー	*enerugī*	energy
オペラ	*opera*	opera
ワシントン	*Washinton*	Washington

But the same three sounds are written へ/ヘ, を/ヲ, and は/ハ when they represent postpositional "auxiliary words" or particles *(joshi)*:

| こんにち<u>は</u> | *konnichi wa* | Hello. |
| テヘラン<u>へ</u> | *Teheran e* | to Teheran |

わた<u>し</u>は<u>は</u>が<u>き</u>をポスト<u>へ</u>いれた。
Watashi wa hagaki o posuto e ireta.
I put the postcard in the mailbox.

11. The word 言う "say" is pronounced ゆう *yū* but written いう *iu*.

USAGE

As mentioned previously, modern texts usually consist of a mixture of kanji and hiragana, with a sprinkling of katakana *(kanji-kana majiri)*. Each of these three scripts serves definite functions. The following rules outline what the kana syllabaries are used for.

■ Usages of hiragana

1. All types of native words other than substantives, verbs, and adjectives:

よく	*yoku*	well, often
たぶん	*tabun*	probably
この	*kono*	this, these
あそこ	*asoko*	there
だから	*dakara*	so, therefore
まだ	*mada*	still, not yet
だけ	*dake*	only
へ	*e*	to

2. Substantives, verbs, and adjectives in certain cases (as when the formerly used kanji have become obsolete):

いす	*isu*	chair
はし	*hashi*	chopsticks
する	*suru*	do, make
できる	*dekiru*	can, be able
きれい	*kirei*	pretty
うれしい	*ureshii*	happy

3. Inflectional endings of all words written with kanji:

行く	*i(ku)*	go
行かない	*i(kanai)*	not go
白い	*shiro(i)*	white
祭り	*matsu(ri)*	festival

Hiragana used for writing word endings *(gobi)* are called *okurigana*. But it must be noted that in many cases not only the inflectional ending but also part of the stem *(gokan)* is written in kana (in particular, this includes adjectives ending in *-shii,* and *ichi-dan* or "vowel" verbs, which end in *-eru* or *-iru*):

新しい	*atara(shii)*	new
大きい	*ō(kii)*	big
食べる	*ta(beru)*	eat
幸せ	*shiawa(se)*	happiness

■ Usages of katakana

1. Foreign-derived words:

ビル	*biru*	building
ビール	*bīru*	beer
パン	*pan*	bread
テーブル	*tēburu*	table
タバコ	*tabako*	tobacco, cigarette

But one also sees:

たばこ	*tabako*	tobacco, cigarette

2. Foreign words and foreign proper names (with the exception of Chinese and Korean proper names, which are written in kanji):

アメリカ	*Amerika*	America
ドイツ	*Doitsu* (from *deutsch*)	Germany
パリ	*Pari* (Fr. pron.)	Paris
シェークスピア	*Shēkusupia*	Shakespeare

In transcribing foreign words and proper names, the basic rule is that the katakana should follow as closely as possible the pronunciation of the original word, the ever-growing vocabulary of foreign-derived words being overwhelmingly of English origin. Despite a general trend toward unification of the transcription rules, one occasionally encounters foreign words and names which are rendered into katakana in more than one way:

ベット	*betto*	bed
ベッド	*beddo*	bed
ジェネレーション	*jenerēshon*	generation
ゼネレーション	*zenerēshon*	generation
ダーウィン	*Dāwin*	Darwin
ダーウイン	*Dāuin*	Darwin

For many foreign sounds there is nothing in the traditional Japanese sound and writing system that corresponds. Diacritical marks and many new combinations of katakana (some written small to show phonetic coalescence into one syllable) are used to represent such sounds:

ティー	*tī*	tea
クォータリー	*quōtarī*	a quarterly
フィリピン	*Firipin*	the Philippines
ダーウィン	*Dāwin*	Darwin

ヴィーン*	*Vīn* (from *Wien*)	Vienna
ジュネーヴ*	*Junēvu* (from *Genève*)	Geneva
デュッセルドルフ*	*Dyusserudorufu*	Düsseldorf

In many cases Japanese prefer to give foreign words a more Japanese-sounding pronunciation:

バイオリン	*baiorin*	violin
ビタミン	*bitamin*	vitamin
チーム	*chīmu*	team
ラジオ	*rajio*	radio
ベートーベン	*Bētōben*	Beethoven

The consonant *l,* which does not occur in the Japanese language, is transcribed with a katakana from the *ra* row of the *gojū-on* table:

| ホール | *hōru* | hall; hole (in golf) |
| ラブレター | *raburetā* | love letter |

Katakana are also used for the following:

3. Names of plants and animals (especially in scientific contexts):

ネズミ	*nezumi*	mouse, rat
マグロ	*maguro*	tuna
サクラ	*sakura*	cherry tree

But kanji and hiragana are also used:

犬	*inu*	dog
桜	*sakura*	cherry tree
みかん	*mikan*	mandarin orange

---

* The Ministry of Education presently recommends that these be written ウイーン *Uīn,* ジュネーブ *Junēbu,* and ジュッセルドルフ *Jusserudorufu.*

4. Some female given names:

| エミ | *Emi* |
| マリ | *Mari* |

5. Onomatopoeic words such as animal cries and other sounds; children's words; exclamations:

ワンワン	*wanwan*	bowwow
ニャーニャー	*nyānyā*	meow
ガタガタ	*gatagata*	(rattling sound)
トントン	*tonton*	(knocking sound)
ビュービュー	*pyūpyū*	(sound of the wind)
アレ/アレッ	*are/are'*	Huh!?
オヤ/オヤッ	*oya/oya'*	Oh!

6. Colloquialisms and slang:

| インチキ | *inchiki* | fake, phony |
| デカ | *deka* | detective |

7. Words and proper names which are to be emphasized:

もうダメだ	*mō dame da*	It's too late.
ナゾの自殺	*nazo no jisatsu*	mysterious suicide
トヨタ	*Toyota*	Toyota (auto company)
ヨコハマ	*Yokohama*	Yokohama (port city)

The limited usage of words written in katakana makes them stand out and often lends them a certain weight. This high visibility, which is often made use of in advertising, has somewhat the same effect that italics have in Western languages.

8. Telegrams:

| カネオクレ | *kane okure* | Send money. |

■ Usages of both hiragana and katakana

1. To show the pronunciation of kanji:

<table>
<tr><td>一^{ひと}つ</td><td>hitotsu</td><td>片^{カタ}</td><td>kata-</td></tr>
<tr><td>平^{ひら}仮^が名^な</td><td>hiragana</td><td>仮^カ</td><td>ka-</td></tr>
<tr><td>漢^{カン}字^ジ</td><td>kanji</td><td>名^ナ</td><td>na</td></tr>
</table>

These small kana, written either above or below the kanji in horizontal writing and to the right of the kanji in vertical writing, are called *furigana* or *rubi*.

2. In transliterating individual kanji, katakana are used for Chinese-derived *(on)* readings, and hiragana for Japanese *(kun)* readings:

人 ジン, ニン, ひと   *jin, nin (on)*; *hito (kun)*   person

■ The repetition symbols *(kurikaeshi fugō)*

If, within a single word, the same two kana symbols occur one after the other, the second one can be replaced by the repetition symbol ゝ :

あゝ	*ā*	Ah! Oh!
かゝし	*kakashi*	scarecrow

The repetition symbol may also be used in combination with the *daku-ten*:

ほゞ	*hobo*	almost, nearly
たゞし	*tadashi*	but, however
すゞり	*suzuri*	inkstone

The repetition symbol for two syllables is used only in vertical writing:

いろ〳 *iroiro* various   わざ〳 *wazawaza* on purpose

There are no compulsory and uniform rules for the usage and nomenclature of the various punctuation marks (*kugiri fugō* or *kutōten*), and this chapter is but an attempt to present in a systematic way a uniform terminology and practical explication of Japanese punctuation as it is used today.

In general, a punctuation mark is given the same amount of space as any other character; that is, on *genkō yōshi* an entire square is used even for a punctuation mark. However, a pair of successive punctuation marks like 「 『 or 。) are written in a single space, the *tensen* is written three dots per space, and some punctuation marks (see examples under 4, 5, 10, and 11 below) extend over several spaces.

Some punctuation marks take different orientations or forms when used in vertical and in horizontal writing:

VERTICAL		HORIZONTAL
﹂, ﹈	⟶	「」, 『』
〝〞	⟶	" "
⌒, ◠	⟶	( ), (( ))
〉	⟶	〜
ひ、る	⟶	ひ る
よる	⟶	よる

1. *Maru* or *kuten* [。]

Indicates the conclusion of a sentence or utterance (a)–(c), like the period in English. When the presence of the question particle *ka* or an interrogative word makes it clear that the sentence is a question, a *maru* is used in preference to a question mark (d), (cf. 12).

(a) 日本は島国です。

(b) 「どうぞ、こちらへ。」

(c) 「おおい、田中君。」

(d) 「どちらへ。」

2. *Ten* or *tōten* [、]

Used like the comma in English to indicate a pause and clarify the structure of the sentence (a)–(e); to separate successive numbers (f); and to divide numbers of four or more digits into three-digit groups (g). To show how the presence or absence of a *ten* can change the meaning of a sentence, (e) has been written with a *ten* ("A large man wearing glasses") and without ("A man wearing large glasses").

(a) はい、そうです。

(b) ただ、例外として、……

(c) 「行きますか」と、彼にきいた。

(d) 見ましたか、今朝の新聞を。

(e) 大きな、めがねをかけた男。
大きなめがねをかけた男。

(f) 二、三日

(g) 二、三二〇円

3. *Nakaten* [・]

Used to separate words of the same type (a), (b); to link words together into one unit, when opposed to *ten* which separates (c), (d); to separate the year, month, and day when citing dates (e); to indicate the decimal point

— 41 —

(f); and to separate the component words of foreign phrases and names written in katakana (g).

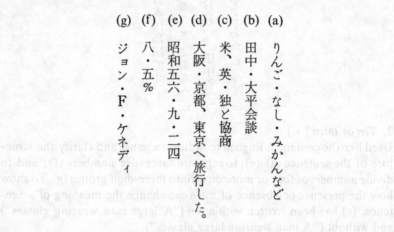

(a) りんご・なし・みかんなど

(b) 田中・大平会談

(c) 米・英・独と協商

(d) 大阪・京都、東京へ旅行した。

(e) 昭和五六・九・二四

(f) 八・五%

(g) ジョン・F・ケネディ

4. *Nakasen* |

Has the same functions as the dash in English. It is used to indicate that a sentence or thought has been broken off while still incomplete (a) or to set off explanatory information inserted into a sentence (b); when used for lengths of time or distance it has the meaning of "from . . . to . . ." or "between . . . and . . ." (c)–(e); and in Japanese addresses it separates the numbers for the *-chōme, -ban,* and *-gō* (f).

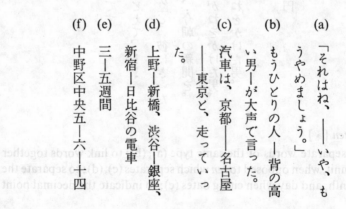

(a) 「それはね、──いや、もうやめましょう。」

(b) もうひとりの人──背の高い男──が大声で言った。

(c) 汽車は、京都──名古屋──東京と、走っていった。

(d) 上野─新橋、渋谷─銀座、新宿─日比谷の電車

(e) 三─五週間

(f) 中野区中央五─六─十四

5. *Tensen* ⁚

Consists of a string of centered dots (usually six), three to a space. It corresponds to the English ellipsis [. . .] and denotes a pause in speech indicating that a sentence or thought has been left uncompleted (a), (cf. 4a), the trailing off of the voice at the end of an utterance (b), or silence (c). Long strings of successive three-dot *tensen* groups are sometimes used in tables of contents and the like to form lines connecting chapter titles and page numbers (d).

(a) 「それからね……いやいや、もうなんにも申し上げますまい。」

(b) 「それもそうだけど……」

(c) 「ごめんネ、由美ちゃん。」「……」

(d) 第一章　序説 ……… 一頁

6. *Kagikakko* 「 」

Correspond to the quotation marks of English (a), (b).

Futaekagi 『 』 Used for quotations within quotations (c), (d).

(a) 国歌「君が代」

(b) 漢字の読み方は「音」と「訓」との二つがある。

(c) 「母も『よろしく』と申しております。」

(d) 彼は「人生に大切なのは『努力』ということだ」と言った。

7. *In'yōfu* „ "

Today often used instead of *kagikakko*, especially with short phrases in the sense of "so-called."

これは有名な"月光の曲"です。

8. *Kakko* or *marugakko* ◯

Used like parentheses in English (a), (b).

Futaegakko ◎ Like brackets in English, used for parentheses within parentheses (c).

Yokogakko ( ) Enclose the numbers or letters that mark off various sections, articles, paragraphs, etc., of a text (d).

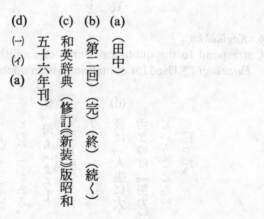

	(d)	(c)	(b)	(a)
	(一)	第二回	完	田中
	(イ)		終	
	(a)	和英辞典	（続く）	
	五十六年刊	（修訂《新装》版昭和		

— 44 —

9. *Namigata* 〰

Used to indicate a range "from . . . to . . ." (a)–(c), (cf. 4c–4e). It is usually read aloud as *kara,* "from."

(a) 一〜三時間

(b) 四月〜六月

(c) 東京〜大阪

10. *Wakiten* ⁝

Used to "italicize" words and phrases (a); also applied to words which for some reason are written in kana instead of the usual kanji (b), and sometimes used to distinguish slang, dialect, or other types of unconventional words (c).

(a) まず、句点は文の終わりにつけると

(b) ひるという言葉は、

(c) いうのが……びんからきりまである。

11. *Wakisen* │

Directs the reader's attention to certain phrases (a), words, or parts of words (b) like a kind of "vertical underlining" (cf. 10a).

(b)　　　　　　　(a)

名辞は、単一の名詞から成ることも
あり、あるいは長い名詞句から成る
こともある。人はパンのみにて生く
るものにあらず。

次の傍線を引いた語について説明せ
よ。そう考えられる。

12. *Gimonfu* [?]

Used in place of the *maru* when it would otherwise be unclear whether the
sentence is a question or a statement (a), (b), (cf. 1d).

(b)　(a)

「ええ？ なんですって？」
「きのう見に行った？」

13. *Kantanfu* [!]

Like the exclamation point in English, indicates emotional intensity and
should be used sparingly.

「ちがう、ちがう、ちがうぞ!」

14. *Piriodo,* "period" [.]
Used in horizontal writing as a delimiter between the year, month, and day in dates (see example), and sometimes also instead of the *maru.*

昭和 16. 9. 14

15. *Konma,* "comma" [,]
Used in horizontal writing instead of the *ten.*

はい, そうです。

--- **5. THE KANJI** ---

BRIEF HISTORICAL OUTLINE

The oldest known Chinese characters date back to the sixteenth century B.C., but their number and advanced form indicate that they had already gone through a development of several hundred years. Like the Egyptian hieroglyphics, the earliest characters started with simple illustrations, which during the course of time became increasingly abstract and took on forms better adapted to the writing tools of the time. These characters, along with many other elements of Chinese culture, came to Japan by way of the Korean peninsula in the fourth century A.D. Since the Japanese had no writing of their own, the Chinese characters soon came to be used for the Japanese language as well.

At first these monosyllabic Chinese characters were used purely phonetically, with no reference to their meanings, to represent similar Japanese sounds:

久尔 *ku-ni* country

This method enabled one to write down any word, but a single multisyllabic Japanese word required several Chinese characters, each consisting of many strokes.

A second method soon developed: the characters were used ideographically, with no reference to their Chinese pronunciations, to represent Japanese words of the same or related meaning:

国 *kuni* country

Both methods are used in the *Manyōshū,* the oldest (eighth-century) Japanese collection of poetry. Here, words denoting concepts are written with the corresponding Chinese characters, which are then given the Japanese pronunciation. All other words, as well as proper names and inflectional endings, are represented phonetically by kanji which are read with a Japanese approximation to their Chinese pronunciations.

The characters used for this latter, phonetic function are called *manyōgana.* The kana syllabaries developed from these characters after great simplification.

For centuries kanji, hiragana, and katakana were used independently of one another, and the number of symbols in use and their readings kept growing. Toward the end of the 1800s, after the Meiji Restoration, the government as part of its modernization program undertook to simplify the writing system for the first time.

The latest major writing reform came shortly after World War II:

1. In 1946 the number of kanji permitted for use in official publications was limited to 1,850 (1,900 in the revised proposal issued in 1977); of these, 881 were selected to be learned in the first six years of schooling.
2. The *on* and *kun* readings of the 1,850 kanji were limited in number to about 3,500 (4,032 readings in the 1977 proposal).
3. Many kanji were simplified or replaced by others easier to write.
4. Uniform rules were prescribed for how to write the kanji (sequence and number of strokes).

The press strives to follow these and other government recommendations concerning how Japanese is to be written. A knowledge of the set of characters treated in this book will therefore be sufficient for reading Japanese newspapers without time-consuming reference to character dictionaries.

In 1951 the government published a supplementary list of 92 kanji permitted for use in personal names.

A Japanese of average education is familiar with about 3,000 characters. At present, roughly 4,000 characters are used in written Japanese, including technical and literary writing. The most comprehensive Japanese character dictionaries include about 10,000 kanji, while Chinese character dictionaries which attempt to record every character that has ever been in use have entries for some 50,000.

FORM AND CONSTRUCTION

Most characters are built up from a limited number of basic elements according to principles which are easily grasped. How these elements are put together is related to the meaning, and often the pronunciation, of a kanji, and therefore familiarity with the most important elements and their use will make it much easier to understand and memorize the 1,900 characters presented in this book, as well as all those not included here. Chinese characters can be divided, according to their origins and structures, into three categories: pictographs, ideographs, and complex characters.

■ Pictographs

The first characters developed from simple illustrations of objects and phenomena of daily life. Even in the abstract form used today, the object depicted can often still be recognized:

山	*yama*	mountain	⋏⋏	(3 towering peaks)
川	*kawa*	river	∫∫∫	(water flowing between banks)
日	*hi*	sun	⊙	(shape of the sun)

There are only a few pictographs which are used today as independent characters. But they serve as building blocks for almost all the other characters in use.

■ Ideographs

For abstract concepts, characters were invented which indicate meaning in only a few strokes:

一	*ichi*	one
二	*ni*	two
上	*ue*	above
下	*shita*	below
中	*naka*	middle

■ Complex characters

To increase the stock of word signs, the characters already available were put together in new combinations. At first two or three pictographs with the same or similar meanings were combined into a single new character (logogram):

林	*hayashi*	woods	(木 tree + 木 tree)
森	*mori*	forest	(木 tree + 木 tree + 木 tree)
明	*mei*	light	(日 sun + 月 moon)

In other cases, the Chinese took the reading of one part of a newly created complex character as the reading of the entire character (phonologogram):

理　　*ri*　reason

The sound-indicating part is in this case the character 里, whose reading is *ri*. Over 90 percent of all kanji are combinations constructed according to this principle, which is therefore often helpful for guessing at the *on* reading of a newly encountered character. Usually the component indicating the pronunciation is on the right, while that on the left indicates the meaning. Most phonologograms can be classed into six groups, corresponding to the positions of the sound- and meaning-indicating components (P = pronunciation, M = meaning):

M on left, P on right:	銅 *dō,* copper	(金 metal ＋ 同 *dō*)
P on left, M on right:	歌 *ka,* sing	(欠 yawn ＋ 可 *ka*)
M on top, P on bottom:	花 *ka,* flower	(艹 grass ＋ 化 *ka*)
P on top, M on bottom:	盛 *sei,* fill	(皿 dish ＋ 成 *sei*)
M outside, P inside:	園 *en,* garden	(囗 enclosure ＋ 袁 *en*)
P outside, M inside:	問 *mon,* ask	(口 mouth ＋ 門 *mon*)

READINGS

When Chinese texts were introduced into Japan, the Japanese adopted not only the Chinese characters but their Chinese readings as well. In being adapted to the Japanese phonetic system, the Chinese pronunciations were modified. For example, the distinctions between the four tones of Chinese were ignored. (This is one reason for the large number of homophones in Japanese.) Later, Chinese characters were used to represent Japanese words of identical or similar meaning and were given Japanese readings. This explains why most kanji have both Chinese-derived *(on)* and native Japanese *(kun)* readings. Moreover, a single kanji may have two or more *on* or *kun* readings, each indicating a different meaning or nuance (in contrast to Chinese, in which each character has only one reading).

In prescribing the basic kanji, the Ministry of Education limited not only the number of characters recognized for general use but also the number of officially authorized readings. Of the 1,900 basic kanji dealt with in this book, 1,160 have both Chinese and Japanese readings, 705 have only Chinese readings, and 35 have only Japanese readings. The kanji which have only a *kun* reading consist almost entirely of characters which were created by Japanese in imitation of the Chinese pattern (*kokuji*). The character 働 meaning "work" is the only *kokuji* to which a pseudo-*on* reading is attached; its *on* reading is *dō* and its *kun* reading is *hatara(ku)*.

Whether a word is to be read with an *on* or with a *kun* reading can be determined in most cases by means of the following criteria:

1. One-character words are read with their *kun* readings:

人	*hito*	person
口	*kuchi*	mouth
日	*hi*	sun; day

The relatively few single-character words which are pronounced with *on* readings have no *kun* readings, so the problem of choosing between two different readings does not arise.

2. Words incorporating *okurigana* are pronounced with *kun* readings:

一つ	*hitotsu*	one
明かり	*akari*	light
大きい	*ōkii*	big
出す	*dasu*	take out
入り口	*iriguchi*	entrance

3. Kanji sequences without *okurigana* are usually read with *on* readings:

見 物	*kenbutsu*	sight-seeing
人 口	*jinkō*	population

4. Personal names are usually read with *kun* readings:

田 中	*Tanaka*	山 田	*Yamada*

The characters composing a given compound word are generally read either all *on* or all *kun*.

Some character combinations have two, and in rare cases three, different readings, which may be associated with similar or with different meanings:

明日	*myōnichi, asu*	tomorrow
一日	*ichinichi, ichijitsu*	1 day
	tsuitachi	1st of the month

Sometimes kanji are used either (a) exclusively to convey the meaning of a word, disregarding the usual readings of the kanji; or (b) exclusively as phonetic symbols, disregarding the meanings of the individual kanji. Both types of kanji are called *ateji*:

(a) 大人	*otona*	adult
お母さん	*okāsan*	mother

The readings *asu* and *tsuitachi* for the compounds 明日 and 一日 given above belong to this group.

(b) 出来る	*dekiru*	can, be able

A number of kanji are used in compounds to refer to countries. Most are *ateji* of the second type, derived from an obsolete phonetic kanji spelling of the name of the country. The following list gives the most frequently encountered kanji which denote countries; those marked with an asterisk [*] are not among the 1,900 basic kanji.

日	*Nichi, Nit-*	Japan	米	*Bei*	America, U.S.A.
中	*Chū*	China	英	*Ei*	Britain, England
韓*	*Kan*	South Korea	独	*Doku*	Germany
越	*Etsu*	Vietnam	仏	*Futsu*	France
印	*In*	India	伊*	*I*	Italy
比	*Hi*	the Philippines	露	*Ro*	Russia
豪, 濠*	*Gō*	Australia	西	*Sei*	Spain

WRITING

At least in the beginning, reading practice should be supplemented by writing practice. Only by repeatedly writing the individual characters and their compounds can one gain confidence in reading. In addition, stroke counting, which is indispensable in using character dictionaries, can be mastered only through writing. Writing the most complex kanji will present no difficulties once one knows how to apply the writing rules to the limited number of elements which make up any kanji. The main problem is active writing: that is, reproducing from memory a character that has already been learned.

The small numbers given at the beginning of each stroke in the kanji illustrations in the following examples, and in the Kanji List, indicate the direction in which each stroke is to be written and the order in which the strokes are to be written, as well as the total number of strokes in the kanji.

■ Stroke direction

1. Horizontal strokes are written from left to right:

2. Vertical or slanting strokes are written from top to bottom:

An exception is the combination of a short slanting down-stroke followed by a short slanting up-stroke, as in the radicals 氵 *sanzui*, 冫 *nisui*, and 疒 *yamaidare* and in 求 *kyū*, *moto(meru)* and other related kanji:

3. A stroke may change direction several times:

■ Stroke order

1. From top to bottom:

2. From left to right:

3. Middle part before short flanking side-strokes:

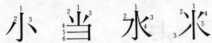

Exceptions:

4. Horizontal stroke before intersecting vertical stroke:

Exceptions:

and elements and characters built from these.

5. When slanting strokes intersect, the one running from upper right to lower left is written first:

文 父 交

6. A piercing vertical stroke is written last:

中 申 車 半 聿 平 手

When the vertical middle stroke protrudes neither above nor below, the writing sequence is: upper part, middle stroke, lower part:

7. A piercing horizontal stroke is written last:

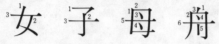

8. First the vertical stroke, then the short horizontal stroke which adjoins it on the right:

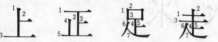

9. The enclosure is written first:

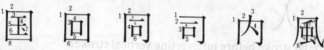

Exceptions:

10. *Shinnyō, shinnyū* ⻌ is written last:

11. The kanji repetition symbol 々 is written:

山 々	*yamayama*	mountains
人 々	*hitobito*	people

In order to avoid confusing the beginner, not all details of the stroke-order rules set forth by the Ministry of Education have been given here.

HOW TO USE A KANJI DICTIONARY

Many people have sought in vain to arrange Chinese characters in some logical way that would make it easy to look up a character whose readings are unknown.

In 1716 a character dictionary known as the *Kōki Jiten* was published in China. In this work 214 character components called "radicals" were used to classify the Chinese characters into an equal number of groups. Since in general a character contains a number of radicals, a decision had to be made concerning which of its constituent radicals each character would be classified under. Unfortunately, this was not decided according to any consistent graphical principle, but rather the radical which indicates the meaning of the character was selected. This classical radical system, despite all its shortcomings, is still used as the basis for almost all character dictionaries. The 214 radicals are arranged in order of stroke count, as are the characters within each group.

This traditional system of arrangement is so complex that even for Japanese it is easier to use an index to locate a character than it is to search for the character directly. The character dictionaries used by Japanese *(kanwa jiten)* usually include three indexes: an index by radicals *(bushu sakuin)*, a stroke-count index *(sōkaku sakuin)*, and an index by readings *(on-kun sakuin)*. This book also includes three such indexes, which makes it possible to quickly look up any of the 1,900 characters presented, and thus use the book as a concise kanji dictionary. The indexes are used as follows:

1. Index by Radicals (p. 343)

When none of the readings of a character are known, one usually locates the character by means of the radical index.

Modern character dictionaries frequently list a number of kanji under different radicals from those under which they were previously classified. This is due partly to the attempt to devise a simpler, more logical reference system, and partly to the fact that many simplified characters have lost the radical under which they were previously listed. In his *Modern Reader's Japanese–English Character Dictionary,* Andrew Nathaniel Nelson undertook to preserve the classical radical system while arranging the characters according to logical and easy-to-understand rules, so that once one has gained some familiarity with the system one can look up kanji directly, without preliminary reference to an index. The arrangement of characters in the indexes of this book follows Nelson's rules, which will now be outlined.

A kanji normally contains several of the 214 radicals, but Nelson's 12-step Radical Priority System allows one to determine speedily and surely under which radical the kanji is listed: one goes down the steps until one finds a description that matches one of the radicals. For example, if a character is clearly divided into left and right halves, one takes left in preference to right, since Step 4 precedes Step 5. Nelson's 12-step priority checklist to determine under which radical a kanji is listed is as follows:

(1) The kanji is itself a radical: 人 日 水

(2) The kanji has only one radical: 乃 及

(3) The kanji has a radical which encloses the rest of the kanji on two or more sides: 原 式 進 同 国

(4) The left side is a radical: 明 畑 休

(5) The right side is a radical: 北 部 故

(6) The top part is a radical: 千 万 分 思 字 空

(7) The bottom part is a radical: 無 想 共 学

(8) The upper left (NW) part is a radical: 報

(9) The upper right (NE) part is a radical: 求

(10) The lower right (SE) part is a radical: 君

(11) The lower left (SW) part is a radical: 来 未 弱

(12) Choose the highest-protruding or highest-positioned radical: 事 更 夫 民 与

Having determined which radical a kanji is listed under, one next looks up this radical in the index by radicals, which is arranged according to stroke count. The characters under each radical are listed in order of total stroke number.

2. Index by Stroke Count (p. 353)

When none of the readings of a character are known and determining its radical seems too troublesome, the character can be located by means of the stroke-count index. Kanji having the same number of strokes are arranged according to their radicals. Using this index, however, requires a sure knowledge of the rules for writing and counting strokes.

3. Index by Readings (p. 361)

The alphabetically arranged index by readings is used when one knows one of the readings of the desired kanji. Since many kanji have the same *on* reading (among the 1,900 basic kanji alone there are 44 characters which have the reading *kan*), one should whenever possible look for the kanji under its *kun* reading. Characters having the same reading are arranged according to radicals, then stroke count.

Character dictionaries list not just the individual characters but also all their important compounds *(jukugo)* with readings and meanings. One usually consults a character dictionary to determine the reading of a compound. The compounds are usually listed under their initial characters, and compounds having the same initial character are arranged in order of the stroke count of the second character.

RADICALS

A knowledge of radicals helps in understanding kanji more thoroughly and memorizing them more easily, and is a prerequisite for efficient use of a character dictionary. In addition, the oral description of Chinese characters (such as in communicating the spelling of proper names by telephone) is possible only when all the participants know what the various radicals are called.

Table 10 lists the most important radicals by the positions in which they are written within characters. The shaded areas in the boxes indicate the position of the radicals following; next to each box appears the Japanese term for radicals in that position, in *rōmaji* and kanji. Each radical is accompanied by its Japanese name and two kanji which incorporate it.

Table 11 (page 62) lists all 214 radicals with their meanings. There is no sure way to derive the meaning of a kanji from its radical and the meanings of its other components, and this is especially true of those kanji which were simplified after World War II. But the learner may find it quite helpful, in remembering which radical goes with which kanji, to know for example that kanji containing Radical No. 61 忄 "heart" are usually associated, at least in some vague way, with the mind or emotions; those containing Radical No. 85 氵 with "water"; those containing Radical No. 149 言 "speak" with something verbal; and those containing Radical No. 167 金 with "metal."

Table 10. THE MOST IMPORTANT RADICALS AND THEIR JAPANESE NAMES

hen 偏

亻	ninben	体	住
冫	nisui	次	冷
口	kuchihen	味	呼
土	tsuchihen	地	場
女	onnahen	好	始
弓	yumihen	引	強
彳	gyōninben	役	御
阝	kozatohen	防	院
忄	risshinben	性	情
扌	tehen	持	招
方	katahen	放	旅
日	hihen	明	曜
木	kihen	林	村
氵	sanzui	海	池
火	hihen	畑	灯
牛	ushihen	物	特
犭	kemonohen	独	犯
王	ōhen	理	現
目	mehen	眼	眠
矢	yahen	知	短
石	ishihen	砂	破
礻	shimesuhen	社	礼
禾	nogihen	和	私
米	komehen	粉	精
糸	itohen	続	約
月	nikuzuki	胴	服
舟	funehen	般	航
衤	koromohen	初	裸
言	gonben	語	話
貝	kaihen	財	貯
車	kurumahen	転	輪
金	kanehen	鉄	針
馬	umahen	駅	験

tsukuri 旁

刂	rittō	別	制
力	chikara	助	効
卩	fushizukuri	印	却
彡	sanzukuri	形	彫
阝	ōzato	都	郡
攵	nobun	故	政
斤	onozukuri	新	断
欠	akubi	歌	欧
殳	rumata	段	殺
隹	furutori	難	雑
頁	ōgai	類	顔

kanmuri 冠

亠	nabebuta	交	京
八	hachigashira	分	公
冖	wakanmuri	写	冠
宀	ukanmuri	家	安
艹	kusakanmuri	花	茶
癶	hatsugashira	発	登
穴	anakanmuri	空	窓
罒	amigashira	買	罪

takekanmuri / etc.

竹	takekanmuri	筆	答
耂	oikanmuri	者	老
雨	amekanmuri	雲	電

ashi 脚

儿	hitoashi	先	免
心	kokoro	想	悪
灬	rekka/renga	無	照
皿	sara	盗	盟
貝	kogai	貨	負

kamae 構

冂	dōgamae	円	同
匚	hakogamae	区	医
囗	kunigamae	国	四
戈	hokogamae	戦	成
行	gyōgamae	街	術
門	mongamae	間	問

tare 垂

厂	gandare	原	厚
尸	shikabane	局	居
广	madare	広	庁
疒	yamaidare	病	痛

nyō 繞

廴	ennyō	建	延
辶	shinnyō	進	返
走	sōnyō	起	超

11. THE 214 RADICALS AND THEIR MEANINGS
(arranged by stroke count)

– 1 Stroke –

1	一	one; (horizontal stroke)
2	｜	(vertical stroke)
3	、	(dot stroke)
4	ノ	(diagonal stroke)
5	乙	No. 2
6	亅	(vertical stroke with hook)

– 2 Strokes –

7	二	two
8	亠	lid, top; up
9	人 , 亻	man, human being
10	儿	legs
11	入	enter
12	八	eight
13	冂	enclose
14	冖	cover
15	冫	ice
16	几	table
17	凵	container
18	刀 , 刂	knife, sword
19	力	power
20	勹	wrap
21	匕	spoon
22	匚	box
23	匸	conceal
24	十	ten
25	卜	oracle
26	卩	stamp, seal

27	厂	cliff
28	厶	private
29	又	again; hand

– 3 Strokes –

30	口	mouth
31	囗	border
32	土	earth
33	士	man; scholar
34	夂	follow
35	夊	go slowly
36	夕	evening
37	大	large
38	女	woman
39	子	child, son
40	宀	roof
41	寸	inch
42	小	small
43	尢	lame
44	尸	corpse
45	屮	sprout
46	山	mountain
47	川	river
48	工	work
49	己	self
50	巾	cloth
51	干	dry; shield
52	幺	young; slight
53	广	slanting roof
54	廴	move
55	廾	folded hands

56	弋	javelin
57	弓	bow (in archery)
58	彑, ヨ	pig's head
59	彡	hair-style; light rays
60	彳	step, stride

– 4 Strokes –

61	心, 忄, 㣺	heart
62	戈	spear
63	戸, 戶	weapon; door
64	手, 扌	hand
65	支	branch
66	攴, 攵	strike, hit
67	文	literature
68	斗	(unit of volume)
69	斤	ax
70	方	direction
71	无	not
72	日	sun; day
73	曰	say
74	月	moon; month
75	木	tree, wood
76	欠	lack
77	止	stop
78	歹	decompose
79	殳	lance shaft
80	毋	mother; not
81	比	compare
82	毛	hair
83	氏	family, clan
84	气	breath, air
85	水, 氵	water
86	火, 灬	fire

87	爪	claw, nail
88	父	father
89	爻	mix
90	爿, 丬	split wood (left half)
91	片	split wood (right half)
92	牙	fang, canine tooth
93	牛	cow, cattle
94	犬, 犭	dog

– 5 Strokes –

95	玄	darkness
96	玉, 王	jewel
97	瓜	melon
98	瓦	tile
99	甘	sweet
100	生	be born, live
101	用	use
102	田	rice paddy
103	疋, 乛	roll of cloth
104	疒	sickness
105	癶	outspread legs
106	白	white
107	皮	skin, hide
108	皿	bowl, dish
109	目	eye
110	矛	halberd
111	矢	arrow
112	石	stone
113	示, 礻	show, announce
114	禸	footprint
115	禾	grain

116	穴	hole
117	立	stand

– 6 Strokes –

118	竹, ⺮	bamboo
119	米	rice
120	糸, 糹	thread
121	缶	earthen jar
122	网, 罒	net
123	羊	sheep
124	羽, 羽	feather
125	老	old
126	而	and also
127	耒	plow
128	耳	ear
129	聿	writing brush
130	肉, 月	flesh, meat
131	臣	retainer, minister
132	自	self
133	至	arrive, reach
134	臼	mortar
135	舌	tongue
136	舛	contrary, err
137	舟	ship, boat
138	艮, 艮	boundary
139	色	color
140	艸, ⺾	grass, plant
141	虍	tiger
142	虫	worm, insect
143	血	blood
144	行	go
145	衣, 衤	clothing
146	西	cover; west

– 7 Strokes –

147	見	see
148	角	horn; corner
149	言	speak, say
150	谷	valley
151	豆	bean
152	豕	pig
153	豸	badger; reptile
154	貝	shell, mussel; money
155	赤	red
156	走	run
157	足	foot, leg
158	身	body
159	車	vehicle, wheel
160	辛	bitter
161	辰	(fifth zodiac sign); 7–9 A.M.
162	辵, 辶	advance, move ahead
163	邑, 阝	community
164	酉	wine jug; bird
165	釆	separate
166	里	(2.44 miles); village

– 8 Strokes –

167	金	metal, gold
168	長	long
169	門	gate, door
170	阜, 阝	hill
171	隶	capture
172	隹	small bird
173	雨	rain

174	靑 , 青	green, blue		198	鹿	deer
175	非	wrong; non-		199	麥	wheat
				200	麻	hemp

– 9 Strokes –

176	面	face; surface		**– 12 Strokes –**		
177	革	leather		201	黃	yellow
178	韋	leather		202	黍	millet
179	韭	leek		203	黑 , 黒	black
180	音	sound, noise		204	黹	embroider
181	頁	head; page				
182	風	wind		**– 13 Strokes –**		
183	飛	fly		205	黽	frog
184	食	food, eat		206	鼎	3-legged kettle
185	首	head		207	鼓	drum
186	香	scent		208	鼠	rat, mouse

– 10 Strokes –

187	馬	horse		**– 14 Strokes –**		
188	骨	bone		209	鼻	nose
189	高	high		210	齊 , 斉	alike
190	髟	long hair				
191	鬥	fighting		**– 15 Strokes –**		
192	鬯	herbs		211	齒 , 歯	tooth
193	鬲	tripod				
194	鬼	demon		**– 16 Strokes –**		
				212	龍 , 竜	dragon

– 11 Strokes –

195	魚	fish		**– 17 Strokes –**		
196	鳥	bird		213	龜 , 亀	turtle
197	鹵	salt		214	龠	flute

— 6. EXPLANATION OF THE KANJI LIST —

A sample entry from the Kanji List appears below, with annotations explaining the arrangement and typography.

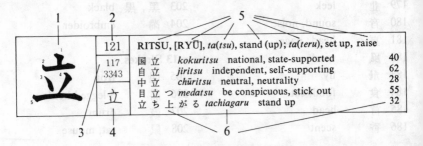

1. The kanji in brush form, with numbers showing stroke order positioned at the beginning of each stroke. Occasionally, to avoid a confusing clutter in a very complex character, one of the stroke-order numbers has been omitted when its position can be easily inferred. Other texts may give slightly different stroke orders and counts for some kanji.
2. Number of the kanji in this book.
3. Radical number (above) and kanji number (below) of the kanji as listed in Nelson's *Japanese–English Character Dictionary*.
4. The kanji in pen form. There are minor differences in style, stroke order, and even stroke count between the brush, pen, and printed forms of a few kanji.
5. *On* readings, in capital letters; *kun* readings, in lowercase italics; readings which are infrequent or used only in special cases, in brackets; *okurigana,* in parentheses; English meanings. All officially recognized readings of the kanji are listed, plus as many of the most important meanings as space allows. *On* readings are listed before *kun* readings, and within these divisions the more frequently used readings are given first.

6. Compounds, with romanization, meanings, and cross-reference numbers to the main entries for the other characters in the compound. Officially sanctioned *ateji* are listed among the compounds. Note that the readings of a kanji often undergo slight modification when it is combined with other kanji to form compounds. An example of this is the voicing of *tatsu* in the compound *medatsu* shown in the sample entry above.

A few other conventions have been used to save space or enhance clarity. The abbreviations "tr." and "intr." indicate where necessary whether a Japanese verb is transitive (that is, can be used with the particle を *o*) or intransitive. Similar English meanings are separated by a comma, but meanings which differ more sharply are marked off by a semicolon: "gem, jewel; ball."

Besides *okurigana,* parentheses enclose explanatory information and examples of usage. Parentheses also contain optional additions: "(sum) total" is short for "total, sum total"; and *nyūmon(sho)* for *nyūmon* or *nyūmonsho*. When additions appear on both the Japanese and English sides of an entry, there is correspondence between them: "*(rōdō) undō* (labor) movement" is a condensed way of writing "*undō* movement" and "*rōdō undō* labor movement." A parenthesized English preposition in the definition of a Japanese word corresponds to a Japanese particle (usually the particle に *ni*); compare "*saga(su)* look for" with "*masa(ru)* be superior (to)."

The slash [/] is used to save space by indicating alternative choices; thus, "comic book/strip" is short for "comic book, comic strip"; *jizen/go* for *jizen* and *jigo;* and *su(mu/mau)* for *su(mu), su(mau)*. When needed, a hyphen is used in conjunction with the slash to make its scope clear: *kigen-zen/go* is short for *kigenzen* and *kigengo*. When slashes appear on both the Japanese and English sides of an entry, they indicate one-to-one correspondence between the respective alternatives: "*hok/nan-kyoku* north/south pole" indicates that *hokkyoku* means "north pole" and *nankyoku* means "south pole."

The articles "a," "an," and "the" are used only when needed to clarify the meaning or connotation of an English definition, for example to indicate a noun which could otherwise be mistaken for a verb: "a jump," "a shout." Many Japanese words can also be used either as nouns or, by attaching a form of *suru,* as verbs. Wherever possible, this happy coincidence has been exploited by giving an English "noun-verb" as the equivalent of a Japanese noun-verb: "*henji* reply." Where this is not possible, usually only the more common form is given.

Here are some recommendations on how to study the 1,900 units of the Kanji List:

1. On the first reading, accentuate with a colored marker those readings and words which you already know. For the compounds, mark the kanji, not the *rōmaji;* try to get away as soon as possible from relying on the romanization, which after all is not even Japanese. The known readings and words will be used later in forming new words and meanings.

2. Write the kanji, first by itself, then as part of the compounds in which it occurs, until you can reproduce it readily from memory.

3. Keep firmly in mind the association between the writing, readings, meanings, and compounds of each character. Learn this information together as a single unit so that you do not wind up knowing, for example, the meaning of a kanji but not its readings. With many kanji you may find it possible to make up your own mnemonics. For example, the kanji 親 *oya,* "parent" is composed of the kanji 立 *ta(tsu),* "stand"; 木 *ki,* "tree"; and 見 *mi(ru),* "see, watch," so one can remember this character by picturing an image of parents standing in a tree watching over their children at play.

4. As you learn each kanji, check its radical number to see which radical it is listed under in Nelson.

5. On each repetition of a unit, learn at least one new reading or character combination and mark it (perhaps in a different color).

6. Test yourself on the writing, readings, and meanings of the characters you have learned. You can use a bookmark to cover up the part which is to be reproduced. Or make a self-testing card, with a notch or window positioned to expose only the desired part of the entry.

THE KANJI LIST

Note: The 1,900 characters in this Kanji List and the 45 characters in the Supplement, which begins on page 385, constitute the 1,945 officially recommended Jōyō Kanji.

	1	JIN, NIN, *hito*, human being, man, person
人	9 339	アメリカ人 *Amerikajin* an American 100 人 *hyakunin* 100 people 5, 6 人 *gorokunin* 5 or 6 people
	人	あ の 人 *ano hito* that person, he, she 人 々 *hitobito* people
	2	ICHI, ITSU, *hito(tsu)*, *hito-*, one
一	1 1	一 ペ ー ジ *ichi pēji* 1 page; page 1 り ん ご 一 つ *ringo hitotsu* 1 apple 一 つ 一 つ *hitotsu-hitotsu* one by one, individually
	一	一 人 *hitori* 1 person; alone 1 一 人 一 人 *hitori-hitori* one by one, one after another 1
	3	NI, *futa(tsu)*, *futa*, two
二	7 273	二 人 *futari, ninin* 2 people 1 一 人 二 人 *hitori futari* 1 or 2 people 2, 1 二 人 ず つ *futarizutsu* two by two, every 2 people 1
	二	二 人 と も *futaritomo* both people, both (of them) 1 二 け た *futaketa* 2 digits; 2-digit, double-digit
	4	SAN, *mit(tsu)*, *mi(tsu)*, *mi*, three
三	1 8	三 人 *sannin* 3 people 1 二, 三 人 *nisannin* 2 or 3 people 3, 1 三 キ ロ *sankiro* 3 kg; 3 km
	三	三 つ ぞ ろ い *mitsuzoroi* 3-piece suit 二 つ 三 つ *futatsu mittsu* 2 or 3 3
	5	NICHI, JITSU, *hi*, *-ka*, day; sun
日	72 2097	一 日 *ichinichi, ichijitsu* 1 day 2 *tsuitachi* 1st of the month 二 日 *futsuka* 2 days; 2nd of the month 3 三 日 *mikka* 3 days; 3rd of the month 4
	日	二, 三 日 *nisannichi* 2 or 3 days 3, 4
	6	SHI, *yot(tsu)*, *yo(tsu)*, *yo*, *yon*, four
四	31 1025	四 人 *yonin* 4 people 1 四 日 *yokka* 4 days; 4th of the month 5 三, 四 日 *san'yokka* 3 or 4 days 4, 5 三, 四 人 *san'yonin* 3 or 4 people 4, 1
	四	四 つ ん ば い *yotsunbai* (on) all fours
	7	GO, *itsu(tsu)*, *itsu*, five
五	1 15	五 人 *gonin* 5 people 1 五 日 *itsuka* 5 days; 5th of the month 5 四, 五 日 *shigonichi* 4 or 5 days 6, 5 四, 五 人 *shigonin* 4 or 5 people ⌜threes 6, 1
	五	三 々 五 々 *sansan-gogo* in small groups, by twos and 4

	8 8 283 六	**ROKU**, *mut(tsu)*, *mu(tsu)*, *mu*, [*mui*], six
六		六 人　　*rokunin*　6 people　　　　　　　　　1 五，六 人 *gorokunin*　5 or 6 people　　　7, 1 六 日　　*muika*　6 days; 6th of the month　5 五，六 日 *gorokunichi*　5 or 6 days　　　7, 5 六 つ ぐ ら い *muttsu-gurai*　about 6

	9 5 261 七	**SHICHI**, *nana(tsu)*, *nana*, [*nano*], seven
七		七 人　　*shichinin*　7 people　　　　　　　　1 七 日　　*nanoka*　7 days; 7th of the month　5 七 メ ー ト ル *nanamētoru*, *shichimētoru*　7 meters 七 五 三 *Shichigosan*　festival day for 3-, 5-, and 　　　　　7-year-olds (Nov. 15)　　　　　　7, 4

	10 12 577 八	**HACHI**, *yat(tsu)*, *ya(tsu)*, *ya*, [*yō*], eight
八		八 人　　*hachinin*　8 people　　　　　　　　1 八 日　　*yōka*　8 days; 8th of the month　　5 八 ミ リ *hachimiri*　8 mm 八 グ ラ ム *hachiguramu*　8 grams お 八 つ *oyatsu*　afternoon snack

	11 4 146 九	**KYŪ**, **KU**, *kokono(tsu)*, *kokono*, nine
九		九 人　　*kyūnin*, *kunin*　9 people　　　　　1 九 日　　*kokonoka*　9 days; 9th of the month　5 九 ド ル *kyūdoru*　9 dollars 九 九　　*kuku*　multiplication table

	12 24 768 十	**JŪ**, **JI'**, *tō*, *to*, ten
十		十 人　　*jūnin*　10 people　　　　　　　　　　1 十 日　　*tōka*　10 days; 10th of the month　　5 二 十 日 *hatsuka*　20 days; 20th of the month　3, 5 十 四 日 *jūyokka*　14 days; 14th of the month　6, 5 十 八 日 *jūhachinichi*　18 days; 18th of the month　10, 5

	13 13 617 円	**EN**, circle; yen; *maru(i)*, round
円		一 円　　*ichien*　1 yen　　　　　　　　　　　2 二 円　　*nien*　2 yen　　　　　　　　　　　　3 三 円　　*san'en*　3 yen　　　　　　　　　　　4 四 円　　*yoen*　4 yen　　　　　　　　　　　　6 十 円　　*jūen*, *tōen*　10 yen　　　　　　　　12

	14 1 33 百	**HYAKU**, hundred
百		百 人　　*hyakunin*　100 people　　　　　　　1 三 百 六 十 五 日 *sanbyaku rokujūgonichi* 　　　　　365 days　　　　　　　　4, 8, 12, 7, 5 八 百 円 *happyakuen*　800 yen　　　　　　10, 13 九 百　　*kyūhyaku*　900　　　　　　　　　　11

千 千	15 4 156	**SEN**, *chi*, thousand	
		一 千　*issen*　1,000	2
		三 千　*sanzen*　3,000	4
		八 千　*hassen*　8,000	10
		千 円　*sen'en*　1,000 yen	13
		千 人　*sennin*　1,000 people	1

万 万	16 1 7	**MAN**, ten thousand; **BAN**, many, all	
		一 万 円　*ichiman'en*　10,000 yen	2, 13
		百 万　*hyakuman*　1 million	14
		一 千 万 円　*issenman'en*　10 million yen	2, 15, 13
		二，三 万 円　*nisanman'en*　20,000–30,000 yen	3, 4, 13
		万 一　*man'ichi*　by any chance, should happen to	2

月 月	17 74 2169	**GETSU**, *tsuki*, moon; month; **GATSU**, month	
		一 月　*ichigatsu*　January	2
		hitotsuki　1 month	
		一 か 月　*ikkagetsu*　1 month	2
		一 月 八 日　*ichigatsu yōka*　January 8	2, 10, 5
		月 ロ ケ ッ ト　*tsuki roketto*　moon rocket	

明 明	18 72 2110	**MEI**, light; **MYŌ**, light; next; *a(kari)*, light, clearness; *aka(rui)*, bright; *aki(raka)*, clear; *a(keru)*, *aka(rumu/ramu)*, become light; *a(ku)*, be open; *a(kasu)*, pass (the night); divulge; *a(kuru)*, next, following	
		明 日　*myōnichi, asu*　tomorrow	5
		明 く る 日　*akuruhi*　the next/following day	5

曜 曜	19 72 2162	**YŌ**, day of the week	
		曜 日　*yōbi*　day of the week	5
		日 曜（日）　*nichiyō(bi)*　Sunday	5
		月 曜（日）　*getsuyō(bi)*　Monday	17, 5

火 火	20 86 2743	**KA**, *hi*, [*ho*], fire	
		火 曜（日）　*kayō(bi)*　Tuesday	19, 5
		九 月 四 日（火）　*kugatsu yokka (ka)*　(Tuesday) 　　　　September 4	11, 6, 17, 5

水 水	21 85 2482	**SUI**, *mizu*, water	
		水 曜（日）　*suiyō(bi)*　Wednesday	19, 5
		水 が め　*mizugame*　water jug/jar	
		水 か さ　*mizukasa*　volume of water (of a river)	

木	22 75 2170 木	**BOKU, MOKU**, *ki*, *[ko]*, tree, wood

<table>
<tr><td rowspan="6">木
<small>1 2</small></td><td>22
75
2170</td><td>**BOKU, MOKU**, *ki*, *[ko]*, tree, wood</td></tr>
<tr><td></td><td>木 曜（日）*mokuyō(bi)* Thursday   19, 5</td></tr>
<tr><td></td><td>木こり *kikori* woodcutter, lumberjack, logger</td></tr>
<tr><td></td><td>木々 *kigi* every tree; many trees</td></tr>
<tr><td>木</td><td>千木 *chigi* ornamental crossbeams on a Shinto shrine 15</td></tr>
<tr><td></td><td>三木 *Miki* (surname)   4</td></tr>
</table>

<table>
<tr><td rowspan="6">金</td><td>23
167
4815</td><td>**KIN, KON**, gold; metal; money; *kane*, money; *[kana]*, metal</td></tr>
<tr><td></td><td>金 曜（日）*kin'yō(bi)* Friday   19, 5</td></tr>
<tr><td></td><td>金メダル *kinmedaru* gold medal</td></tr>
<tr><td>金</td><td>金ばく *kinpaku* gold leaf/foil</td></tr>
<tr><td></td><td>金もうけ *kanemōke* making money</td></tr>
</table>

<table>
<tr><td rowspan="5">土</td><td>24
32
1050</td><td>**DO, TO**, *tsuchi*, earth, soil, ground</td></tr>
<tr><td></td><td>土 曜（日）*doyō(bi)* Saturday   19, 5</td></tr>
<tr><td></td><td>土木 *doboku* civil engineering   22</td></tr>
<tr><td>土</td><td>土人 *dojin* native, aborigine   1</td></tr>
<tr><td></td><td>土のう *donō* sandbag</td></tr>
</table>

<table>
<tr><td rowspan="5">本</td><td>25
2
96</td><td>**HON**, book; origin; main; this; (counter for long, thin objects); *moto*, origin</td></tr>
<tr><td></td><td>日本（人）*Nippon(jin)*, *Nihon(jin)* (a) Japan(ese)   5, 1</td></tr>
<tr><td></td><td>本日 *honjitsu* today   5</td></tr>
<tr><td>本</td><td>本だな *hondana* bookshelf</td></tr>
<tr><td></td><td>ビール六本 *bīru roppon* 6 bottles of beer   8</td></tr>
</table>

<table>
<tr><td rowspan="5">大</td><td>26
37
1171</td><td>**DAI, TAI**, *ō(kii)*, *ō-*, big, large; *ō(i ni)*, very much, greatly</td></tr>
<tr><td></td><td>大金 *taikin* large amount of money   23</td></tr>
<tr><td></td><td>大きさ *ōkisa* size</td></tr>
<tr><td>大</td><td>大水 *ōmizu* flooding, overflow   21</td></tr>
<tr><td></td><td>大みそか *Ōmisoka* New Year's Eve
大人 *otona* adult   1</td></tr>
</table>

<table>
<tr><td rowspan="5">小</td><td>27
42
1355</td><td>**SHŌ**, *chii(sai)*, *ko-*, *o-*, little, small</td></tr>
<tr><td></td><td>小人 *kobito* dwarf, midget   1
shōjin insignificant person; small-minded man
shōnin child</td></tr>
<tr><td>小</td><td>大小 *daishō* large and small; size   26</td></tr>
<tr><td></td><td>小金 *kogane* small sum of money; small fortune   23</td></tr>
</table>

<table>
<tr><td rowspan="5">中</td><td>28
2
81</td><td>**CHŪ**, *naka*, middle; inside; throughout</td></tr>
<tr><td></td><td>日本中 *Nipponjū*, *Nihonjū* all over Japan   5, 25</td></tr>
<tr><td></td><td>一日中 *ichinichijū* all day long   2, 5</td></tr>
<tr><td>中</td><td>日中 *nitchū* during the daytime   5
Nit-Chū Japanese-Chinese, Sino-Japanese</td></tr>
<tr><td></td><td>中小 *chūshō* medium and small, smaller, minor   27</td></tr>
</table>

風	29	FŪ, [FU], wind; appearance; style; *kaze*, [*kaza*], wind	
	182	日本風 *nihonfū* Japanese-style	5, 25
	5148	風土 *fūdo* natural features, climate	24
		中風 *chūfū, chūbu, chūbū* paralysis, palsy	28
	風	そよ風 *soyokaze* gentle breeze	

雨	30	U, *ame*, [*ama*], rain	
	173	風雨 *fūu* wind and rain	29
	5042	大雨 *ōame* heavy rain, downpour	26
		小雨 *kosame* light/fine rain	27
		にわか雨 *niwakaame* sudden shower	
	雨	雨水 *amamizu* rainwater	21

下	31	KA, GE, *shita*, *moto*, lower, base; *shimo*, lower part; *sa(geru)*, *o(rosu)*, *kuda(su)*, lower, hand down (a verdict); *sa(garu)*, hang down, fall; *o(riru)*, get out of/off (a vehicle); *kuda(ru)*, go/come down; *kuda(saru)*, give	
	1 9		
		下水 *gesui* sewer system, drainage	21
	下	風下 *kazashimo* leeward side	29

上	32	JŌ, [SHŌ], *ue*, upper; *kami*, [*uwa-*], upper part; *a(geru)*, raise; *a(garu)*, *nobo(ru)*, rise; *nobo(seru/su)*, bring up (a topic)	
	25 798		
		水上 *suijō* on the water	21
		上下 *jōge* high and low, rise and fall	31
	上	上り下り *noborikudari* ascent and descent, ups and downs	31

川	33	SEN, *kawa*, river	
	47	川上 *kawakami* upstream	32
	1447	川下 *kawashimo* downstream	31
		小川 *ogawa* stream, brook, creek	27
		ミシシッピー川 *Mishishippī-gawa* Mississippi River	
	川	中川 *Nakagawa* (surname)	28

山	34	SAN, *yama*, mountain	
	46	山水 *sansui* landscape, natural scenery	21
	1407	火山 *kazan* volcano	20
		下山 *gezan* descent from a mountain	31
		小山 *koyama* hill	27
	山	山々 *yamayama* mountains	

田	35	DEN, *ta*, rice field, paddy	
	102	水田 *suiden* rice paddy	21
	2994	田中 *Tanaka* (surname)	28
		本田 *Honda* (surname)	25
		山田 *Yamada* (surname)	34
	田	下田 *Shimoda* (city on Izu Peninsula)	31

	36	*hata*, *hatake*, cultivated field	
畑	86 2757 畑	田 畑 *tahata* fields	35
		み か ん 畑 *mikan-batake* mandarin orange/tangerine orchard	

	37	TŌ, *katana*, sword, knife	
刀	18 665 刀	日 本 刀 *nihontō* Japanese sword	5, 25
		大 刀 *daitō* long sword	26
		小 刀 *shōtō* short sword	27
		kogatana knife, pocketknife	
		山 刀 *yamagatana* woodsman's hatchet	34

	38	BUN, portion; BU, portion, 1 percent; FUN, minute (of time/arc); *wa(keru/katsu)*, divide, share, distinguish; *wa-(kareru)*, be separated; *wa(karu)*, understand	
分	12 578 分	十 分 *jūbun* enough, sufficient, adequate (cf. No. 828)	12
		jippun 10 minutes	
		水 分 *suibun* water content	21

	39	SETSU, [SAI], *ki(ru)*, cut; *ki(reru)*, cut well; break off; run out of	
切	18 667 切	大 切 *taisetsu* important; precious	26
		一 切 れ *hitokire* slice, piece	2
		切 り 上 げ *kiriage* conclusion; rounding up; revaluation	32
		切 り 下 げ *kirisage* reduction; devaluation	31

	40	KOKU, *kuni*, country	
国	31 1037 国	大 国 *taikoku* large/great country, major power	26
		万 国 *bankoku* all countries, world	16
		六 か 国 *rokkakoku* 6 countries	8
		四 国 *Shikoku* (one of the 4 main islands of Japan)	6
		中 国 *Chūgoku* China; (region in western Honshu)	28

	41	JI, *tera*, temple	
寺	32 1054 寺	国 分 寺 *Kokubunji* (common temple name)	40, 38
		山 寺 *yamadera* mountain temple	34

	42	JI, *toki*, time; hour	
時	72 2126 時	四 時 二 十 分 *yoji nijippun* 4:20	6, 3, 12, 38
		一 時 *ichiji* for a time; 1 o'clock	2
		hitotoki, *ittoki* a while, moment	
		時 々 *tokidoki* sometimes	
		日 時 *nichiji* time, date, day and hour	5

間 間	**43** 169 4949	**KAN, KEN**, *aida*, interval (between); *ma*, interval (between); a room
		時 間　*jikan*　time; hour 42
		中 間　*chūkan*　middle, intermediate 28
		人 間　*ningen*　human being 1
		間 も な く　*mamonaku*　presently, in a little while, soon

生 生	**44** 100 2991	**SEI, SHŌ**, life; *i(kiru/keru)*, be alive; *i(kasu)*, revive, bring to life; let live; *u(mu)*, bear (a child); *u(mareru)*, be born; *ha-(yasu/eru)*, *o(u)*, grow; *nama*, raw, draft (beer); *ki-*, pure
		人 生　*jinsei*　(human) life 1
		一 生　*isshō*　one's whole life 2

年 年	**45** 4 188	**NEN**, *toshi*, year
		生 年 月 日　*seinengappi*　date of birth 44, 17, 5
		1981 年　*sen kyūhyaku hachijūichinen*　1981
		五 年 間　*gonenkan*　for 5 years 7, 43
		年 金　*nenkin*　pension, annuity 23
		三 年 生　*sannensei*　third-year student, junior 4, 44

以 以	**46** 9 348	**I**, (prefix)
		以 上　*ijō*　or more; more than; above-mentioned 32
		三 時 間 以 上　*sanjikan ijō*　at least 3 hours ... 4, 42, 43, 32
		以 下　*ika*　or less; less than; as follows 31
		三 つ 以 下　*mittsu ika*　3 or fewer 4, 31

前 前	**47** 12 595	**ZEN**, *mae*, before, in front of; earlier
		以 前　*izen*　ago, previously, formerly 46
		前 も っ て　*maemotte*　beforehand, in advance
		人 前 (で)　*hitomae (de)*　before others, in public 1
		分 け 前　*wakemae*　one's share 38
		二 人 前　*nininmae, futarimae*　enough for 2 people 3, 1

後 後	**48** 60 1610	**GO**, *nochi*, after, later; **KŌ**, *ushi(ro)*, behind; *ato*, afterward, subsequent; back, retro-; *oku(reru)*, be late, lag behind
		以 後　*igo*　hereafter; since then 46
		前 後　*zengo*　approximately; front and rear 47
		明 後 日　*myōgonichi*　day after tomorrow 18, 5
		そ の 後　*sonogo*　thereafter, later

午 午	**49** 4 162	**GO**, noon
		午 前　*gozen*　A.M. 47
		午 後　*gogo*　afternoon; P.M. 48
		午 前 中　*gozenchū*　all morning, before noon 47, 28
		午 前 も 午 後 も　*gozen mo gogo mo*　both morning 47, 48
		午 後 四 時　*gogo yoji*　4:00 P.M.　⌊and afternoon 6, 48, 42

	50	**SEN**, *saki*, earlier; ahead; priority; future; destination; the tip
先	10 571	先日 *senjitsu* recently, the other day ... 5
		先月 *sengetsu* last month ... 17
		先々月 *sensengetsu* month before last ... 17
	先	先生 *sensei* teacher ... 44

	51	**KON, KIN**, *ima*, now
今	9 352	今日 *konnichi, kyō* today ... 5
		今月 *kongetsu* this month ... 17
		今年 *kotoshi* this year ... 45
		今後 *kongo* after this, from now on ... 48
	今	今ごろ *imagoro* about this time (of day)

	52	**NYŪ**, *hai(ru)*, *i(ru)*, go/come/get in, enter; *i(reru)*, put/let in
入	11 574	入国 *nyūkoku* entry into a country ... 40
		金入れ *kaneire* cashbox; purse, wallet ... 23
		日の入り *hi no iri* sunset ... 5
	入	入り日 *irihi* setting sun ... 5

	53	**SHUTSU, [SUI]**, *da(su)*, take out; send; *de(ru)*, go/come out
出	2 97	出火 *shukka* outbreak of fire ... 20
		出入り *deiri* coming and going (of people) ... 52
		人出 *hitode* turnout, crowds ... 1
	出	日の出 *hi no de* sunrise ... 5

	54	**KŌ, KU**, *kuchi*, mouth
口	30 868	人口 *jinkō* population, number of inhabitants ... 1
		入(り)口 *iriguchi* entrance ... 52
		出口 *deguchi* exit ... 53
		川口 *kawaguchi* mouth of a river ... 33
	口	口出し *kuchidashi* meddling, butting in ... 53

	55	**MOKU, [BOKU]**, *me*, [*ma*], eye; (suffix for ordinals)
目	109 3127	一目 *ichimoku, hitome* a glance ... 2
		人目 *hitome* notice, public attention ... 1
		目上 *meue* one's superior/senior ... 32
		目下 *meshita* one's subordinate/junior ... 31
	目	*mokka* at present

	56	**JI**, *mimi*, ear
耳	128 3697	耳目 *jimoku* eye and ear; attention, notice ... 55
		中耳 *chūji* the middle ear ... 28
	耳	耳たぶ *mimitabu* earlobe

	57	SHU, *te*, [*ta*], hand	
	64	切手 *kitte* (postage) stamp	39
	1827	小切手 *kogitte* (bank) check	27, 39
		手本 *tehon* model, example, pattern	25
		上手 *jōzu* skilled, good (at)	32
	手	下手 *heta* unskilled, poor (at)	31

	58	SOKU, *ashi*, foot, leg; *ta(ru/riru)*, be enough, sufficient; *ta(su)*, add up, add (to)	
	157		
	4546	一足 *issoku* 1 pair (of shoes/socks)	2
		hitoashi a step	
		手足 *teashi* hands and feet, limbs	57
	足	足下に *ashimoto ni* at one's feet; (watch your) step	31

	59	SHIN, *mi*, body	
	158	身上 *shinjō* strong point, merit; personal back-	32
	4601	*shinshō* one's fortune, property ⌐ground	
		出身 *-shusshin* (be) from . . .	53
		前身 *zenshin* one's past life; predecessor	47
	身	身分 *mibun* one's social standing; identity	38

	60	KYŪ, *yasu(mu)*, rest; *yasu(meru)*, give it a rest; *yasu(maru)*, be rested	
	9		
	380	休日 *kyūjitsu* holiday, day off	5
		一休み *hitoyasumi* short rest	2
		中休み *nakayasumi* a break, recess	28
	休	休み中 *yasumichū* Closed (shop sign)	28

	61	TAI, TEI, *karada*, body	
	9	身体 *shintai* body	59
	405	人体 *jintai* the human body	1
		五体 *gotai* the whole body	7
		大体 *daitai* gist; on the whole, generally	26
	体	風体 *fūtei, fūtai* (outward) appearance	29

	62	JI, SHI, *mizuka(ra)*, self	
	132	自分 *jibun* oneself, one's own	38
	3841	自身 *jishin* oneself, itself	59
		自体 *jitai* one's own body; itself	61
		自国 *jikoku* one's own country	40
	自	自らの手で *mizukara no te de* with one's own hands	57

	63	KEN, *mi(ru)*, see; *mi(eru)*, be visible; *mi(seru)*, show	
	147	一見 *ikken* (quick) glance	2
	4284	先見 *senken* foresight	50
		見本 *mihon* sample (of merchandise)	25
		見出し *midashi* heading, headline	53
	見	見分ける *miwakeru* tell apart, recognize	38

	64	BUN, MON, *ki(ku)*, hear; heed; ask; *ki(koeru)*, be audible
聞	169	見 聞 *kenbun* information, observation, experience 63
	4959	風 聞 *fūbun* hearsay, rumor 29
		聞 き 手 *kikite* listener 57
聞		聞 き 入 れ る *kikiireru* accede to, comply with 52

	65	SHU, *to(ru)*, take
取	128	取 り 出 す *toridasu* take out; pick out 53
	3699	取 り 上 げ る *toriageru* take up; adopt; take away 32
		聞 き 取 る *kikitoru* catch, follow (what someone says) 64
取		日 取 り *hidori* appointed day 5
		足 取 り *ashidori* way of walking, gait 58

	66	GEN, GON, -*koto*, word; *i(u)*, say
言	149	一 言 *ichigon, hitokoto* a word, brief comment 2
	4309	一 言 二 言 *hitokoto futakoto* a word or two 2, 3
		言 明 *genmei* declaration, definite statement 18
言		小 言 *kogoto* a scolding; complaints, griping 27
		言 い 分 *iibun* one's say; objection 38

	67	GO, word; *kata(ru)*, talk, relate; *kata(rau)*, converse
語	149	日 本 語 *Nihongo* Japanese language 5, 25
	4374	国 語 *kokugo* national/Japanese language 40
		言 語 *gengo* speech, language 66
語		一 語 一 語 *ichigo-ichigo* word for word, verbatim 2
		語 り 手 *katarite* narrator, storyteller 57

	68	KŌ, [AN], *i(ku)*, *yu(ku)*, go; GYŌ, line (of text); *okona(u)*, do, perform, carry out
行	144	一 行 *ikkō* party, retinue 2
	4213		*ichigyō* a line (of text)
		行 間 *gyōkan* space between lines (of text) 43
行		行 き 先 *ikisaki, yukisaki* destination 50

	69	RAI, *ku(ru)*, *kita(ru)*, come; *kita(su)*, bring about
来	4	来 年 *rainen* next year 45
	202	来 月 *raigetsu* next month 17
		来 日 *rainichi* come to Japan 5
来		本 来 *honrai* originally, primarily 25
		以 来 *irai* (ever) since 46

	70	HŌ, direction, side; *kata*, direction; person; method
方	70	一 方 *ippō* one side; on the other hand; only 2
	2082	四 方 *shihō* north, south, east, west; all directions 6
		八 方 *happō* all directions, all sides 10
方		方 言 *hōgen* dialect 66
		目 方 *mekata* weight 55

	71	**TŌ**, *higashi*, east	
東	4 213	東方 *tōhō* the eastward, east	70
		中東 *Chūtō* Middle East	28
		東大 *Tōdai* Tokyo University (abbrev. for 東京大学	
	東	*Tōkyō Daigaku*)	26
		東アジア *Higashi Ajia* East Asia	

	72	**SEI, SAI**, *nishi*, west	
西	146 4273	西方 *seihō* the westward, west	70
		東西 *tōzai* east and west	71
		西風 *seifū, nishikaze* westerly wind	29
	西	西日 *nishibi* the afternoon sun	5
		西ドイツ *Nishi Doitsu* West Germany	

	73	**HOKU**, *kita*, north	
北	21 751	北方 *hoppō* the northward, north	70
		北風 *hokufū, kitakaze* wind from the north	29
		東北 *Tōhoku* (region in northern Honshu)	71
	北	北東 *hokutō* northeast	71
		北北東 *hokuhokutō* north-northeast	71

	74	**NAN, [NA]**, *minami*, south	
南	24 778	西南 *seinan* southwest	72
		東南アジア *Tōnan Ajia* Southeast Asia	71
		南北 *nanboku* south and north, north-south	73
	南	南アルプス *Minami Arupusu* Southern (Japan) Alps	
		南口 *minamiguchi* southern entrance/exit	54

	75	**SA**, *hidari*, left	
左	48 1455	左方 *sahō* left side	70
		左手 *hidarite* left hand; (on) the left	57
		左足 *hidariashi* left foot/leg	58
	左	左目 *hidarime* left eye	55
		左上 *hidariue* upper left	32

	76	**U, YŪ**, *migi*, right	
右	30 878	右方 *uhō* right side	70
		左右 *sayū* left and right; control	75
		右手 *migite* right hand; (on) the right	57
	右	右足 *migiashi* right foot/leg ⌐quickly	58
		右から左へ *migi kara hidari e* from right to left;	75

	77	**TŌ**, *a(teru/taru)*, hit, be on target	
当	42 1359	本当 *hontō* truth; really	25
		当時 *tōji* at present; at that time	42
		当分 *tōbun* for now, for a while ⌐treatment	38
	当	手当て *teate* allowance, compensation; medical	57
		一人当たり *hitoriatari* per person, per capita	2, 1

	78	SEKI, [SHAKU], *ishi*, stone; [KOKU], (unit of volume, about 180 liters)
石	112 3176 石	石けん *sekken* soap 木 石 *bokuseki* trees and stones; inanimate objects 22 小 石 *koishi* small stone, pebble 27 石 切 り *ishikiri* stonecutting, quarrying 39
物	79 93 2857 物	BUTSU, MOTSU, *mono*, object, thing 人 物 *jinbutsu* person, personage 1 生 物 *seibutsu* living beings, life 44 見 物 *kenbutsu* sightseeing 63 物 語 *monogatari* tale, story 67 本 物 *honmono* genuine, the real thing 25
事	80 6 272 事	JI, [ZU], *koto*, thing, affair 人 事 *jinji* human/personnel affairs 1 火 事 *kaji* a fire 20 事 前/後 *jizen/go* before/after the fact 47, 48 大 事 *daiji* great thing, important 26 出 来 事 *dekigoto* event, occurrence 53, 69
夕	81 36 1167 夕	SEKI, *yū*, evening 一 夕 *isseki* one evening 2 夕 方 *yūgata* evening 70 夕 日 *yūhi* evening/setting sun 5 夕 月 *yūzuki* evening moon 17 七 夕 *Tanabata* Star Festival (July 7) 9
名	82 36 1170 名	MEI, MYŌ, *na*, name, reputation 人 名 *jinmei* name of a person 1 名 人 *meijin* master, expert, virtuoso 1 名 物 *meibutsu* noted product (of a locality) 79 大 名 *daimyō* (Japanese) feudal lord 26 名 前 *namae* a name 47
外	83 36 1168 外	GAI, GE, *soto*, outside; *hoka*, other; *hazu(reru/su)*, slip off; miss 外 (国) 人 *gai(koku)jin* foreigner 40, 1 外 来 語 *gairaigo* word of foreign origin, loanword 69, 67 外 出 *gaishutsu* go out 53 以 外 *igai* besides, except (for) 46
内	84 2 82 内	NAI, [DAI], *uchi*, inside 国 内 *kokunai* domestic, internal 40 体 内 *tainai* inside the body 61 内 外 *naigai* inner and outer; domestic and foreign 83 年 内 に *nennai ni* before the year is out 45 一 年 以 内 に *ichinen inai ni* within a year 2, 45, 46

死	**85**	**SHI**, death; *shi(nu)*, die
78	死体	*shitai* dead body, corpse	61
2439	死人	*shinin* dead person, the dead	1
	死後	*shigo* after death	48
死	水死	*suishi* drowning	21
	死語	*shigo* dead language	67

部	**86**	**BU**, part, section; copy of a publication
163	一部	*ichibu* a part	2
4767	部分	*bubun* a part	38
	大部分	*daibubun* greater part, most	26, 38
部	本部	*honbu* headquarters	25
	北部	*hokubu* the north (of a country)	73

倍	**87**	**BAI**, double, times, -fold
9	一倍	*ichibai* as much again	2
483	二倍	*nibai* double, twice as much	3
	三倍	*sanbai* 3 times as much, threefold	4
倍	三倍以上	*sanbai ijō* at least 3 times as much	4, 46, 32
	倍にする	*bai ni suru* double	

半	**88**	**HAN**, *naka(ba)*, half
3	半分	*hanbun* half	38
132	半年	*hantoshi* half a year, 6 months	45
	三時半	*sanjihan* 3:30	4, 42
半	前半	*zenhan, zenpan* first half	47
	大半	*taihan* greater part, majority	26

全	**89**	**ZEN**, *matta(ku)*, all, whole, entirely
9	全部	*zenbu* all	86
384	全国	*zenkoku* the whole country	40
	全体	*zentai* the whole, (in) all	61
全	全身	*zenshin* the entire body	59
	万全	*banzen* perfect, absolutely sure	16

回	**90**	**KAI**, [E], times, repetitions; *mawa(su)*, send around, rotate; *mawa(ru)*, go around, revolve
31	十回	*jikkai* 10 times	12
1028	今/前回	*kon/zenkai* this/last time	51, 47
	言い回し	*iimawashi* expression, turn of phrase	66
回	上回る	*uwamawaru* be more than, exceed	32

周	**91**	**SHŪ**, *mawa(ri)*, lap, circumference; surroundings
13	一周	*isshū* 1 lap, 1 revolution	2
622	半周	*hanshū* semicircle, halfway around	88
	円周	*enshū* circumference of a circle	13
周	百周年	*hyakushūnen* 100th anniversary	14, 45

	92	SHŪ, week	
週	162 4707	二 週 間 *nishūkan* 2 weeks 先 週 *senshū* last week 今 週 *konshū* this week 来 週 *raishū* next week 週 日 *shūjitsu* weekday	3, 43 50 51 69 5
	週		

	93	MU, BU, *na(i)*, not be; (prefix) un-, without, -less	
無	86 2773	無 名 *mumei* anonymous; unknown 無 口 *mukuchi* taciturn, laconic 無 言 *mugon* silent, mute 無 休 *mukyū* no holidays, always open (shop) 無 事 *buji* safe and sound	82 54 66 60 80
	無		

	94	FU, BU, (prefix) not, un-	
不	1 17	不 足 *fusoku* insufficiency, shortage 不 十 分 *fujūbun* not enough, inadequate 行方不明 *yukue fumei* whereabouts unknown, 68, 70, 18 不 当 *futō* improper, unjust ⌊missing 不 死 身 *fujimi* invulnerable	58 12, 38 77 85, 59
	不		

	95	CHŌ, long; chief, head; *naga(i)*, long	
長	168 4938	部 長 *buchō* department head, director 身 長 *shinchō* person's height 長 時 間 *chōjikan* long time, many hours 長 年 *naganen* many/long years 長 い 間 *nagai aida* for a long time	86 59 42, 43 45 43
	長		

	96	HATSU, HOTSU, emit; start from; depart	
発	105 3092	発 明 *hatsumei* invention 発 見 *hakken* discovery 発 行 *hakkō* publish, issue 出 発 *shuppatsu* departure, start out 発 足 *hossoku* start, inauguration	18 63 68 53 58
	発		

	97	SHIN, *kokoro*, heart, mind; core	
心	61 1645	中 心 *chūshin* center, midpoint 心 身 *shinshin* body and mind/spirit 本 心 *honshin* one's right mind; real intention 内 心 *naishin* one's inmost heart, true intent 一 心 に *isshin ni* with singlehearted devotion, fervently	28 59 25 84 2
	心		

	98	SEI, sex; nature (of); SHŌ, temperament	
性	61 1666	中 性 *chūsei* neuter gender 性 行 *seikō* character and conduct 発 が ん 性 *hatsugansei* carcinogenic, cancer-causing 性 分 *shōbun* nature, temperament 本 性 *honshō, honsei* true nature/character	28 68 96 38 25
	性		

	99	**SHI**, *omo(u)*, think, believe	
思	102 3001 思	思い出 *omoide* memories 思い出す *omoidasu* remember 思い切って *omoikitte* resolutely, daringly 思いやり *omoiyari* compassion, considerateness 思い上がった *omoiagatta* conceited, cocky	53 53 39 32
	100	**RYOKU, RIKI**, *chikara*, force, power	
力	19 715 力	体力 *tairyoku* physical strength 水力 *suiryoku* water/hydraulic power 風力 *fūryoku* force of the wind 全力 *zenryoku* all one's power, utmost efforts 無力 *muryoku* powerless, helpless	61 21 29 89 93
	101	**DAN, NAN**, *otoko*, man, human male	
男	102 2996 男	男性 *dansei* man; masculine gender 長男 *chōnan* eldest son 男の人 *otoko no hito* man 山男 *yamaotoko* mountain dweller; mountaineer 大男 *ōotoko* giant, tall man	98 95 1 34 26
	102	**JO, NYO, [NYŌ]**, *onna*, woman; *me*, feminine	
女	38 1185 女	女性 *josei* woman; feminine gender 長女 *chōjo* eldest daughter 男女 *danjo* men and women 女中 *jochū* maid 女の人 *onna no hito* woman	98 95 101 28 1
	103	**SHI, SU**, *ko*, child	
子	39 1264 子	男子 *danshi* boy, man 男の子 *otoko no ko* boy 女子 *joshi* girl, woman 女の子 *onna no ko* girl 分子 *bunshi* molecule; numerator of a fraction	101 101 102 102 38
	104	**KŌ**, *kono(mu)*, *su(ku)*, like	
好	38 1191 好	好物 *kōbutsu* favorite food 好人物 *kōjinbutsu* good-natured person 物好き *monozuki* idle curiosity 好き好き *sukizuki* matter of individual preference 大好き *daisuki* like very much	79 1, 79 79 26
	105	**AN**, peace, peacefulness; *yasu(i)*, cheap	
安	40 1283 安	安心 *anshin* feel relieved/reassured 安全 *anzen* safety 不安 *fuan* unease, anxiety, fear 安らか *yasuraka* peaceful, tranquil 安物 *yasumono* cheap goods	97 89 94 79

	106	AN, plan, proposal
案	40 1308 案	案内 *annai* guidance, information 84 案外 *angai* contrary to expectations 83 名案 *meian* good idea 82 思案 *shian* consideration, reflection 99 案出 *anshutsu* contrive, devise 53
用	107 101 2993 用	YŌ, business; usage; *mochi(iru)*, use 用事 *yōji* business affair; errand 80 用水 *yōsui* city/tap water 21 用語 *yōgo* (technical) term, vocabulary 67 無用 *muyō* useless; unnecessary 93 男子用 *danshiyō* for men, men's 101, 103
電	108 173 5050 電	DEN, electricity 電力 *denryoku* electrical power/energy 100 電子 *denshi* electron 103 発電 *hatsuden* generation of electricity 96 外電 *gaiden* telegram from abroad ⌈train 83 国電 *kokuden* (Japanese) National Railways electric 40
学	109 39 1271 学	GAKU, science, study; *mana(bu)*, learn 大学 *daigaku* university, college 26 学部 *gakubu* academic department; faculty 86 入学 *nyūgaku* entry/admission into a school 52 学生 *gakusei* student 44 語学 *gogaku* linguistics 67
字	110 40 1281 字	JI, character, letter; *aza*, village section 国字 *kokuji* national/Japanese script 40 当て字 *ateji* kanji used phonetically/for meaning 77 ローマ字 *rōmaji* roman letters 字体 *jitai* form of a character, type font 61 十字 *jūji* a cross 12
文	111 67 2064 文	BUN, MON, literature, text, sentence; *fumi*, letter, note 文字 *moji, monji* letter, character 110 文学 *bungaku* literature 109 本文 *honbun, honmon* text, wording 25 文語 *bungo* the written language 67 文明 *bunmei* civilization 18
母	112 80 2466 母	BO, *haha*, mother 母子 *boshi* mother and child 103 生母 *seibo* one's biological mother 44 母国語 *bokokugo* one's mother tongue 40, 67 母方 *hahakata* on the mother's side, maternal 70 お母さん *okāsan* mother

	113	FU, *chichi*, father	
父	88 2832 父	父母 *fubo, chichihaha* father and mother 父子 *fushi* father and child/son 父方 *chichikata* on the father's side, paternal 父上 *chichiue* father お父さん *otōsan* father	112 103 70 32

	114	KŌ, intersection; coming and going; *ma(jiru/zaru)*, (intr.) mix; *maji(eru)*, *ma(zeru)*, (tr.) mix; *maji(waru)*, *ka(u)*, associate (with); *ka(wasu)*, exchange (greetings)	
交	8 290 交	国交 *kokkō* diplomatic relations 外交 *gaikō* foreign policy, diplomacy 性交 *seikō* sexual intercourse	40 83 98

	115	KŌ, school; (printing) proof	
校	75 2260 校	学校 *gakkō* school 小学校 *shōgakkō* elementary school 中学校 *chūgakkō* junior high school 母校 *bokō* alma mater 校長 *kōchō* principal, headmaster	109 27, 109 28, 109 112 95

	116	MAI, every, each	
毎	80 2467 毎	毎年 *mainen, maitoshi* every year, yearly, annual 毎月 *maigetsu, maitsuki* every month, monthly 毎週 *maishū* every week, weekly 毎日 *mainichi* every day, daily 毎時 *maiji* every hour, hourly, per hour	45 17 92 5 42

	117	KAI, *umi*, sea, ocean	
海	85 2553 海	大海 *taikai* an ocean 海上 *kaijō* ocean, seagoing, marine 海外 *kaigai* overseas, abroad 内海 *uchiumi, naikai* inland sea 日本海 *Nihonkai* Sea of Japan	26 32 83 84 5, 25

	118	CHI, JI, earth, land	
地	32 1056 地	土地 *tochi* land, soil 地下 *chika* underground, subterranean 地方 *chihō* region, area 地名 *chimei* place name 生地 *kiji* material, cloth	24 31 70 82 44

	119	CHI, *ike*, pond	
池	85 2489 池	用水池 *yōsuichi* water reservoir 電池 *denchi* battery 池田 *Ikeda* (surname)	107, 21 108 35

他	120 9 361 他	**TA, other, another** 他人　　*tanin*　another person; stranger　　1 他国　　*takoku*　another/foreign country　　40 他方　　*tahō*　the other side/party/direction　　70 自他　　*jita*　oneself and others　　62 その他　*sonota*　and so forth
立	121 117 3343 立	**RITSU, [RYŪ], *ta(tsu)*, stand (up); *ta(teru)*, set up, raise** 国立　　*kokuritsu*　national, state-supported　　40 自立　　*jiritsu*　independent, self-supporting　　62 中立　　*chūritsu*　neutral, neutrality　　28 目立つ　*medatsu*　be conspicuous, stick out　　55 立ち上がる *tachiagaru*　stand up　　32
位	122 9 401 位	**I, *kurai*, rank, position** 地位　　*chii*　position, rank　　118 学位　　*gakui*　academic degree　　109 上位　　*jōi*　higher rank　　32 本位　　*hon'i*　monetary standard; basis, principle　　25 位取り　*kuraidori*　position (before/after decimal point)　　65
法	123 85 2535 法	**HŌ, HA', HO', law** 国法　　*kokuhō*　laws of the country　　40 立法　　*rippō*　enactment of legislation　　121 法案　　*hōan*　bill, legislative proposal　　106 文法　　*bunpō*　grammar　　111 方法　　*hōhō*　method　　70
和	124 115 3268 和	**WA, [O], peace, harmony; *yawa(rageru/ragu)*, *nago(mu)*, soften, calm down; *nago(yaka)*, mild, gentle, congenial** 和文　　*wabun*　Japanese script　　111 和風　　*wafū*　Japanese style　　29 不和　　*fuwa*　disharmony, discord, enmity　　94 大和　　*Yamato*　(old) Japan　　26
私	125 115 3265 私	**SHI, *watakushi*, I; private** 私事　　*shiji*　personal affairs　　80 私物　　*shibutsu*　private property　　79 私用　　*shiyō*　private use　　107 私立　　*shiritsu*　private, privately supported　　121 私自身　*watakushi jishin*　personally, as for me　　62, 59
公	126 12 579 公	**KŌ, *ōyake*, public, official** 公安　　*kōan*　public peace/security　　105 公法　　*kōhō*　public law　　123 公立　　*kōritsu*　public　　121 公海　　*kōkai*　international waters　　117 公言　　*kōgen*　public declaration, avowal　　66

	127	**RIN**, *hayashi*, woods, forest
林	75 2210	山 林　　*sanrin*　mountains and forests; mountain forest　34 (山) 林 学　(*san*)*ringaku*　forestry　　34, 109 林 立　　*rinritsu*　stand close together in large numbers 121 小 林　　*Kobayashi*　(surname)　27

	128	**SHIN**, *mori*, woods, forest
森	75 2301	森 林　　*shinrin*　woods, forest　127 大 森　　*Ōmori*　(area of Tokyo)　26

	129	**CHIKU**, *take*, bamboo
竹	118 3366	竹 林　　*chikurin, takebayashi*　bamboo grove/thicket 127 竹 刀　　*shinai*　bamboo sword (for Kendo)　37 さ お 竹　*saodake*　bamboo pole 竹 の つ え　*take no tsue*　bamboo cane 竹 や ぶ　*takeyabu*　bamboo thicket

	130	**HITSU**, *fude*, writing brush
筆	118 3397	万 年 筆　*mannenhitsu*　fountain pen　16, 45 自 筆　　*jihitsu*　one's own handwriting; autograph　62 筆 名　　*hitsumei*　pen name, pseudonym　82 文 筆　　*bunpitsu*　literary work, writing　111 筆 先　　*fudesaki*　tip of the writing brush　50

	131	**SHO**, *ka(ku)*, write
書	129 3719	書 物　　*shomotsu*　book　79 文 書　　*bunsho*　(in) writing, document　111 書 名　　*shomei*　book title　82 前 書 き　*maegaki*　foreword, preface　47 書 き 取 り　*kakitori*　dictation　65

	132	**I**, will, heart, mind, thought; meaning, sense
意	180 5113	意 見　　*iken*　opinion　63 用 意　　*yōi*　preparations, readiness　107 好 意　　*kōi*　goodwill, good wishes, kindness　104 意 外　　*igai*　unexpected, surprising　83 不 意　　*fui*　sudden, unexpected　94

	133	**SHA**, *kuruma*, vehicle; wheel
車	159 4608	電 車　　*densha*　electric train　108 人 力 車　*jinrikisha*　rickshaw　1, 100 発 車　　*hassha*　departure　96 下 車　　*gesha*　get off (a train)　31 水 車　　*suisha*　waterwheel　21

	134	KI, KE, spirit, soul, mood	
気	84 2480 気	人 気 *ninki* popularity 気 分 *kibun* feeling, mood 本 気 *honki* seriousness, (in) earnest 気 体 *kitai* a gas 電 気 *denki* electricity	1 38 25 61 108
汽	135 85 2507 汽	KI, steam 汽 車 *kisha* train drawn by steam locomotive	 133
原	136 27 825 原	GEN, original, fundamental; *hara*, plain, field; wilderness 原 案 *gen'an* the original plan/proposal 原 書 *gensho* (in) the original (text) 原 文 *genbun* the text, the original 原 生 林 *genseirin* primeval/virgin forest 原 子 *genshi* atom	 106 131 111 44, 127 103
元	137 7 275 元	GEN, yuan, yüan (Chinese monetary unit); GAN, *moto*, origin, foundation 元 日 *ganjitsu* New Year's Day 元 金 *gankin* principal (vs. interest) 元 気 *genki* healthy, peppy 地 元 *jimoto* local	 5 23 134 118
光	138 42 1358 光	KŌ, *hikari*, light; *hika(ru)*, shine 日 光 *nikkō* sunlight, sunshine 月 光 *gekkō* moonlight 光 年 *kōnen* light-year 発 光 *hakkō* luminosity, emit light 電 光 *denkō* electric light, lightning	 5 17 45 96 108
工	139 48 1451 工	KŌ, KU, artisan; manufacturing, construction 工 事 (中) *kōji(chū)* (under) construction 大 工 *daiku* carpenter 女 工 *jokō* woman factory-worker 工 学 *kōgaku* engineering 人 工 *jinkō* man-made, artificial	 80, 28 26 102 109 1
空	140 116 3317 空	KŪ, *sora*, sky; *a(keru/ku)*, make/be unoccupied; *kara*, empty 空 気 *kūki* air (時 間 と) 空 間 (*jikan to*) *kūkan* (time and) space 空 車 *kūsha* empty car, For Hire (taxi) 空 手 *karate* Karate 大 空 *ōzora* sky, firmament	 134 42, 43 133 57 26

— 90 —

	141	TEN, *ame*, [*ama*], heaven
天	1 16 天	天 気 *tenki* weather 134 天 文 学 *tenmongaku* astronomy 111, 109 天 国 *tengoku* paradise 40 天 性 *tensei* nature, natural constitution 98 天 の 川 *amanogawa* Milky Way 33

	142	RI, (old unit of length, about 2.9 km); *sato*, village; one's parents' home
里	166 4813 里	千 里 *senri* 1,000 *ri*; a great distance 15 海 里 *kairi* nautical mile 117 里 子 *satogo* foster child 103 里 心 *satogokoro* homesickness 97

	143	RI, reason, logic, principle
理	96 2942 理	地 理 (学) *chiri(gaku)* geography 118, 109 心 理 学 *shinrigaku* psychology 97, 109 理 学 部 *rigakubu* department of science 109, 86 無 理 *muri* unreasonable; impossible; (by) force 93 理 事 *riji* director 80

	144	SHŌ, *suko(shi)*, a little; *suku(nai)*, little, few, slight
少	4 166 少	少 年 *shōnen* boy 45 少 年 法 *shōnenhō* the Juvenile Law 45, 123 少 女 *shōjo* girl 102 少 々 *shōshō* a little 少 し ず つ *sukoshizutsu* little by little, a little at a time

	145	SEI, *kaeri(miru)*, reflect upon, give heed to; SHŌ, (government) ministry; *habu(ku)*, omit; cut down on
省	4 218 省	自 省 *jisei* reflection, introspection 62 内 省 *naisei* introspection 84 人 事 不 省 *jinjifusei* unconsciousness, fainting 1, 80, 94 文 部 省 *Monbushō* Ministry of Education 111, 86

	146	SŌ, aspect, phase; SHŌ, (government) minister; *ai-*, together, fellow, each other
相	75 2241 相	相 当 *sōtō* suitable, appropriate 77 文 相 *bunshō* minister of education 111 外 相 *gaishō* foreign minister 83 相 手 *aite* the other party, partner, opponent 57

	147	SŌ, [SO], idea, thought
想	61 1728 想	思 想 *shisō* idea, thought 99 回 想 *kaisō* retrospection, reminiscence 90 理 想 *risō* an ideal 143 空 想 *kūsō* fantasy, daydream 140 め い 想 *meisō* meditation

	148	**SHU**, *kubi*, neck, head	
首	185	首相 *shushō* prime minister	146
	5186	元首 *genshu* sovereign, ruler	137
		首位 *shui* leading position, top spot	122
	首	部首 *bushu* radical of a kanji	86
		手首 *tekubi* wrist	57

	149	**DŌ**, [TŌ], *michi*, street, way, path	
道	162	国道 *kokudō* national highway	40
	4724	水道 *suidō* water conduits, running water	21
		北海道 *Hokkaidō* (northernmost of the 4 main	73, 117
	道	書道 *shodō* calligraphy ⌊islands of Japan)	131
		回り道 *mawarimichi* a detour	90

	150	**TSŪ**, [TSU], *tō(ru)*, go through, pass; *tō(su)*, let through; *kayo(u)*, commute	
通	162		
	4703	交通 *kōtsū* traffic, transportation	114
		文通 *buntsū* correspondence, exchange of letters	111
	通	通学 *tsūgaku* attend school	109
		見通し *mitōshi* prospects, outlook	63

	151	**RO**, *-ji*, street, way	
路	157	道路 *dōro* street, road	149
	4561	十字路 *jūjiro* intersection, crossroads	12, 110
		水路 *suiro* waterway, aqueduct	21
	路	海路 *kairo* sea route	117
		通路 *tsūro* passageway, walkway, aisle	150

	152	**KO**, *to*, door	
戸	63	戸外で *kogai de* outdoors, in the open air	83
	1817	下戸 *geko* nondrinker, teetotaler	31
		戸口 *toguchi* doorway	54
	戸	戸だな *todana* closet, cupboard	
		雨戸 *amado* storm door, shutter	30

	153	**SHO**, *tokoro*, place	
所	63	案内所 *annaijo* inquiry office, information desk	106, 84
	1821	名所 *meisho* noted place, sights (to see)	82
		所長 *shochō* director, head, manager	95
	所	長所 *chōsho* strong point, merit, advantage	95
		発電所 *hatsudensho* power plant	96, 108

	154	**JŌ**, *ba*, place	
場	32	工場 *kōjō, kōba* factory, plant	139
	1113	出場 *shutsujō* stage appearance; participation	53
		場所 *basho* place, location	153
	場	立ち場 *tachiba* standpoint, point of view	121
		相場 *sōba* market price	146

	155	**SHU, [SU]**, *nushi*, lord, master; main; *omo*, main, principal
主	8	主 人　　*shujin*　husband, head of household … 1
	285	主 人 公　*shujinkō*　hero, main character … 1, 126
		自 主　　*jishu*　independence, autonomy … 62
主		主 語　　*shugo*　subject (in grammar) … 67
		地 主　　*jinushi*　landowner, landlord … 118

	156	**JŪ**, *su(mu/mau)*, live, dwell, reside
住	9	住 所　　*jūsho*　an address … 153
	404	住 人　　*jūnin*　inhabitant, resident … 1
		安 住　　*anjū*　peaceful living … 105
住		住 ま い　*sumai*　residence, where one lives, address
		住 み 心 地　*sumigokochi*　comfortableness, livability 97, 118

	157	**SHIN**, faith, trust, belief
信	9	信 用　　*shin'yō*　trust … 107
	454	不 信　　*fushin*　bad faith, insincerity; distrust … 94
		自 信　　*jishin*　(self-)confidence … 62
信		所 信　　*shoshin*　one's conviction, opinion ⌈patch 153
		通 信　　*tsūshin*　communication, correspondence, dis- … 150

	158	**KAI**, meeting; association; **E**, *a(u)*, meet
会	9	国 会　　*kokkai*　parliament, diet, congress … 40
	381	大 会　　*taikai*　mass meeting; sports meet, tournament 26
		学 会　　*gakkai*　learned/academic society … 109
会		会 見　　*kaiken*　interview, news conference … 63
		出 会 う　*deau*　happen to meet, run into … 53

	159	**GŌ, GA'**, [**KA'**], *a(u)*, fit; *a(waseru/wasu)*, put together
合	9	合 意　　*gōi*　mutual consent, agreement … 132
	383	場 合　　*baai, bawai*　(in this) case … 154
		(お) 見 合 い *(o)miai*　marriage interview … 63
合		見 合 わ せ る *miawaseru*　look at each other; postpone 63
		間 に 合 う *ma ni au*　be in time (for); will do, suffice 43

	160	**TŌ**, *kota(e)*, an answer; *kota(eru)*, answer
答	118	回 答　　*kaitō*　an answer, reply … 90
	3394	口 答　　*kōtō*　oral answer … 54
		筆 答　　*hittō*　written answer … 130
答		名 答　　*meitō*　correct answer … 82
		答 案　　*tōan*　examination paper … 106

	161	**MON**, *kado*, gate
門	169	入 門 (書) *nyūmon(sho)*　introduction, primer … 52, 131
	4940	部 門　　*bumon*　group, category, branch … 86
		名 門　　*meimon*　distinguished/illustrious family … 82
門		門 下 生 *monkasei*　(someone's) pupil … 31, 44
		門 口　　*kadoguchi*　front door, entrance … 54

	162	**MON**, *to(i)*, [*ton*], question, problem; *to(u)*, matter, care about	
問	169 4944	問 答 *mondō* questions and answers, dialogue	160
		学 問 *gakumon* learning, science	109
	問	問 い 合 わ せ る *toiawaseru* inquire, ask	159
		問 い た だ す *toitadasu* inquire, question	
	163	**IN**, member	
員	30 928	会 員 *kaiin* member (of a society)	158
		海 員 *kaiin* seaman, sailor	117
		工 員 *kōin* factory worker	139
	員	人 員 *jin'in* staff, personnel	1
		全 員 *zen'in* all members, entire staff	89
	164	**SHA**, *mono*, person	
者	125 3685	学 者 *gakusha* scholar	109
		日 本 学 者 *Nihongakusha* Japanologist	5, 25, 109
		筆 者 *hissha* writer, author	130
	者	信 者 *shinja* believer, the faithful	157
		後 者 *kōsha* the latter	48
	165	**KA, KE**, *ie*, *ya*, house; family	
家	40 1311	家 事 *kaji* family affairs; household chores	80
		家 内 *kanai* (one's own) wife	84
		家 来 *kerai* retainer, vassal	69
	家	国 家 *kokka* state, nation	40
		家 主 *yanushi* landlord, house owner	155
	166	**SHITSU**, a room; *muro*, greenhouse; cellar	
室	40 1300	和 室 *washitsu* Japanese-style room	124
		私 室 *shishitsu* private room	125
		室 内 *shitsunai* in a room, indoor	84
	室	分 室 *bunshitsu* isolated room; annex	38
		室 長 *shitsuchō* senior roommate; section chief	95
	167	**OKU**, *ya*, roof, house; shop, dealer	
屋	44 1392	家 屋 *kaoku* house, building	165
		屋 上 *okujō* roof, rooftop	32
		部 屋 *heya* a room	86
	屋	小 屋 *koya* cottage, hut, shack	27
		八 百 屋 *yaoya* vegetable shop, greengrocer	10, 14
	168	**TEN**, *mise*, shop, store	
店	53 1509	書 店 *shoten* bookstore	131
		本 店 *honten* head office, main shop	25
		店 員 *ten'in* store employee, clerk	163
	店	店 先 *misesaki* storefront	50
		出 店 *demise* branch store	53

	169	TEN, point	
	25	出発点 *shuppatsuten* starting point	53, 96
	804	原点 *genten* starting point; origin (of coordinates)	136
		合点 *gaten, gatten* understanding; consent	159
	点	点字 *tenji* Braille	110
		点火 *tenka* ignite	20

	170	KYOKU, bureau, office	
	44	当局 *tōkyoku* the authorities, responsible officials	77
	1384	局長 *kyokuchō* director of a bureau; postmaster	95
		局員 *kyokuin* staff member of a bureau	163
	局	局外者 *kyokugaisha* outsider, onlooker	83, 164
		時局 *jikyoku* the situation	42

	171	KYO, i(ru), be (present), exist	
	44	住居 *jūkyo* dwelling, residence	156
	1387	居住地 *kyojūchi* place of residence	156, 118
		居間 *ima* living room	43
	居	長居 *nagai* stay (too) long	95
		居合わせる *iawaseru* (happen to) be present	159

	172	KO, furu(i), old; furu(su), wear out	
	24	古風 *kofū* old customs; antiquated	29
	770	古語 *kogo* archaic word; old adage	67
		古文 *kobun* classical literature, ancient classics	111
	古	古今東西 *kokon-tōzai* all ages and countries	51, 71, 72
		古本 *furuhon* secondhand/used book	25

	173	KO, deceased; yue, reason, cause; circumstances	
	66	故人 *kojin* the deceased	1
	2044	故事 *koji* historical event	80
		事故 *jiko* accident	80
	故	故国 *kokoku* one's homeland, native country	40
		故意 *koi* intention, purpose	132

	174	SHIN, atara(shii), ara(ta), nii-, new	
	69	新聞 *shinbun* newspaper	64
	2080	古新聞 *furushinbun* old newspapers	172
		新年 *shinnen* the New Year	45
	新	新人 *shinjin* newcomer, new face	1
		一新 *isshin* renovation, reform	2

	175	SHIN, intimacy; parent; oya, parent; shita(shii), intimate, close (friend); shita(shimu), get to know better	
	147	親切 *shinsetsu* kind, friendly	39
	4293	親日 *shin-Nichi* pro-Japanese	5
		母親 *hahaoya* mother	112
	親	親子 *oyako* parent and child	103

	176	SHITSU, quality, nature; SHICHI, [CHI], hostage; pawn
質	154 4518 質	質問 *shitsumon* a question 162 性質 *seishitsu* nature, property 98 物質 *busshitsu* matter, material, substance 79 本質 *honshitsu* essence, substance 25 人質 *hitojichi* hostage 1
	177	MIN, *tami*, people, nation
民	1 25 民	国民 *kokumin* people, nation, citizen 40 人民 *jinmin* the people, citizens 1 (原)住民 *(gen)jūmin* (aboriginal) native of a place 136, 156 民間 *minkan* private (not public) 43 民意 *min'i* will of the people 132
	178	TAKU, house, home, residence
宅	40 1279 宅	住宅 *jūtaku* house, residence 156 自宅 *jitaku* one's own home, private residence 62 私宅 *shitaku* one's private residence 125 宅地 *takuchi* land for housing, residential site 118 家宅 *kataku* house, the premises 165
	179	SHUKU, *yado*, lodging, inn; *yado(ru)*, take shelter; be pregnant; *yado(su)*, give shelter; conceive (a child)
宿	40 1317 宿	下宿 *geshuku* room and board; boardinghouse 31 合宿 *gasshuku* lodging together 159 民宿 *minshuku* private house providing tourist 177 宿屋 *yadoya* inn ⌊lodging 167
	180	SHI, *kami*, paper
紙	120 3510 紙	和紙 *washi* Japanese paper 124 日本紙 *nihonshi* Japanese paper 5, 25 新聞紙 *shinbunshi* newspaper; newsprint 174, 64 質問用紙 *shitsumon yōshi* questionnaire 176, 162, 107 手紙 *tegami* letter 57
	181	SHI, city; *ichi*, market
市	8 284 市	市長 *shichō* mayor 95 市会 *shikai* municipal assembly, city council 158 市立 *shiritsu* municipal 121 市民 *shimin* citizen, townspeople 177 市場 *ichiba, shijō* marketplace, market 154
	182	CHŌ, *machi*, town, quarter
町	102 2995 町	町民 *chōmin* townsman, townsfolk 177 町人 *chōnin* merchant; townsfolk 1 町内 *chōnai* neighborhood 84 下町 *shitamachi* (low-lying) downtown area 31 室町 *Muromachi* (historical period, 1392–1573) 166

	183	**KU**, municipal administrative district, ward	
区	22 757	地区 *chiku* district, area, zone	118
		区間 *kukan* section, interval	43
		区切る *kugiru* partition; punctuate	39
		区分 *kubun* division, partition; classification	38
	区	北区 *Kita-ku* Kita Ward (Tokyo)	73

	184	**CHŌ**, even number; (counter for blocks of houses/blocks of tofu/guns/dishes of prepared food); **TEI**, **D**, No. 4 (in a series); adult; **т** shape	
丁	1 2	丁目 *chōme* city block (in addresses)	55
		丁年 *teinen* (age of) majority, adulthood	45
	丁	丁字路 *teijiro* **T**-shaped street intersection	110, 151

	185	**BAN**, keeping watch; number, order	
番	165 4811	一番 *ichiban* the first; number one, most	2
		二番目 *nibanme* the second, No. 2	3, 55
		番地 *banchi* lot/house number	118
	番	局番 *kyokuban* exchange (part of a phone number)	170
		交番 *kōban* police box	114

	186	**GAI**, [**KAI**], *machi*, street	
街	60 1626	街路 *gairo* street	151
		街道 *kaidō* street, highway	149
		市街 *shigai* the streets (of a city); town	181
	街	名店街 *meitengai* arcade of well-known stores	82, 168
		地下街 *chikagai* underground shopping mall	118, 31

	187	**JUTSU**, art, technique; means; conjury	
術	60 1621	手術 *shujutsu* (surgical) operation	57
		手術室 *shujutsushitsu* operating room	57, 166
		学術 *gakujutsu* science, learning	109
	術	(学)術(用)語 *(gaku)jutsu(yō)go* technical term, terminology	109, 107, 67

	188	**TO**, **TSU**, *miyako*, capital (city)	
都	163 4769	(大)都市 *(dai)toshi* (major/large) city	26, 181
		都会 *tokai* city	158
		首都 *shuto* capital (city)	148
	都	都内 *tonai* in (the city of) Tokyo	84
		都合 *tsugō* circumstances, reasons	159

	189	**KYŌ**, **KEI**, the capital	
京	8 295	東京(都) *Tōkyō(-to)* (City of) Tokyo	71, 188
		京都(市) *Kyōto(-shi)* (City of) Kyoto	188, 181
		上京 *jōkyō* go/come to Tokyo	32
	京	北京 *Pekin* Peking, Beijing	73

— 97 —

	190	**KŌ**, *taka(i)*, high; expensive; *taka*, amount, quantity; *taka-(maru)*, rise; *taka(meru)*, raise	
高	189 5248 高	高原 *kōgen* plateau, heights, tableland 高校 *kōkō* senior high school (cf. No. 569) 名高い *nadaka(i)* renowned, famous	136 115 82

	191	**SON**, *mura*, village	
村	75 2191 村	市町村 *shichōson* cities, towns, and villages 村会 *sonkai* village assembly 村長 *sonchō* village mayor 村民 *sonmin* villager 村人 *murabito* villager	181, 182 158 95 177 1

	192	**FU**, *tsu(ku)*, be attached, belong (to); *tsu(keru)*, attach, apply (cf. No. 1843)	
付	9 363 付	交付 *kōfu* deliver, hand over 日付け *hizuke* date (of a letter) 気付く *kizuku* (take) notice 付き物 *tsukimono* what (something) entails, adjunct	114 5 134 79

	193	**GUN**, county, district	
郡	163 4764 郡	郡部 *gunbu* rural district 新田郡 *Nitta-gun* Nitta District (in Gunma Prefecture)	86 174, 35

	194	**KEN**, prefecture, province	
県	42 1362 県	郡県 *gunken* districts/counties and prefectures 県立 *kenritsu* prefectural, provincial 県道 *kendō* prefectural highway 県会 *kenkai* prefectural assembly 山口県 *Yamaguchi-ken* Yamaguchi Prefecture	193 121 149 158 34, 54

	195	**SHŪ**, state, province; *su*, sandbank, shoals	
州	2 99 州	本州 *Honshū* (largest of the 4 main islands of Japan) カリフォルニア州 *Kariforunia-shū* (State of) California 五大州 *godaishū* Asia, Africa, Europe, America, and Australia 中州 *nakasu* sandbank in a river	25 7, 26 28

	196	**KYŌ**, *tomo*, together, both, all	
共	12 581 共	共学 *kyōgaku* coeducation 共通 *kyōtsū* (in) common (with) 公共 *kōkyō* the public, community 共和国 *kyōwakoku* republic	109 150 126 124, 40

	197	**KYŌ**, [KU], *tomo*, retinue, attendant; serve; *sona(eru)*, offer	
供	9 431	供出 *kyōshutsu* delivery	53
		自供 *jikyō* confession, admission	62
		供物 *kumotsu* votive offering	79
		子供 *kodomo* child	103
供		（お）供 *(o)tomo* accompany (someone)	

	198	**DŌ**, *ona(ji)*, same	
同	13 619	同時に *dōji ni* at the same time, simultaneously	42
		共同 *kyōdō* joint, communal, cooperative	196
		合同 *gōdō* combination, merger, joint	159
		同意 *dōi* agreement, consent	132
同		同居 *dōkyo* live in the same house	171

	199	**KŌ**, *mu(kau)*, face (toward); proceed (to); *mu(ku/keru)*, (intr./tr.) turn; *mu(kō)*, opposite side	
向	2 101	方向 *hōkō* direction	70
		向上 *kōjō* elevation, betterment	32
		意向 *ikō* intention, inclination	132
向		外人向け *gaijinmuke* for foreigners	83, 1

	200	**RYŌ**, both; (obsolete Japanese coin)	
両	1 34	両親 *ryōshin* parents	175
		両方 *ryōhō* both	70
		両手 *ryōte* both hands	57
		両立 *ryōritsu* coexist, be compatible (with)	121
両		車両 *sharyō* car, vehicle	133

	201	**MAN**, *mi(chiru)*, become full; *mi(tasu)*, fill; fulfill	
満	85 2636	満足 *manzoku* satisfaction	58
		不満 *fuman* dissatisfaction, discontent	94
		満員 *man'in* full to capacity	163
		満点 *manten* perfect score	169
満		円満 *enman* harmonious, peaceful, perfect	13

	202	**HEI, BYŌ**, *tai(ra)*, *hira*, flat, level	
平	1 26	平行 *heikō* parallel	68
		平和 *heiwa* peace	124
		不平 *fuhei* discontent, complaint	94
		平家 *Heike* (historical clan name)	165
平		平屋 *hiraya* 1-story house	

	203	**JITSU**, truth, actuality; *mi*, fruit, nut; *mino(ru)*, bear fruit	
実	40 1297	事実 *jijitsu* fact	80
		口実 *kōjitsu* pretext, excuse	54
		実行 *jikkō* put into practice, carry out, realize	68
		実力 *jitsuryoku* actual ability, competence	100
実		実用 *jitsuyō* practical use	107

	204	**SHOKU, SHIKI**, *iro*, color; erotic passion	
色	139 3889 色	原色 *genshoku* primary color	136
		好色 *kōshoku* sensuality, lust, eroticism	104
		色紙 *shikishi* (type of calligraphy paper)	180
		irogami colored paper	
		金色 *kin'iro, kinshoku, konjiki* gold color	23

	205	**HAKU, BYAKU**, *shiro(i)*, *shiro*, [*shira*], white	
白	106 3095 白	白紙 *hakushi* white/blank paper	180
		白書 *hakusho* a white paper (on), report	131
		白人 *hakujin* a white, Caucasian	1
		自白 *jihaku* confession, admission	62
		空白 *kūhaku* a blank; vacuum	140

	206	**KOKU**, *kuro(i)*, *kuro*, black	
黒	203 5403 黒	黒人 *kokujin* a black, Negro	1
		黒白 *kuroshiro, kokubyaku* black and/or white;	
		right and wrong	205
		黒字 *kuroji* (in the) black, black figures	110
		黒子 *kuroko* black-clad Kabuki stagehand	103

	207	**SEKI, [SHAKU]**, *aka(i)*, *aka*, red; *aka(ramu)*, become red, blush; *aka(rameru)*, make red, blush	
赤	155 4534 赤	赤十字 *Sekijūji* Red Cross	12, 110
		赤道 *sekidō* equator	149
		赤字 *akaji* deficit, red figures, (in the) red	110
		赤ちゃん *akachan* baby	

	208	**SEI, [SHŌ]**, *ao(i)*, *ao*, blue, green; unripe	
青	174 5076 青	青年 *seinen* young man/people	45
		青少年 *seishōnen* young people, youth	144, 45
		青空 *aozora* blue sky	140
		青空市場 *aozora ichiba* open-air market	140, 181, 154
		青物 *aomono* green vegetables	79

	209	**JŌ, [SEI]**, *nasa(ke)*, emotion, sympathy; circumstances	
情	61 1714 情	人情 *ninjō* human feelings, humanity	1
		同情 *dōjō* sympathy	198
		無情 *mujō* heartlessness, callousness	93
		事情 *jijō* circumstances, situation	80
		実情 *jitsujō* actual situation, the facts	203

	210	**TEKI**, (attributive suffix); *mato*, target	
的	106 3097 的	目的 *mokuteki* purpose, aim, goal	55
		一時的 *ichijiteki* temporary	2, 42
		民主的 *minshuteki* democratic	177, 155
		理想的 *risōteki* ideal	143, 147
		自発的 *jihatsuteki* voluntary, spontaneous	62, 96

	211	**YAKU**, approximately; promise	
約	120 3499	公 約 *kōyaku* public commitment	126
		口 約 *kōyaku* verbal promise ⌈gagement	54
		先 約 (が あ る) *sen'yaku (ga aru)* (have a) previous en-	50
約		約半分 *yaku hanbun* approximately half	88, 38
		約 三 キ ロ *yaku sankiro* approximately 3 km/kg	4

	212	**KYŪ**, *yumi*, bow (for archery/violin)	
弓	57 1560	弓 術 *kyūjutsu* (Japanese) archery	187
弓		弓 道 *kyūdō* (Japanese) archery	149

	213	**SHI**, *ya*, arrow	
矢	111 3168	弓矢 *yumiya* bow and arrow	212
矢			

	214	**CHI**, *shi(ru)*, know	
知	111 3169	通 知 *tsūchi* a notification, communication	150
		周 知 *shūchi* common knowledge, generally known	91
		知事 *chiji* governor (of a prefecture)	80
知		知人 *chijin* an acquaintance	1
		知 り 合 い *shiriai* an acquaintance	159

	215	**TAN**, *mijika(i)*, short	
短	111 3172	長 短 *chōtan* (relative) length; good and bad points	95
		短刀 *tantō* short sword, dagger	37
		短気 *tanki* short temper, touchiness, hastiness	134
短		短所 *tansho* defect, shortcoming	153
		短大 *tandai* junior college (cf. No. 449)	26

	216	**IN**, *hi(ku)*, pull; attract; *hi(keru)*, be ended; make cheaper	
引	57 1562	引力 *inryoku* attraction, gravitation	100
		引用 *in'yō* quotation, citation	107
		引 き 出 し *hikidashi* drawer	53
引		取 り 引 き *torihiki* transaction, trade	65
		引 き 上 げ *hikiage* raise, increase	32

	217	**KYŌ, GŌ**, *tsuyo(i)*, strong; *tsuyo(maru)*, become strong(er); *tsuyo(meru)*, make strong(er), strengthen; *shi(iru)*, force	
強	57 1571	強力 *kyōryoku* strength, power	100
		強国 *kyōkoku* strong country, great power	40
		強情 *gōjō* stubbornness, obstinacy	209
強		強引 に *gōin ni* by force	216

	218	JAKU, *yowa(i)*, weak; *yowa(ru/maru)*, become weak(er); *yowa(meru)*, make weak(er), weaken	
弱	15 650	強弱 *kyōjaku* strengths and weaknesses, strength	217
		弱点 *jakuten* a weakness, weak point	169
		弱体 *jakutai* weak	61
弱		弱気 *yowaki* faintheartedness; bearishness	134

	219	DOKU, *hito(ri)*, alone	
独	94 2884	独立 *dokuritsu* independence	121
		独身 *dokushin* unmarried, single	59
		独学 *dokugaku* self-study 「German	109
独		日独 *Nichi-Doku* Japan and Germany, Japanese-	5
		和独 *Wa-Doku* Japanese-German (dictionary)	124

	220	I, medicine, healing	
医	22 763	医学 *igaku* medicine	109
		医学部 *igakubu* medical department/school	109, 86
		医学用語 *igaku yōgo* medical term	109, 107, 67
医		医者 *isha* physician, doctor	164
		女医 *joi* woman physician, lady doctor	102

	221	ZOKU, family, tribe	
族	70 2090	家族 *kazoku* family	165
		親族 *shinzoku* relative, kin	175
		一族 *ichizoku* one's whole family, kin	2
族		部族 *buzoku* tribe	86
		民族 *minzoku* race, people, nation	177

	222	RYO, *tabi*, trip, travel	
旅	70 2088	旅行 *ryokō* trip, travel	68
		旅行者 *ryokōsha* traveler, tourist	68, 164
		旅人 *tabibito* traveler, wayfarer	1
旅		旅先 *tabisaki* destination	50
		旅立つ *tabidatsu* start on a journey	121

	223	NIKU, meat, flesh	
肉	130 3724	肉屋 *nikuya* butcher (shop)	167
		肉体 *nikutai* the body, the flesh	61
		肉親 *nikushin* blood relationship/relative	175
肉		肉付きのよい *nikuzuki no yoi* well-fleshed, plump	192
		肉筆 *nikuhitsu* one's own handwriting; autograph	130

	224	BEI, MAI, *kome*, rice	
米	119 3461	白米 *hakumai* polished rice	205
		新米 *shinmai* new rice; novice	174
		外米 *gaimai* imported rice	83
米		日米 *Nichi-Bei* Japan and America, Japanese-U.S.	5
		南米 *Nanbei* South America	74

	225	SŪ, [SU], *kazu*, number; *kazo(eru)*, count	
数	66 2057	数字　*sūji*　digit, numeral, figures	110
		数学　*sūgaku*　mathematics	109
		人数　*ninzū*　number of people	1
	数	無数　*musū*　countless, innumerable	93
		手数　*tesū*　trouble, bother	57

	226	RUI, kind, type, genus	
類	181 5138	親類　*shinrui*　relative, kin	175
		人類　*jinrui*　mankind	1
		書類　*shorui*　papers, documents	131
	類	分類　*bunrui*　classification	38
		類語　*ruigo*　synonym	67

	227	JŪ, CHŌ, *omo(i)*, heavy; *kasa(naru/neru)*, lie/pile on top of one another; *-e*, -fold, -ply	
重	4 224	体重　*taijū*　body weight	61
		重力　*jūryoku*　gravity, gravitation	100
		重大　*jūdai*　weighty, grave, important	26
	重	二重　*nijū, futae*　double, twofold	3

	228	SHU, kind, type; seed; *tane*, seed; species; cause	
種	115 3295	種類　*shurui*　kind, type, sort	226
		一種　*isshu*　kind, sort	2
		人種　*jinshu*　a human race	1
	種	種子　*shushi*　seed, pit	103
		不安の種　*fuan no tane*　cause of unease	94, 105

	229	TA, *ō(i)*, much, many, numerous	
多	36 1169	多少　*tashō*　much or little, many or few; some	144
		多数　*tasū*　large number (of); majority	225
		大多数　*daitasū*　the overwhelming majority	26, 225
	多	多元的　*tagenteki*　pluralistic	137, 210
		数多く　*kazuōku*　many, great number (of)	225

	230	HIN, refinement; article; *shina*, goods; quality	
品	30 923	上品　*jōhin*　refined, elegant, graceful	32
		下品　*gehin*　unrefined, gross, vulgar	31
		品質　*hinshitsu*　quality	176
	品	部品　*buhin*　(spare/machine) parts	86
		品物　*shinamono*　merchandise	79

	231	DŌ, *ugo(ku/kasu)*, (intr./tr.) move	
動	19 730	自動車　*jidōsha*　automobile, car	62, 133
		動物　*dōbutsu*　animal	79
		動力　*dōryoku*　moving force, (electric) power	100
	動	行動　*kōdō*　action	68
		動員　*dōin*　mobilize	163

	232	DŌ, *hatara(ku)*, work
働	9 532	実働時間 *jitsudō jikan* actual working hours 203, 42, 43
		働き *hataraki* work; functioning; ability
		働き口 *hatarakiguchi* job, position 54
働		働き者 *hatarakimono* hard worker 164
		働き手 *hatarakite* worker, breadwinner; capable man 57

	233	RŌ, labor, toil
労	19 720	労働 *rōdō* work, labor 232
		労働者 *rōdōsha* worker, laborer 232, 164
		労働時間 *rōdō jikan* working hours 232, 42, 43
労		労力 *rōryoku* trouble, effort; labor 100
		心労 *shinrō* worry, concern 97

	234	KYŌ, cooperation
協	24 774	協力 *kyōryoku* cooperation 100
		協力者 *kyōryokusha* collaborator, coworker 100, 164
		協同 *kyōdō* cooperation, collaboration, partnership 198
協		協会 *kyōkai* society, association 「Japan Society 158
		日米協会 *Nichi-Bei Kyōkai* the America- 5, 224, 158

	235	MU, *tsuto(meru)*, work, serve
務	110 3167	事務所 *jimusho* office 80, 153
		公務員 *kōmuin* government employee 126, 163
		国務 *kokumu* affairs of state 40
務		外務省 *Gaimushō* Ministry of Foreign Affairs 83, 145
		法務省 *Hōmushō* Ministry of Justice 123, 145

	236	YA, *no*, field, plain
野	166 4814	野生 *yasei* wild (animal/plant) 44
		平野 *heiya* a plain 202
		Hirano (surname)
野		分野 *bun'ya* field (of endeavor) 38
		野原 *nohara* field, plain 136

	237	KATSU, life, activity
活	85 2552	生活 *seikatsu* life 44
		活発 *kappatsu* active, lively 96
		活動 *katsudō* activity 231
活		活用 *katsuyō* practical use; conjugate, inflect 107
		活字 *katsuji* printing/movable type 110

	238	WA, *hanashi*, conversation, story; *hana(su)*, speak
話	149 4358	会話 *kaiwa* conversation 158
		電話 *denwa* telephone 108
		立ち話 *tachibanashi* chat while standing 121
話		話し手 *hanashite* speaker 57
		話し合う *hanashiau* talk over, discuss 159

	239	**BAI**, *u(ru)*, sell; *u(reru)*, be sold	
売	32 1067	売店　　*baiten*　stand, newsstand, kiosk 売り子　*uriko*　store salesclerk 売り手　*urite*　seller 売り切れ　*urikire*　sold out 小売り　*kouri*　retailing, retail	168 103 57 39 27
	240	*kai*, shellfish (cf. No. 453)	
貝	154 4486	貝類　　*kairui*　shellfish (plural) ほら貝　*horagai*　trumpet shell, conch 貝ボタン　*kaibotan*　shell button	226
	241	**BAI**, *ka(u)*, buy	
買	122 3637	売買　　*baibai*　buying and selling, trade, dealing 買い物　*kaimono*　shopping, purchase 買い手　*kaite*　buyer 買い主　*kainushi*　buyer 買い入れる　*kaiireru*　purchase, stock up on	239 79 57 155 52
	242	**SHI**, *ito*, thread	
糸	120 3492	一糸まとわぬ　*isshi matowanu*　stark naked 糸口　　*itoguchi*　end of a thread; beginning; clue 糸車　　*itoguruma*　spinning wheel 糸目　　*itome*　a fine thread 生糸　　*kiito*　raw silk	2 54 133 55 44
	243	**ZOKU**, *tsuzu(ku/keru)*, (intr./tr.) continue	
続	120 3544	続出　　*zokushutsu*　appear one after another 続行　　*zokkō*　continuation 相続　　*sōzoku*　succession; inheritance 手続き　*tetsuzuki*　procedures, formalities 「ruptedly 引き続いて　*hikitsuzuite*　continuously, uninter-	53 68 146 57 216
	244	**DOKU, TOKU**, [**TŌ**], *yo(mu)*, read	
読	149 4375	読者　　*dokusha*　reader 読書　　*dokusho*　reading 読本　　*tokuhon*　reader, book of readings 読み物　*yomimono*　reading matter 読み方　*yomikata*　reading, pronunciation (of a word)	164 131 25 79 70
	245	**KYŌ**, *oshi(eru)*, teach; *oso(waru)*, be taught, learn	
教	66 2052	教室　　*kyōshitsu*　classroom 教員　　*kyōin*　teacher, instructor; teaching staff 教会　　*kyōkai*　church 回教　　*kaikyō*　Islam, Muhammadanism 教え方　*oshiekata*　teaching method	166 163 158 90 70

	246	IKU, *soda(tsu)*, grow up; *soda(teru)*, raise	
育	8 296	教育 *kyōiku* education 体育 *taiiku* physical education 発育 *hatsuiku* growth, development 生育 *seiiku* growth, development 育 て の 親 *sodate no oya* foster/adoptive parent	245 61 96 44 175

	247	RYŪ, a current; style, school (of thought); [RU], *naga-(reru)*, flow; *naga(su)*, pour	
流	85 2576	流通 *ryūtsū* circulation, distribution, ventilation 海流 *kairyū* ocean current 流行 *ryūkō* fashion, fad, popularity 一流 *ichiryū* first class	150 117 68 2

	248	SŌ, [SA'], *haya(i)*, early; fast; *haya(maru)*, be hasty; *haya-(meru)*, hasten	
早	72 2100	早々 *sōsō* early, immediately 早目 に *hayame ni* a little early (leaving leeway) 早耳 *hayamimi* quick-eared, in the know 手早 い *tebayai* quick, nimble, agile	 55 56 57

	249	SŌ, *kusa*, grass, plants	
草	140 3939	草原 *sōgen* grassy plain, grasslands 草木 *sōmoku, kusaki* plants and trees, vegetation 草本 *sōhon* herb 草書 *sōsho* (cursive script form of kanji) 草案 *sōan* (rough) draft	136 22 25 131 106

	250	*shiba*, lawn	
芝	140 3893	芝生 *shibafu* lawn 芝草 *shibakusa* lawn 人工芝 *jinkō shiba* artificial turf 芝居 *shibai* stage play, theater 芝居小屋 *shibai-goya* playhouse, theater	44 249 1, 139 171 171, 27, 167

	251	CHA, SA, tea	
茶	140 3940	茶色 *chairo* brown 茶畑 *chabatake* tea plantation 茶室 *chashitsu* tea-ceremony room 茶 の 間 *cha no ma* living room 茶道 *chadō, sadō* tea ceremony	204 36 166 43 149

	252	SEI, SE, *yo*, world, era	
世	2 95	二世 *nisei* second generation 中世 *chūsei* Middle Ages 世間 *seken* the world, public, people 出世 *shusse* success in life, getting ahead 世話 *sewa* taking care of, looking after	3 28 43 53 238

	253	YŌ, *ha*, leaf, foliage	
葉	140 4001	葉書 *hagaki* postcard	131
		青葉 *aoba* green foliage	208
		言葉 *kotoba* word; language	66
		木の葉 *ko no ha* tree leaves, foliage	22
葉		千葉 *Chiba* (prefecture east of Tokyo)	15

	254	KA, KE, *ba(keru)*, turn oneself (into); *ba(kasu)*, bewitch	
化	9 350	文化 *bunka* culture	111
		化学 *kagaku* chemistry	109
		強化 *kyōka* strengthening	217
		合理化 *gōrika* rationalization, streamlining	159, 143
化		化け物 *bakemono* spook, ghost, monster	79

	255	KA, *hana*, flower, blossom	
花	140 3909	草花 *kusabana* flower, flowering plant	249
		生け花 *ikebana* flower arranging	44
		花屋 *hanaya* flower shop, florist	167
		花見 *hanami* viewing cherry blossoms	63
花		花火 *hanabi* fireworks	20

	256	DAI, generation; age; price; TAI, *ka(waru)*, represent; *ka(eru)*, replace; *yo*, generation; *shiro*, price; substitution	
代	9 364	時代 *jidai* era, period	42
		古代 *kodai* ancient times, antiquity	172
		世代 *sedai* generation	252
代		代理 *dairi* representation; agent	143

	257	HEN, *ka(waru/eru)*, (intr./tr.) change	
変	8 306	変化 *henka* change, alteration	254
		変動 *hendō* change, fluctuation	231
		変種 *henshu* variety, strain	228
		変人 *henjin* an eccentric	1
変		不変 *fuhen* immutability, constancy	94

	258	REN, *koi*, (romantic) love; *ko(u)*, be in love; *koi(shii)*, dear, fond, long for	
恋	8 313	恋人 *koibito* boyfriend, girlfriend, lover	1
		恋文 *koibumi* love letter	111
		恋心 *koigokoro* (awakening of) love	97
恋		道ならぬ恋 *michi naranu koi* forbidden love	149

	259	AI, love	
愛	87 2829	恋愛 *ren'ai* love	258
		愛情 *aijō* love	209
		愛国心 *aikokushin* patriotic sentiment, patriotism	40, 97
		愛読 *aidoku* like to read	244
愛		愛想 *aisō* amiability, sociability	147

	260	JU, u(keru), receive; u(karu), pass (an exam)	
受	87 2826 受	受理 juri acceptance	143
		受動 judō passive	231
		受け身 ukemi passivity; passive (in grammar)	59
		受(け)付(け) uketsuke receptionist, reception desk	192
		受け取る uketoru receive, accept, take	65

	261	SEI, [JŌ], na(ru), become; consist (of); na(su), do; form	
成	62 1799 成	成長 seichō growth	95
		成年 seinen (age of) majority, adulthood	45
		成立 seiritsu establishment, founding	121
		合成 gōsei composition, synthesis	159
		成り行き nariyuki course (of events), development	68

	262	KAN, feeling, sensation	
感	61 1731 感	五感 gokan the 5 senses	7
		感心 kanshin admire	97
		感想 kansō one's thoughts, impressions	147
		感情 kanjō feelings, emotion	209
		感受性 kanjusei sensibility, sensitivity	260, 98

	263	SAI, motto(mo), highest, most	
最	72 2146 最	最後 saigo end; last	48
		最新 saishin newest, latest	174
		最大 saidai maximum, greatest, largest	26
		最高 saikō maximum, highest, best	190
		最上 saijō best, highest	32

	264	YŪ, tomo, friend	
友	29 858 友	友人 yūjin friend	1
		学友 gakuyū fellow student, classmate; alumnus	109
		親友 shin'yū close friend	175
		友好 yūkō friendship	104
		友情 yūjō friendliness, friendship	209

	265	YŪ, U, a(ru), be, exist, have	
有	130 3727 有	国有 kokuyū state-owned	40
		私有 shiyū privately owned	125
		所有 shoyū possession, ownership	153
		有名 yūmei famous	82
		有力 yūryoku influential, powerful	100

	266	GŌ, number; pseudonym	
号	30 882 号	番号 bangō (identification) number	185
		三号室 sangōshitsu Room No. 3	4, 166
		年号 nengō name/year of a reign era	45
		信号 shingō signal	157
		号外 gōgai an extra (edition of a newspaper)	83

	267	**BETSU**, different, separate; another, special; *waka(reru)*, diverge, part, bid farewell
別	18 674	区別 *kubetsu* difference, distinction 183
		分別 *funbetsu* discretion, good judgment 38
		別人 *betsujin* different person 1
別		別居 *bekkyo* (legal) separation; live separately 171

	268	**ZAI**, outskirts, country; be located; *a(ru)*, be, exist
在	32 1055	所在地 *shozaichi* (prefectural) capital, (county) seat; location 153, 118
		在日 *zainichi* (stationed) in Japan 5
		在外 *zaigai* overseas, abroad 83
在		不在 *fuzai* absence 94

	269	**SON, ZON**, exist; know, believe
存	39 1267	存在 *sonzai* existence 268
		生存 *seizon* existence, life 44
		存続 *sonzoku* continuance, duration 243
		共存 *kyōson* coexistence 196
存		存分に *zonbun ni* as much as one likes, freely 38

	270	**BAKU**, *mugi*, wheat, barley, rye, oats
麦	199 5385	小麦 *komugi* wheat 27
		大麦 *ōmugi* barley 26
		麦畑 *mugibatake* wheat field 36
麦		麦わら *mugiwara* (wheat) straw
		麦茶 *mugicha* wheat tea, barley water 251

	271	**SO**, element; beginning; **SU**, naked, uncovered, simple
素	120 3511	素質 *soshitsu* nature, makeup 176
		質素 *shisso* simple, plain 176
		元素 *genso* chemical element 137
		水素 *suiso* hydrogen 21
素		素人 *shirōto* amateur, layman 1

	272	**HYŌ**, table, chart; surface; expression; *omote*, surface, obverse; *arawa(reru)*, be expressed; *arawa(su)*, express
表	2 108	時間表 *jikanhyō* timetable, schedule 42, 43
		代表的 *daihyōteki* representative, typical 256, 210
		表情 *hyōjō* facial expression 209
表		発表 *happyō* announcement, publication 96

	273	**RI**, *ura*, reverse side, back, rear
裏	8 327	表裏 *hyōri* inside and outside; double-dealing 272
		裏口 *uraguchi* back door, rear entrance 54
		裏道 *uramichi* back street; secret path 149
		裏付け *urazuke* backing, support; corroboration 192
裏		裏切る *uragiru* betray, double-cross 39

面 176 5087 面	274	**MEN**, face, mask, surface, aspect; *omote, omo, tsura*, face	
	方面	*hōmen* direction, side	70
	表面	*hyōmen* surface, exterior	272
	面会	*menkai* interview, meeting	158
	面目	*menmoku, menboku* face, honor, dignity	55

正 1 27 正	275	**SEI, SHŌ**, *tada(shii)*, correct, just; *tada(su)*, correct; *masa (ni)*, just, exactly; certainly	
	校正	*kōsei* proofreading	115
	不正	*fusei* injustice	94
	正面	*shōmen* front, front side	274
	正月	*shōgatsu* January; New Year	17

頭 151 4469 頭	276	**TŌ, [TO], ZU**, *atama, kashira*, head, leader, top	
	後頭(部)	*kōtō(bu)* back of the head	48, 86
	出頭	*shuttō* appearance, attendance, presence (at	53
	先頭	*sentō* (in the) front, lead ⌊official proceeding⌋	50
	口頭	*kōtō* oral, verbal	54
	頭上	*zujō* overhead	32

顔 181 5139 顔	277	**GAN**, *kao*, face	
	顔面	*ganmen* face	274
	顔色	*kaoiro* complexion; a look	204
	素顔	*sugao* face without makeup	271
	新顔	*shingao* stranger; newcomer	174
	知らん顔	*shirankao* pretend not to notice, ignore	214

産 117 3354 産	278	**SAN**, childbirth; production; property; *u(mu)*, give birth/ rise to; *u(mareru)*, be born; *ubu*, birth; infant	
	出産	*shussan* childbirth, delivery	53
	生産	*seisan* production	44
	産物	*sanbutsu* product	79
	不動産	*fudōsan* immovable property, real estate	94, 231

業 3 143 業	279	**GYŌ**, occupation, business, undertaking; **GŌ**, karma; *waza*, act, deed, work, art	
	工業	*kōgyō* industry	139
	産業	*sangyō* industry	278
	事業	*jigyō* undertaking, enterprise	80
	実業家	*jitsugyōka* businessman, industrialist	203, 165

犬 94 2868 犬	280	**KEN**, *inu*, dog	
	番犬	*banken* watchdog	185
	愛犬	*aiken* pet/favorite dog	259
	野犬	*yaken* stray dog	236
	小犬	*koinu* puppy	27
	犬小屋	*inugoya* doghouse	27, 167

	281	GYŪ, *ushi*, cow, bull, cattle		
牛	93	牛 肉	*gyūniku* beef	223
	2852	野 牛	*yagyū* buffalo, bison	236
		水 牛	*suigyū* water buffalo	21
		小/子 牛	*koushi* calf	27, 103
牛		牛 小 屋	*ushigoya* cowshed, barn	27, 167

	282	TOKU, special		
特	93	特 別	*tokubetsu* special	267
	2860	特 色	*tokushoku* distinguishing characteristic	204
		特 有	*tokuyū* characteristic, peculiar (to)	265
		独 特	*dokutoku* peculiar, original, unique	219
特		特 長	*tokuchō* strong point, forte	95

	283	BA, *uma*, [*ma*], horse		
馬	187	馬 車	*basha* horse-drawn carriage	133
	5191	馬 力	*bariki* horsepower	100
		馬 術	*bajutsu* horseback riding, dressage	187
		竹 馬	*takeuma*, *chikuba* stilts	129
馬		馬 小 屋	*umagoya* a stable	27, 167

	284	EKI, (train) station		
駅	187	東 京 駅	*Tōkyō-eki* Tokyo Station	71, 189
	5199	当 駅	*tōeki* this station	77
		駅 前	*ekimae* (in) front of/opposite the station	47
		駅 長	*ekichō* stationmaster	95
駅		駅 員	*ekiin* station employee	163

	285	CHŌ, *tori*, bird		
鳥	196	白 鳥	*hakuchō* swan	205
	5340	野 鳥	*yachō* wild bird	236
		花 鳥	*kachō* flowers and birds	255
		一 石 二 鳥	*isseki-nichō* killing 2 birds with 1 stone	2, 78, 3
鳥		鳥 居	*torii* torii, Shinto shrine archway	171

	286	TŌ, *shima*, island		
島	4	半 島	*hantō* peninsula	88
	230	島 民	*tōmin* islander	177
		無 人 島	*mujintō* uninhabited island	93, 1
		島 国	*shimaguni* island country	40
島		島 々	*shimajima* (many) islands	

	287	MŌ, *ke*, hair, fur, feather, down		
毛	82	原 毛	*genmō* raw wool	136
	2473	毛 筆	*mōhitsu* brush (for writing/painting)	130
		不 毛	*fumō* barren, sterile	94
		毛 糸	*keito* wool yarn, knitting wool	242
毛		ま ゆ 毛	*mayuge* eyebrow	

羊	288	**YŌ**, *hitsuji*, sheep	
	123	羊 毛 *yōmō* wool	287
	3656	羊 肉 *yōniku* mutton	223
	羊	小/子 羊 *kohitsuji* lamb	27, 103

洋	289	**YŌ**, ocean; foreign, Western	
	85	大 洋 *taiyō* ocean	26
	2550	東 洋 *tōyō* the East, Orient	71
		西 洋 *seiyō* the West, Occident	72
	洋	大 西 洋 *Taiseiyō* Atlantic Ocean	26, 72
		洋 書 *yōsho* foreign/Western book	131

魚	290	**GYO**, *sakana*, *uo*, fish	
	195	魚 類 *gyorui* a variety of fish	226
	5281	金 魚 *kingyo* goldfish	23
		魚 肉 *gyoniku* fish (meat)	223
	魚	魚 市 場 *uoichiba* fish market	181, 154
		魚 屋 *sakanaya* fish shop/dealer	167

義	291	**GI**, justice, honor; meaning; in-law; artificial	
	123	民 主 主 義 *minshu shugi* democracy	177, 155
	3668	義 務 *gimu* obligation, duty	235
		義 理 *giri* duty, debt of gratitude	143
	義	同 義 語 *dōgigo* synonym	198, 67
		類 義 語 *ruigigo* word of similar meaning, synonym	226, 67

議	292	**GI**, deliberation; proposal	
	149	会 議 *kaigi* conference, meeting	158
	4448	協 議 *kyōgi* council, conference	234
		議 会 *gikai* parliament, diet, congress	158
	議	議 員 *giin* M.P., dietman, congressman	163
		不 思 議 *fushigi* marvel, wonder, mystery	94, 99

論	293	**RON**, discussion, argument; thesis, dissertation	
	149	論 理 *ronri* logic	143
	4391	理 論 *riron* theory	143
		世 論 *yoron, seron* public opinion	252
	論	論 議 *rongi* discussion, argument	292
		論 文 *ronbun* thesis, essay	111

王	294	**Ō**, king	
	96	王 国 *ōkoku* kingdom	40
	2922	国 王 *kokuō* king	40
		女 王 *joō* queen	102
	王	王 子 *ōji* prince	103
		法 王 *hōō* pope	123

	295	GYOKU, *tama*, gem, jewel; sphere, ball	
玉	96	玉 石 *gyokuseki* wheat and chaff, good and bad	78
	2923	玉 子 *tamago* egg (cf. No. 1058)	103
		水 玉 *mizutama* drop of water	21
		目 玉 *medama* eyeball	55
	玉	十 円 玉 *jūendama* 10-yen piece/coin	12, 13

	296	HŌ, *takara*, treasure	
宝	40	宝 石 *hōseki* precious stone, gem	78
	1293	宝 玉 *hōgyoku* precious stone, gem	295
		国 宝 *kokuhō* national treasure	40
		家 宝 *kahō* family heirloom	165
	宝	宝 物 *hōmotsu, takaramono* treasure, prized possession	79

	297	KŌ, Ō, emperor	
皇	106	天 皇 *tennō* emperor	141
	3100	皇 女 *kōjo* imperial princess	102
		皇 居 *kōkyo* imperial palace	171
		皇 室 *kōshitsu* imperial household	166
	皇	皇 位 *kōi* imperial throne	122

	298	GEN, present; *arawa(reru)*, appear; *arawa(su)*, show	
現	96	現 代 *gendai* contemporary, modern	256
	2943	現 在 *genzai* current, present; present tense	268
		現 金 *genkin* cash	23
		表 現 *hyōgen* an expression	272
	現	実 現 *jitsugen* realize, attain; come true	203

	299	SEN, line	
線	120	光 線 *kōsen* light, light ray	138
	3580	内 線 *naisen* (telephone) extension	84
		無 線 *musen* wireless, radio	93
		二 番 線 *nibansen* Track No. 2	3, 185
	線	地 平 線 *chiheisen* horizon	118, 202

	300	TAN, single, simple	
単	3	単 語 *tango* word	67
	139	単 位 *tan'i* unit, denomination	122
		単 一 *tan'itsu* single, simple, individual	2
		単 数 *tansū* singular (in grammar)	225
	単	単 独 *tandoku* independent, single-handed	219

	301	SEN, *tataka(u)*, wage war, fight; *ikusa*, war, battle	
戦	62	内 戦 *naisen* civil war	84
	1810	交 戦 *kōsen* war, warfare	114
		合 戦 *kassen* battle; contest	159
		休 戦 *kyūsen* truce, cease-fire	60
	戦	戦 後 *sengo* postwar	48

	302	SŌ, *araso(u)*, dispute, argue, contend for	
争	4	戦 争 *sensō* war	301
	186	争 議 *sōgi* dispute, strife	292
		論 争 *ronsō* argument, controversy	293
	争	争 点 *sōten* point of contention, issue	169
		言 い 争 う *iiarasou* quarrel, argue	66

	303	KYŪ, urgent, sudden; *iso(gu)*, be in a hurry	
急	61	急 行 *kyūkō* an express (train)	68
	1667	特 急 *tokkyū* a special express (train)	282
		急 変 *kyūhen* sudden change	257
	急	急 用 *kyūyō* urgent business	107
		急 性 *kyūsei* acute	98

	304	AKU, O, *waru(i)*, bad, evil	
悪	1	悪 化 *akka* change for the worse	254
	62	悪 性 *akusei* malignant, vicious	98
		悪 事 *akuji* evil deed	80
	悪	最 悪 *saiaku* the worst, at worst	263
		悪 口 *akkō, warukuchi* abusive language, speaking ⌈ill of	54

	305	MATSU, BATSU, *sue*, end	
末	4	週 末 *shūmatsu* weekend	91
	177	月 末 *getsumatsu* end of the month	17
		年 末 *nenmatsu* year's end	45
	末	末 代 *matsudai* all ages to come, eternity	256
		末 っ 子 *suekko* youngest child	103

	306	MI, not yet	
未	4	未 来 *mirai* future	69
	179	未 知 *michi* unknown	214
		前 代 未 聞 *zendaimimon* unprecedented	47, 256, 64
	未	未 満 *miman* less than, under	201
		未 明 *mimei* early dawn, before daybreak	18

	307	MI, *aji*, taste; *aji(wau)*, taste; relish, appreciate	
味	30	意 味 *imi* meaning, significance, sense	132
	913	正 味 *shōmi* net (amount/weight/price)	275
		不 気 味 *bukimi* uncanny, eerie, ominous	94, 134
	味	地 味 *jimi* plain, subdued, undemonstrative	118
		三 味 線 *shamisen* samisen (3-stringed instrument)	4, 299

	308	SHA, Shinto shrine; company, firm; *yashiro*, Shinto shrine	
社	113	社 会 *shakai* society, social	158
	3231	会 社 *kaisha* company, firm	158
		本 社 *honsha* head office	25
	社	社 長 *shachō* company president	95
		社 員 *shain* employee, staff member	163

	309	**SHIN**, *mō(su)*, say; be named	
申	2 93 申	答 申 *tōshin* report, findings 上 申 *jōshin* report (to a superior) 内 申 *naishin* unofficial/confidential report 申 し 入 れ *mōshiire* offer, proposal, notice 申 し 合 わ せ *mōshiawase* an understanding	160 32 84 52 159
	310	**SHIN, JIN**, *kami*, [*kan*], [*kō*], god, God	
神	113 3245 神	神 道 *shintō* Shintoism 神 社 *jinja* Shinto shrine 神 話 *shinwa* myth, mythology 神 父 *shinpu* (Catholic) priest, Father 神 風 *kamikaze* divine wind; kamikaze	149 308 238 113 29
	311	**SHITSU**, *ushina(u)*, lose	
失	4 178 失	失 業 *shitsugyō* unemployment 失 意 *shitsui* disappointment, despair 失 神 *shisshin* faint, lose consciousness 失 恋 *shitsuren* unrequited love 見 失 う *miushinau* lose sight of	279 132 310 258 63
	312	**TETSU**, iron	
鉄	167 4844 鉄	鉄 道 *tetsudō* railroad 地 下 鉄 *chikatetsu* subway 国 鉄 *Kokutetsu* Japanese National Railways 私 鉄 *shitetsu* private railway 鉄 か ぶ と *tetsukabuto* steel helmet	149 118, 31 40 125
	313	**GIN**, silver	
銀	167 4855 銀	銀 行 *ginkō* bank 日 銀 *Nichigin* the Bank of Japan 銀 色 *gin'iro* silver color 水 銀 *suigin* mercury 銀 メ ダ ル *ginmedaru* silver medal	68 5 204 21
	314	**KON**, root; perseverance; *ne*, root, base, origin	
根	75 2261 根	大 根 *daikon* daikon, Japanese radish 根 本 的 *konponteki* fundamental; radical 根 気 *konki* patience, perseverance 屋 根 *yane* roof 根 強 い *nezuyoi* deep-rooted, firmly established	26 25, 210 134 167 217
	315	**FU**, [**FŪ**], *otto*, husband	
夫	4 164 夫	夫 人 *fujin* wife, Mrs. 人 夫 *ninpu* laborer 水 夫 *suifu* sailor, seaman 工 夫 *kōfu* laborer *kufū* contrivance, scheme, means	1 1 21 139

	316	FU, woman, wife	
婦	38 1237	夫婦 *fūfu* husband and wife, married couple	315
		主婦 *shufu* housewife	155
		婦人 *fujin* lady, woman	1
婦		婦女 (子) *fujo(shi)* woman	102, 103
		婦長 *fuchō* head nurse	95

	317	KI, *kae(ru)*, return; *kae(su)*, let return, dismiss	
帰	58 1582	帰国 *kikoku* return to one's country	40
		帰宅 *kitaku* return/come/get home	178
		帰路 *kiro* the way home	151
帰		帰化 *kika* become naturalized	254
		日帰り *higaeri* go and return in a day	5

	318	SHI, branch; support; *sasa(eru)*, support	
支	65 2039	支出 *shishutsu* expenditure, disbursement	53
		支社 *shisha* branch (office)	308
		支店 *shiten* branch office/store	168
支		支部 *shibu* branch, local chapter	86
		支流 *shiryū* tributary (of a river)	247

	319	RYŌ, materials; fee	
料	119 3468	料理 *ryōri* cooking, cuisine; dish, food	143
		原料 *genryō* raw materials	136
		料金 *ryōkin* fee, charge, fare	23
料		手数料 *tesūryō* fee; commission	57, 225
		有/無料 *yū/muryō* pay, toll, charging a fee/free	265, 93

	320	KA, academic course, department, faculty	
科	115 3272	科学 *kagaku* science	109
		理科 *rika* natural sciences (department)	143
		外科 *geka* surgery	83
科		産婦人科医 *sanfujinkai* gynecologist	278, 316, 1, 220
		教科書 *kyōkasho* textbook, schoolbook	245, 131

	321	RYŌ, *yo(i)*, good	
良	138 3885	良好 *ryōkō* good, favorable, satisfactory	104
		良質 *ryōshitsu* good quality	176
		最良 *sairyō* best	263
良		不良 *furyō* bad, unsatisfactory; delinquency	94
		良心 *ryōshin* conscience	97

	322	SHOKU, [JIKI], food; eating; *ta(beru)*, *ku(u/rau)*, eat	
食	184 5154	食事 *shokuji* meal, dinner	80
		食料品 *shokuryōhin* food, foodstuffs	319, 230
		和/洋食 *wa/yō-shoku* Japanese/Western food	124, 289
食		夕食 *yūshoku* evening meal, supper	81
		食べ物 *tabemono* food	79

	323	**IN**, *no(mu)*, drink
飲	184 5159	飲 食 *inshoku* food and drink, eating and drinking 322
		飲 料 *inryō* drink, beverage 319
		飲料水 *inryōsui* drinking water 319, 21
飲		飲 み 水 *nomimizu* drinking water 21
		飲 み 物 *nomimono* (something to) drink, beverage 79

	324	**HAN**, [**HON**], anti-; [**TAN**], (unit of land/cloth measurement); *so(ru/rasu)*, (intr./tr.) warp, bend back
反	27 817	反 発 *hanpatsu* repulsion, repellence; opposition 96
		反 日 *han-Nichi* anti-Japanese 5
		反 面 *hanmen* the other side ⌈ation 274
反		反 省 *hansei* reflection, introspection; reconsider- 145

	325	**HAN**, *meshi*, cooked rice; meal, food
飯	184 5158	ご 飯 *gohan* cooked rice; meal, food
		赤 飯 *sekihan* (festive) rice boiled with red beans 207
		夕 飯 *yūhan, yūmeshi* evening meal, supper, dinner 81
飯		飯 ご う *hangō* mess kit, eating utensils
		飯 場 *hanba* construction camp/bunkhouse 154

	326	**KAN**, government, authorities
官	40 1295	半官半民 *hankan-hanmin* semigovernmental 88, 177
		国 務 長 官 *kokumu chōkan* secretary of state 40, 235, 95
		外 交 官 *gaikōkan* diplomat 83, 114
官		高 官 *kōkan* high government official/office 190
		神 官 *shinkan* Shinto priest 310

	327	**KAN**, (large) building, hall
館	184 5174	旅 館 *ryokan* Japanese-style inn 222
		水 族 館 *suizokukan* aquarium 22, 221
		会 館 *kaikan* (assembly) hall 158
館		本 館 *honkan* main building 25
		別 館 *bekkan* annex, extension 267

	328	**KAN**, pipe; wind instrument; control; *kuda*, pipe, tube
管	118 3416	管 内 *kannai* (area of) jurisdiction 84
		管 理 *kanri* administration, supervision 143
		水 道 管 *suidōkan* water pipe/conduit 21, 149
管		気 管 *kikan* windpipe, trachea 134
		鉄 管 *tekkan* iron tube/pipe 312

	329	**RI**, advantage; (loan) interest; *ki(ku)*, take effect, work
利	115 3264	有 利 *yūri* profitable, advantageous 265
		利 子 *rishi* interest (on a loan) 103
		利 用 *riyō* make use of 107
利		利 口 *rikō* smart, clever, bright 54
		左 利 き *hidarikiki* left-hander 75

	330	**BEN**, convenience; excrement; **BIN**, opportunity; mail; *tayo(ri)*, news, tidings	
便	9 450,451	便利　　*benri*　convenient, handy	329
		不便　　*fuben*　inconvenient	94
		便所　　*benjo*　toilet	153
	便	別便　　*betsubin*　separate mail	267

	331	**SHI**, use; messenger; *tsuka(u)*, use	
使	9 432	大使　　*taishi*　ambassador	26
		公使　　*kōshi*　minister, envoy	126
		天使　　*tenshi*　angel	141
	使	使用法　*shiyōhō*　how to use, directions for use	107, 123
		使い方　*tsukaikata*　how to use, way to handle	70

	332	**SHI**, history, chronicles	
史	2 91	日本史　*nihonshi*　Japanese history	5, 25
		中世史　*chūseishi*　medieval history	28, 252
		文学史　*bungakushi*　history of literature	111, 109
	史	史実　　*shijitsu*　historical fact	203
		女史　　*joshi*　(honorific) Madame, Miss, Mrs.	102

	333	**SHI**, [**JI**], *tsuka(eru)*, serve	
仕	9 362	仕事　　*shigoto*　work, job	80
		仕立て屋　*shitateya*　tailor; dressmaker	121, 167
		仕方　　*shikata*　way, method, means	70
	仕	仕手　　*shite*　protagonist, leading role (in Noh)	57
		仕上げる　*shiageru*　finish up, complete	32

	334	**NIN**, duty, responsibility, office; *maka(seru/su)*, entrust (to)	
任	9 374	主任　　*shunin*　person in charge, manager, head	155
		信任　　*shinnin*　confidence, trust	157
		後任　　*kōnin*　successor	48
	任	任務　　*ninmu*　duty, office, mission	235
		任意　　*nin'i*　optional, voluntary	132

	335	**KEN**, [**GON**], authority, power; right	
権	75 2360	権利　　*kenri*　a right	329
		人権　　*jinken*　human rights	1
		特権　　*tokken*　special right, privilege	282
	権	主権　　*shuken*　sovereignty　　　　┌powers	155
		三権分立　*sanken bunritsu*　separation of	4, 38, 121

	336	**KYOKU**, end, pole: **GOKU**, very, extremely; *kiwa(mi)*, height, end; *kiwa(meru/maru)*, carry to/reach its end	
極	75 2305	北/南極　*hok/nan-kyoku*　north/south pole	73, 74
		極東　　*kyokutō*　the Far East	71
		極上　　*gokujō*　finest, top quality	32
	極	見極める　*mikiwameru*　see through, discern	63

	337	**KU**, phrase, sentence, verse	
句 20 745 句		語 句 *goku* words and phrases	67
		成 句 *seiku* set phrase, idiom	261
		文 句 *monku* words, expression; objection	111
		句 読 点 *kutōten* punctuation mark	244, 169
		引 用 句 *in'yōku* quotation	216, 107

	338	**JUN**, 10-day period	
旬 20 747 旬		上 旬 *jōjun* first 10 days of a month (1st to 10th)	32
		中 旬 *chūjun* second 10 days of a month (11th to 20th)	28
		下 旬 *gejun* last third of a month (21st to end)	31

	339	**ZU**, drawing, diagram, plan; **TO**, *haka(ru)*, plan	
図 31 1034 図		地 図 *chizu* map	118
		図 表 *zuhyō* chart, table, graph	272
		合 図 *aizu* signal, sign, gesture	159
		意 図 *ito* intention	132
		図 書 館 *toshokan* library	131, 327

	340	**KEI**, measuring; plan; total; *haka(ru)*, measure, compute; *haka(rau)*, arrange, dispose of, see about	
計 149 4312 計		時 計 *tokei* clock, watch	42
		会 計 *kaikei* accounting; paying a bill	158
		合 計 *gōkei* total	159
		家 計 *kakei* household finances	165

	341	**SHIN**, *hari*, needle	
針 167 4817 針		方 針 *hōshin* course, line, policy	70
		針 路 *shinro* course (of a ship)	151
		長/分 針 *chō/funshin* minute hand	95, 38
		短 針 *tanshin* hour hand	215
		針 金 *harigane* wire	23

	342	**CHŌ**, *shira(beru)*, investigate, check; *totono(eru)*, prepare, arrange, put in order; *totono(u)*, be prepared, arranged	
調 149 4392 調		協 調 *kyōchō* cooperation, harmony	234
		好 調 *kōchō* good, favorable	104
		調 子 *chōshi* tone; mood; condition	103
		取 り 調 べ *torishirabe* investigation, questioning	65

	343	**GA**, picture; **KAKU**, stroke (in writing kanji)	
画 1 50 画		画 家 *gaka* painter ⌈painting	165
		日 本/洋 画 *nihon/yō-ga* Japanese/Western-style	5, 25, 289
		画 用 紙 *gayōshi* drawing paper	107, 180
		画 面 *gamen* (TV/movie) screen	274
		計 画 *keikaku* plan, project	340

演	344	**EN**, performance, presentation, play	
	85	上演 *jōen* performance, dramatic presentation	32
	2685	公演 *kōen* public performance	126
		独演 *dokuen* solo performance	219
		出演 *shutsuen* appearance, performance	53
	演	演出 *enshutsu* production, staging (of a play)	53

絵	345	**KAI, E**, picture	
	120	絵画 *kaiga* pictures, paintings, drawings	343
	3537	絵葉書 *ehagaki* picture postcard	253, 131
		絵本 *ehon* picture book	25
		口絵 *kuchie* frontispiece	54
	絵	大和絵 *Yamato-e* ancient Japanese-style painting	26, 124

給	346	**KYŪ**, supply	
	120	給料 *kyūryō* pay, wages, salary	319
	3538	月給 *gekkyū* monthly salary	17
		支給 *shikyū* supply, provisioning, allowance	318
		供給 *kyōkyū* supply	197
	給	給水 *kyūsui* water supply	21

音	347	**ON, IN**, *oto*, *ne*, sound	
	180	発音 *hatsuon* pronunciation	96
	5110	表音文字 *hyōon moji* phonetic symbol	272, 111, 110
		母音 *boin* vowel	112
		本音 *honne* one's true intention	25
	音	足音 *ashioto* sound of footsteps	58

暗	348	**AN**, *kura(i)*, dark, dim	
	72	暗黒 *ankoku* darkness	206
	2154	暗室 *anshitsu* darkroom	166
		暗号 *angō* (secret) code, cipher	266
		明暗 *meian* light and darkness, shading	18
	暗	暗がり *kuragari* darkness	

韻	349	**IN**, rhyme	
	180	音韻学 *on'ingaku* phonology	347, 109
	5115	韻文 *inbun* verse, poetry	111
		韻語 *ingo* rhyming words	67
	韻	頭韻 *tōin* alliteration	276

損	350	**SON**, loss, damage; *soko(nau/neru)*, harm, injure; *-soko-(nau)*, fail to, err in	
	64		
	1979	損失 *sonshitsu* loss	311
		大損 *ōzon* great loss	26
		見損なう *misokonau* miss (seeing); misjudge	63
	損	読み損なう *yomisokonau* misread	244

	351	Ō, center, middle
央	2 86 央	中 央　　　*chūō*　center　28 中 央 口　*chūōguchi*　main/middle exit　28, 54 中 央 部　*chūōbu*　central part, middle　28, 86 中 央 線　*Chūō-sen*　the Chuo (train) Line　28, 299 中 央 区　*Chūō-ku*　Chuo Ward (Tokyo)　28, 183

	352	EI, *utsu(su)*, reflect, project; *utsu(ru)*, be reflected, projected; *ha(eru)*, shine, be brilliant
映	72 2118 映	映 画　*eiga*　movie　343 反 映　*han'ei*　reflection　324 上 映　*jōei*　showing, screening (of a movie)　32 夕 映 え　*yūbae*　the glow of sunset　81

	353	EI, brilliant, talented, gifted
英	140 3927 英	英 気　*eiki*　energetic spirit, enthusiasm　134 石 英　*sekiei*　quartz　78 英 語　*Eigo*　the English language　67 和 英　*Wa-Ei*　Japanese-English　124 英 会 話　*Eikaiwa*　English conversation　158, 238

	354	DAI, topic, theme; title
題	72 2164 題	問 題　*mondai*　problem, question　162 議 題　*gidai*　topic for discussion, agenda　292 話 題　*wadai*　topic　238 表 題　*hyōdai*　title, caption　272 宿 題　*shukudai*　homework　179

	355	TEI, JŌ, *sada(meru)*, determine, decide; *sada(maru)*, be determined, decided; *sada(ka)*, certain, definite
定	40 1296 定	安 定　*antei*　stability, equilibrium　105 協 定　*kyōtei*　agreement, pact　234 定 食　*teishoku*　meal of fixed menu, complete meal　322 未 定　*mitei*　undecided, unsettled, not yet fixed　306

	356	KETSU, *ki(meru)*, decide; *ki(maru)*, be decided
決	85 2509 決	決 定　*kettei*　decision, determination　355 決 心　*kesshin*　determination, resolution　97 決 意　*ketsui*　determination, resolution　132 議 決　*giketsu*　decision (of a committee)　292 未 決　*miketsu*　pending　306

	357	CHŪ, note, comment; *soso(gu)*, pour, flow
注	85 2531 注	注 意　*chūi*　attention, caution, warning　132 注 目　*chūmoku*　attention, notice　55 注 文　*chūmon*　order, commission　111 発 注　*hatchū*　order, commission　96 注 入　*chūnyū*　injection; pour into, infuse　52

358 楽

75
2324

楽

GAKU, music; RAKU, pleasure; *tano(shimu)*, enjoy; *tano-(shii)*, fun, enjoyable, pleasant

音楽	*ongaku*	music	347
文楽	*bunraku*	Japanese puppet theater	111
楽天家	*rakutenka*	optimist	141, 165
安楽死	*anrakushi*	euthanasia	105, 85

359 薬

140
4074

薬

YAKU, *kusuri*, medicine

薬学	*yakugaku*	pharmacy	109
薬品	*yakuhin*	medicines, drugs	230
薬味	*yakumi*	spices	307
薬局	*yakkyoku*	pharmacy	170
薬屋	*kusuriya*	drugstore, pharmacy	167

360 作

9
407

作

SAKU, SA, *tsuku(ru)*, make

作家	*sakka*	writer	165
作品	*sakuhin*	literary work	230
作戦	*sakusen*	military operation, tactics	301
作り話	*tsukuribanashi*	made-up story, fabrication	238
手作り	*tezukuri*	handmade	57

361 昨

72
2119

昨

SAKU, past, yesterday

昨年	*sakunen*	last year	45
昨日	*sakujitsu, kinō*	yesterday	5
一昨日	*issakujitsu*	day before yesterday	2, 5
一昨年	*issakunen*	year before last	2, 45
昨今	*sakkon*	these days, recent	51

362 段

79
2452

段

DAN, step; stairs; rank; column

一段	*ichidan*	step; single-stage	2
石段	*ishidan*	stone stairway	78
段々畑	*dandanbatake*	terraced fields	36
手段	*shudan*	means, measure	57
段取り	*dandori*	program, plan, arrangements	65

363 由

2
89

由

YU, YŪ, [YUI], *yoshi*, reason, cause; significance

由来	*yurai*	origin, derivation	69
理由	*riyū*	reason, grounds	143
自由	*jiyū*	freedom	62
不自由	*fujiyū*	discomfort; want, privation	94, 62
事由	*jiyū*	reason, cause	80

364 油

85
2534

油

YU, *abura*, oil

石油	*sekiyu*	oil, petroleum	78
原油	*gen'yu*	crude oil	136
油田	*yuden*	oil field	35
給油所	*kyūyusho, kyūyujo*	filling/gas station	346, 153
油絵	*aburae*	oil painting	345

	365	**TAI**, against; **TSUI**, pair	
対	67 2067	反対 *hantai* opposite; opposition	324
		対立 *tairitsu* confrontation	121
		対決 *taiketsu* showdown	356
対		対面 *taimen* interview, meeting	274
		対話 *taiwa* conversation, dialogue	238

	366	**KYOKU**, curve; melody, musical composition; *ma(geru)*, bend, distort; *ma(garu)*, (intr.) bend, turn	
曲	2 103	作曲 *sakkyoku* musical composition	360
		名曲 *meikyoku* famous/well-known melody	82
		曲線 *kyokusen* a curve	299
曲		曲がり道 *magarimichi* winding street	149

	367	**TEN**, law code; ceremony	
典	12 588	古典 *koten* classical literature, the classics	172
		百科事典 *hyakkajiten* encyclopedia	14, 320, 80
		法典 *hōten* code of laws	123
典		出典 *shutten* literary source, authority	53
		特典 *tokuten* special favor, privilege	282

	368	**KŌ, KYŌ**, interest; entertainment; liveliness; prosperity; *oko(ru)*, flourish, prosper; *oko(su)*, revive, retrieve	
興	12 615	興行 *kōgyō* entertainment industry; performance	68
		興信所 *kōshinjo* private inquiry/detective agency	157, 153
		興業 *kōgyō* industrial enterprise	279
興		興味 *kyōmi* interest	307

	369	**NŌ**, agriculture	
農	161 4658	農業 *nōgyō* agriculture	279
		農村 *nōson* farm village	191
		農民 *nōmin* farmer, peasant	177
農		農家 *nōka* farmhouse, farm household; farmer	165
		農産物 *nōsanbutsu* agricultural product	278, 79

	370	**KO, KI**, *onore*, self	
己	49 1462	自己 *jiko* self-	62
		自己中心 *jiko chūshin* egocentric	62, 28, 97
		利己 *riko* selfishness, egoism	329
己		利己的 *rikoteki* selfish, self-centered	329, 210
		知己 *chiki* acquaintance	214

	371	**KI**, *shiru(su)*, write/note down	
記	149 4318	記者 *kisha* newspaperman, journalist	164
		記事 *kiji* article, report	80
		日記 *nikki* diary	5
記		暗記 *anki* memorize	348
		記号 *kigō* mark, symbol	266

	372	**KI**, narrative, history	
紀	120 3497	紀 元 *kigen* era (of year reckoning) 紀 元 前/後 *kigen-zen/go* B.C./A.D. 世 紀 *seiki* century 紀 行(文) *kikō(bun)* account of a journey 風 紀 *fūki* discipline, public morals	137 137, 47, 48 252 68, 111 29
紀			

	373	**KI**, awakening, rise, beginning; *o(kiru)*, get/wake/be up; *o(koru)*, occur; *o(kosu)*, give rise to; wake (someone) up	
起	156 4541	起 原 *kigen* origin, beginning 起 点 *kiten* starting point 早 起 き *hayaoki* get up early 起 き 上 が る *okiagaru* get up, pick oneself up	136 169 248 32
起			

	374	**TOKU**, profit, advantage; *e(ru)*, *u(ru)*, gain, acquire	
得	60 1622	損 得 *sontoku* profit and loss 所 得 *shotoku* income 得 点 *tokuten* one's score, points made 得 意 *tokui* prosperity; pride; one's strong point 心 得 る *kokoroeru* know, understand	350 153 169 132 97
得			

	375	**YAKU**, service, use; office, post; **EKI**, battle; service	
役	60 1598	役 所 *yakusho* government office/bureau 役 人 *yakunin* public official 役 員 *yakuin* (company) officer, director 役 者 *yakusha* player, actor 使 役 *shieki* employment, service	153 1 163 164 331
役			

	376	**SEN**, *fune*, [*funa*], ship	
船	137 3873	船 長 *senchō* captain 船 員 *sen'in* crewman, seaman, sailor 船 室 *senshitsu* cabin 汽 船 *kisen* steamship, steamer 船 旅 *funatabi* sea voyage	95 163 166 135 222
船			

	377	**DO**, [**TAKU**], [**TO**], degree, measure, limit; times; *tabi*, times	
度	53 1511	一 度 *ichido* once; 1 degree (of temperature/arc) 今 度 *kondo* this time; soon; next time 年 度 *nendo* business/fiscal year 高 度 成 長 *kōdo seichō* high growth 支/仕 度 *shitaku* preparations	2 51 45 190, 261, 95 318, 333
度			

	378	**TO**, *wata(ru)*, cross; *wata(su)*, hand over	
渡	85 2635	渡 来 *torai* introduction (into); visit 渡 し 船 *watashibune* ferryboat 渡 り 鳥 *wataridori* migratory bird 見 渡 す *miwatasu* look out over 手 渡 す *tewatasu* hand deliver, hand over	69 376 285 63 57
渡			

	379	**SEKI**, seat, place	
53		出席	*shusseki* attendance	53
1513		満席	*manseki* full, fully occupied	201
		議席	*giseki* seat (in parliament)	292
席		主席	*shuseki* top seat, head, chief	155
		席上	*sekijō* (at) the meeting; (on) the occasion	32

	380	**BYŌ**, [**HEI**], *ya(mu)*, fall ill, suffer from; *yamai*, illness	
104		病気	*byōki* sickness, disease	134
3042		重病	*jūbyō* serious illness	227
		急病	*kyūbyō* sudden illness	303
病		性病	*seibyō* venereal disease	98
		病人	*byōnin* sick person	1

	381	**OKU**, remember, think	
61		記憶	*kioku* memory, recollection	371
1780		憶病	*okubyō* cowardice, timidity	380
憶				

	382	**OKU**, 100 million	
9		一億	*ichioku* 100 million	2
551		億万長者	*okuman chōja* multimillionaire	16, 95, 164
		数億年	*sūokunen* hundreds of millions of years	225, 45
億				

	383	**KETSU**, *ka(ku)*, lack; *ka(keru)*, be lacking	
76		欠点	*ketten* defect, flaw	169
2412		出欠	*shukketsu* attendance (and/or absence)	53
		欠席	*kesseki* absence, nonattendance	379
欠		欠員	*ketsuin* vacant position, opening	163
		欠損	*kesson* deficit, loss	350

	384	**JI**, **SHI**, *tsugi*, next; *tsu(gu)*, come/rank next	
15		次官	*jikan* vice-minister	326
638		次男	*jinan* second-oldest son	101
		二次	*niji* second, secondary	3
次		目次	*mokuji* table of contents	55
		相次ぐ	*aitsugu* follow/happen one after another	146

	385	**SHOKU**, employment, job, occupation, office	
128		職業	*shokugyō* occupation, profession	279
3718		職場	*shokuba* place of work, jobsite	154
		職員	*shokuin* personnel, staff, staff member	163
職		現職	*genshoku* one's present post	298
		無職	*mushoku* unemployed	93

	386	NŌ, ability, function; Noh play	
能	28 853 能	能力 *nōryoku* capacity, talent 本能 *honnō* instinct 能筆 *nōhitsu* calligraphy, skilled penmanship 能楽 *nōgaku* Noh play 能面 *nōmen* Noh mask	100 25 130 358 274
態	61 1743 態	態度 *taido* attitude 生態 *seitai* mode of life, ecology 変態 *hentai* metamorphosis; abnormality 事態 *jitai* situation, state of affairs 実態 *jittai* actual conditions/situation	377 44 257 80 203
	387	TAI, condition, appearance	
可	1 24 可	可能(性) *kanō(sei)* possibility 不可能 *fukanō* impossible 不可欠 *fukaketsu* indispensable, essential 不可分 *fukabun* indivisible 可決 *kaketsu* approval (of a proposed law)	386, 98 94, 386 94, 383 94, 38 356
	388	KA, good; possible; approval	
河	85 2530 河	河川 *kasen* rivers 河口 *kakō, kawaguchi* mouth of a river 大河 *taiga, ōkawa* large river 銀河 *ginga* the Milky Way 河原 *kawara* dry riverbed	33 54 26 313 136
	389	KA, *kawa*, river	
何	9 409 何	何事 *nanigoto* what, whatever 何曜日 *nan(i)yōbi* what day of the week 何日 *nannichi* how many days; what day of the month 何時 *nanji* what time 何時間 *nanjikan* how many hours	80 19, 5 5 42 42, 43
	390	KA, *nani*, [*nan*], what, which, how many	
荷	140 3956 荷	在荷 *zaika* stock, inventory 入荷 *nyūka* fresh supply/arrival of goods 出荷 *shukka* shipment, shipping (手)荷物 *(te)nimotsu* (hand)baggage, luggage 重荷 *omoni* heavy burden	268 52 53 57, 79 227
	391	KA, *ni*, load, cargo, baggage	
歌	76 2422 歌	歌手 *kashu* singer 国歌 *kokka* national anthem 和歌 *waka* 31-syllable Japanese poem 短歌 *tanka* (synonym for *waka*) 流行歌 *ryūkōka* popular song	57 40 124 215 247, 68
	392	KA, *uta*, poem, song; *uta(u)*, sing	

	393	**YO, previously, in advance**	
予	6 271	予約 *yoyaku* subscription, reservation, booking	211
		予定 *yotei* plan; expectation	355
		予想 *yosō* expectation, supposition	147
予		予知 *yochi* foresee, predict	214
		予言 *yogen* prophecy, prediction	66

	394	**YO, azu(keru/karu), entrust/receive for safekeeping**	
預	181 5123	預金 *yokin* deposit, bank account ⌈house	23
		預かり所 *azukarisho, azukarijo* depository, ware-	153
預		手荷物一時預かり(所) *tenimotsu ichiji azukari(sho/jo)* (place for) temporary handbaggage storage 57, 391, 79, 2, 42, 153	

	395	**KEI, GYŌ, katachi, kata, form, shape**	
形	59 1589	円形 *enkei* round/circular shape	13
		正方形 *seihōkei* square	275, 70
		無形 *mukei* formless, immaterial, intangible	93
形		人形 *ningyō* doll, puppet	1
		手形 *tegata* (bank) bill, note, draft	57

	396	**KAI, opening, development; a(ku/keru), (intr./tr.) open; hira(keru), become developed; hira(ku), (tr.) open**	
開	169 4950	公開 *kōkai* open to the public	126
		開会 *kaikai* opening of a meeting	158
開		未開 *mikai* uncivilized, backward, savage	306
		開発 *kaihatsu* development	96

	397	**HEI, shi(meru), to(jiru/zasu), close, shut; shi(maru), become closed**	
閉	169 4945	開閉 *kaihei* opening and closing	396
		閉会 *heikai* closing, adjournment	158
閉		閉店 *heiten* store closing	168
		閉口 *heikō* be dumbfounded	54

	398	**KAN, seki, barrier**	
関	169 4958	関門 *kanmon* gateway, barrier	161
		関心 *kanshin* interest	97
		関東 *Kantō* (region including Tokyo)	71
関		関西 *Kansai* (region including Osaka and Kyoto)	72
		関所 *sekisho* barrier station, checkpoint	153

	399	**ZEI, tax**	
税	115 3287	税金 *zeikin* tax	23
		所得税 *shotokuzei* income tax	153, 374
		関税 *kanzei* customs, duty, tariff	398
税		税関 *zeikan* customs, customshouse	398
		無税 *muzei* tax-free, duty-free	93

	400	SETSU, opinion, theory; ZEI, *to(ku)*, explain; persuade	
説	149 4373	説 明 *setsumei* explanation	18
		社 説 *shasetsu* an editorial	308
		小 説 *shōsetsu* novel, story	27
		演 説 *enzetsu* a speech	344
説		説 教 *sekkyō* sermon	245

	401	BI, *utsuku(shii)*, beautiful	
美	123 3658	美 術 館 *bijutsukan* art museum/gallery	187, 327
		美 学 *bigaku* esthetics	109
		美 人 *bijin* beautiful woman	1
		美 化 *bika* beautification	254
美		美 点 *biten* beauty, merit, good point	169

	402	YŌ, *yashina(u)*, rear; adopt; support; recuperate	
養	123 3671	養 育 *yōiku* upbringing, nurture	246
		養 成 *yōsei* training, cultivation	261
		教 養 *kyōyō* culture, education	245
		養 子 *yōshi* adopted child	103
養		休 養 *kyūyō* rest, recreation; recuperation	60

	403	YŌ, way, manner; similarity; condition; *sama*, condition; Mr., Mrs., Miss	
様	75 2341	様 子 *yōsu* situation, aspect, appearance	103
		同 様 *dōyō* same	198
		多 様 *tayō* diversity, variety	229
様		神 様 *kamisama* God	310

	404	DAI, (prefix for ordinals), degree	
第	118 3385	第 一 *daiichi* No. 1; first, best, main	2
		毎 月 第 二 土 曜 日 *maitsuki daini doyōbi* second Saturday of every month	116, 17, 3, 24, 19, 5
		第 三 者 *daisansha* third person/party	4, 164
第		次 第 *shidai* sequence; circumstances; as soon as	384

	405	TEI, [DAI], [DE], *otōto*, younger brother	
弟	12 584	義 弟 *gitei* younger brother-in-law	291
		子 弟 *shitei* sons, children	103
		弟 子 *deshi* pupil, apprentice, disciple	103
		門 弟 *montei* pupil, follower	161
弟		弟 分 *otōtobun* like a younger brother	38

	406	KEI, [KYŌ], *ani*, elder brother	
兄	30 875	兄 弟 *kyōdai* brothers, brothers and sisters	405
		父 兄 *fukei* parents and brothers; guardians	113
		義 兄 *gikei* elder brother-in-law	291
		実 兄 *jikkei* one's brother by blood	203
兄		兄 さ ん *niisan* elder brother	

	407	**SHI**, *ane*, elder sister	
姉	38 1207	義姉 *gishi* elder sister-in-law 姉さん *nēsan* elder sister; young lady	291
	姉		

	408	**MAI**, *imōto*, younger sister	
妹	38 1204	姉妹 *shimai* sisters 姉妹都市 *shimai toshi* sister cities 弟妹 *teimai* younger brothers and sisters 義妹 *gimai* younger sister-in-law	407 407, 188, 181 405 291
	妹		

	409	**SHI**, teacher; army	
師	2 113	教師 *kyōshi* teacher, instructor 医師 *ishi* physician 法師 *hōshi* Buddhist priest 山師 *yamashi* speculator; adventurer; charlatan 師弟 *shitei* master and pupil	245 220 123 34 405
	師		

	410	**DŌ**, *warabe*, child	
童	117 3357	学童 *gakudō* schoolchild 童話 *dōwa* nursery story, fairy tale 童顔 *dōgan* childlike/boyish face 童心 *dōshin* child's mind/feelings 神童 *shindō* child prodigy	109 238 277 97 310
	童		

	411	**RYŌ**, quantity; *haka(ru)*, (tr.) measure, weigh	
量	72 2141	大/少量 *tai/shōryō* large/small quantity 雨量 *uryō* (amount of) rainfall 大量生産 *tairyō seisan* mass production 分量 *bunryō* quantity, amount; dosage 重量 *jūryō* weight	26, 144 30 26, 44, 278 38 227
	量		

	412	**SHŌ**, *akina(u)*, deal (in), trade	
商	8 321	商人 *shōnin* merchant, dealer 商品 *shōhin* goods, merchandise 商業 *shōgyō* commerce, business 商売 *shōbai* trade, business; one's trade 商工 *shōkō* commerce and industry	1 230 279 239 139
	商		

	413	**KA**, *su(giru)*, pass, exceed, too much; *su(gosu)*, spend (time); *ayama(tsu)*, err; *ayama(chi)*, error	
過	162 4723	過度 *kado* excessive, too much 通過 *tsūka* passage, transit 過半数 *kahansū* majority, more than half 食べ過ぎる *tabesugiru* eat too much, overeat	377 150 88, 225 322
	過		

	414	**KYO, KO**, *sa(ru)*, leave, move away; pass, elapse	
去	32 1051	去年　　*kyonen*　last year	45
		死去　　*shikyo*　death	85
		去来　　*kyorai*　coming and going	69
		過去　　*kako*　past	413
去		立ち去る *tachisaru*　leave, go away	121

	415	**TEKI**, fit, be suitable	
適	162 4738	適当　　*tekitō*　suitable, appropriate	77
		適度　　*tekido*　to a proper degree, moderate	377
		適切　　*tekisetsu*　pertinent, appropriate	39
		適用　　*tekiyō*　application (of a rule)	107
適		適合　　*tekigō*　conformity, compatibility	159

	416	**TEKI**, *kataki*, enemy, opponent, competitor	
敵	66 2060	宿敵　　*shukuteki*　old/hereditary enemy	179
		強敵　　*kyōteki*　powerful foe, formidable rival	217
		敵意　　*tekii*　enmity, hostility	132
		敵対　　*tekitai*　hostility, antagonism	365
敵		不敵　　*futeki*　fearless, daring	94

	417	**TEI**, *hodo*, degree, extent	
程	115 3285	程度　　*teido*　degree, extent, grade	377
		過程　　*katei*　a process	413
		工程　　*kōtei*　progress of the work; manufacturing	139
		日程　　*nittei*　schedule for the day　⌊process	5
程		音程　　*ontei*　musical interval, step	347

	418	**SO**, *kumi*, group, crew, class, gang; *ku(mu)*, put together	
組	120 3520	組成　　*sosei*　composition, makeup	261
		番組　　*bangumi*　(TV) program	185
		労働組合 *rōdō kumiai*　labor union	233, 232, 159
		組み立て *kumitate*　construction; assembling	121
組		組み合わせる *kumiawaseru*　combine, fit together	159

	419	**YŌ**, main point, necessity; *i(ru)*, need, be necessary	
要	146 4274	重要　　*jūyō*　important	227
		主要　　*shuyō*　principal, major	155
		要点　　*yōten*　main point, gist	169
		要素　　*yōso*　element, factor	271
要		要約　　*yōyaku*　summary	211

	420	**GU**, tool	
具	109 3128	具体的 *gutaiteki*　concrete, specific	61, 210
		道具　　*dōgu*　tool, implement	149
		家具　　*kagu*　furniture	165
		金具　　*kanagu*　metal fitting	23
具		不具　　*fugu*　deformity, crippled	94

	421	KA, *atai*, price, value
9	物価	*bukka* prices (of commodities) 79
422	米価	*beika* price of rice 224
	単価	*tanka* unit price 300
価	定価	*teika* fixed/list price 355
	現金正価	*genkin seika* cash price 298, 23, 275

	422	SHIN, truth, genuineness, reality; *ma*, true, pure, exactly
24	真実	*shinjitsu* the truth, a fact 203
783	真理	*shinri* truth 143
	真相	*shinsō* the truth, the facts 146
真	真空	*shinkū* vacuum 140
	真っ暗	*makkura* pitch-dark 348

	423	CHOKU, JIKI, honest, frank, direct; *nao(su)*, fix, correct; *nao(ru)*, be fixed, corrected; *tada(chi ni)*, immediately
24		
775	直線	*chokusen* straight line 299
	直前/後	*choku-zen/go* immediately before/after 47, 48
直	正直	*shōjiki* honest, upright 275
	書き直す	*kakinaosu* write over again, rewrite 131

	424	SHOKU, *u(eru)*, plant; *u(waru)*, be planted
75	植物	*shokubutsu* a plant 79
2303	動植物	*dōshokubutsu* animals and plants 231, 79
	植民地	*shokuminchi* colony 177, 118
植	植木	*ueki* garden/potted plant 22
	田植え	*taue* rice planting 35

	425	CHI, *ne*, *atai*, value, price
9	価値	*kachi* value 421
488	値うち	*neuchi* value; public estimation
	値段	*nedan* price 362
値	値上げ	*neage* price increase 32
	値切る	*negiru* haggle over the price, bargain 39

	426	CHI, *o(ku)*, put, set; leave behind/as is
122	位置	*ichi* position, location 122
3644	置き物	*okimono* ornament; figurehead 79
	物置き	*monooki* storeroom, shed 79
置	前置き	*maeoki* introductory remarks, preface 47
	一日置き	*ichinichioki* every other day 2, 5

	427	SEI, system; regulations
18	制度	*seido* system 377
683	税制	*zeisei* system of taxation 399
	新制	*shinsei* new order, reorganization 174
制	強制	*kyōsei* compulsion, force 217
	管制	*kansei* control 328

	428	**SEI**, produce, manufacture, make	
製	145	製作　*seisaku*　a work, production	360
	4249	製品　*seihin*　product	230
		製鉄　*seitetsu*　iron manufacturing	312
製		木製　*mokusei*　wooden, made of wood	22
		日本製　*nihonsei*　Japanese-made, Made in Japan	5, 25

	429	**SŌ**, *hashi(ru)*, run	
走	156	走路　*sōro*　(race) track, course	151
	4539	走行時間　*sōkō jikan*　travel time	68, 42, 43
		走り回る　*hashirimawaru*　run around	90
走		走り書き　*hashirigaki*　flowing/hasty handwriting	131
		口走る　*kuchibashiru*　babble, blurt out	54

	430	**TO**, on foot; companions; vain, useless	
徒	60	生徒　*seito*　pupil, student	44
	1614	教徒　*kyōto*　believer, adherent	245
		使徒　*shito*　apostle	331
徒		徒手　*toshu*　empty-handed; penniless	57
		徒労　*torō*　vain effort	233

	431	**HO, BU**, [FU], *aru(ku)*, *ayu(mu)*, walk	
歩	77	歩道　*hodō*　footpath, sidewalk	149
	2433	歩行者　*hokōsha*　pedestrian	68, 164
		一歩　*ippo*　a step	2
歩		歩調　*hochō*　pace, step	342
		歩合　*buai*　rate, percentage; commission	159

	432	**SHŌ**, cross over; have to do with	
渉	85	交渉　*kōshō*　negotiations	114
	2591		
渉			

	433	**TEN**, *koro(bu/garu/geru)*, roll over, fall down; *koro(gasu)*, roll, knock down	
転	159	自転車　*jitensha*　bicycle	62, 133
	4615	回転　*kaiten*　rotation, revolution	90
		空転　*kūten*　idling (of an engine)	140
転		転任　*tennin*　transfer of assignments/personnel	334

	434	**DEN**, *tsuta(eru)*, transmit, impart; *tsuta(waru)*, be transmitted, imparted; *tsuta(u)*, go along	
伝	9	伝記　*denki*　biography	371
	379	伝説　*densetsu*　legend, folklore	400
		伝道　*dendō*　evangelism, missionary work	149
伝		手伝い　*tetsudai*　help, helper	57

	435	GEI, art, craft	
芸	140 3908		
		芸者 *geisha* geisha	164
		芸術 *geijutsu* art	187
		文芸 *bungei* literary art, literature	111
芸		演芸 *engei* performance, entertainment	344
		民芸 *mingei* folkcraft	177

	436	SHŪ, *atsu(maru/meru)*, (intr./tr.) gather; *tsudo(u)*, (intr.) gather	
集	172 5031		
		集金 *shūkin* bill collecting	23
		集中 *shūchū* concentration	28
		全集 *zenshū* the complete works	89
集		特集 *tokushū* special edition	282

	437	SHIN, *susu(mu)*, advance, progress; *susu(meru)*, advance, promote	
進	162 4709		
		進歩 *shinpo* progress, improvement	431
		進行 *shinkō* progress, onward movement	68
		前進 *zenshin* advance, forward movement	47
進		先進国 *senshinkoku* developed/advanced country	50, 40

	438	GUN, army, troops, war	
軍	14 628		
		軍人 *gunjin* soldier, military man	1
		軍事 *gunji* military affairs, military	80
		海軍 *kaigun* navy	117
軍		敵軍 *tekigun* enemy army/troops	416
		軍国主義 *gunkoku shugi* militarism	40, 155, 291

	439	UN, fate, luck; *hako(bu)*, carry, transport	
運	162 4725		
		運転手 *untenshu* driver, chauffeur	433, 57
		(労働)運動 *(rōdō) undō* (labor) movement	233, 232, 231
		運動不足 *undōbusoku* lack of exercise	231, 94, 58
運		運河 *unga* canal	389
		不運 *fuun* misfortune	94

	440	REN, group, accompaniment; *tsu(reru)*, take (someone); *tsura(naru)*, stand in a row; *tsura(neru)*, link, put in a row	
連	162 4702		
		連続 *renzoku* series, continuity	243
		連合 *rengō* combination, league, coalition	159
		国連 *Kokuren* United Nations	40
連		家族連れ *kazokuzure* with the family	165, 221

	441	SŌ, *oku(ru)*, send	
送	162 4683		
		運送 *unsō* transport, shipment	439
		回送 *kaisō* forwarding	90
		送金 *sōkin* remittance	23
送		送別会 *sōbetsukai* going-away/farewell party	267, 158
		見送る *miokuru* see (someone) off; escort	63

返 返	442 162 4670	**HEN**, *kae(ru/su)*, (intr./tr.) return

返事　　*henji*　reply ⌐postcard　　80
返信用葉書　*henshin'yō hagaki*　reply　157, 107, 253, 131
見返す　*mikaesu*　look back; triumph over (an old enemy)　63
読み返す　*yomikaesu*　reread　244
送り返す　*okurikaesu*　send back　441

坂 坂	443 32 1061	**HAN**, *saka*, slope, hill

急な坂　*kyū na saka*　steep slope/hill　303
坂道　　*sakamichi*　road on a slope　149
上り坂　*noborizaka*　ascent　32
下り坂　*kudarizaka*　descent; decline　31
赤坂　　*Akasaka*　(area of Tokyo)　207

逆 逆	444 162 4685	**GYAKU**, reverse, inverse, opposite; treason; *saka*, reverse, inverse; *saka(rau)*, be contrary (to)

逆転　　*gyakuten*　reversal　433
逆説　　*gyakusetsu*　paradox　400
反逆　　*hangyaku*　treason　324
逆立つ　*sakadatsu*　stand on end　121

近 近	445 162 4671	**KIN**, *chika(i)*, near, close

近所　　*kinjo*　vicinity, neighborhood　153
付近　　*fukin*　vicinity, environs　192
最近　　*saikin*　recent; most recent, latest　263
近代　　*kindai*　modern times, modern　256
近道　　*chikamichi*　shortcut, shorter way　149

遠 遠	446 162 4733	**EN**, [ON], *tō(i)*, far, distant

遠方　　*enpō*　great distance, (in) the distance　70
遠近法　*enkinhō*　(law of) perspective　445, 123
遠足　　*ensoku*　excursion, outing　58
遠心力　*enshinryoku*　centrifugal force　97, 100
遠回し　*tōmawashi*　indirect, roundabout　90

園 園	447 31 1047	**EN**, *sono*, garden

公園　　　*kōen*　(public) park　126
動物園　　*dōbutsuen*　zoo　231, 79
植物園　　*shokubutsuen*　botanical garden　424, 79
学園　　　*gakuen*　educational institution, academy　109
楽園　　　*rakuen*　paradise　358

達 達	448 162 4721	**TATSU**, reach, arrive at

上達　　*jōtatsu*　progress; proficiency　32
発達　　*hattatsu*　development　96
達成　　*tassei*　achieve, attain　261
達人　　*tatsujin*　expert, master　1
友達　　*tomodachi*　friend　264

	449	**KI**, [GO], time, period, term	
期	130 3785	期 間 *kikan* period of time, term 定 期 *teiki* fixed period 過 渡 期 *katoki* transition period 学 期 *gakki* semester, trimester, school term 短 期 大 学 *tanki daigaku* junior college	43 355 413, 378 109 215, 26, 109

	450	**KI**, *moto, motoi*, basis, foundation, origin	
基	32 1098	基 本 *kihon* basics, fundamentals; standard 基 金 *kikin* fund, endowment 基 地 *kichi* (military) base 基 石 *kiseki* foundation stone, cornerstone 基 調 *kichō* keynote	25 23 118 78 342

	451	**JI**, *mo(tsu)*, have, possess; hold, maintain	
持	64 1903	支 持 *shiji* support 持 続 *jizoku* continuance, maintenance 持 ち 主 *mochinushi* owner, possessor 金 持 ち *kanemochi* rich person 気 持 ち *kimochi* mood, feeling	318 243 155 23 134

	452	**TAI**, *ma(tsu)*, wait for	
待	60 1609	期 待 *kitai* expectation, anticipation 特 待 *tokutai* special treatment, distinction 待 ち 合 い 室 *machiaishitsu* waiting room 待 ち 合 わ せ る *machiawaseru* wait for (as previously 待 ち ぼ う け *machibōke* getting stood up ⌊arranged)	449 282 159, 166 159

	453	**KAI**, shellfish (cf. No. 240); be in between, mediate	
介	9 347	介 入 *kainyū* intervention 介 在 *kaizai* lie/stand/come between 魚 介 *gyokai* fish and shellfish, marine products 一 介 の *ikkai no* mere, only	52 268 290 2

	454	**KAI**, world	
界	102 2998	世 界 *sekai* world 世 界 史 *sekaishi* world history 学 界 *gakkai* academic world 外 界 *gaikai* external world, outside 下 界 *gekai* this world, the earth below	252 252, 332 109 83 31

	455	**SHŌ**, *mane(ku)*, beckon to, invite, cause	
招	64 1882	招 待 *shōtai* invitation 手 招 き *temaneki* beckoning	452 57

456

SHŌ, introduction

120	紹 介	*shōkai* introduction, presentation	453
3516	自 己 紹 介	*jiko shōkai* introduce oneself	62, 370, 453

紹

457

KAN, coldest season, coldness; *samu(i)*, cold

40	寒 気	*kanki* the cold	134
1322	寒 中	*kanchū* the cold season	28
	極 寒	*gokkan* severe cold	336
	寒 村	*kanson* poor/lonely village	191
	寒 空	*samuzora* wintry sky, cold weather	140

寒

458

SHŪ, *o(waru/eru)*, come/bring to an end

120	最 終	*saishū* last	263
3521	終 戦	*shūsen* end of the war	301
	終 点	*shūten* end of the line, last stop, terminus	169
	終 身	*shūshin* for life, lifelong	59
	終 日	*shūjitsu* all day long	5

終

459

TŌ, *fuyu*, winter

34	立 冬	*rittō* first day of winter	121
1161	真 冬	*mafuyu* midwinter, the dead of winter	422
	冬 向 き	*fuyumuki* for winter	199
	冬 物	*fuyumono* winter clothing	79
	冬 空	*fuyuzora* winter sky	140

冬

460

SHUN, *haru*, spring

72	春 分 （の 日）	*shunbun (no hi)* vernal equinox	38, 5
2122	立 春	*risshun* beginning of spring	121
	青 春	*seishun* springtime of life, youth	208
	売 春	*baishun* prostitution	239
	春 画	*shunga* obscene picture, pornography	343

春

461

KA, [GE], *natsu*, summer

1	夏 期	*kaki* the summer period	449
58	立 夏	*rikka* beginning of summer	121
	真 夏	*manatsu* midsummer, height of summer	422
	夏 物	*natsumono* summer clothing	79
	夏 休 み	*natsuyasumi* summer vacation	60

夏

462

SHŪ, *aki*, fall, autumn

115	春 夏 秋 冬	*shunkashūtō* all the year round	460, 461, 459
3273	春 秋	*shunjū* spring and autumn; years, age	460
	秋 分 （の 日）	*shūbun (no hi)* autumnal equinox	38, 5
	秋 気	*shūki* the autumn air	134
	秋 風	*akikaze* autumn breeze	29

秋

	463	**SOKU**, immediately; conform (to); namely, i.e.	
即	138 3886	即時 *sokuji* instantly, immediately, on the spot	42
		即日 *sokujitsu* on the same day	5
		即金 *sokkin* cash; payment in cash	23
即		即席 *sokuseki* extemporaneous, impromptu	379
		即興 *sokkyō* improvised, ad-lib	368

	464	**SETSU**, [SECHI], season; occasion; section, paragraph; verse; *fushi*, joint, knuckle; melody; point	
節	118 3402	時節 *jisetsu* time of year; the times	42
		調節 *chōsetsu* adjustment, regulation	342
		使節 *shisetsu* envoy, mission	331
節		節約 *setsuyaku* economizing, thrift	211

	465	**KI**, season	
季	115 3266	季節 *kisetsu* season, time of year	464
		四季 *shiki* the 4 seasons	6
		季節風 *kisetsufū* seasonal wind, monsoon	464, 29
季		季節外れ *kisetsuhazure* out of season	464, 83
		季語 *kigo* word indicating the season (in haiku)	67

	466	**I**, entrust	
委	115 3267	委任 *inin* trust, mandate, authorization	334
		委員 *iin* committee member	163
委		委員会 *iinkai* committee	163, 158

	467	**KO**, *mizuumi*, lake	
湖	85 2628	湖水 *kosui* lake	21
		火口湖 *kakōko* crater lake	20, 54
		湖面 *komen* surface of a lake	274
湖		山中湖 *Yamanaka-ko* (lake near Mt. Fuji)	34, 28
		十和田湖 *Towada-ko* (lake in Tohoku)	12, 124, 35

	468	**CHŌ**, *shio*, tide; salt water; opportunity	
潮	85 2702	満潮 *manchō* high tide	201
		潮流 *chōryū* tidal current; trend of the times	247
		風潮 *fūchō* tide; tendency, trend	29
潮		潮時 *shiodoki* favorable tide; opportunity	42
		黒潮 *Kuroshio* Japan Current	206

	469	**CHŌ**, morning; dynasty; *asa*, morning	
朝	130 3788	朝食 *chōshoku* breakfast	322
		平安朝 *Heianchō* Heian period (794–1185)	202, 105
		朝日 *asahi* morning/rising sun	5
朝		毎朝 *maiasa* every morning	116
		今朝 *kesa, konchō* this morning	51

	470	CHŪ, *hiru*, daytime, noon	
昼	1 53	昼 食 *chūshoku* lunch	322
		白 昼 に *hakuchū ni* in broad daylight	205
		昼 飯 *hirumeshi* lunch	325
		昼 間 *hiruma* daytime	43
昼		昼 休 み *hiruyasumi* lunch break, noon recess	60

	471	YA, *yoru, yo*, night	
夜	8 298	昼 夜 *chūya* day and night	470
		今 夜 *kon'ya* tonight	51
		夜 行 *yakō* traveling by night; night train	68
		夜 学 *yagaku* evening class	109
夜		夜 明 け *yoake* dawn, daybreak	18

	472	EKI, liquid, fluid	
液	85 2599	液 体 *ekitai* liquid, fluid	61
		液 化 *ekika* liquefaction	254
液		だ 液 *daeki* saliva	

	473	KAKU, angle, corner; *kado*, corner, angle; *tsuno*, horn, antlers	
角	148 4301	角 度 *kakudo* degrees of an angle, angle	377
		三 角 (形) *sankaku(kei)* triangle	4, 395
		直 角 *chokkaku* right angle	423
角		街 角 *machikado* street corner	186

	474	KAI, GE, *to(ku)*, untie; solve; *to(keru)*, come loose; be solved; *to(kasu)*, comb	
解	148 4306	理 解 *rikai* understanding	143
		解 説 *kaisetsu* explanation, commentary	400
		解 決 *kaiketsu* solution, settlement	356
解		和 解 *wakai* compromise	124

	475	KIKU, chrysanthemum	
菊	140 3981	白 菊 *shiragiku* white chrysanthemum	205
		菊 の 花 *kiku no hana* chrysanthemum	255
		菊 作 り *kikuzukuri* chrysanthemum growing	360
		菊 人 形 *kikuningyō* chrysanthemum doll	1, 395
菊		菊 地 *Kikuchi* (surname)	118

	476	Ō, *oku*, interior	
奥	4 240	奥 義 *ōgi, okugi* secrets, hidden mysteries	291
		奥 行 き *okuyuki* depth (vs. height and width)	68
		山 奥 *yamaoku* deep in the mountains	34
		奥 付 け *okuzuke* colophon	192
奥		奥 さ ん *okusan* wife; ma'am	

477 SHI, to(maru/meru), come/bring to a stop

止

止

77	終 止	*shūshi*	termination, end	458
2429	休 止	*kyūshi*	pause, suspension ⌈oughfare	60
	通 行 止 め	*tsūkōdome*	Road Closed, No Thor-	150, 68
	口 止 め 料	*kuchidomeryō*	hush money	54, 319
	足 止 め	*ashidome*	keep indoors, confinement	58

478 SHI, ha, tooth

歯

歯

211	門/犬 歯	*mon/kenshi*	incisor/canine	161, 280
5428	義 歯	*gishi*	false teeth, dentures	291
	歯 科 医	*shikai*	dentist	319, 220
	歯 医 者	*haisha*	dentist	220, 164
	歯 車	*haguruma*	toothed wheel, gear	133

479 SAI, year, years old; [SEI], year

歳

歳

77	満 四 歳	*man'yonsai*	4 (full) years old	201, 6
2434	二 十 歳	*hatachi*	20 years old	3, 12
	万 歳	*banzai*	Hurrah! Long live . . . !	16
	歳 月	*saigetsu*	time, years ⌈penditure	17
	歳 入 歳 出	*sainyū-saishutsu*	yearly revenue and ex-	52, 53

480 REKI, continuation, passing of time

歴

歴

27	歴 史	*rekishi*	history	332
835	学 歴	*gakureki*	school career, academic background	109
	前 歴	*zenreki*	one's personal history, background	47
	歴 任	*rekinin*	successive holding of various posts	334

481 KI, kuwada(teru), plan, undertake, attempt

企

企

9	企 業	*kigyō*	enterprise, undertaking	279
373	中 小 企 業	*chūshō kigyō*	small- and medium-size	
			enterprises	28, 27, 279
	企 画	*kikaku*	planning, plan	343
	企 図	*kito*	plan, project, scheme	339

482 KIN, prohibition

禁

禁

113	禁 止	*kinshi*	prohibition	477
3251	解 禁	*kaikin*	lifting of a ban	474
	禁 制	*kinsei*	prohibition, ban	427
	禁 物	*kinmotsu*	forbidden things, taboo	79
	発 禁	*hakkin*	prohibition of sale	96

483 SEI, [SHŌ], matsurigoto, government, rule

政

政

66	政 局	*seikyoku*	political situation	170
2045	行 政	*gyōsei*	administration	68
	内 政	*naisei*	domestic politics, internal affairs	84
	市 政	*shisei*	municipal government ⌈keeping	181
	家 政	*kasei*	management of a household, house-	165

証	484	SHŌ, proof, evidence, certificate	
	149 4341	証明 *shōmei* proof, testimony, corroboration	18
		証人 *shōnin* witness	1
		証言 *shōgen* testimony	66
証		反証 *hanshō* counterproof, counterevidence	324
		内証 *naisho, naishō* secret	84

結	485	KETSU, *musu(bu)*, tie, bind; conclude (a contract); bear (fruit); *yu(waeru)*, tie; *yu(u)*, do up (one's hair)	
	120 3540	結論 *ketsuron* conclusion	293
		結成 *kessei* formation, organization	261
		結合 *ketsugō* union, combination	159
結		終結 *shūketsu* conclusion, termination	458

接	486	SETSU, touch, contact; *tsu(gu)*, join together	
	64 1951	直接 *chokusetsu* direct	423
		間接 *kansetsu* indirect	43
		面接 *mensetsu* interview	274
		接続 *setsuzoku* connection, joining	243
接		接待 *settai* reception, welcome; serving, offering	452

果	487	KA, fruit; result; *ha(tasu)*, carry out, complete; *ha(teru)*, come to an end; *ha(te)*, end, limit; result	
	2 107	結果 *kekka* result	485
		成果 *seika* result	261
		果実 *kajitsu* fruit	203
果		果物 *kudamono* fruit	79

課	488	KA, lesson; section	
	149 4389	第一課 *daiikka* Lesson 1	404, 2
		課目 *kamoku* subject (in school)	55
		課程 *katei* course, curriculum	417
		課長 *kachō* section chief	95
課		人事課 *jinjika* personnel section	1, 80

保	489	HO, *tamo(tsu)*, keep, preserve, maintain	
	9 455	保証 *hoshō* guarantee, warranty	484
		保証人 *hoshōnin* guarantor, sponsor	484, 1
		保存 *hozon* preservation	269
		保育所 *hoikusho, hoikujo* daycare nursery	246, 153
保		保養所 *hoyōsho, hoyōjo* sanatorium, rest home	402, 153

守	490	SHU, [SU], *mamo(ru)*, protect; obey, abide by; *mori*, baby-sitter, (lighthouse) keeper	
	40 1282	保守的 *hoshuteki* conservative	489, 210
		子守 *komori* baby-sitting; baby-sitter, nursemaid	103
		子守歌 *komoriuta* lullaby	103, 392
守		見守る *mimamoru* keep watch over; stare at	63

	491	**DAN, [TON], group**	
団	31 1027 団	団体(旅行) *dantai* (*ryokō*) group (tour) 61, 222, 68 集団 *shūdan* group, mass 436 団地 *danchi* public housing development/complex 118 団結 *danketsu* unity, solidarity 485 師団 *shidan* (army) division 409	

	492	**DAI, TAI, stand, pedestal, platform, plateau**	
台	28 848 台	台所 *daidokoro* kitchen 153 天文台 *tenmondai* observatory 141, 111 高台 *takadai* high ground, a height 190 台本 *daihon* script, screenplay, libretto 25 台風 *taifū* typhoon 29	

	493	**JI, CHI, peace; government; healing; *osa(meru)*, govern; suppress; *osa(maru)*, be at peace, quelled; *nao(ru/su)*, (intr./tr.) heal**	
治	85 2528 治	政治 *seiji* politics 483 自治 *jichi* self-government, autonomy 62 明治時代 *Meiji jidai* Meiji era (1868–1912) 18, 42, 256	

	494	**SHI, *haji(maru/meru)*, (intr./tr.) start, begin**	
始	38 1208 始	始末 *shimatsu* circumstances; management, disposal 305 始終 *shijū* from first to last, all the while 458 始発 *shihatsu* the first (train) departure 96 開始 *kaishi* beginning, opening 396 原始的 *genshiteki* primitive, original 136, 210	

	495	**TŌ, party, faction**	
党	42 1363 党	政党 *seitō* political party 483 野党 *yatō* party out of power, the opposition 236 党員/首 *tōin/shu* party member/leader 163, 148 徒党 *totō* confederates, clique, conspiracy 430 社会党 *Shakaitō* Socialist Party 308, 158	

	496	**DŌ, temple; hall**	
堂	42 1365 堂	食堂 *shokudō* dining hall, restaurant 322 能楽堂 *nōgakudō* Noh theater 386, 358 公会堂 *kōkaidō* public hall, community center 126, 158 本堂 *hondō* main temple 25 国会議事堂 *kokkai gijidō* Diet Building 40, 158, 292, 80	

	497	**JŌ, *tsune*, normal, usual, continual; *toko-*, ever-, always**	
常	42 1364 常	日常生活 *nichijō seikatsu* everyday life 5, 44, 237 正常 *seijō* normal 275 通常 *tsūjō* ordinary, usual 150 常任委員 *jōnin iin* member of a standing committee 334, 466, 163	

	498	**HI**, mistake; (prefix) non-, un-
非	175 5080	非 常 口 *hijōguchi* emergency exit 497, 54
		非 常 事 態 *hijō jitai* state of emergency 497, 80, 387
		非 公 開 *hikōkai* not open to the public, private 126, 396
	非	非 人 間 的 *hiningenteki* inhuman, impersonal 1, 43, 210
		非 合 法 *higōhō* illegal 159, 123

	499	**SHŌ**, palm of the hand; administer
掌	42 1366	合 掌 *gasshō* clasp one's hands (in prayer) 159
		掌 中 *shōchū* pocket (edition), in the hand 28
		掌 中 の 玉 *shōchū no tama* apple of one's eye,
	掌	one's jewel 28, 295
		車 掌 *shashō* (train) conductor 133

	500	**SHŌ**, prize; praise
賞	42 1372	文 学 賞 *bungaku-shō* prize for literature 111, 109
		ノ ー ベ ル賞 *Nōberu-shō* Nobel Prize
		賞 品 *shōhin* a prize 230
	賞	賞 金 *shōkin* cash prize, prize money 23
		受 賞 者 *jushōsha* prizewinner 260, 164

	501	**SOKU**, *taba*, bundle, sheaf
束	4 196	一 束 *issoku, hitotaba* a bundle 2
		約 束 *yakusoku* promise, appointment 211
		結 束 *kessoku* unity, union, bond 485
	束	花 束 *hanataba* bouquet 255
		束 ね る *tabaneru* tie in a bundle; control

	502	**SOKU**, *haya(i)*, *sumi(yaka)*, fast, quick, prompt; *haya(meru)*, quicken, accelerate
速	162 4700	速 力/度 *soku-ryoku/do* speed, velocity 100, 377
		高 速 道 路 *kōsoku dōro* expressway, freeway 190, 149, 151
	速	速 達 *sokutatsu* special/express delivery 448
		速 記 *sokki* shorthand, stenography 371

	503	**SEI**, *totono(eru)*, put in order, prepare; *totono(u)*, be put in order, prepared
整	77 2436	整 理 *seiri* arrangement, adjustment 143
		調 整 *chōsei* adjustment, modulation 342
	整	整 形 外 科 *seikei geka* plastic surgery 395, 83, 320
		整 数 *seisū* integer 225

	504	**FU**, storehouse; government office; capital city
府	53 1507	政 府 *seifu* government 483
		無 政 府 *museifu* anarchy 93, 483
		首 府 *shufu* the capital 148
	府	京 都 府 *Kyōto-fu* Kyoto Prefecture ⌐tures 189, 188
		都 道 府 県 *todōfuken* the Japanese prefec- 188, 149, 194

符	**505** 118 3383 符	**FU**, sign, mark; amulet

切 符　　　*kippu*　ticket　　　　　　　　　　「dow　39
切符売り場　*kippu uriba*　ticket office/win-　39, 239, 154
音 符　　　*onpu*　diacritical mark; musical note　347
符 号　　　*fugō*　mark, symbol　　　　　　266
符 合　　　*fugō*　coincidence, agreement, correspondence　159

券	**506** 18 678 券	**KEN**, ticket, certificate

入 場 券　*nyūjōken*　admission ticket　　　52, 154
旅 券　　　*ryoken*　passport　　　　　　　222
回 数 券　*kaisūken*　coupon ticket　　　　90, 225
定 期 券　*teikiken*　commutation ticket, (train) pass　355, 449
(有 価) 証 券　*(yūka) shōken*　securities　265, 421, 484

巻	**507** 49 1466 巻	**KAN**, *maki*, roll, reel; volume; *ma(ku)*, roll, wind

上/中/下巻　*jō/chū/ge-kan*　first/middle/last volume　32, 28, 31
第 一 巻　*daiikkan*　Volume 1　　　　　　404, 2
絵 巻 (物)　*emaki(mono)*　picture scroll　345, 79
葉 巻　　　*hamaki*　cigar　　　　　　　　253
取り巻く　*torimaku*　surround, encircle　65

圏	**508** 31 1045 圏	**KEN**, circle, range, sphere

共 産 圏　*kyōsanken*　the Communist bloc/countries　196, 278
極 地 圏　*kyokuchiken*　polar region　　336, 118
北/南 極 圏　*hok/nan-kyokuken*　Artic/Antarctic　73, 74, 336
首 都 圏　*shutoken*　the capital region　148, 188
圏 内/外　*kennai/gai*　within/outside the range (of)　「Circle　84, 83

勝	**509** 130 3787 勝	**SHŌ**, *ka(tsu)*, win; *masa(ru)*, be superior (to)

勝 利　　　*shōri*　victory　　　　　　　　329
勝 (利) 者　*shō(ri)sha*　victor, winner　329, 164
決 勝　　　*kesshō*　decision (of a competition)　356
連 勝　　　*renshō*　series of victories, winning streak　440
勝ち通す　*kachitōsu*　win successive victories　150

負	**510** 154 4488 負	**FU**, *ma(keru)*, be defeated, lose; give a discount; *ma(kasu)*, beat, defeat; *o(u)*, carry, bear; owe

勝 負　　　*shōbu*　victory or defeat; game, match　509
自 負　　　*jifu*　conceit, self-importance　62
負けん気　*makenki*　unyielding/competitive spirit　134
負け犬　　*makeinu*　loser　　　　　　　　280

敗	**511** 154 4494 敗	**HAI**, *yabu(reru)*, be defeated, beaten, frustrated

敗 北　　　*haiboku*　defeat　　　　　　　73
勝 敗　　　*shōhai*　victory or defeat, outcome　509
失 敗　　　*shippai*　failure, blunder　　　311
敗 戦　　　*haisen*　lost battle, defeat　　301
敗 者　　　*haisha*　the defeated, loser　　164

	512	HŌ, *hana(tsu)*, set free, release; fire (a gun); emit; *hana(su)*, set free, release; *hana(reru)*, get free of	
放	70 2084	解 放　*kaihō*　liberation, emancipation	474
		放 送　*hōsō*　(radio/TV) broadcasting	441
	放	放 火　*hōka*　arson	20
		放 置　*hōchi*　let alone, leave as is, leave to chance	426

	513	BŌ, *fuse(gu)*, defend/protect from, prevent	
防	170 4980	防 止　*bōshi*　prevention, keeping in check	477
		予 防　*yobō*　prevention, precaution	393
		国 防　*kokubō*　national defense	40
	防	防 火　*bōka*　fire prevention/fighting	20
		防 水　*bōsui*　waterproof, watertight	21

	514	KAI, *arata(meru)*, alter, renew, reform; *arata(maru)*, be altered, renewed, corrected	
改	49 1464	改 正　*kaisei*　improvement; revision	275
		改 良　*kairyō*　improvement, reform	321
		改 新　*kaishin*　renovation, reformation	174
	改	改 名　*kaimei*　changing one's name	82

	515	HAI, *kuba(ru)*, distribute, pass out	
配	164 4779	心 配　*shinpai*　worry, concern	97
		支 配　*shihai*　management, administration, rule	318
		配 達　*haitatsu*　deliver	448
	配	配 置　*haichi*　arrangement, placement	426
		気 配　*kehai*　sign, indication	134

	516	SAN, *su(i)*, acid, sour	
酸	164 4789	酸 味　*sanmi*　acidity, sourness	307
		酸 性　*sansei*　acidity	98
		酸 化　*sanka*　oxidation	254
	酸	酸 素　*sanso*　oxygen	271
		青 酸　*seisan*　prussic acid, hydrogen cyanide	208

	517	SHU, *sake*, [*saka*], sakè, rice wine, liquor	
酒	85 2573	日 本 酒　*nihonshu*　sakè, Japanese rice wine	5, 25
		ぶどう酒　*budōshu*　(grape) wine	
		禁 酒　*kinshu*　abstinence from drink; temperance	482
	酒	酒 屋　*sakaya*　wine dealer, liquor store	167
		酒 場　*sakaba*　bar, saloon, tavern	154

	518	GAI, injury, harm, damage	
害	40 1306	公 害　*kōgai*　pollution	126
		水 害　*suigai*　flood damage, flooding	21
		損 害　*songai*　injury, loss	350
	害	利 害　*rigai*　advantages and disadvantages, interests	329
		防 害　*bōgai*　hindrance, obstruction	513

	519	KATSU, *wa(ru)*, divide, separate, split; *wa(reru)*, break, crack/split apart; *wari*, proportion; profit; 10 percent; *sa(ku)*, cut up; separate; spare (time)
割 18 703 割		分 割 *bunkatsu* division, partitioning 38
		割 合 *wariai* rate, proportion, percentage 159
		割 引 き *waribiki* discount 216

	520	HITSU, *kanara(zu)*, surely, (be) sure (to), without fail
必 3 129 必		必 要 *hitsuyō* necessary, requisite 419
		必 死 *hisshi* certain death; desperation 85
		必 読 *hitsudoku* required reading 244
		必 勝 *hisshō* sure victory ⌜sarily 509
		必 ず し も … な い *kanarazushimo . . . nai* not neces-

	521	KEN, law
憲 40 1342 憲		憲 法 *kenpō* constitution 123
		改 憲 *kaiken* constitutional revision 514
		憲 政 *kensei* constitutional government 483
		立 憲 *rikken* constitutional 121
		官 憲 *kanken* the (government) authorities 326

	522	DOKU, poison
毒 80 2468 毒		毒 薬 *dokuyaku* poison 359
		有 毒 *yūdoku* poisonous 265
		中 毒 *chūdoku* poisoning 28
		毒 草 *dokusō* poisonous plant 249
		気 の 毒 *kinodoku* pitiable, regrettable, unfortunate 134

	523	JŌ, *no(ru)*, get in/on, ride, take (a train); be fooled; *no(seru)*, let ride, take aboard; deceive, trick, take in
乗 4 223 乗		乗 用 車 *jōyōsha* passenger car 107, 133
		乗 車 券 *jōshaken* (passenger) ticket 133, 506
		乗 組 員 *norikumiin* (ship's) crew 418, 163
		乗 っ 取 る *nottoru* take over, commandeer, hijack 65

	524	YŪ, mail
郵 163 4768 郵		郵 便 局 *yūbinkyoku* post office 330, 170
		郵 便 配 達(人) *yūbin haitatsu(nin)* mailman 330, 515, 448, 1
		郵 便 料 金 *yūbin ryōkin* postage 330, 319, 23
		郵 税 *yūzei* postage 399
		郵 送 料 *yūsōryō* postage 441, 319

	525	SHIKI, ceremony, rite; style, form, method; formula
式 56 1556 式		正 式 *seishiki* prescribed form, formal 275
		公 式 *kōshiki* formula (in mathematics); formal, 126
		様 式 *yōshiki* mode, style ⌊official 403
		方 式 *hōshiki* formula, mode; method, system 70
		新 式 *shinshiki* new type 174

	526	**SHI**, *kokoro(miru)*, *tame(su)*, give it a try, try out, attempt	
試	149 4361	試合 *shiai* game, match	159
		試作 *shisaku* trial manufacture/cultivation	360
		試食 *shishoku* sample, taste	322
試		試運転 *shiunten* trial run	439, 433
		試金石 *shikinseki* touchstone; test	23, 78

	527	**KI**, *utsuwa*, container, apparatus; capacity, ability	
器	30 994	楽器 *gakki* musical instrument	358
		器楽 *kigaku* instrumental music	358
		器具 *kigu* utensil, appliance, tool, apparatus	420
器		食器 *shokki* eating utensils	322
		(無)器用 *(bu)kiyō* (not) dexterous	93, 107

	528	**KI**, opportunity; machine; *hata*, loom	
機	75 2379	機関 *kikan* engine; machinery, organ, medium	398
		制動機 *seidōki* a brake	427, 231
		起重機 *kijūki* crane	373, 227
機		機能 *kinō* a function	386
		機会 *kikai* opportunity, occasion, chance	158

	529	**KAI**, fetters; machine	
械	75 2264	器械 *kikai* instrument, apparatus, appliance	527
		機械 *kikai* machine, machinery	528
		機械化 *kikaika* mechanization	528, 254
械		機械文明 *kikai bunmei* technological civilization	528, 111, 18

	530	**HI**, *to(bu)*, fly; *to(basu)*, let fly; skip over, omit	
飛	183 5152	飛行 *hikō* flight, aviation	68
		飛行機 *hikōki* airplane	68, 528
		飛行場 *hikōjō* airport	68, 154
飛		飛び石 *tobiishi* stepping-stones	78
		飛び火 *tobihi* flying sparks, leaping flames	20

	531	**KEN**, investigation, inspection	
検	75 2304	検事 *kenji* public procurator/prosecutor	80
		検定 *kentei* official approval, inspection	355
		検証 *kenshō* verification, inspection	484
検		検死 *kenshi* coroner's inquest, autopsy	85
		点検 *tenken* inspection, examination	169

	532	**KEN**, effect; testing; [GEN], beneficial effect	
験	187 5220	実験 *jikken* experiment	203
		試験 *shiken* examination, test	526
		入学試験 *nyūgaku shiken* entrance exam	52, 109, 526
験		体験 *taiken* experience	61
		受験 *juken* take a test/exam	260

陰

険

533	KEN, *kewa(shii)*, steep, inaccessible; stern, harsh	
170	保険 *hoken* insurance	489
5000	険悪 *ken'aku* dangerous, threatening	304
	険路 *kenro* steep path	151
	険しい路 *kewashii michi* steep/treacherous road	149
	険しい顔つき *kewashii kaotsuki* stern/fierce look	277

危

534	KI, *abu(nai)*, *aya(ui)*, dangerous	
4	危険 *kiken* danger	533
187	危機 *kiki* crisis, critical moment	528
	危急 *kikyū* emergency, crisis	303
	危害 *kigai* injury, harm	518
	危ぐ *kigu* fear, misgivings, apprehension	

探

535	TAN, *sagu(ru)*, search/grope for; *saga(su)*, look for	
64	探検/険 *tanken* exploration, expedition	531, 533
1949	探知 *tanchi* detection	214
	探てい小説 *tantei shōsetsu* detective story	27, 400
	探り出す *saguridasu* spy/sniff out (a secret)	53
	探し回る *sagashimawaru* look/search around for	90

深

536	SHIN, *fuka(i)*, deep; *fuka(meru/maru)*, make/become deeper, more intense	
85		
2606	深度 *shindo* depth, deepness	377
	深夜 *shin'ya* dead of night, late at night	471
	情け深い *nasakebukai* compassionate, merciful	209
	興味深い *kyōmibukai* very interesting	368, 307

緑

537	RYOKU, [ROKU], *midori*, green	
120	緑地 *ryokuchi* green tract of land	118
3564	新緑 *shinryoku* fresh verdure/greenery	174
	葉緑素 *yōryokuso* chlorophyll	253, 271
	緑青 *rokushō* verdigris, green/copper rust	208
	緑色 *midoriiro* green, green-colored	204

録

538	ROKU, record	
167	記録 *kiroku* record	371
4879	録音 *rokuon* (sound) recording	347
	録画 *rokuga* videotape recording	274
	目録 *mokuroku* catalog, inventory, list	55
	付録 *furoku* supplement, appendix, addendum	192

与

539	YO, *ata(eru)*, give, grant	
1	与党 *yotō* party in power, government	495
6	関与 *kan'yo* participation	398
	給与 *kyūyo* allowance, wage	346
	供与 *kyōyo* give, grant, furnish	197
	賞与 *shōyo* bonus	500

	540	**SHA**, *utsu(su)*, copy down; copy, duplicate; depict; photograph; *utsu(ru)*, be taken, turn out (photo)	
写	14 626	写真　　*shashin*　photograph	422
		映写機　*eishaki*　projector	352, 528
		写生　　*shasei*　sketch, painting from nature	44
	写	写実的　*shajitsuteki*　realistic, graphic	203, 210
	541	**KŌ**, *kanga(eru)*, think, consider	
考	125 3684	思考　　*shikō*　thinking, thought	99
		考案　　*kōan*　conception, idea, design	106
		考証　　*kōshō*　historical research	484
		考古学　*kōkogaku*　archaeology	172, 109
	考	考え方　*kangaekata*　way of thinking, viewpoint	70
	542	**KŌ**, filial piety	
孝	24 773	(親)孝行　(*oya*)*kōkō*　filial piety, obedience to 　　　　　　　　　　　parents	175, 68
		孝養　　*kōyō*　discharge of filial duties	402
	孝	(親)不孝　(*oya*)*fukō*　undutifulness to one's parents	175, 94
	543	**RŌ**, *o(iru)*, *fu(keru)*, grow old	
老	125 3683	老人　　*rōjin*　old man/woman/people	1
		長老　　*chōrō*　elder, senior member	95
		元老　　*genrō*　genro; elder statesman	137
		老夫婦　*rōfūfu*　old married couple	315, 316
	老	老子　　*Rōshi*　Laozi, Lao-tzu	103
	544	**JAKU**, [**NYAKU**], *waka(i)*, young; *mo(shikuwa)*, or	
若	140 3926	老若　　*rōnyaku, rōjaku*　young and old, youth and age	543
		若者　　*wakamono*　young man/people	164
		若手　　*wakate*　young man, younger member	57
		若人　　*wakōdo*　young man, a youth	1
	若	若死に　*wakajini*　die young	85
	545	**KU**, *kuru(shimu)*, suffer; *kuru(shimeru)*, torment; *kuru(shii)*, painful; *niga(i)*, bitter; *niga(ru)*, scowl	
苦	140 3928	苦労　　*kurō*　trouble, hardship, adversity	233
		苦心　　*kushin*　pains, efforts	97
		病苦　　*byōku*　the pain of illness	380
	苦	重苦しい　*omokurushii*　oppressed, gloomy, ponderous	227
	546	**YU**, send, transport	
輸	159 4634	輸入　　*yunyū*　import	52
		輸出　　*yushutsu*　export	53
		輸送　　*yusō*　transport	441
		運輸　　*un'yu*　transport, conveyance	439
	輸	空輸　　*kūyu*　air transport, shipment by air	140

軽	547	**KEI, *karu(i)*, *karo(yaka)*, light**	
	159	軽工業 *keikōgyō* light industry	139, 279
	4620	軽食 *keishoku* light meal	322
		軽音楽 *keiongaku* light music	347, 358
	軽	気軽 *kigaru* lighthearted, cheerful, feel free (to)	134
		手軽 *tegaru* easy, light, simple, cheap	57

経	548	**KEI, longitude; sutra; passage of time; KYŌ, sutra; *he(ru)*, pass, elapse**	
	120	経験 *keiken* experience	532
	3523	経歴 *keireki* one's life history, career	480
		経理 *keiri* accounting	143
	経	神経 *shinkei* a nerve	310

済	549	**SAI, *su(mu)*, come to an end; be paid; suffice; *su(masu)*, finish, settle; pay; make do, manage**	
	85	経済 *keizai* economy, economics	548
	2597	返済 *hensai* payment, repayment	442
		決済 *kessai* settlement of accounts	356
	済	使用済み *shiyōzumi* used up	331, 107

剤	550	**ZAI, medicine, dose**	
	210	薬剤 *yakuzai* medicine, drug	359
	5424	薬剤師 *yakuzaishi* pharmacist, druggist	359, 409
		調剤 *chōzai* compounding/preparation of medicines	342
	剤	下剤 *gezai* laxative	31
		解毒剤 *gedokuzai* antidote	474, 522

才	551	**SAI, talent, genius**	
	6	天才 *tensai* a genius	141
	270	才子 *saishi* talented person	103
		才能 *sainō* talent, ability	386
	才	多才 *tasai* many-talented	229
		十八才 *jūhassai* 18 years old	12, 10

材	552	**ZAI, wood; material; talent**	
	75	材料 *zairyō* materials, ingredients	319
	2189	取材 *shuzai* collection of material, news gathering	65
		教材 *kyōzai* teaching materials	245
	材	題材 *daizai* subject matter, theme	354
		材木 *zaimoku* wood, lumber	22

財	553	**ZAI, [SAI], money, wealth, property**	
	154	財産 *zaisan* estate, assets, property	278
	4490	財政 *zaisei* finances, financial affairs	483
		財務 *zaimu* financial affairs	235
	財	財界 *zaikai* financial world, business circles	454
		文化財 *bunkazai* cultural asset	111, 254

	554	IN, cause; yo(ru), depend (on); be limited (to)	
因	31 1026	原 因　gen'in　cause	136
		主 因　shuin　primary/main cause	155
		死 因　shiin　cause of death	85
		要 因　yōin　important factor, chief cause	419
因		因 果　inga　cause and effect	487

	555	ON, kindness, goodness; favor; gratitude	
恩	61 1684	恩 給　onkyū　pension	346
		恩 賞　onshō　a reward	500
		恩 人　onjin　benefactor; patron	1
		恩 返し　ongaeshi　repayment of a favor	442
恩		恩 知らズ　onshirazu　ingratitude; ingrate	214

	556	KAN, Han (Chinese dynasty), China; man, fellow	
漢	85 2662	漢 字　kanji　Chinese character	110
		漢 文　kanbun　Chinese writing; Chinese classics	111
		漢 時代　Kan jidai　Han dynasty/period	42, 256
		好/悪 漢　kō/ak-kan　nice fellow/scoundrel, villain	104, 304
漢		門 外 漢　mongaikan　outsider, layman	161, 83

	557	NAN, muzuka(shii), kata(i), difficult	
難	172 5038	難 題　nandai　difficult problem/question	354
		難 病　nanbyō　incurable disease	380
		難 民　nanmin　refugees	177
		海 難　kainan　disaster at sea, shipwreck	117
難		非 難　hinan　adverse criticism	498

	558	KON, koma(ru), be distressed	
困	31 1033	困 難　konnan　difficulty, trouble	557
		困 苦　konku　hardships, adversity	545
		困り 果てる　komarihateru　be greatly troubled, non-plussed	487
困		困り 切る　komarikiru　be in a bad fix, at a loss	39

	559	KIN, [GON], tsuto(meru), be employed; tsuto(maru), be fit for	
勤	19 732	勤 労　kinrō　work, labor	233
		勤 務　kinmu　service, being on duty/at work	235
		通 勤　tsūkin　going to work, commuting	150
勤		転 勤　tenkin　be transferred (to another job)	433

	560	TEI, resist	
抵	64 1878	抵 当　teitō　mortgage, hypothec	77
		大 抵　taitei　generally, for the most part, usually	26
抵			

561	**TEI**, *hiku(i)*, low; *hiku(meru/maru)*, make/become lower			
9	最低	*saitei*	lowest, minimum	263
406	低地	*teichi*	low ground, lowlands	118
	低所得	*teishotoku*	low income	153, 374
低	低成長	*teiseichō*	low growth	261, 95
	低能	*teinō*	weak intellect, mental deficiency	386

562	**TEI**, *soko*, bottom			
53	根底	*kontei*	base, foundation	314
1508	海底	*kaitei*	bottom of the sea, ocean floor	117
	河底	*katei*	bottom of a river, riverbed	389
底	底力	*sokojikara*	latent energy/power	100
	底値	*sokone*	rock-bottom price	425

563	**TEI**, mansion, residence			
163	公邸	*kōtei*	official residence	126
4759	官邸	*kantei*	official residence	326
	私邸	*shitei*	one's private residence	125
邸	邸宅	*teitaku*	residence, mansion	178
	邸内	*teinai*	the grounds, the premises	84

564	**JŌ**, article, clause; line, stripe			
34	条約	*jōyaku*	treaty	211
1164	条文	*jōbun*	the text, provisions	111
	第一条	*daiichijō*	Article 1 (in a law/contract/treaty)	404, 2
条	条理	*jōri*	logic, reason	143
	信条	*shinjō*	a belief, article of faith	157

565	**KEI**, *chigi(ru)*, pledge, vow, promise			
37	契約	*keiyaku*	contract	211
1177	契機	*keiki*	opportunity, chance	528
契				

566	**SHI**, family, surname; Mr.; *uji*, family, lineage			
83	氏名	*shimei*	(full) name	82
2478	坂本氏	*Sakamoto-shi*	Mr. Sakamoto	443, 25
	同氏	*dōshi*	the said person, he	198
氏	両氏	*ryōshi*	both (gentlemen)	200
	氏神	*ujigami*	tutelary deity, genius loci	310

567	**KON**, marriage			
38	結婚	*kekkon*	marriage	485
1236	結婚式	*kekkonshiki*	marriage ceremony, wedding	485, 525
	婚約	*kon'yaku*	engagement	211
婚	未婚	*mikon*	unmarried	306
	新婚旅行	*shinkon ryokō*	honeymoon	174, 222, 68

	568	**KYŪ**, rank, class	
級	120	進級 *shinkyū* (school/military) promotion	437
	3496	高級 *kōkyū* high rank; high class, de luxe	190
		上級 *jōkyū* upper grade, senior	32
		学級 *gakkyū* class in school	109
級		同級生 *dōkyūsei* classmate	198, 44

	569	**TŌ**, class, grade; equality; etc.; *hito(shii)*, equal	
等	118	等級 *tōkyū* class, grade, rank	568
	3396	一等 *ittō* first class	2
		平等 *byōdō* equality	202
		同等 *dōtō* equality, same rank	198
等		高等学校 *kōtō gakkō* senior high school	190, 109, 115

	570	**SHI**, poetry, poem	
詩	149	詩人 *shijin* poet	1
	4360	詩歌 *shiika, shika* poetry	392
		詩情 *shijō* poetic sentiment	209
		詩集 *shishū* collection of poems	436
詩		漢詩 *kanshi* Chinese poem/poetry	556

	571	**JI**, *samurai*, samurai	
侍	9	侍者 *jisha* attendant, valet, page	164
	427	侍女 *jijo* lady-in-waiting, lady's attendant	102
		侍医 *jii* court physician	220
		侍気質 *samurai katagi* the samurai spirit	134, 176
侍		七人の侍 *Shichinin no Samurai* (The Seven Samurai)	9, 1

	572	**SHI**, samurai, man, scholar	
士	33	人間同士 *ningen dōshi* fellow human being	1, 43, 198
	1160	力士 *rikishi* sumo wrestler	100
		代議士 *daigishi* dietman, congressman, M.P.	256, 292
		学士 *gakushi* university graduate	109
士		税理士 *zeirishi* (licensed) tax accountant	399, 143

	573	**SHI**, *kokorozashi*, will, intention, aim; *kokoroza(su)*, intend, aim at, have in view	
志	32		
	1064	意志 *ishi* will	132
		志向 *shikō* intention, inclination	199
		同志 *dōshi* like-minded (person)	198
志		有志 *yūshi* voluntary; those interested	265

	574	**SHI**, write down, chronicle; magazine	
誌	149	誌上 *shijō* in a magazine	32
	4366	誌面 *shimen* page of a magazine	274
		日誌 *nisshi* diary	5
		地誌 *chishi* a topography, geographical description	118
誌		書誌学 *shoshigaku* bibliography	131, 109

		575	ZATSU, ZŌ, miscellany, a mix	
雑	172 5032 雑		雑誌　　　*zasshi*　magazine 雑音　　　*zatsuon*　noise, static 雑感　　　*zakkan*　miscellaneous thoughts/impressions 雑草　　　*zassō*　weeds 雑木林　　*zōkibayashi*　thicket of assorted trees	574 347 262 249 22, 127
殺	79 2454 殺	576	SATSU, [SAI], [SETSU], *koro(su)*, kill 自殺　　　*jisatsu*　suicide 暗殺　　　*ansatsu*　assassination 毒殺　　　*dokusatsu*　killing by poison 殺人　　　*satsujin*　a murder 人殺し　　*hitogoroshi*　murder, murderer	62 348 522 1 1
設	149 4325 設	577	SETSU, *mō(keru)*, establish, set up, prepare 設立　　　*setsuritsu*　establishment, founding 設置　　　*setchi*　establishment, founding, institution 設定　　　*settei*　establishment, creation 新設　　　*shinsetsu*　newly established/organized 私設　　　*shisetsu*　private	121 426 355 174 125
命	9 430 命	578	MEI, command; fate; life; MYŌ, *inochi*, life 生命 (保険)　*seimei (hoken)*　life (insurance) 運命　　　*unmei*　fate 使命　　　*shimei*　mission, errand 短命　　　*tanmei*　a short life 任命　　　*ninmei*　appointment, nomination	44, 489, 533 439 331 215 334
念	9 424 念	579	NEN, thought, idea; desire; concern, attention 記念日　　*kinenbi*　memorial day, anniversary 記念切手　*kinen kitte*　commemorative stamp 理念　　　*rinen*　idea, doctrine, ideology 信念　　　*shinnen*　belief, faith, conviction 念入り　　*nen'iri*　careful, scrupulous, thorough	371, 5 371, 39, 57 143 157 52
源	85 2656 源	580	GEN, *minamoto*, source, origin 起源　　　*kigen*　origin 根源　　　*kongen*　origin 財源　　　*zaigen*　source of revenue 源平　　　*Gen-Pei*　Genji and Heike clans　「Genji) 源氏物語　*Genji Monogatari*　(The Tale of	373 314 553 202 566, 79, 67
願	4 255 願	581	GAN, *nega(u)*, petition, request, desire 大願　　　*taigan*　great ambition, earnest wish 念願　　　*nengan*　one's heart's desire 出願　　　*shutsugan*　application 願書　　　*gansho*　written request, application 志願　　　*shigan*　application, volunteering, desire	26 579 53 131 573

	582	FUTSU, hara(u), pay; sweep away	
払	64 1828	払底 *futtei* shortage, scarcity	562
		支払い *shiharai* payment	318
		前払い *maebarai* payment in advance	47
		現金払い *genkinbarai* cash payment	298, 23
払		分割払い *bunkatsubarai* payment in installments	38, 519

	583	BUTSU, hotoke, Buddha	
仏	9 351	仏教 *bukkyō* Buddhism	245
		大仏 *daibutsu* great statue of Buddha	26
		石仏 *sekibutsu* stone image of Buddha	78
		念仏 *nenbutsu* Buddhist prayer	579
仏		日仏 *Nichi-Futsu* Japanese-French	5

	584	KAN, hi(ru), get dry; ho(su), dry; drink up	
干	51 1492	(潮の)干満 (*shio no*) *kanman* tide, ebb and flow	467, 201
		干潮 *kanchō* ebb/low tide	467
		干渉 *kanshō* interfere, meddle	432
		若干 *jakkan* some, a number of	544
干		物干し *monohoshi* frame for drying clothes	79

	585	KAN, publish	
刊	51 1493	週刊(誌) *shūkan(shi)* weekly magazine	92, 574
		日刊紙 *nikkanshi* daily newspaper	5, 180
		夕刊 *yūkan* evening newspaper/edition	81
		新刊 *shinkan* new publication	174
刊		未刊行 *mikankō* unpublished	306, 68

	586	GAN, kishi, bank, shore, coast	
岸	46 1413	西岸 *seigan* west bank/coast	72
		対岸 *taigan* opposite shore	365
		海岸 *kaigan* seashore, coast	117
		河岸 *kawagishi, kagan* riverbank	389
岸		川岸 *kawagishi* riverbank	33

	587	KAI, mina, all	
皆	81 2471	皆済 *kaisai* payment in full	549
		皆勤 *kaikin* perfect attendance (at work/school)	559
		皆さん *minasan* everybody; Ladies and Gentlemen!	
		皆目 *kaimoku* utterly; (not) at all	55
皆		皆無 *kaimu* nothing/none at all	93

	588	KAI, stair, story, level	
階	170 5011	三階 *sangai, sankai* third floor	4
		階段 *kaidan* stairs, stairway	362
		段階 *dankai* stage, phase	362
		階級 *kaikyū* social class	568
階		音階 *onkai* musical scale	347

	589	**HEI**, steps (of the throne)
陛	170 4988	天皇陛下 *tennō-heika* H.M. the Emperor 141, 297, 31
		国王陛下 *kokuō-heika* H.M. the King 40, 294, 31
		女王陛下 *joō-heika* H.M. the Queen 102, 294, 31
陛		両陛下 *ryōheika* Their Majesties the Emperor and Empress 200, 31

	590	**U**, *ha, hane*, feather, wing
羽	124 3673	羽毛 *umō* feather, plumage 287
		白羽 *shiraha* white feather 205
		羽音 *haoto* flapping of wings 347
		一羽 *ichiwa* 1 bird 2
羽		羽田 *Haneda* (airport in Tokyo) 35

	591	**SHŪ**, *nara(u)*, learn
習	124 3675	学習 *gakushū* learning, study 109
		独習 *dokushū* self-study 219
		予習 *yoshū* preparation of lessons 393
		常習 *jōshū* custom; habit 497
習		習字 *shūji* penmanship, calligraphy 110

	592	**YOKU**, the next, following
翌	124 3674	翌朝 *yokuasa, yokuchō* the next morning 469
		翌日 *yokujitsu* the next/following day 5
		翌週 *yokushū* the following week, the week after that 92
		翌年 *yokunen* the following year 45
翌		翌々日 *yokuyokujitsu* 2 days later/thereafter 5

	593	**DAN**, conversation
談	149 4388	会談 *kaidan* a conversation, conference 158
		対談 *taidan* face-to-face talk, conversation 365
		談話 *danwa* conversation 238
		相談 *sōdan* consultation 146
談		下相談 *shitasōdan* preliminary negotiations 31, 146

	594	**YAKU**, translation; *wake*, reason; meaning; circumstances
訳	149 4327	通訳 *tsūyaku* interpreting, interpreter 150
		英訳 *eiyaku* a translation into English 353
		全訳 *zen'yaku* a complete translation 89
		訳者 *yakusha* translator 164
訳		言い訳 *iiwake* apology; excuse 66

	595	**SHAKU**, explanation
釈	165 4809	解釈 *kaishaku* interpretation, construal 474
		釈明 *shakumei* explanation, vindication 18
		釈放 *shakuhō* release, discharge 512
		保釈 *hoshaku* (prison) bail 489
釈		注釈 *chūshaku* comments, annotation 357

翻 124 3681 翻	**596**	**HON,** *hirugae(su)*, (tr.) turn over; change (one's opinion); wave (a flag); *hirugae(ru)*, (intr.) turn over; wave
	翻 訳	*hon'yaku* translation, translate 594
	翻 案	*hon'an* an adaptation 106
	翻 意	*hon'i* change one's mind 132
	翻 ろ う	*honrō* trifle with, make sport of

橋 75 2378 橋	**597**	**KYŌ,** *hashi*, bridge
	歩 道 橋	*hodōkyō* pedestrian bridge 431, 149
	鉄 橋	*tekkyō* iron bridge; railway bridge 312
	石 橋	*ishibashi* stone bridge 78
	つ り 橋	*tsuribashi* suspension bridge
	日 本 橋	*Nihonbashi* (area of Tokyo) 5, 25

柱 75 2236 柱	**598**	**CHŪ,** *hashira*, pillar, column, pole
	支 柱	*shichū* prop, support, strut 318
	電 柱	*denchū* utility/electric pole 108
	水 銀 柱	*suiginchū* column of mercury 21, 313
	円 柱	*enchū* column, cylinder 13
	大 黒 柱	*daikokubashira* central pillar, mainstay 26, 206

駐 187 5209 駐	**599**	**CHŪ,** stop; reside
	駐 車 場	*chūshajō* parking lot 133, 154
	駐 在	*chūzai* stay, residence 268
	駐 日	*chūnichi* resident/stationed in Japan 5
	進 駐	*shinchū* stationing, occupation 437
	駐 と ん 地	*chūtonchi* (army) post 118

専 41 1350 専	**600**	**SEN,** *moppa(ra)*, entirely, exclusively
	専 門 家	*senmonka* specialist, expert 161, 165
	専 任	*sennin* exclusive duty, full-time 334
	専 制	*sensei* absolutism, despotism 427
	専 売	*senbai* monopoly ⌈vate (parking lot) 239
	専 用 (駐 車 場)	*sen'yō (chūshajō)* pri- 107, 599, 133, 154

博 24 787 博	**601**	**HAKU, [BAKU],** extensive, broad, many
	博 物 館	*hakubutsukan* museum 79, 327
	博 学	*hakugaku* broad knowledge, erudition 109
	博 士	*hakase, hakushi* doctor 572
	博 愛	*hakuai* philanthropy 259
	万 博	*banpaku* international exhibition 16

授 64 1946 授	**602**	**JU,** *sazu(keru)*, grant, teach; *sazu(karu)*, be granted, taught
	授 業	*jugyō* teaching, instruction 279
	教 授	*kyōju* instruction; professor 245
	授 受	*juju* giving and receiving, transfer 260
	授 与	*juyo* conferment, presentation 539
	授 賞	*jushō* receiving a prize 500

確	603 112 3217 確	KAKU, *tashi(ka)*, certain; *tashi(kameru)*, make sure of, verify		
		確立	*kakuritsu* establishment, settlement	121
		確定	*kakutei* decision, settlement	355
		確実	*kakujitsu* certain, reliable	203
		確信	*kakushin* firm belief, conviction	157
		正確	*seikaku* accurate, precise, correct	275
観	604 147 4296 観	KAN, appearance, view		
		観光	*kankō* sight-seeing, tourism	138
		外観	*gaikan* (external) appearance	83
		主観的	*shukanteki* subjective	155, 210
		楽観的	*rakkanteki* optimistic	358, 210
		観念	*kannen* idea; sense (of duty/justice)	579
覚	605 147 4288 覚	KAKU, *obo(eru)*, remember, bear in mind, learn; feel; *sa-(meru/masu)*, (intr./tr.) awake, wake up		
		感覚	*kankaku* sense, sensation, feeling	262
		直覚	*chokkaku* intuition, insight	423
		見覚え	*mioboe* recognition, knowing by sight ⌈clock 63	
		目覚まし (時計)	*mezamashi(-dokei)* alarm	55, 42, 340
視	606 113 3248 視	SHI, seeing, regarding as		
		視力	*shiryoku* visual acuity, eyesight	100
		近視	*kinshi* nearsightedness, shortsightedness	445
		重視	*jūshi* attach importance to, stress	227
		無視	*mushi* ignore, disregard	93
		視界	*shikai* field of vision	454
規	607 147 4285 規	KI, standard, measure		
		規定	*kitei* stipulations, provisions, regulations	355
		定規	*jōgi* ruler, square; standard, norm	355
		正規	*seiki* regular, formal, regulation	275
		新規	*shinki* new	174
		法規	*hōki* laws and regulations, legislation	123
則	608 154 4487 則	SOKU, rule, law		
		規則	*kisoku* rule, regulation	607
		原則	*gensoku* general rule, principle	136
		法則	*hōsoku* a law	123
		変則	*hensoku* irregularity, anomaly	257
		会則	*kaisoku* rules of an association	158
側	609 9 509 側	SOKU, *kawa*, side		
		側面	*sokumen* side, flank	274
		側近者	*sokkinsha* one's close associates	445, 164
		左側	*hidarigawa* left side	75
		反対側	*hantaigawa* opposite side	324, 365
		日本側	*Nippongawa, Nihongawa* the Japanese side	5, 25

	610	SOKU, *haka(ru)*, measure	
測	85 2632	測 量 *sokuryō* measurement, surveying	411
		測 定 *sokutei* measuring	355
		観 測 *kansoku* observation	604
		目 測 *mokusoku* measurement by eye, estimation	55
測		予 測 *yosoku* estimate, forecast	393

	611	RETSU, row	
列	78 2438	列 車 *ressha* train	133
		列 島 *rettō* chain of islands, archipelago	286
		列 国 *rekkoku* world powers, nations	40
		行 列 *gyōretsu* queue; procession; matrix	68
列		後 列 *kōretsu* back row	48

	612	REI, example; custom, precedent; *tato(eru)*, compare	
例	9 428	例 外 *reigai* exception	83
		特 例 *tokurei* special case, exception	282
		先 例 *senrei* previous example, precedent	50
		例 年 *reinen* normal year; every year	45
例		条 例 *jōrei* regulations, ordinance	564

	613	KAN, completion	
完	40 1288	完 結 *kanketsu* completion	485
		完 全 *kanzen* complete, perfect	89
		完 成 *kansei* completion, accomplishment	261
		未 完 成 *mikansei* incomplete, unfinished	306, 261
完		完 敗 *kanpai* complete defeat	511

	614	IN, institution	
院	170 4991	病 院 *byōin* hospital	380
		入 院 *nyūin* admission to a hospital	52
		大 学 院 *daigakuin* graduate school	26, 109
		養 老 院 *yōrōin* old folks' home 「Parliament)	402, 543
院		両 院 *ryōin* both houses (of the Diet/Congress/	200

	615	JI, SHI, *shime(su)*, show	
示	113 3228	公 示 *kōji* public announcement	126
		明 示 *meiji* clear statement	18
		教 示 *kyōji* instruction, teaching	245
		暗 示 *anji* hint, suggestion	348
示		示 談 *jidan* out-of-court settlement	593

	616	SHŪ, SŌ, religion, sect	
宗	40 1294	宗 教 *shūkyō* religion	245
		宗 門 *shūmon* sect	161
		宗 徒 *shūto* adherent, believer	430
		改 宗 *kaishū* conversion, become a convert	514
宗		宗 家 *sōke* the head family	165

祭 祭	617 113 3247	SAI, *matsu(ru)*, deify, worship; *matsu(ri)*, festival	
		祭 日 *saijitsu* holiday; festival day	5
		百 年 祭 *hyakunensai* centennial	14, 45
		文 化 祭 *bunkasai* cultural festival	111, 254
		秋 祭 り *akimatsuri* autumn festival	462
		後 の 祭 り *ato no matsuri* Too late!	48

際 際	618 170 5018	SAI, time, occasion; *kiwa*, side, brink, edge	
		国 際 *kokusai* international	40
		交 際 *kōsai* association, company, acquaintance	114
		実 際 *jissai* truth, reality, actual practice	203
		水 際 *mizugiwa* water's edge, shore	21
		際 立 つ *kiwadatsu* be conspicuous, stand out	121

察 察	619 40 1334	SATSU, surmise, judge, understand, sympathize	
		観 察 *kansatsu* observation	604
		検 察 *kensatsu* criminal investigation, prosecution	531
		視 察 *shisatsu* inspection, observation	606
		考 察 *kōsatsu* consideration, examination	541
		明 察 *meisatsu* discernment, keen insight	18

礼 礼	620 113 3229	REI, RAI, courtesy; salutation; gratitude, remuneration	
		祭 礼 *sairei* religious festival	617
		礼 式 *reishiki* etiquette	525
		失 礼 *shitsurei* rudeness	311
		非 礼 *hirei* impoliteness	498
		無 礼 *burei* rudeness, impertinence, affront	93

祈 祈	621 113 3234	KI, *ino(ru)*, pray	
		祈 念 *kinen* a prayer	579
		祈 願 *kigan* a prayer	581
		祈 とう(書) *kitō(sho)* prayer (book)	131
		祈 り *inori* a prayer	
		主 の 祈 り *shu no inori* the Lord's Prayer	155

祖 祖	622 113 3243	SO, ancestor	
		祖 先 *sosen* ancestor, forefather	50
		祖 母/父 *sobo/fu* grandmother/father	112, 113
		祖 国 *sokoku* one's homeland/fatherland	40
		元 祖 *ganso* originator, founder, inventor	137
		宗 祖 *shūso* founder of a sect	616

助 助	623 19 719	JO, *tasu(keru)*, help, rescue; *tasu(karu)* be helped, rescued; *suke*, assistance	
		助 力 *joryoku* help, assistance	100
		助 言 *jogen* advice	66
		助 手 *joshu* helper, assistant	57
		助 け 合 う *tasukeau* help each other	159

	624	**SA,** investigate	
査	75 2235 查	調査 *chōsa* investigation, inquiry, observation 検査 *kensa* inspection, examination 査問 *samon* inquiry, hearing 査察 *sasatsu* inspection, observation 査定 *satei* assessment	342 531 162 619 355
宣	625 40 1301 宣	**SEN,** announce 宣言 *sengen* declaration, manifesto ⌈dependence 独立宣言 *dokuritsu sengen* declaration of in- 219, 121, 66 宣伝 *senden* propaganda; advertising, publicity 宣戦 *sensen* declaration of war 宣教師 *senkyōshi* a missionary	66 434 301 245, 409
状	626 90 2839 状	**JŌ,** condition, circumstances; form: letter 状態 *jōtai* circumstances, situation 現状 *genjō* present situation 白状 *hakujō* confession 礼状 *reijō* letter of thanks 招待状 *shōtaijō* written invitation	387 298 205 620 455, 452
将	627 90 2840 将	**SHŌ,** commander, general; soon 将来 *shōrai* future 将軍 *shōgun* shogun, general 大将 *taishō* general, leader 主将 *shushō* (team) captain 将校 *shōkō* officer	69 438 26 155 115
提	628 64 1967 提	**TEI,** present, submit; *sa(geru)*, carry (in the hand) 提案 *teian* proposition, proposal 提供 *teikyō* offer 提議 *teigi* proposal, suggestion 提出 *teishutsu* presentation, filing 前提 *zentei* premise	106 197 292 53 47
太	629 37 1172 太	**TAI, TA,** *futo(i),* fat, thick; *futo(ru),* get fat/thick 太平洋 *Taiheiyō* Pacific Ocean 皇太子 *kōtaishi* crown prince 太古 *taiko* ancient times, antiquity 太字 *futoji* thick character, boldface 太刀 *tachi* (long) sword	202, 289 297, 103 172 110 37
陽	630 170 5012 陽	**YŌ,** positive, male; sun 太陽 *taiyō* sun 陽光 *yōkō* sunshine, sunlight 陽気 *yōki* season, weather; cheerfulness, gaiety 陽性 *yōsei* positive 陽子 *yōshi* proton	629 138 134 98 103

	631	YŌ, a(geru), raise; fry; a(garu), rise	
揚	64 1966	高揚 *kōyō* uplift, surge	190
		揚水車 *yōsuisha* scoop wheel	21, 133
		意気揚々 *ikiyōyō* triumphantly, exultantly	132, 134
		荷揚げ *niage* unloading, discharge, landing	391
揚		引き揚げ *hikiage* withdrawal, evacuation	216

	632	TŌ, yu, hot water	
湯	85 2633	湯治 *tōji* hot-spring cure	493
		湯元 *yumoto* source of a hot spring	137
		湯ぶね *yubune* bathtub	
		茶の湯 *cha no yu* tea ceremony	251
湯		湯上がり *yuagari* just after a bath	32

	633	SHŌ, kizu, wound, injury; ita(mu), hurt; ita(meru), injure	
傷	9 535	負傷 *fushō* wound, injury	510
		傷害 *shōgai* injury, damage	518
		重/軽傷 *jū/keishō* severe/minor injuries	227, 547
		死傷者 *shishōsha* the killed and injured, casualties 85, 164	
傷		中傷 *chūshō* slander	28

	634	ON, atata(kai/ka), warm; atata(maru/meru), (intr./tr) warm up	
温	85 2634	温度 *ondo* temperature ⌈perature	377
		気/水/体温 *ki/sui/tai-on* air/water/body tem-	134, 21, 61
		温室 *onshitsu* hothouse, greenhouse	166
温		温和 *onwa* mild, gentle	124

	635	DAN, atata(kai/ka), warm; atata(maru/meru), (intr./tr.) warm up	
暖	72 2153	寒暖計 *kandankei* thermometer	457, 340
		温暖 *ondan* warm	634
		暖流 *danryū* warm ocean current	247
暖		暖冬 *dantō* warm/mild winter	459

	636	UN, kumo, cloud	
雲	173 5046	風雲 *fūun* wind and clouds; situation	29
		暗雲 *an'un* dark clouds	348
		雨雲 *amagumo* rain cloud	30
		入道雲 *nyūdōgumo* cumulonimbus, thunderhead 52, 149	
雲		出雲大社 *Izumo Taisha* Izumo Shrine	53, 26, 308

	637	DON, kumo(ru), cloud up, get cloudy	
曇	72 2160	曇天 *donten* cloudy/overcast sky	141
		花曇り *hanagumori* cloudy weather in cherry- blossom season	255
		曇りがち *kumorigachi* broken clouds, mostly cloudy	
曇		曇りガラス *kumorigarasu* ground/frosted/mat glass	

	638	SHO, *atsu(i)*, hot (weather)	
暑	72 2138 暑	寒暑 *kansho* cold and heat 暑気 *shoki* the heat 暑中 *shochū* middle of summer　「July 24) 大暑 *taisho* Japanese Midsummer Day (about 暑苦しい *atsukurushii* oppressively hot, sultry	457 134 28 26 545
	639	KŌ, *atsu(i)*, thick; kind, cordial	
厚	27 824 厚	厚意 *kōi* kind intentions, kindness 厚顔 *kōgan* impudence, effrontery　「fare 厚生省 *Kōseishō* Ministry of Health and Wel-　44, 145 厚相 *kōshō* minister of health and welfare 厚紙 *atsugami* thick paper, cardboard	132 277 146 180
	640	EN, feast, banquet	
宴	40 1304 宴	宴会 *enkai* dinner party, banquet 宴席 *enseki* (one's seat in) a banquet hall 酒宴 *shuen* feast, drinking bout きょう宴 *kyōen* banquet, feast, dinner	158 379 517
	641	KYAKU, KAKU, guest, customer	
客	40 1302 客	客間/室 *kyaku-ma/shitsu* guest room 客船 *kyakusen* passenger ship 乗客 *jōkyaku* passenger 旅客 *ryokaku* passenger, traveler 客観的 *kyakkanteki* objective	43, 166 376 523 222 604, 210
	642	KAKU, *onoono*, each, every; various	
各	34 1163 各	各地 *kakuchi* every area; various places 各国 *kakkoku* all/various countries 各種 *kakushu* every kind, various types 各人 *kakujin* each person, everyone 各自 *kakuji* each person, everyone	118 40 228 1 62
	643	KAKU, [KŌ], status, rank; standard, rule; case	
格	75 2259 格	人格 *jinkaku* personality, character 性格 *seikaku* character, personality 価格 *kakaku* price; value 合格 *gōkaku* pass (an exam) 格子 *kōshi* lattice, bars, grating, grille	1 98 421 159 103
	644	GAN, *maru(i)*, round; *maru(meru)*, make round, form into a ball; -*maru*, (suffix for names of ships)	
丸	4 155 丸	丸薬 *gan'yaku* pill 丸太小屋 *marutagoya* log cabin　629, 27, 167 日本丸 *Nihonmaru* the ship *Nihon* 日の丸 *Hi no Maru* (Japanese) Rising-Sun Flag	359 5, 25 5

	645	NETSU, heat, fever; *atsu(i)*, hot (food)	
熱	86 2797 熱	熱病 *netsubyō* fever 高熱 *kōnetsu* high fever 熱湯 *nettō* boiling water 情熱 *jōnetsu* passion 熱心 *nesshin* enthusiasm, zeal	380 190 632 209 97

	646	SEI, *ikio(i)*, force, energy, vigor; trend	
勢	19 735 勢	勢力 *seiryoku* influence, force 国勢 *kokusei* state/condition of a country 情勢 *jōsei* the situation 大勢 *taisei* general situation/trend *ōzei* many people, large crowd	100 40 209 26

	647	RIKU, land	
陸	170 5005 陸	大陸 *tairiku* continent, mainland 陸上 *rikujō* land, ground 上陸 *jōriku* landing, going ashore 陸路 *rikuro* land route 陸軍 *rikugun* army	26 32 32 151 438

	648	SEN, money; 1/100 yen; *zeni*, money	
銭	167 4851 銭	金銭 *kinsen* money 口銭 *kōsen* commission, percentage 悪銭 *akusen* ill-gotten money 銭湯 *sentō* public bath 小銭 *kozeni* small change	23 54 304 632 27

	649	SEN, *asa(i)*, shallow	
浅	85 2549 浅	浅海 *senkai* shallow sea 浅見 *senken* superficial view 浅学 *sengaku* superficial knowledge 浅黒い *asaguroi* dark-colored, swarthy 遠浅 *tōasa* shoaling beach	117 63 109 206 446

	650	ZAN, *noko(su/ru)*, leave/remain behind	
残	78 2445 残	残念 *zannen* regret, disappointment, too bad 残業 *zangyō* overtime 残高 *zandaka* balance, remainder 残り物 *nokorimono* leftovers 生き残る *ikinokoru* survive	579 279 190 79 44

	651	ZEN, NEN, as, like	
然	86 2770 然	全然 *zenzen* (not) at all; completely 当然 *tōzen* naturally, (as a matter) of course 必然 *hitsuzen* inevitability, necessity 自然 *shizen* nature 天然 *tennen* natural	89 77 520 62 141

	652	NEN, mo(eru), (intr.) burn; mo(yasu/su), (tr.) burn
燃	86 2808 燃	燃料　　nenryō　fuel　　　319 不燃性　funensei　nonflammable, fireproof　　94, 98 可燃性　kanensei　flammable, combustible ⌈engine 388, 98 内燃機関　nainen kikan　internal-combustion 84, 528, 398 燃え上がる　moeagaru　blaze up, burst into flames　32

	653	KOKU, tani, valley
谷	150 4458 谷	谷間　　tanima　valley　　43 谷底　　tanisoko　bottom of a ravine/gorge　562 谷川　　tanigawa　mountain stream　33 長谷川　Hasegawa　(surname)　95, 33 四ツ谷　Yotsuya　(area of Tokyo)　6

	654	YŌ, form, appearance; content
容	40 1309 容	美容院　biyōin　beauty parlor, hairdresser's　401, 614 形容　　keiyō　form; metaphor　395 内容　　naiyō　content　84 容器　　yōki　container　527 容量　　yōryō　capacity, volume　411

	655	SEKI, se(meru), condemn, censure; torture
責	154 4492 責	責任　　sekinin　responsibility　334 重責　　jūseki　heavy responsibility　227 責務　　sekimu　duty, obligation　235 自責　　jiseki　self-reproach, pangs of conscience　62 引責　　inseki　assume responsibility　216

	656	SEKI, tsu(mu), heap up, load; tsu(moru), be piled up, accumulate; tsu(mori), intention; estimate
積	115 3306 積	面積　　menseki　(surface) area　274 積極的　sekkyokuteki　positive, active　336, 210 積み重ねる　tsumikasaneru　stack up one on another 227 見積(書)　mitsumori(sho)　(written) estimate　63, 131

	657	CHAKU, [JAKU], arrival; clothing; ki(ru), tsu(keru), put on, wear; ki(seru), dress (someone); tsu(ku), arrive
着	123 3665 着	着陸　　chakuriku　(airplane) landing　647 決着　　ketchaku　conclusion, settlement, decision　356 着物　　kimono　kimono; clothing　79 下着　　shitagi　underwear　31

	658	SA, difference; sa(su), hold (an umbrella); wear (a sword); offer (a cup of sakè); thrust
差	123 3662 差	時差　　jisa　time difference/lag　42 差別　　sabetsu　discrimination　267 交差点　kōsaten　intersection　114, 169 差し支え　sashitsukae　impediment; objection　318

精	659 119 3480 精	**SEI, [SHŌ], spirit; energy, vitality**	
		精力　　*seiryoku*　energy, vigor, vitality	100
		精神　　*seishin*　mind, spirit	310
		精液　　*seieki*　semen, sperm	472
		精進　　*shōjin*　diligence, devotion; purification	437
		不/無精　*bushō*　sloth, laziness, indolence	94, 93

清	660 85 2605 清	**SEI, [SHŌ], *kiyo(i)*, pure, clean, clear; *kiyo(meru)*, purify, cleanse; *kiyo(maru)*, be purified, cleansed**	
		清酒　　*seishu*　refined sakè	517
		清書　　*seisho*　fair/clean copy	131
		清水　　*seisui, shimizu*　pure/clear water	21
		Kiyomizu　(temple in Kyoto)	

請	661 149 4390 請	**SEI, SHIN, *ko(u)*, ask for; *u(keru)*, receive**	
		請願　　*seigan*　petition, application	581
		要請　　*yōsei*　demand, requirement, request	419
		申請　　*shinsei*　application, petition	309
		強請　　*kyōsei*　importunate demand; extortion	217
		下請け　*shitauke*　subcontract	31

晴	662 72 2143 晴	**SEI, *ha(reru/rasu)*, (intr./tr.) clear up**	
		晴天　　*seiten*　clear sky, fine weather	141
		晴曇　　*seidon*　changeable, fair to cloudy	637
		秋晴れ　*akibare*　clear autumn weather	462
		見晴らし　*miharashi*　view, vista	63
		気晴らし　*kibarashi*　pastime, diversion	134

静	663 174 5077 静	**SEI, [JŌ], *shizu, shizu(ka)*, quiet, peaceful, still; *shizu(meru/maru)*, make/become peaceful**	
		静物　　*seibutsu*　still life	79
		静止　　*seishi*　stillness, rest, stationary	477
		安静　　*ansei*　rest, quiet, repose	105
		平静　　*heisei*　calm, serenity	202

浄	664 85 2548 浄	**JŌ, pure**	
		清浄　　*seijō*　purity, cleanliness	660
		浄化　　*jōka*　purification	254
		不浄　　*fujō*　dirtiness, impurity	94
		浄土宗　*Jōdoshū*　the Jodo sect (of Buddhism)	24, 616

破	665 112 3186 破	**HA, *yabu(ru)*, tear, break; *yabu(reru)*, get torn/broken**	
		破産　　*hasan*　bankruptcy	278
		破局　　*hakyoku*　catastrophe, ruin	170
		破約　　*hayaku*　breach of contract/promise	211
		破れ目　*yabureme*　a tear, split	55
		見破る　*miyaburu*　see through	63

666	**HA**, *nami*, wave	
85 2529	波止場 *hatoba* wharf, pier	477, 154
	電波 *denpa* electric/radio wave	108
	短波 *tanpa* shortwave	215
波	波長 *hachō* wavelength	95
	波乗り *naminori* surfing	523

667	**RITSU**, [RICHI], law, regulation	
60 1608	法律 *hōritsu* law	123
	規律 *kiritsu* order, discipline, regulations	607
	不文律 *fubunritsu* unwritten law	94, 111
律	韻律 *inritsu* rhythm, meter	349
	自律神経 *jiritsu shinkei* autonomic nerve	62, 310, 548

668	**SHIN**, *tsu*, harbor, ferry	
85 2543	津波 *tsunami* tsunami, "tidal" wave	666
	興味津々 *kyōmi-shinshin* very interesting	368, 307
津	津軽半島 *Tsugaru Hantō* Tsugaru Peninsula	547, 88, 286

669	**KŌ**, *minato*, harbor, port	
85 2630	空港 *kūkō* airport	140
	商/軍港 *shō/gunkō* trading/naval port	412, 438
	内港 *naikō* inner harbor	84
港	港内 *kōnai* in the harbor	84
	港町 *minatomachi* port city	182

670	**WAN**, bay	
85 2627	東京湾 *Tōkyō-wan* Tokyo Bay	71, 189
	湾曲 *wankyoku* curvature, bend	366
	港湾 *kōwan* harbor ⌈borer, longshoreman	669
湾	港湾労働者 *kōwan rōdōsha* port la-	669, 233, 232, 164
	台湾 *Taiwan* Taiwan, Formosa	492

671	**SAI**, *tsuma*, wife	
38 1206	夫妻 *fusai* husband and wife, Mr. and Mrs.	315
	妻子 *saishi* wife and child/children, family	103
	後妻 *gosai* second wife	48
妻	良妻 *ryōsai* good wife	321
	老妻 *rōsai* one's aged wife	543

672	**BŌ** [MŌ], die; *na(i)*, dead, deceased	
8 281	死亡者 *shibōsha* the dead	85, 164
	亡父 *bōfu* one's late father	113
	亡夫 *bōfu* one's late husband	315
亡	未亡人 *mibōjin* widow	306, 1
	亡命 *bōmei* fleeing one's country, going into exile	578

望	673 96 2940 望	**BŌ, MŌ**, *nozo(mu)*, desire, wish, hope for	
		志望 *shibō* wish, aspiration	573
		宿望 *shukubō* long-cherished desire	179
		要望 *yōbō* demand, wish	419
		失望 *shitsubō* despair, disappointment	311
		大望 *taimō* great desire, ambition	26

聖	674 96 2960 聖	**SEI**, holy	
		聖人 *seijin* sage, holy man	1
		神聖 *shinsei* sacredness, sanctity	310
		聖書 *Seisho* the Bible	131
		聖堂 *seidō* Confucian temple; church	496
		聖母 *seibo* the Holy Mother, the Blessed Mary	112

布	675 50 1468 布	**FU**, spread; cloth; *nuno*, a cloth	
		財布 *saifu* purse, wallet	553
		毛布 *mōfu* a blanket	287
		分布 *bunpu* distribution, range	38
		配布 *haifu* distribution, distributing widely	515
		公布 *kōfu* official announcement, promulgation	126

希	676 50 1470 希	**KI**, hope, desire; rarity, scarcity	
		希望 *kibō* wish, hope	673
		メーカー希望価格 *mēkā kibō kakaku* manufac- turer's suggested price, list price	673, 421, 643
		希少 *kishō* scarce, rare	144
		希少価値 *kishō kachi* scarcity value	144, 421, 425

衣	677 145 4214 衣	**I**, *koromo*, garment, clothes	
		衣類 *irui* clothing	226
		黒衣 *kokui* black clothes	206
		法衣 *hōi* priestly robes, vestment	123
		衣食住 *ishokujū* food, clothing, and shelter	322, 156
		羽衣 *hagoromo* robe of feathers	590

依	678 9 426 依	**I**, [E], depend on, be due to; request	
		依存(度) *izon(do)* (extent of) dependence	269, 377
		依然として *izen toshite* as ever, as before	651
		帰依 *kie* faith, devotion; conversion	317

初	679 145 4215 初	**SHO**, *haji(me)*, beginning; *haji(mete)*, for the first time; *hatsu-,* *ui-*, first; *-so(meru)*, begin to	
		最初 *saisho* beginning, first	263
		初歩 *shoho* rudiments, ABCs	431
		初演 *shoen* first performance, premiere	344
		初恋 *hatsukoi* one's first love	258

	680	**SHOKU, SHIKI,** *o(ru),* weave	
	120	織機　　　*shokki*　loom	528
	3613	組織　　　*soshiki*　organization, structure; tissue	418
		織物　　　*orimono*　cloth, fabric, textiles	79
	織	毛織(物)　*keori(mono)*　woolen fabric	287, 79
		羽織　　　*haori*　haori, Japanese half-coat	590

	681	**SHIKI,** know, discriminate	
	149	意識　　　*ishiki*　consciousness	132
	4438	知識　　　*chishiki*　knowledge	214
		常識　　　*jōshiki*　common sense/knowledge	497
	識	学識　　　*gakushiki*　learning	109
		識別　　　*shikibetsu*　discrimination, recognition	267

	682	**HEN,** *a(mu),* knit, crochet; compile, edit	
	120	編集　　　*henshū*　editing	436
	3583	短編小説　*tanpen shōsetsu*　short novel, story	215, 27, 400
		編成　　　*hensei*　organizing, formation	261
	編	編み物　　*amimono*　knitting; knitted goods	79
		手編み　　*teami*　knitting by hand	57

	683	**FUKU,** clothes, dress; dose	
	130	衣服　　　*ifuku*　clothing	677
	3741	洋/和服　*yō/wa-fuku*　Western/Japanese clothing	289, 124
		心服　　　*shinpuku*　admiration and devotion	97
	服	着服　　　*chakufuku*　embezzlement, misappropriation	657
		服役　　　*fukueki*　penal servitude; military service	375

	684	**KŌ,** *saiwa(i), shiawa(se), sachi,* happiness, good fortune	
	32	幸運　　　*kōun*　good fortune, luck	439
	1073	不幸　　　*fukō*　unhappiness, misfortune	94
	幸		

	685	**HŌ,** news, report; remuneration; *muku(iru),* reward, requite	
	32	天気予報　*tenki yohō*　weather forecast	141, 134, 393
	1114	報道機関　*hōdō kikan*　news media, the press	149, 528, 398
		情報　　　*jōhō*　information	209
	報	報知　　　*hōchi*　information, news, intelligence	214
		電報　　　*denpō*　telegram	108

	686	**SHITSU, SHŪ,** *to(ru),* take, grasp; carry out, execute	
	32	執行　　　*shikkō*　execution, performance	68
	1097	執権　　　*shikken*　regent	335
		執心　　　*shūshin*　devotion, attachment, infatuation	97
	執	執着　　　*shūjaku, shūchaku*　attachment to; tenacity	657
		執念　　　*shūnen*　tenacity of purpose; vindictiveness	579

熟 86 2795 熟	687	**JUKU**, *u(reru)*, ripen, come to maturity
	円 熟	*enjuku* maturity, mellowness 13
	成 熟	*seijuku* ripeness, maturity 261
	未 熟	*mijuku* unripe, immature, green 306
	半 熟	*hanjuku* half-cooked, soft-boiled (egg) 88
	熟 語	*jukugo* compound word; phrase 67
辞 135 3860 辞	688	**JI**, word; resignation; *ya(meru)*, quit, resign
	辞 書/典	*jisho/ten* dictionary 131, 367
	(お)世 辞	*(o)seji* compliment, flattery 252
	式 辞	*shikiji* address, oration 525
	辞 職	*jishoku* resignation 385
	辞 表	*jihyō* (letter of) resignation 272
乱 135 3856 乱	689	**RAN**, riot, rebellion; disorder; *mida(su/reru)*, put/get in disorder, confusion
	反 乱	*hanran* rebellion, insurgency, insurrection 324
	内 乱	*nairan* internal strife, civil war 84
	乱 雑	*ranzatsu* disorder, confusion 575
	乱 筆	*ranpitsu* hasty writing, scrawl 130
告 30 900 告	690	**KOKU**, *tsu(geru)*, tell, announce, inform
	報 告	*hōkoku* report 685
	通 告	*tsūkoku* notice, notification 150
	申 告	*shinkoku* report, declaration, (tax) return 309
	告 発	*kokuhatsu* prosecution, indictment, accusation 96
	告 白	*kokuhaku* confession, avowal, profession 205
造 162 4701 造	691	**ZŌ**, *tsuku(ru)*, produce, build
	製 造	*seizō* manufacture, production 428
	造 船	*zōsen* shipbuilding 376
	木 造	*mokuzō* made of wood, wooden 22
	人 造	*jinzō* man-made, artificial 1
	手 造 り	*tezukuri* handmade 57
洗 85 2551 洗	692	**SEN**, *ara(u)*, wash
	洗 剤	*senzai* detergent 550
	洗 面 器	*senmenki* wash basin 274, 527
	洗 面 所	*senmenjo* washroom, lavatory 274, 153
	(お)手 洗 い	*(o)tearai* washroom, lavatory ⌈out 57
	洗 い 立 て る	*araitateru* inquire into, rake up, ferret 121
汚 85 2494 汚	693	**O**, *kitana(i)*, *kega(rawashii)*, dirty; *yogo(reru/su)*, *kega(reru/su)*, become/make dirty
	汚 職	*oshoku* corruption, bribery 385
	汚 物	*obutsu* dirt, filth; sewage 79
	汚 点	*oten* blot, blotch, blemish, tarnish 169
	汚 名	*omei* stigma, stain on one's name, dishonor 82

広 広	694 53 1499	KŌ, *hiro(i)*, broad, wide; *hiro(geru)*, extend, enlarge; *hiro-* *(garu)*, spread, expand; *hiro(meru)*, broaden, propagate; *hiro-* *(maru)*, spread, be propagated	
		広告 *kōkoku* advertisement	690
		広大 *kōdai* vast, extensive, huge	26
		広場 *hiroba* plaza, public square	154
細 細	695 120 3522	SAI, narrow, small, fine; *hoso(i)*, thin, narrow, slender; *hoso-* *(ru)*, get thinner; *koma(kai/ka)*, small, detailed	
		委細 *isai* details, particulars	466
		細工 *saiku* work, workmanship; artifice, trick	139
		細説 *saisetsu* detailed explanation	400
		細長い *hosonagai* long and thin, lean and lanky	95
松 松	696 75 2212	SHŌ, *matsu*, pine	
		松原 *matsubara* pine grove	136
		松林 *matsubayashi* pine woods	127
		松葉 *matsuba* pine needle	253
		門松 *kadomatsu* pine decoration for New Year's	161
		松島 *Matsushima* (scenic coastal area near Sendai)	286
総 総	697 120 3567	SŌ, general, overall	
		総会 *sōkai* general meeting, plenary session	158
		総合 *sōgō* synthesis, comprehensive	159
		総計 *sōkei* (sum) total	340
		総理 *sōri* prime minister (cf. No. 835) 「product	143
		国民総生産 *kokumin sōseisan* gross nat'l 40, 177, 44, 278	
窓 窓	698 116 3326	SŌ, *mado*, window	
		同窓生 *dōsōsei* schoolmate, alumnus	198, 44
		車窓 *shasō* car window	133
		窓口 *madoguchi* (ticket) window	54
		二重窓 *nijūmado* double window 「window 3, 227	
		窓際の席 *madogiwa no seki* seat next to the 618, 379	
漁 漁	699 85 2684	GYO, RYŌ, fishing	
		漁業 *gyogyō* fishery, fishing industry	279
		漁船 *gyosen* fishing boat/vessel	376
		漁場 *gyojō* fishing ground/banks	154
		漁村 *gyoson* fishing village	191
		漁師 *ryōshi* fisherman	409
鯨 鯨	700 195 5307	GEI, *kujira*, whale	
		白鯨 *Hakugei* (Moby Dick, or The White Whale —Melville)	205
		鯨肉 *geiniku* whale meat	223
		鯨油 *geiyu* whale oil	364
		鯨飲 *geiin* drink like a fish, guzzle	323

	701	SEN, *aza(yaka)*, fresh, vivid, clear, brilliant	
鮮	195	新 鮮 *shinsen* fresh	174
	5295	鮮 明 *senmei* clear, distinct	18
		鮮 度 *sendo* (degree of) freshness	377
	鮮	鮮 魚 *sengyo* fresh fish	290
		朝 鮮 *Chōsen* Korea	469

	702	CHI, *oso(i)*, late, tardy; slow; *oku(reru)*, be late (for); be slow (clock); *oku(rasu)*, defer, put back (a clock)	
遅	162	遅 着 *chichaku* late arrival	657
	4722	遅 配 *chihai* delay in apportioning/delivery	515
		遅 速 *chisoku* speed	502
	遅	乗 り 遅 れ る *noriokureru* be too late to catch, miss (a bus) 523	

	703	DŌ, *michibi(ku)*, lead, guide	
導	41	主 導 *shudō* leadership, guidance	155
	1354	先 導 *sendō* guidance, leadership	50
		導 入 *dōnyū* introduction	52
	導	導 火 線 *dōkasen* fuse; cause, occasion	20, 299
		半 導 体 *handōtai* semiconductor	88, 61

	704	SON, *tatto(bu)*, *tōto(bu)*, value, esteem, respect; *tatto(i)*, *tōto(i)*, valuable, precious, noble, august	
尊	12	尊 重 *sonchō* value, respect, pay high regard to	227
	607	自 尊(心) *jison(shin)* self-respect, pride	62, 97
		尊 大 *sondai* haughtiness, arrogance	26
	尊	本 尊 *honzon* Buddha; idol; he himself, she herself	25

	705	KEI, *uyama(u)*, respect, revere	
敬	66	尊 敬 *sonkei* respect, deference	704
	2055	敬 意 *keii* respect, homage	132
		敬 老 *keirō* respect for the aged	543
	敬	敬 遠 *keien* keep at a respectful distance	446
		敬 語 *keigo* an honorific, term of respect	67

	706	KEI, admonish, warn	
警	149	警 察 *keisatsu* police	619
	4439	警 官 *keikan* policeman	326
		警 視 *keishi* police superintendent	606
	警	警 告 *keikoku* warning, admonition	690
		警 報 *keihō* warning (signal), alarm	685

	707	*oro(su)*, sell wholesale; *oroshi*, wholesaling	
卸	26	卸 商 *oroshishō* wholesaler	412
	812	卸 値 *oroshine* wholesale price	425
	卸	卸 し 売 り 物 価 *oroshiuri bukka* wholesale prices	239, 79, 421

	708	GYO, GO, *on*-, (honorific prefix)	
御	60	制御 *seigyo* control, governing, suppression	427
	1628	御飯 *gohan* boiled rice; meal	325
		御用の方 *goyō no kata* customer, inquirer	107, 70
御		御所 *gosho* imperial palace	153
		御中 *onchū* Dear sirs:, Gentlemen:, Messrs.	28

	709	KA, *kuwa(eru)*, add, append; *kuwa(waru)*, join, take part (in)	
加	19	加入 *kanyū* joining	52
	716	加工 *kakō* processing	139
		加法 *kahō* addition (in mathematics)	123
加		倍加 *baika* doubling	87
		付加価値税 *fukakachizei* value-added ⌐tax 192, 421, 425, 399	

	710	SAN, three (in documents); go, come, visit; *mai(ru)*, go, come, visit, visit a temple/shrine	
参	28	参加 *sanka* participation	709
	850	参列 *sanretsu* attendance, presence	611
		参議院 *Sangiin* (Japanese) House of Councilors	292, 614
参		参考書 *sankōsho* reference book/work	541, 131

	711	BEN, speech, dialect; discrimination; petal; valve	
弁	28	弁当 *bentō* box/sack lunch	77
	846	駅弁 *ekiben* box lunch sold at a train station	284
		答弁 *tōben* reply, answer	160
弁		弁解 *benkai* explanation, justification, excuse	474
		関西弁 *Kansai-ben* Kansai dialect/accent	398, 72

	712	ZŌ, *ma(su)*, *fu(eru)*, increase, rise; *fu(yasu)*, increase, raise	
増	32	増加 *zōka* increase, rise, growth	709
	1137	増産 *zōsan* increase in production	278
		増税 *zōzei* tax increase	399
増		増進 *zōshin* increase, furtherance, improvement	437

	713	FU, [FŪ], *tomi*, wealth; *to(mu)*, be/become rich	
富	40	国富 *kokufu* national wealth	40
	1321	富強 *fukyō* wealth and power	217
		富力 *furyoku* wealth, resources	100
富		富者 *fusha, fūsha* rich person, the wealthy	164
		富士山 *Fuji-san* Mount Fuji	572, 34

	714	FUKU, assistant, accompany, supplement	
副	18	副社長 *fukushachō* company vice-president	308, 95
	699	副業 *fukugyō* side business, sideline	279
		副産物 *fukusanbutsu* by-product	278, 79
副		副作用 *fukusayō* side effects	360, 107
		副題 *fukudai* subtitle, subheading	354

	715	GEN, *he(ru)*, decrease, diminish; *he(rasu)*, decrease, shorten
減	85 2637 減	増 減 *zōgen* increase and/or decrease ⌈health 712 加 減 *kagen* addition and subtraction; state of 709 減 少 *genshō* decrease, reduction 144 半 減 *hangen* reduction by half 88 減 法 *genpō* subtraction (in mathematics) 123
	716	EKI, [YAKU], profit, use, advantage
益	12 597 益	利 益 *rieki* profit, advantage 329 公 益 *kōeki* the public good 126 有 益 *yūeki* useful, beneficial, profitable 265 無 益 *mueki* useless, in vain 93 益 鳥 *ekichō* beneficial bird 285
	717	MEI, oath; alliance
盟	108 3119 盟	連 盟 *renmei* league, federation 440 同 盟 *dōmei* alliance, confederation 198 加 盟 *kamei* joining, affiliation 709 盟 主 *meishu* the leader, leading power 155 盟 約 *meiyaku* pledge, pact; alliance 211
	718	SEI, *makoto*, truth, reality; sincerity, fidelity
誠	149 4352 誠	誠 実 *seijitsu* sincere, faithful, truthful 203 誠 意 *seii* sincerity, good faith 132 誠 心 誠 意 *seishin-seii* sincerely, wholeheartedly 97, 132 誠 に *makoto ni* truly, indeed; sincerely; very
	719	SEI, [JŌ], *saka(n)*, prosperous, energetic; *saka(ru)*, flourish, prosper; *mo(ru)*, serve (food); heap up
盛	108 3116 盛	盛 大 *seidai* thriving, grand, magnificent 26 全 盛 *zensei* height of prosperity, zenith, heyday 89 最 盛 期 *saiseiki* golden age, zenith 263, 449 花 盛 り *hanazakari* in full bloom, at its best 255
	720	JŌ, *shiro*, castle
城	32 1078 城	城 下 町 *jōkamachi* castle town 31, 182 城 主 *jōshu* feudal lord of a castle 155 開 城 *kaijō* surrender of a fortress, capitulation 396 城 門 *jōmon* castle gate 161 古 城 *kojō* old castle 172
	721	KYŪ, GŪ, [KU], *miya*, shrine, palace, prince
宮	40 1310 宮	宮 城 *kyūjō* imperial palace 720 神 宮 *jingū* Shinto shrine 310 宮 参 り *miyamairi* visit to a shrine 710 宮 城 県 *Miyagi-ken* Miyagi Prefecture 720, 194 子 宮 *shikyū* uterus, womb 103

営 営	**722** 30 963	**EI,** *itona(mu)*, perform (a ceremony); conduct (business)	
		経営 *keiei* management, administration	548
		運営 *un'ei* operation, management, running	439
		公営 *kōei* public management, municipally run	126
		営業 *eigyō* (running a) business	279
		営利 *eiri* profit, profit-making	329
栄 栄	**723** 75 2239	**EI,** *ha(e)*, glory, honor, splendor; *ha(eru)*, shine, be brilliant; *saka(eru)*, thrive, prosper	
		栄養 *eiyō* nutrition	402
		光栄 *kōei* honor, glory	138
		栄光 *eikō* glory	138
		見栄え *mibae* outward appearance	63
求 求	**724** 3 137	**KYŪ,** *moto(meru)*, want; request, demand, seek	
		請求 *seikyū* a claim, demand	661
		要求 *yōkyū* demand	419
		求職 *kyūshoku* seeking employment, job hunting	385
		求人 *kyūjin* job offer, Help Wanted	1
		探求 *tankyū* research, investigation	535
救 救	**725** 66 2051	**KYŪ,** *suku(u)*, rescue, aid	
		救急 *kyūkyū* first aid	303
		救助 *kyūjo* rescue, relief	623
		救済 *kyūsai* relief, aid, redemption, salvation	549
		救命ボート *kyūmei bōto* lifeboat	578
		救世軍 *Kyūseigun* Salvation Army	252, 438
球 球	**726** 96 2941	**KYŪ,** *tama*, ball, sphere	
		野球 *yakyū* baseball	236
		球場 *kyūjō* baseball stadium, ball park	154
		電球 *denkyū* light bulb	108
		(軽)気球 *(kei)kikyū* (hot-air/helium) balloon	547, 134
		地球 *chikyū* the earth, globe	118
儀 儀	**727** 9 554	**GI,** rule; ceremony; affair, matter	
		礼儀 *reigi* politeness, courtesy, propriety	620
		礼儀正しい *reigi tadashii* courteous, decorous	620, 275
		儀式 *gishiki* ceremony, formality, ritual	525
		儀典長 *gitenchō* chief of protocol	367, 95
		地球儀 *chikyūgi* a globe	118, 726
犠 犠	**728** 93 2865	**GI,** sacrifice	

	729	**SEI**, sacrifice	
牲	93	犠牲 *gisei* sacrifice	728
	2858	犠牲者 *giseisha* victim	728, 164
牲			

	730	**SEI**, [**SHŌ**], *hoshi*, star	
星	72	火星 *kasei* Mars	20
	2121	明星 *myōjō* morning star, Venus	18
		すい星 *suisei* comet	
星		流れ星 *nagareboshi* shooting star, meteor	247
		星空 *hoshizora* starry sky	140

	731	**BOKU**, *maki*, pasture	
牧	93	牧場 *bokujō, makiba* pasture, meadow	154
	2856	牧草地 *bokusōchi* pasture, grassland, meadow-	249, 118
		放牧 *hōboku* pasturage, grazing ⌊land	512
牧		牧羊者 *bokuyōsha* sheep raiser, shepherd	288, 164
		牧師 *bokushi* pastor, minister	409

	732	**KEN**, matter, affair, case	
件	9	事件 *jiken* incident, affair, case	80
	368	条件 *jōken* condition, terms, stipulation	564
		要件 *yōken* important matter; condition, requisite	419
件		用件 *yōken* (item of) business	107
		案件 *anken* matter, case, item	106

	733	**MEN**, *manuka(reru)*, escape, avoid, be exempt from	
免	10	御免 *gomen* pardon; declining, refusal	708
	573	免責 *menseki* exemption from responsibility	655
		免税 *menzei* tax exemption	399
免		免状 *menjō* diploma; license	626
		免職 *menshoku* dismissal from one's job/office	385

	734	**ITSU**, idleness; diverge, deviate from	
逸	162	逸話 *itsuwa* anecdote	238
	4708	逸品 *ippin* superb article, masterpiece	230
		放逸 *hōitsu* self-indulgence, licentiousness	512
逸			

	735	**BEN**, effort, hard work	
勉	4	勤勉 *kinben* industriousness, diligence, hard work	559
	228	勉強 *benkyō* studying; diligence; sell cheap	217
		勉強家 *benkyōka* diligent student; hard worker	217, 165
勉		勉学 *bengaku* study, pursuit of one's studies	109

	736	**BAN, evening, night**	
晚 72 2145 晚		今 晚　　*konban*　this evening, tonight	51
		毎 晚　　*maiban*　every evening	116
		一 晚　　*hitoban*　a night, all night　⌈night	2
		朝 晚　　*asaban*　mornings and evenings, day and	469
		晚 年　　*bannen*　latter part of one's life	45

	737	**KYO, *yuru(su)*, permit, allow**	
許 149 4324 許		免 許　　*menkyo*　permission, license	733
		許 可　　*kyoka*　permission, approval, authorization	388
		許 容　　*kyoyō*　permission, tolerance	654
		特 許　　*tokkyo*　special permission; patent	282
		特 許 法 *tokkyohō*　patent law	282, 123

	738	**NIN, *mito(meru)*, perceive; recognize; approve of**	
認 149 4370 認		認 可　　*ninka*　approval	388
		認 定　　*nintei*　approval, acknowledgment	355
		確 認　　*kakunin*　confirmation, certification	603
		公 認　　*kōnin*　official recognition/sanction	126
		認 識　　*ninshiki*　cognition, recognition, perception	681

	739	**SHŌ, image, shape; ZŌ, elephant**	
象 152 4472 象		具 象 的 *gushōteki*　concrete, embodied	420, 210
		現 象　　*genshō*　phenomenon	298
		対 象　　*taishō*　object, subject, target	365
		気 象 学 *kishōgaku*　meteorology	134, 109
		象 げ　　*zōge*　ivory	

	740	**ZŌ, statue, image**	
像 9 540 像		仏 像　　*butsuzō*　statue/image of Buddha	583
		自 画 像 *jigazō*　self-portrait	62, 343
		受 像 機 *juzōki*　television set	260, 528
		現 像　　*genzō*　(photographic) development	298
		想 像　　*sōzō*　imagination	147

	741	***kabu*, share, stock; stump**	
株 75 2257 株		株 式 会 社 *kabushiki-gaisha/kaisha*　Co., Ltd. 525, 158, 308	
		株 券　　*kabuken*　share/stock certificate	506
		株 主　　*kabunushi*　stockholder　⌈of shareholders	155
		株 主 総 会 *kabunushi sōkai*　general meeting 155, 697, 158	
		切 り 株 *kirikabu*　(tree) stump, (grain) stubble	39

	742	**ZETSU, *ta(eru)*, die out, end; *ta(tsu)*, cut off, interrupt, eradicate; *ta(yasu)*, kill off, let die out**	
絶 120 3539 絶		絶 対　　*zettai*　absolute	365
		絶 大　　*zetsudai*　greatest, immense	26
		絶 望　　*zetsubō*　despair	673
		根 絶　　*konzetsu*　root out, eradicate, stamp out	314

	743	REN, *ne(ru)*, knead; train; polish up	
練	120 3565	練習 *renshū* practice, exercise	591
		教練 *kyōren* (military) drill	245
		試練 *shiren* trial, test, ordeal	526
	練	熟練 *jukuren* practiced skill, expertness, mastery	687
		洗練 *senren* polish, refine	692

	744	TAI, *ka(eru)*, replace; *ka(waru)*, be replaced	
替	72 2140	代替 *daitai, daigae* substitution	256
		両替 *ryōgae* exchanging/changing money	200
		取り替え *torikae* exchange, swap, replacement	65
	替	切り替え *kirikae* renewal, changeover	39
		着替える *kigaeru, kikaeru* change clothes	657

	745	SAN, praise; agreement	
賛	154 4516	賛成 *sansei* agreement, approbation	261
		賛助 *sanjo* support, backing	623
		協賛 *kyōsan* approval, consent, support	234
	賛	賞賛 *shōsan* praise, admiration	500
		賛美 *sanbi* praise, glorification	401

	746	SEI, [SHŌ], *koe*, [*kowa-*], voice	
声	32 1066	声明 *seimei* declaration, statement, proclamation	18
		名声 *meisei* fame, renown, reputation	82
		音声学 *onseigaku* phonetics	347, 109
	声	声変わり *koegawari* change/cracking of voice	257
		声色 *kowairo* imitated/assumed voice	204

	747	SAN, calculate	
算	118 3415	計算 *keisan* calculation, computation	340
		公算 *kōsan* probability, likelihood	126
		予算 *yosan* an estimate; budget	393
	算	清算 *seisan* exact calculation, (fare) adjustment	660
		暗算 *anzan* mental arithmetic/calculation	348

	748	TAI, *ka(su)*, rent out	
貸	154 4503	貸与 *taiyo* lend, loan	539
		貸し家 *kashiya* house for rent, rented house	165
		貸しボート *kashibōto* boat for rent, rented boat	
	貸	貸し出す *kashidasu* lend/hire out	53
		貸し切り *kashikiri* reservations, booking	39

	749	HI, *tsui(yasu)*, spend; *tsui(eru)*, be wasted	
費	154 4497	経費 *keihi* expenses, cost	548
		費用 *hiyō* expense, cost	107
		生活費 *seikatsuhi* living expenses, cost of living	44, 237
	費	光熱費 *kōnetsuhi* heating and lighting expenses	138, 645
		旅費 *ryohi* traveling expenses	222

	750	SHI, resources, capital, funds	
資	154	資 源 *shigen* resources	580
	4510	資 本 *shihon* capital	25
		資 金 *shikin* funds	23
	資	物 資 *busshi* goods, (raw) materials	79
		資 格 *shikaku* qualification, competence	643

	751	CHIN, rent, wages, fare, fee	
賃	154	賃 金 *chingin* wages, pay	23
	4509	賃 上 げ *chin'age* raise in wages	32
		運 賃 *unchin* passenger fare; shipping charges	439
	賃	電 車 賃 *denshachin* train fare	108, 133
		家 賃 *yachin* rent	165

	752	KA, freight; goods, property	
貨	154	貨 物 *kamotsu* freight	79
	4493	百 貨 店 *hyakkaten* department store	14, 168
		通 貨 *tsūka* currency	150
	貨	外 貨 *gaika* foreign goods/currency	83
		銀 貨 *ginka* silver coin	313

	753	HIN, BIN, *mazu(shii)*, poor	
貧	12	貧 富 *hinpu* poverty and wealth, the rich and poor	713
	600	貧 困 *hinkon* poverty, need	558
		貧 弱 *hinjaku* poor, meager, scanty	218
	貧	貧 相 *hinsō* poor-looking, seedy	146
		清 貧 *seihin* honest poverty	660

	754	BŌ, *tobo(shii)*, scanty, meager, scarce	
乏	4	貧 乏 *binbō* poor	753
	150	欠 乏 *ketsubō* shortage, deficiency	383
	乏		

	755	KA, *ka(keru)*, hang, build (bridge); *ka(karu)*, hang, be built	
架	75	架 設 *kasetsu* construction, laying	577
	2237	架 橋 *kakyō* bridge building	597
		書 架 *shoka* bookshelf	131
	架	十 字 架 像 *jūjikazō* crucifix	12, 110, 740
		架 空 *kakū* overhead, aerial; fanciful	140

	756	GA, congratulations, felicitations	
賀	154	賀 状 *gajō* greeting card	626
	4501	年 賀 *nenga* New Year's greetings	45
		年 賀 状 *nengajō* New Year's card	45, 626
	賀	賀 正 *gashō* New Year's greetings	275
		志 賀 高 原 *Shiga Kōgen* Shiga Plateau	573, 190, 136

	757	SHŪ, osa(meru), obtain, collect; osa(maru), be obtained, end	
収	29 860	収支 shūshi income and expenditures	318
		収入 shūnyū income, earnings, receipts	52
		買収 baishū purchase; buying off, bribery	241
	収	収益 shūeki earnings, proceeds, profit	716
		収容 shūyō admission, accommodation	654

	758	NŌ, [TŌ], [NA], [NA'], [NAN], osa(meru), pay; supply; accept, store; osa(maru), be paid (in), supplied	
納	120 3508	納税 nōzei payment of taxes	399
		出納 suitō receipts and disbursements	53
	納	納得 nattoku consent, understanding	374
		納屋 naya (storage) shed	167

	759	EKI, divination; I, yasa(shii), easy	
易	72 2107	易者 ekisha fortune-teller	164
		不易 fueki immutability, unchangeableness	94
		交易 kōeki trade, commerce, barter	114
	易	容易 yōi easy, simple	654
		難易 (度) nan'i(do) (degree of) difficulty	557, 377

	760	BŌ, exchange, trade	
貿	154 4499	貿易 bōeki trade	759
		自由貿易 jiyū bōeki free trade	62, 363, 759
		貿易会社 bōeki-gaisha trading firm/company	759, 158, 308
	貿	貿易収支 bōeki shūshi balance of trade	759, 757, 318
		日米貿易 Nichi-Bei bōeki Japan-U.S. trade	5, 224, 759

	761	RYŪ, [RU], to(meru), fasten down; hold, keep (in); to(maru), stay, settle	
留	102 3003	留学 ryūgaku study abroad	109
		留守 rusu absence from home	490
	留	書留 kakitome registered mail	131
		局留 (め) kyokudome general delivery	170

	762	CHO, storage	
貯	154 4502	貯金 chokin savings, deposit	23
	貯	貯水池 chosuichi reservoir	21, 119

	763	CHŌ, government office, agency	
庁	53 1498	官庁 kanchō government office, agency	326
		警視庁 Keishichō Metropolitan Police Department	706, 606
	庁	気象庁 Kishōchō Meteorological Agency	134, 739
		県庁 kenchō prefectural office	194

	764	SEKI, [SHAKU], *mukashi*, antiquity, long ago	
昔	72 2108 昔	今昔　　　　*konjaku*　past and present 大昔　　　　*ōmukashi*　remote antiquity, time immemorial 昔々　　　　*mukashimukashi*　Once upon a time . . . 昔話　　　　*mukashibanashi*　old tale, legend 昔の事　*mukashi no koto*　thing of the past	51 26 238 80
惜	765 61 1712 惜	SEKI, *o(shii)*, regrettable; precious; wasteful; *o(shimu)*, regret; value; begrudge, be sparing of 惜敗　　　　*sekihai*　narrow defeat (after a hard-fought 愛惜　　　　*aiseki*　be loath to part　　　　⌊contest) 口惜しい　*kuchioshii* regrettable, vexing　　　⌈feat 負け惜しみ *makeoshimi* unwillingness to admit de-	 511 259 54 510
借	766 9 490 借	SHAKU, *ka(riru)*, borrow, rent 借金　　　　*shakkin*　debt 借財　　　　*shakuzai*　debt 貸借　　　　*taishaku*　debits and credits 転借　　　　*tenshaku*　subleasing 賃借/借り　*chin-shaku/gari*　lease	23 553 748 433 751
散	767 66 2056 散	SAN, *chi(rakasu)*, scatter, disarrange; *chi(rakaru)*, lie scattered, be in disorder; *chi(ru/rasu)*, (intr./tr.) scatter 解散　　　　*kaisan*　breakup, dissolution, disbanding 散会　　　　*sankai*　adjournment 散文　　　　*sanbun*　prose 散歩　　　　*sanpo*　walk, stroll	 474 158 111 431
備	768 9 519 備	BI, *sona(eru)*, furnish, provide (for); *sona(waru)*, possess 設備　　　　*setsubi*　equipment, facilities 整備　　　　*seibi*　maintenance, servicing 軍備　　　　*gunbi*　military preparations, armaments 予備費　　*yobihi*　reserves, reserve funds 備考　　　　*bikō*　explanatory notes, remarks	 577 503 438 393, 749 541
順	769 47 1450 順	JUN, order, sequence 順番　　　　*junban*　order, one's turn 順位　　　　*jun'i*　ranking, standing 語順　　　　*gojun*　word order　　　　　⌈labary 五十音順　*gojū-on jun*　in order of the kana syl- 順調　　　　*junchō*　favorable, smooth, without a hitch	 185 122 67 7, 12, 347 342
序	770 53 1502 序	JO, beginning; preface; order, precedence 順序　　　　*junjo*　order, method, procedure 序説　　　　*josetsu*　introduction, preface 序論　　　　*joron*　introduction, preface 序文　　　　*jobun*　preface, foreword, introduction 序曲　　　　*jokyoku*　overture, prelude	769 400 293 111 366

	771	**KUN,** Japanese reading of a kanji; teaching, precept	
訓	149	訓育 *kun'iku* education, discipline	246
	4317	教訓 *kyōkun* teaching, precept, moral	245
		訓練 *kunren* training	743
訓		訓辞 *kunji* an admonitory speech, instructions	688
		音訓 *on-kun* Chinese and Japanese readings	347

	772	**JUN,** *tate,* shield	
盾	4	後ろ盾 *ushirodate* support, backing, supporter,	
	215	backer	48
盾			

	773	**MU,** *hoko,* halberd	
矛	110	矛盾 *mujun* contradiction	772
	3164	矛先 *hokosaki* point of a spear; aim of an attack	50
矛			

	774	**JŪ, NYŪ,** *yawa(rakai/raka),* soft	
柔	110	柔道 *jūdō* Judo	149
	3166	柔術 *jūjutsu* jujitsu	187
		柔弱 *nyūjaku* weakness, enervation	218
柔		柔和 *nyūwa* gentle, mild(-mannered)	124
		物柔らか *monoyawaraka* mild(-mannered), quiet, gentle	79

	775	**HEN,** *ata(ri),* *-be,* vicinity	
辺	162	近辺 *kinpen* neighborhood, vicinity	445
	4661	周辺 *shūhen* periphery, environs	91
		辺地 *henchi* remote/out-of-the-way place	118
辺		多辺形 *tahenkei* polygon	229, 395
		海辺 *umibe* beach, seashore	117

	776	*ko(mu),* be crowded, congested; *ko(meru),* include, count in; load (a gun); concentrate	
込	162	巻き込む *makikomu* entangle, involve, implicate	507
	4660	払い込む *haraikomu* pay in	582
		申し込み *mōshikomi* proposal, offer, application	309
込		見込み *mikomi* prospects, outlook	63

	777	**JUN,** *megu(ru),* go around	
巡	162	巡回 *junkai* tour, patrol, one's rounds	90
	4667	巡視 *junshi* tour of inspection, round of visits	606
		巡査 *junsa* policeman, cop	624
巡		巡礼 *junrei* pilgrimage, pilgrim	620
		巡業 *jungyō* tour (of a troupe/team)	279

	778	JUN, semi-, quasi-; level; correspond (to)	
準	24 791	水準 *suijun* water level; level, standard 基準 *kijun* standard, criterion 規準 *kijun* criterion, standard, norm 準備 *junbi* preparation 準決勝 *junkesshō* semifinal game/round	21 450 607 768 356, 509
準			
	779	SEN, *so(meru)*, dye, color; *so(maru)*, be dyed, imbued; *shi-(miru)*, soak into; be infected; smart, hurt; *shi(mi)*, stain, blot, smudge	
染	75 2240	(大気)汚染 (*taiki*) *osen* (air) pollution 伝染病 *densenbyō* contagious disease 感染 *kansen* infection	26, 134, 693 434, 380 262
染			
	780	KŌ, Ō, *ki*, [*ko*], yellow	
黄	201 5399	黄葉 *kōyō* yellow (autumn) leaves 黄熱(病) (*k*)*ōnetsu*(*byō*) yellow fever 黄金 *ōgon, kogane* gold 黄色 *kiiro* yellow 黄身 *kimi* egg yolk	253 645, 380 23 204 59
黄			
	781	Ō, *yoko*, side	
横	75 2361	専横 *sen'ō* arbitrariness, tyranny 横道 *yokomichi* side street; side issue, digression 横切る *yokogiru* cross, traverse 横顔 *yokogao* profile 横目 *yokome* side glance; amorous glance	600 149 39 277 55
横			
	782	SAI, [SA], *futata(bi)*, once more, again, twice	
再	1 35	再会 *saikai* meeting again, reunion 再開 *saikai* reopening 再編成 *saihensei* reorganization 再婚 *saikon* second marriage, remarriage 再来週 *saraishū* week after next	158 396 682, 261 567 69, 92
再			
	783	KŌ, club; lecture, study	
講	149 4425	講義 *kōgi* lecture 講演 *kōen* lecture, address 講師 *kōshi* lecturer, instructor 講堂 *kōdō* lecture hall 講和 *kōwa* (make) peace	291 344 409 496 124
講			
	784	HEI, HYŌ, soldier	
兵	4 201	兵器 *heiki* weapon 兵士 *heishi* soldier 歩兵 *hohei* infantry; infantryman, foot soldier 志願兵 *shiganhei* a volunteer (soldier) 兵役 *heieki* military service, conscription	527 572 431 573, 581 375
兵			

	785	**HIN**, *hama*, beach	
浜	85 2567	海浜 *kaihin* seashore, beach	117
		京浜 *Kei-Hin* Tokyo-Yokohama	189
		横浜 *Yokohama* (port city near Tokyo)	781
	浜	浜辺 *hamabe* beach, seashore	775
		浜田 *Hamada* (surname)	35

	786	**ZA**, seat; theater; constellation; *suwa(ru)*, sit down	
座	53 1515	座席 *zaseki* seat ⌜sium	379
		座談会 *zadankai* round-table discussion, sympo-	593, 158
		(通信)講座 *(tsūshin) kōza* (correspondence)	150, 157, 783
	座	口座 *kōza* (savings) account ⌊course	54
		銀座 *Ginza* (area of Tokyo)	313

	787	**SOTSU**, soldier, private; end	
卒	8 294	卒業 *sotsugyō* graduation ⌜amination	279
		卒業試験 *sotsugyō shiken* graduation ex-	279, 526, 532
		卒業証書 *sotsugyō shōsho* diploma	279, 484, 131
	卒	卒中 *sotchū* cerebral stroke, apoplexy	28
		兵卒 *heisotsu* a private, common soldier	784

	788	**SOTSU**, *hiki(iru)*, lead, command; **RITSU**, rate, proportion	
率	8 319	率直 *sotchoku* straightforward, frank	423
		軽率 *keisotsu* rash, hasty, heedless	547
		能率 *nōritsu* efficiency	386
	率	倍率 *bairitsu* (degree of) magnification	87
		成長率 *seichōritsu* rate of growth	261, 95

	789	**KETSU**, *chi*, blood	
血	143 4205	血液 *ketsueki* blood	472
		血管 *kekkan* blood vessel	328
		(内)出血 *(nai)shukketsu* (internal) hemorrhage	84, 53
	血	止血剤 *shiketsuzai* a hemostatic, styptic (agent)	477, 550
		流血 *ryūketsu* bloodshed	247

	790	**SAN**, *kasa*, umbrella	
傘	9 518	傘下 *sanka* affiliated	31
		日傘 *higasa* parasol	5
		雨傘 *amagasa* umbrella	30
	傘	傘立て *kasatate* umbrella stand	121
		こうもり傘 *kōmorigasa* umbrella, parasol	

	791	**SHA**, house, hut, quarters	
舎	9 423	国民宿舎 *kokumin shukusha* government- sponsored hostels	40, 177, 179
		校舎 *kōsha* schoolhouse, school building	115
	舎	兵舎 *heisha* barracks	784
		田舎 *inaka* the country, rural areas	35

	792	SHŪ, [SHU], multitude, populace
衆	143 4210	公衆(電話) *kōshū (denwa)* public (telephone) 126, 108, 238 大衆文学 *taishū bungaku* popular literature 26, 111, 109 民衆 *minshū* the people, masses 177
衆		アメリカ合衆国 *Amerika Gasshūkoku* United States of America 159, 40
	793	KUN, (suffix for male personal names); ruler; *kimi*, you (in masculine speech); ruler
君	30 899	和夫君 *Kazuo-kun* Kazuo 124, 315 君主 *kunshu* monarch, sovereign 155
君		立憲君主政(国) *rikken kunshusei (koku)* constitutional monarchy 121, 521, 155, 483, 40
	794	GUN, *mu(re)*, [*mura*], group, herd; *mu(reru)*, crowd, flock
群	123 3667	群衆 *gunshū* crowd of people 792 群集 *gunshū* crowd of people 436 群像 *gunzō* group of people (in an artwork) 740 魚群 *gyogun* school of fish 290
群		群島 *guntō* group of islands, archipelago 286
	795	TAI, party, squad, unit
隊	170 5010	軍隊 *guntai* troops, army, the military 438 部隊 *butai* military unit, squad 86 兵隊 *heitai* soldier, troops ⌈group 784
隊		探検隊 *tankentai* expedition, expeditionary 535, 531 楽隊 *gakutai* (musical) band 358
	796	TON, *buta*, pig
豚	130 3772	養豚 *yōton* pig raising 402 豚カツ *tonkatsu* pork cutlet 豚肉 *butaniku* pork 223
豚		豚小屋 *butagoya* pigsty, pigpen 27, 167
	797	GEKI, drama, play
劇	4 247	劇場 *gekijō* theater, playhouse 154 演劇 *engeki* drama, theatrical performance 344 歌劇 *kageki* opera 392 劇的 *gekiteki* dramatic 210
劇		劇薬 *gekiyaku* powerful medicine; virulent poison 359
	798	HI, *kura(beru)*, compare
比	81 2470	比率 *hiritsu* ratio 788 比例 *hirei* proportion 612 対比 *taihi* contrast, contradistinction 365 比重 *hijū* specific gravity 227
比		見比べる *mikuraberu* compare 63

	799	KON, *ma(zeru)*, mix; *ma(zaru/jiru)*, be mixed	
混	85 2604	混乱 *konran* confusion, disorder, chaos	689
		混雑 *konzatsu* confusion, congestion	575
		混合 *kongō* mixture ⌈half-breed	159
混		混血の人 *konketsu no hito* person of mixed race,	789, 1
		混ぜ物 *mazemono* adulteration	79

	800	SEN, *era(bu)*, choose, select	
選	162 4744	当選 *tōsen* be elected	77
		改選 *kaisen* reelection	514
		精選 *seisen* careful selection	659
選		予選 *yosen* preliminary match; primary election	393
		選手 *senshu* (sports) player	57

	801	KYO, all, whole; arrest, capture; name, give, cite; *a(geru)*, name, give, enumerate; arrest, apprehend; *a(garu)*, be ap- prehended; be found, recovered	
挙	64 1902	選挙 *senkyo* election	800
		挙党 *kyotō* the whole party	495
挙		検挙 *kenkyo* arrest, apprehension, roundup	531

	802	YO, *homa(re)*, glory, honor	
誉	149 4353	栄誉 *eiyo* honor, glory	723
		名誉 *meiyo* honor	82
		名誉職 *meiyoshoku* honorary post	82, 385
誉		名誉教授 *meiyo kyōju* professor emeritus	82, 245, 602
		名誉市民 *meiyo shimin* honorary citizen	82, 181, 177

	803	HŌ, *ho(meru)*, praise	
褒	8 331	褒賞 *hōshō* prize	500
		褒美 *hōbi* reward	401
		過褒 *kahō* excessive/undeserved praise	413
褒		褒め上げる *homeageru* praise very highly, extol	32
		褒め立てる *hometateru* admire, praise highly	121

	804	HŌ, *tsutsu(mu)*, wrap up	
包	4 176	包容力 *hōyōryoku* capacity; tolerance, catho-	654, 100
		包丁 *hōchō* kitchen knife ⌊licity	184
		小包み *kozutsumi* parcel	27
包		紙包み *kamizutsumi* parcel wrapped in paper	180
		包み紙 *tsutsumigami* wrapping paper, wrapper	180

	805	KIN, equal, even	
均	32 1065	平均 *heikin* average	202
		均一 *kin'itsu* uniform	2
		均等 *kintō* equality, uniformity, parity	569
均		均質 *kinshitsu* homogeneous	176
		均分 *kinbun* divide equally	38

	806	MITSU, close, dense, crowded; minute, fine; secret	
密	40	機密 *kimitsu* a secret	528
	1316	密輸 *mitsuyu* smuggling	546
		(人口)密度 (*jinkō*) *mitsudo* (population) density 1, 54, 377	
密		密接 *missetsu* close, intimate	486
		精密 *seimitsu* minute, accurate, precision	659

	807	HI, *hi(meru)*, keep secret	
秘	115	秘密 *himitsu* a secret	806
	3281	極秘 *gokuhi* strict secrecy, top secret	336
		秘書 *hisho* secretary	131
秘		神秘 *shinpi* mystery	310
		便秘 *benpi* constipation	330

	808	HŌ, country; Japan	
邦	163	(在米)邦人 (*zaibei*) *hōjin* Japanese (living in America)	268, 224, 1
	4758	邦字新聞 *hōji shinbun* Japanese-language 110, 174, 64	
邦		連邦 *renpō* federation, federal ⌐newspaper 440	
		連邦政府 *renpō seifu* federal government 440, 483, 504	

	809	RIN, *tonari*, next door; *tona(ru)*, be neighboring	
隣	170	隣国 *ringoku* neighboring country/province	40
	5023	隣席 *rinseki* next seat, seat next to one	379
		隣接 *rinsetsu* border on, be contiguous, adjoin	486
隣		隣人 *rinjin* a neighbor	1
		隣り合う *tonariau* adjoin/be next door to each other 159	

	810	BU, *ma(u)*, dance, flutter about; *mai*, dance	
舞	136	舞台 *butai* the stage	492
	3862	舞楽 *bugaku* old Japanese court-dance music	358
		歌舞き *kabuki* Kabuki	392
舞		仕舞 *shimai* end, conclusion ⌐health] 333	
		(お)見舞 (*o*)*mimai* visit, inquiry (after someone's	63

	811	MU, *yume*, dream	
夢	140	夢想 *musō* dream, vision, fancy	147
	4028	悪夢 *akumu* bad dream, nightmare	304
		夢中 *muchū* rapture; absorption, intentness; fran-	28
夢		夢を見る *yume o miru* (have a) dream ⌐tic 63	
		夢にも *yume nimo* (not) even in a dream	

	812	SŌ, *hōmu(ru)*, bury, inter	
葬	140	葬儀/式 *sō-gi/shiki* funeral	727, 525
	4000	火葬 *kasō* cremation	20
		葬列 *sōretsu* funeral procession	611
葬		副葬品 *fukusōhin* burial accessories	714, 230
		改葬 *kaisō* reburial, reinterment	514

鼻	**813**	**BI**, *hana*, nose	
	209	耳鼻いんこう専門医 *jibiinkō senmon'i* ear,	
	5421	nose, and throat specialist	56, 600, 161, 220
		鼻先 *hanasaki* tip of the nose	50
鼻		鼻血 *hanaji* nosebleed, bloody nose	789
		鼻薬 *hanagusuri* a bribe	359

違	**814**	**I**, *chiga(u)*, be different; be mistaken; *chiga(eru)*, alter	
	162	相違 *sōi* difference, disparity	146
	4720	違反 *ihan* violation	324
		違法 *ihō* illegal	123
違		違憲 *iken* unconstitutionality	521
		間違い *machigai* mistake, error; accident, mishap	43

衛	**815**	**EI**, defend, protect	
	60	防衛 *bōei* defense	513
	1639	自衛隊 *Jieitai* (Japanese) Self-Defense Forces	62, 795
		衛生 *eisei* hygiene, sanitation	44
衛		衛星 *eisei* satellite	730
		前衛 *zen'ei* advance guard; avant-garde	47

効	**816**	**KŌ**, *ki(ku)*, be effective	
	19	効力 *kōryoku* effectiveness, effect, validity	100
	722	効果 *kōka* effect, effectiveness	487
		有効 *yūkō* validity, effectiveness	265
効		無効 *mukō* invalidity, ineffectiveness	93
		時効 *jikō* prescription (in statute of limitations)	42

郊	**817**	**KŌ**, suburbs, rural areas	
	163	近郊 *kinkō* suburbs, outskirts	445
	4761	郊外 *kōgai* suburbs, outskirts	83
郊			

功	**818**	**KŌ**, [**KU**], merits, success	
	48	成功 *seikō* success	261
	1454	功労 *kōrō* meritorious service	233
		功業 *kōgyō* achievement, exploit	279
功		功名 *kōmyō* great achievement, glorious deed	82
		年功 *nenkō* long service/experience	45

攻	**819**	**KŌ**, *se(meru)*, attack	
	48	攻勢 *kōsei* the offensive	646
	1457	攻防 *kōbō* offense and defense	513
		攻守 *kōshu* offense and defense	490
攻		攻城 *kōjō* siege	720
		専攻 *senkō* one's major (study)	600

	820	KŌ, [KU], *kurenai,* deep red; *beni,* rouge, lipstick	
紅	120 3500	紅葉　　*kōyō, momiji* red (autumn) leaves; maple tree 紅茶　　*kōcha*　black tea 紅白　　*kōhaku*　red and white 真紅　　*shinku*　crimson, scarlet 口紅　　*kuchibeni*　lipstick	253 251 205 422 54
	821	KŌ, *e,* inlet, bay	
江	85 2491	江湖　　*kōko*　the public, world 入り江　*irie*　inlet, small bay 江ノ島　*Enoshima*　(island near Kamakura) 江戸　　*Edo*　(old name for Tokyo) 江戸っ子　*Edokko*　true Tokyoite	467 52 286 152 152, 103
	822	GEN, [GON], *kibi(shii),* severe, strict, rigorous, intense; *ogoso(ka),* solemn, grave, stately	
厳	4 253	厳重　　*genjū*　strict, stringent, rigid 厳格　　*genkaku*　strict, stern, severe 厳禁　　*genkin*　strict prohibition 尊厳　　*songen*　dignity	227 643 482 704
	823	KŌ, navigation, sailing	
航	137 3867	航空便　*kōkūbin*　airmail 航空券　*kōkūken*　flight/airplane ticket 航路　　*kōro*　sea route, course 航海　　*kōkai*　sea voyage/navigation 巡航　　*junkō*　a cruise	140, 330 140, 506 151 117 777
	824	KŌ, resist	
抗	64 1852	対抗　　*taikō*　opposition, confrontation 抵抗　　*teikō*　resistance 反抗　　*hankō*　resistance, opposition 抗議　　*kōgi*　protest 抗争　　*kōsō*　contention, dispute	365 560 324 292 302
	825	KO, [KU], storehouse	
庫	53 1512	車庫　　*shako*　garage 金庫　　*kinko*　a safe 国庫　　*Kokko*　the (National) Treasury 文庫本　*bunkobon*　small cheap paperback 在庫品　*zaikohin*　goods in stock, inventory	133 23 40 111, 25 268, 230
	826	SHŌ, *toko,* bed; floor; *yuka,* floor	
床	53 1503	起床　　*kishō*　rise, get up (from bed) 病床　　*byōshō*　sickbed 温床　　*onshō*　hotbed, breeding ground 床屋　　*tokoya*　barber, barbershop 床の間　*tokonoma*　alcove in Japanese-style room	373 380 634 167 43

	827	Ō, reply, respond; comply with; fulfill, satisfy	
応	53	反 応 *hannō* reaction	324
	1504	順 応 *junnō* adaptation, adjustment	769
		相 応 *sōō* correspond, be suitable	146
		応 用 *ōyō* (practical) application	107
応		応 接 間 *ōsetsuma* reception room	486, 43

	828	JŪ, fill; a(*teru*), allot, allocate, apply (to)	
充	8	充 分 *jūbun* enough, sufficient (cf. No. 38)	38
	289	充 満 *jūman* fullness, abundance	201
		充 足 *jūsoku* sufficiency	58
		充 実 *jūjitsu* repletion, perfection	203
充		充 血 した 目 *jūketsu shita me* bloodshot eyes	789, 55

	829	JŪ, gun	
銃	167	銃 器 *jūki* firearm	527
	4854	小 銃 *shōjū* rifle	27
		短 銃 *tanjū* pistol, revolver	215
		機 関 銃 *kikanjū* machine gun	528, 398
銃		銃 殺 *jūsatsu* shoot dead	576

	830	TŌ, su(*beru*), govern, control	
統	120	統 制 *tōsei* control, regulation	427
	3536	統 治 *tōchi, tōji* reign, rule	493
		統 一 *tōitsu* unity, unification	2
		統 計 *tōkei* statistics	340
統		伝 統 *dentō* tradition	434

	831	REI, order, command	
令	9	命 令 *meirei* an order	578
	360	号 令 *gōrei* an order, command	266
		訓 令 *kunrei* instructions, directive	771
		政 令 *seirei* cabinet order, government ordinance	483
令		発 令 *hatsurei* official announcement	96

	832	REI, tsume(*tai*), cold; hi(*yasu*), sa(*masu*), chill, cool; hi(*eru*), sa(*meru*), become cold; hi(*ya*), cold water; cold sakè; hi-(*yakasu*), poke fun at, tease; browse	
冷	15		
	642		
		冷 水 *reisui* cold water	21
		冷 戦 *reisen* cold war	301
冷		冷 静 *reisei* calm, cool, dispassionate	663

	833	REI, age	
齢	211	年 齢 *nenrei* age	45
	5431	学 齢 *gakurei* (of) school age	109
		老 齢 *rōrei* old age	543
		高 齢 *kōrei* old/advanced age	190
齢		月 齢 *getsurei* phase of the moon; age in months	17

	834	RYŌ, govern, rule	
領	181	領土/地 *ryōdo/chi* territory	24, 118
	5124	大統領 *daitōryō* president	26, 830
		領事 *ryōji* consul	80
領		領収書/証 *ryōshū-sho/shō* receipt	757, 131, 484
		横領 *ōryō* usurpation, embezzlement	781

	835	SHIN, JIN, retainer, subject	
臣	131	大臣 *daijin* (government) minister	26
	3837	総理大臣 *sōri daijin* prime minister	697, 143, 26
		臣民 *shinmin* subject	177
臣		臣下 *shinka* subject, retainer ⌈ruled	31
		君臣 *kunshin* sovereign and subject, ruler and	793

	836	RIN, *nozo(mu)*, face, confront; attend, assist at	
臨	131	臨時 *rinji* temporary, provisional, extraordinary	42
	3840	臨床 *rinshō* clinical	826
		臨終 *rinjū* one's last moments/deathbed	458
臨		臨席 *rinseki* attendance, presence	379
		君臨 *kunrin* reign, rule	793

	837	KAKU, tower, palace; the cabinet	
閣	169	内閣 *naikaku* the cabinet	84
	4957	閣議 *kakugi* meeting of the cabinet	292
		組閣 *sokaku* formation of a cabinet	418
閣		閣下 *kakka* Your/His Excellency	31
		金閣寺 *Kinkakuji* Temple of the Golden Pavilion	23, 41

	838	GAKU, amount; framed picture; *hitai*, forehead	
額	181	金額 *kingaku* amount of money	23
	5136	額面 *gakumen* face value, par	274
		総額 *sōgaku* total amount, sum total	697
額		差額 *sagaku* the difference, balance	658
		半額 *hangaku* half the amount/price	88

	839	RAKU, *o(chiru)*, fall; *o(tosu)*, drop; lose	
落	140	転落 *tenraku* a fall	433
	4003	落第 *rakudai* failure in an examination	404
		部落 *buraku* village, settlement	86
落		落語 *rakugo* Japanese comic storytelling	67
		落ち着いた *ochitsuita* calm, composed	657

	840	RAKU, *kara(mu/maru)*, get entangled	
絡	120	連絡 *renraku* contact, liaison, communication	440
	3533	連絡駅 *renraku-eki* connecting station, junction	440, 284
		連絡線 *renraku-sen* connecting line	440, 299
絡		絡み付く *karamitsuku* coil around, cling to	192
		絡み合う *karamiau* intertwine	159

	841	RYAKU, abbreviation, omission	
略	102	省略 *shōryaku* omission, abridgment, abbreviation	145
	3007	略語 *ryakugo* abbreviation	67
		略歴 *ryakureki* brief personal history	480
		計略 *keiryaku* plan, strategem, scheme	340
略		戦略 *senryaku* strategy	301

	842	SHI, administer, conduct	
司	30	司法 *shihō* administration of justice, judicial	123
	877	司令 *shirei* commandant, commanding officer	831
		司会者 *shikaisha* master of ceremonies, chair-	158, 164
		司書 *shisho* librarian ⌐man	131
司		上司 *jōshi* one's superior (officer)	32

	843	SHI, words	
詞	149	品詞 *hinshi* part of speech	230
	4335	名詞 *meishi* noun	82
		(他)動詞 *(ta)dōshi* (transitive) verb	120, 231
		歌詞 *kashi* lyrics, words to a song	392
詞		賀詞 *gashi* congratulations, greetings	756

	844	SHŌ, resemble	
肖	42	肖像画 *shōzōga* portrait	740, 343
	1360	不肖 *fushō* unlike/unworthy of one's father;	
		(humble) I	94
肖			

	845	SHŌ, *ke(su)*, extinguish; *ki(eru)*, go out; disappear	
消	85	消防(車) *shōbō(sha)* fire fighting (engine)	513, 133
	2574	消火器 *shōkaki* fire extinguisher	20, 527
		消費者 *shōhisha* consumer	749, 164
		消化 *shōka* digestion	254
消		消極的 *shōkyokuteki* negative, passive	336, 210

	846	TAI, *shirizo(ku)*, retreat; *shirizo(keru)*, drive away, repel	
退	162	退職 *taishoku* retirement, resignation	385
	4684	退院 *taiin* leave/be discharged from the hospital	614
		退学 *taigaku* leave/drop out of school	109
		引退 *intai* retire (from public life)	216
退		進退 *shintai* advance or retreat, movement	437

	847	GEN, *kagi(ru)*, limit	
限	170	無限 *mugen* unlimited, infinite	93
	4987	制限 *seigen* restriction, limitation	427
		限度 *gendo* a limit	377
		期限 *kigen* term, time limit, deadline	449
限		権限 *kengen* authority, competence, jurisdiction	335

	848	GAN, [GEN], *manako*, eye	
眼	109	両眼 *ryōgan* both eyes	200
	3140	近眼 *kingan* nearsightedness, shortsightedness	445
		眼科医 *gankai* eye doctor, ophthalmologist	320, 220
眼		眼識 *ganshiki* discernment, insight	681
		千里眼 *senrigan* clairvoyance, clairvoyant	15, 142

	849	MIN, *nemu(ru)*, sleep; *nemu(i)*, tired, sleepy	
眠	109	不眠 *fumin* sleeplessness, insomnia	94
	3132	安眠 *anmin* a quiet/sound sleep	105
		冬眠 *tōmin* hibernation	459
眠		居眠り *inemuri* a doze, falling asleep in one's seat	171
		眠り薬 *nemurigusuri* sleeping drug/pills	359

	850	KYŌ, circumstances, situation	
況	85	状/情況 *jōkyō* conditions, situation	626, 209
	2516	現況 *genkyō* present situation	298
		実況 *jikkyō* actual state of affairs	203
況		市況 *shikyō* market conditions, the market	181
		不況 *fukyō* recession, economic slump	94

	851	SHUKU, [SHŪ], *iwa(u)*, celebrate, congratulate	
祝	113	祝辞 *shukuji* (speech of) congratulations	688
	3244	祝電 *shukuden* telegram of congratulations	108
		祝賀 *shukuga* celebration; congratulations	756
祝		祝日 *shukujitsu* festival day, holiday	5
		祝儀 *shūgi* (wedding) celebration; gift	727

	852	KYŌ, KEI, *kiso(u)*, compete, vie for; *se(ru)*, compete, vie; bid for	
競	117		
	3364	競争 *kyōsō* competition	302
		競走 *kyōsō* race	429
		競売 *kyōbai* auction	239
競		競馬 *keiba* horse racing	283

	853	KEI, view, scene	
景	72	景色 *keshiki* scenery	204
	2142	風景 *fūkei* scenery	29
		景勝(地) *keishō(chi)* (place of) picturesque sce-「nery	509, 118
景		景気 *keiki* business conditions	134
		不景気 *fukeiki* hard times, recession	94, 134

	854	EI, *kage*, light; shadow, silhouette; figure; trace	
影	59	影像 *eizō* image, shadow	740
	1594	人影 *hitokage, jin'ei* silhouette, human figure	1
		影法師 *kagebōshi* person's shadow	123, 409
影		影絵 *kagee* shadow picture, silhouette	345
		面影 *omokage* face, traces, vestiges	274

	855	KYŌ, village, native place; GŌ, rural area, country	
郷	163 4766	故 郷 *kokyō* one's hometown, native place	173
		郷 里 *kyōri* one's hometown, native place	142
		郷 土 *kyōdo* one's hometown ⌈gia	24
郷		望 郷 の 念 *bōkyō no nen* homesickness, nostal-	673, 579
		近 郷 *kingō* neighboring districts	445

	856	KYŌ, *hibi(ku)*, sound, resound, be echoed; affect	
響	180 5114	影 響 *eikyō* effect, influence	854
		反 響 *hankyō* echo, response	324
		音 響 *onkyō* sound	347
響		交 響 曲/楽 *kōkyō-kyoku/gaku* symphony	114, 366, 358
		響 き 渡 る *hibikiwataru* resound, reverberate	378

	857	SHŌ, chapter; badge, mark	
章	180 5112	文 章 *bunshō* composition, writing	111
		第 三 章 *daisanshō* Chapter 3	404, 4
		第 三 楽 章 *daisan gakushō* third movement	404, 4, 358
章		憲 章 *kenshō* charter, constitution	521
		記 章 *kishō* medal, badge	371

	858	SHŌ, *sawa(ru)*, hinder, interfere with; harm, hurt	
障	170 5019	保 障 *hoshō* guarantee, security	489
		支 障 *shishō* hindrance, impediment	318
		障 害 *shōgai* obstacle, impediment	518
障		故 障 *koshō* trouble, breakdown, out of order	173
		障 子 *shōji* Japanese sliding paper door	103

	859	CHO, *arawa(su)*, write, publish; *ichijiru(shii)*, marked, striking, remarkable, conspicuous	
著	140 3983	著 者 *chosha* author	164
		著 書 *chosho* a (literary) work	131
著		名 著 *meicho* a famous/great work	82
		著 名 *chomei* prominent, well-known	82

	860	SHO, government office, station	
署	122 3642	税 務 署 *zeimusho* tax office	399, 235
		消 防 署 *shōbōsho* fire station, firehouse	845, 513
		警 察 署 *keisatsusho* police station	706, 619
署		部 署 *busho* one's post/place of duty	86
		署 名 *shomei* signature, autograph	82

	861	SHO, all, various	
諸	149 4393	諸 国 *shokoku* all/various countries	40
		諸 島 *shotō* islands	286
		諸 説 *shosetsu* various views/accounts	400
諸		諸 事 *shoji* various matters/affairs	80
		諸 君 *shokun* (Ladies and) Gentlemen!	793

	862	SHO, [CHO], beginning; *o*, cord, strap, thong	
緒	120	緒戦 *shosen, chosen* beginning of a war	301
	3557	緒論 *shoron, choron* introduction	293
		由緒 *yuisho* history; pedigree, lineage	363
		情緒 *jōcho, jōsho* emotion, feeling	209
緒		鼻緒 *hanao* clog thong, geta strap	813

	863	KYŌ, *kagami*, mirror	
鏡	167	鏡台 *kyōdai* dressing table	492
	4912	三面鏡 *sanmenkyō* a dresser with 3 mirrors	4, 274
		望遠鏡 *bōenkyō* telescope	673, 446
		手鏡 *tekagami* hand mirror	57
鏡		眼鏡 *megane, gankyō* eyeglasses	848

	864	KYŌ, [KEI], *sakai*, boundary	
境	32	国境 *kokkyō* border	40
	1135	境界 *kyōkai* boundary, border	454
		苦境 *kukyō* distress, difficulties	545
		境内 *keidai* precincts, grounds	84
境		境目 *sakaime* borderline; crisis	55

	865	KAN, ring, surround	
環	96	環境 *kankyō* environment	864
	2970	環状 *kanjō* ring-shaped, annular	626
		光環 *kōkan* corona	138
環		一環 *ikkan* a link, part	2

	866	KAN, return	
還	162	返還 *henkan* return, restoration; repayment	442
	4750	帰還 *kikan* return home, repatriation	317
		送還 *sōkan* sending home, repatriation	441
還		還元 *kangen* restoration; reduction	137

	867	IN, negative, hidden; shadow, secret; *kage*, shadow; back; *kage(ru)*, get dark/clouded	
陰	170	陰陽 *in'yō* yin and yang, positive and negative	630
	5006	陰性 *insei* negative; dormant, latent	98
		陰気 *inki* gloomy, dismal, melancholy	134
陰		日/木陰 *hi/ko-kage* shade from the sun/of a tree	5, 22

	868	IN, *kaku(reru/su)*, (intr./tr.) hide	
隠	170	隠者 *inja* hermit	164
	5020	隠居 *inkyo* retirement from active life	171
		隠し芸 *kakushigei* parlor trick, hidden talent	435
隠		隠し引き出し *kakushi hikidashi* secret compartment (in a chest)	216, 53

	869	ON, *oda(yaka)*, calm, quiet, mild, peaceful, moderate	
穏	115	穏和 *onwa* mild, gentle, genial	124
	3305	平穏 *heion* calmness, quiet, serenity	202
		平穏無事 *heion-buji* peace and quiet	202, 93, 80
	穏	穏当 *ontō* proper, appropriate; gentle	77
		穏便 *onbin* gentle, quiet, amicable	330

	870	SHI, *eda*, branch	
枝	75	枝葉 *shiyō, edaha* branches and leaves; digression	253
	2211	大枝 *ōeda* bough, limb	26
		小枝 *koeda* twig	27
	枝	枝切り *edakiri* lopping off/pruning of branches	39
		枝接ぎ *edatsugi* grafting	486

	871	GI, *waza*, technique; ability; feat	
技	64	技術 *gijutsu* technique, technology	187
	1853	技師 *gishi* engineer	409
		技能 *ginō* technical skill, ability	386
	技	演技 *engi* acting, performance	344
		競技 *kyōgi* match, contest, competition	852

	872	KI, forked road	
岐	46	分岐 *bunki* divergence, branching	38
	1410	分岐点 *bunkiten* point of divergence, junction	38, 169
	岐	岐路 *kiro* fork in the road, crossroads	151

	873	CHŪ, *mushi*, bug, insect	
虫	142	益/害虫 *eki/gaichū* beneficial/harmful insect	716, 518
	4115	殺虫剤 *satchūzai* insecticide	576, 550
		毛虫 *kemushi* hairy caterpillar	287
	虫	油虫 *aburamushi* cockroach; hanger-on, parasite	364
		虫歯 *mushiba* decayed tooth, cavity	478

	874	SHOKU, *sawa(ru)*, *fu(reru)*, touch	
触	148	触覚 *shokkaku* sense of touch	605
	4305	接触 *sesshoku* touch, contact	486
		感触 *kanshoku* the touch, feel	262
	触	触角 *shokkaku* feeler, antenna, tentacle	473
		抵触 *teishoku* conflict	560

	875	SŌ, *sawa(gu)*, make noise	
騒	187	騒音 *sōon* noise	347
	5221	騒動 *sōdō* disturbance, riot	231
		騒然 *sōzen* noisy, tumultuous	651
	騒	大騒ぎ *ōsawagi* clamor, uproar, hullabaloo	26
		騒ぎ立てる *sawagitateru* raise a great fuss/furor	121

	876	**KAI**, *imashi(meru)*, admonish, warn	
戒	62	警 戒 *keikai* caution, precaution, warning	706
	1801	訓 戒 *kunkai* admonition, warning	771
		厳 戒 *genkai* strict watch/guard	822
		戒 律 *kairitsu* (Buddhist) precepts	667
戒		十 戒 *jikkai* the Ten Commandments	12

	877	**KI**, *iku*, how much/many, some	
幾	52	幾 何 学 *kikagaku* geometry	390, 109
	1496	幾 日 *ikunichi* how many days, what day of the	5
		幾 分 *ikubun* some, a portion ⌐month	38
		幾 つ *ikutsu* how much/many/old	
幾		幾 ら *ikura* how much/long/expensive	

	878	**KEN**, thrifty, simple, modest	
倹	9	倹 約 *ken'yaku* thriftiness, economy	211
	479	節 倹 *sekken* frugality, economy	464
		勤 倹 *kinken* diligence and thrift	559
倹			

	879	**KEN**, *tsurugi*, sword	
剣	18	剣 道 *kendō* Kendo, Japanese fencing	149
	696	刀 剣 *tōken* swords	37
		短 剣 *tanken* short sword, dagger	215
		剣 劇 *kengeki* swordplay/samurai drama	797
剣		真 剣 *shinken* serious, earnest	422

	880	**SAKU**, plan, means, measure, policy	
策	118	政 策 *seisaku* policy	483
	3393	対 策 *taisaku* measure, countermeasure	365
		具体策 *gutaisaku* specific measure	420, 61
		策 略 *sakuryaku* strategem, scheme, tactic	841
策		術 策 *jussaku* artifice, strategem, intrigue	187

	881	**SHI**, *sa(su)*, pierce; *sa(saru)*, stick, get stuck	
刺	18	名 刺 *meishi* name/business card	82
	682	風 刺 *fūshi* satire	29
		刺 し 殺 す *sashikorosu* stab to death	576
		刺 し 傷 *sashikizu* a stab; (insect) bite	633
刺		刺 身 *sashimi* sashimi, sliced raw fish	59

	882	**HAN**, *oka(su)*, commit (a crime), violate, defy	
犯	94	犯 人 *hannin* criminal, culprit	1
	2869	犯 行 *hankō* crime	68
		現 行 犯 で *genkōhan de* in the act, red-handed	298, 68
		共 犯 *kyōhan* complicity	196
犯		防 犯 *bōhan* crime prevention/fighting	513

	883	KYŌ, *kuru(u)*, go crazy; run amuck; get out of order; *kuru(oshii)*, be nearly mad (with worry/grief)	
狂	94 2872 狂	狂言 *kyōgen* play, drama; Noh farce 発狂 *hakkyō* insanity, madness 狂気 *kyōki* insanity, madness 狂乱 *kyōran* frenzy, madness	66 96 134 689

	884	GOKU, prison	
獄	94 2906 獄	地獄 *jigoku* hell ⌈aminations 受験地獄 *juken jigoku* the ordeal of ex- 獄舎 *gokusha* prison, jail (building) 出獄 *shutsugoku* release from prison 獄死 *gokushi* die in prison	118 260, 532, 118 791 53 85

	885	ZAI, *tsumi*, crime, sin, guilt	
罪	122 3643 罪	犯罪 *hanzai* crime 罪人 *zainin* criminal *tsumibito* sinner 有罪 *yūzai* guilty 罪業 *zaigō* sin	882 1 265 279

	886	BATSU, punishment, penalty; BACHI, (divine) punishment	
罰	122 3646 罰	罰金 *bakkin* a fine 体罰 *taibatsu* corporal punishment 厳罰 *genbatsu* severe punishment 天罰 *tenbatsu* punishment from God/heaven 罰当たり *bachiatari* damned, cursed	23 61 822 141 77

	887	KEI, penalty, punishment, sentence	
刑	18 670 刑	刑事 *keiji* criminal case; (police) detective 刑法 *keihō* criminal law, the Criminal Code 刑罰 *keibatsu* punishment, penalty 死刑 *shikei* capital punishment 刑務所 *keimusho* prison	80 123 886 85 235, 153

	888	KEI, *kata*, model, form	
型	32 1077 型	類型的 *ruikeiteki* stereotyped; typical 原型 *genkei* prototype, model 紙型 *kamigata, shikei* papier-mâché mold 血液型 *ketsuekigata* blood type 大型トラック *ōgata torakku* large truck	226, 210 136 180 789, 472 26

	889	HO, *ogina(u)*, supply, make up for, compensate for	
補	145 4242 補	補給 *hokyū* supply, replenishment 補正 *hosei* revision, compensation 補助 *hojo* assistance, supplement, subsidy 補充 *hojū* supplement, replacement ⌈cation 補習教育 *hoshū kyōiku* continuing edu-	346 275 623 828 591, 245, 246

	890 64 1919 捕	**HO**, *to(ru/raeru)*, *tsuka(maeru)*, catch, grasp; *to(rawareru)*, *tsuka(maru)*, be caught; hold on to
		捕鯨 *hogei* whaling 700
		捕鯨船 *hogeisen* whaling ship 700, 376
		だ捕 *daho* capture, seize
		生け捕り *ikedori* capturing alive 44

	891 162 4706 逮	**TAI**, chase
		逮捕 *taiho* arrest 890
		逮捕状 *taihojō* arrest warrant 890, 626
		逮夜 *taiya* eve of the anniversary of a death 471

	892 54 1549 建	**KEN**, [**KON**], *ta(teru)*, build; *ta(tsu)*, be built
		建設 *kensetsu* construction 577
		建立 *konryū* erection, building 121
		建物 *tatemono* a building 79
		二階建て *nikaidate* 2-story 3, 588
		建て前 *tatemae* erection of the framework; principle 47

	893 9 512 健	**KEN**, *suko(yaka)*, healthy
		保健 *hoken* preservation of health, hygiene 489
		穏健 *onken* moderate, sound 869
		強健 *kyōken* robust health, strong physique 217
		健在 *kenzai* healthy, sound 268
		健勝 *kenshō* healthy 509

	894 53 1518 康	**KŌ**, peace, composure
		健康 *kenkō* health 893
		不健康 *fukenkō* not healthy, unhealthful 94, 893
		小康 *shōkō* lull, brief respite 27

	895 116 3314 究	**KYŪ**, *kiwa(meru)*, investigate thoroughly/exhaustively
		究明 *kyūmei* study, investigation, inquiry 18
		探究 *tankyū* research, investigation 535
		学究 *gakkyū* scholar, student 109
		究極 *kyūkyoku* final, ultimate 336
		論究 *ronkyū* discuss thoroughly 293

	896 112 3180 研	**KEN**, *to(gu)*, whet, hone, sharpen; polish; wash (rice)
		研究 *kenkyū* research 895
		研究所 *kenkyūjo* research institute 895, 153
		研学 *kengaku* study 109

	897	KYŪ, *kiwa(maru)*, reach an extreme; come to an end; *kiwa-(meru)*, carry to extremes; bring to an end
窮	116 3337	窮極目的 *kyūkyoku mokuteki* ultimate goal 336, 55, 210
		窮地/境 *kyūchi/kyō* predicament 118, 864
窮		窮乏 *kyūbō* poverty 754
		困窮 *konkyū* poverty 558

	898	TOTSU, *tsu(ku)*, thrust, poke, strike
突	116 3316	突然 *totsuzen* suddenly 651
		突破 *toppa* break through, overcome 665
		突入 *totsunyū* rush in, storm 52
突		突き当たる *tsukiataru* run/bump into; reach the end 77
		羽根突き *hanetsuki* Japanese badminton 590, 314

	899	KETSU, *ana*, hole; cave
穴	116 3313	穴居人 *kekkyojin* caveman 171, 1
		落とし穴 *otoshiana* pitfall, trap 839
		穴あけ器 *ana akeki* punch, perforator 527
穴		送り穴 *okuriana* (film) perforations, sprocket holes 441
		穴子 *anago* conger eel 103

	900	SHA, *i(ru)*, shoot
射	158 4603	発射 *hassha* fire, launch 96
		射殺 *shasatsu* shoot dead 576
		注射 *chūsha* injection, shot 357
射		放射能 *hōshanō* radioactivity 512, 386
		反射 *hansha* reflection; reflex 324

	901	SHA, gratitude; apology; *ayama(ru)*, apologize
謝	149 4423	感謝 *kansha* gratitude 262
		謝礼 *sharei* remuneration, honorarium 620
		月謝 *gessha* monthly tuition 17
謝		謝罪 *shazai* apology 885
		代謝 *taisha* metabolism (cf. No. 1405) 256

	902	SHI, utmost; *ita(ru)*, arrive, lead to
至	133 3845	必至 *hisshi* inevitable 520
		至急 *shikyū* urgency, urgent 303
		夏至 *geshi* summer solstice 461
至		至る所 *itaru tokoro* everywhere 「map] 153
		至東京 *itaru Tōkyō* To Tokyo (at the edge of a 71, 189

	903	CHI, *ita(su)*, do (deferential, used like *suru*); bring about
致	133 3847	一致 *itchi* agreement, consistency 2
		合致 *gatchi* agreement, consistency 159
		致命傷 *chimeishō* fatal wound 578, 633
致		致死量 *chishiryō* lethal dose 85, 411
		風致地区 *fūchi chiku* scenic area 29, 118, 183

	904	TŌ, arrive, reach	
到	133 3846	到着　tōchaku　arrival	657
		到来　tōrai　arrival, advent	69
		到達　tōtatsu　reach, attain	448
到		殺到　sattō　rush, stampede	576
		周到　shūtō　meticulous	91

	905	TŌ, tao(reru), fall over, collapse; tao(su), knock down, topple, defeat	
倒	9 487	卒倒　sottō　faint	787
		倒産　tōsan　bankruptcy	278
		倒閣　tōkaku　overthrowing the cabinet	837
倒		共倒れ　tomodaore　mutual destruction, common ruin	196

	906	GO, ayama(ru), err, make a mistake	
誤	149 4372	誤解　gokai　misunderstanding	474
		誤報　gohō　erroneous report/information	685
		誤算　gosan　miscalculation	747
誤		誤植　goshoku　a misprint	424
		読み誤る　yomiayamaru　misread	244

	907	GO, taga(i), mutual, reciprocal, each other	
互	1 14	相互　sōgo　mutual	146
		交互　kōgo　mutual; alternating	114
		互助　gojo　mutual aid	623
互		互選　gosen　mutual election	800
		互い違いに　tagaichigai ni　alternately	814

	908	KEI, system; lineage, group	
系	4 195	体系　taikei　system	61
		系統　keitō　system; lineage, descent	830
		日系　nikkei　of Japanese descent	5
系		直系　chokkei　direct descent	423
		系図　keizu　genealogy, family tree	339

	909	KEI, kaka(ru), relate to, concern; kakari, charge, duty; person in charge, clerk	
係	9 449	関係　kankei　relation, relationship, connection	398
		連係　renkei　connection, link, contact	440
		係争　keisō　dispute, contention	302
係		係員　kakariin　clerk in charge, attendant	163

	910	SON, mago, grandchild	
孫	39 1273	子孫　shison　descendant	103
		皇孫　kōson　imperial grandchild/descendant	297
		天孫　tenson　of divine descent	141
孫		そう孫　sōson　great-grandchild	
		ひ孫　himago　great-grandchild	

	911	**KEN, [KE],** *ka(karu)*, hang; *ka(keru)*, offer, give	
懸	61	一生懸命 *isshōkenmei* utmost effort, all 2, 44, 578	
	1790	懸案 *ken'an* unsettled problem ⌊one's might 106	
		懸賞 *kenshō* offer of a prize 500	
懸		懸念 *kenen* fear, apprehension 579	
		命懸け *inochigake* risking one's life 578	

	912	**HA,** group, faction, sect, school (of thought)	
派	85	宗派 *shūha* sect 616	
	2547	党派 *tōha* party, faction 495	
		左/右派 *sa/uha* the left/right wing 75, 76	
派		派出所 *hashutsujo* branch office; police box 53, 153	
		特派員 *tokuhain* correspondent 282, 163	

	913	**MYAKU,** pulse, vein, blood vessel	
脈	130	動脈 *dōmyaku* artery 231	
	3764	静脈 *jōmyaku* vein 663	
		山脈 *sanmyaku* mountain range 34	
脈		文脈 *bunmyaku* context 111	
		脈絡 *myakuraku* logical connection, coherence 840	

	914	**KAN,** *tsuranu(ku)*, pierce; carry out	
貫	80	一貫 *ikkan* consistency, coherence, integrated 2	
	2469	貫通 *kantsū* pass through, pierce 150	
		貫流 *kanryū* flow through 247	
貫		突貫 *tokkan* rush, storm 898	
		貫き通す *tsuranukitōsu* carry out (one's will) 150	

	915	**KAN,** *na(reru)*, get used (to); *na(rasu)*, make used (to); tame	
慣	61	習慣 *shūkan* custom, practice 591	
	1756	慣習 *kanshū* custom, practice 591	
		慣例 *kanrei* custom, convention 612	
慣		見慣れる *minareru* get used to seeing 63	

	916	**FUKU,** double, multiple, composite, again	
複	145	複雑 *fukuzatsu* complicated 575	
	4255	複合 *fukugō* composition, compound, complex 159	
		重複 *chōfuku, jūfuku* duplication, overlapping 227	
複		複製 *fukusei* reproduction, duplicate, facsimile 428	
		複数 *fukusū* plural 225	

	917	**FUKU,** return, be restored	
復	60	復習 *fukushū* review 591	
	1627	反復 *hanpuku* repetition 324	
		復活 *fukkatsu* revival 237	
復		復興 *fukkō* reconstruction, revival 368	
		回復 *kaifuku* recovery, recuperation 90	

	918	**Ō, go**	
往	60 1605 往	往復 *ōfuku* round trip 往来 *ōrai* comings and goings, traffic 立ち往生 *tachiōjō* standstill, getting stalled 右往左往 *uōsaō* rush about in confusion 往年 *ōnen* the past, formerly	917 69 121, 44 76, 75 45
	919	**EN, kemuri, smoke; kemu(ru), smoke, smolder; kemu(i), smoky**	
煙	86 2784 煙	禁煙 *kin'en* No Smoking 煙突 *entotsu* chimney 発煙 *hatsuen* emitting smoke, fuming 黒煙 *kokuen* black smoke	482 898 96 206
	920	**SHŌ, ya(keru), (intr.) burn; be roasted, broiled, baked; ya(ku), (tr.) burn; roast, broil, bake**	
焼	86 2772 焼	全焼 *zenshō* be totally destroyed by fire 焼(き)鳥 *yakitori* grilled chicken 日焼け *hiyake* sunburn, suntan 夕焼け *yūyake* glow of sunset	89 285 5 81
	921	**SEN, move, change; climb**	
遷	162 4743 遷	変遷 *hensen* undergo changes 左遷 *sasen* demotion 遷都 *sento* transfer of the capital	257 75 188
	922	**HYŌ, slip of paper, ballot, vote**	
票	146 4276 票	一票 *ippyō* a vote 得票 *tokuhyō* votes obtained 反対票 *hantaihyō* no vote 開票 *kaihyō* vote counting 伝票 *denpyō* slip of paper	2 374 324, 365 396 434
	923	**HYŌ, sign, mark**	
標	75 2359 標	目標 *mokuhyō* goal, purpose 標語 *hyōgo* slogan, motto 標準語 *hyōjungo* the standard language 標本 *hyōhon* specimen, sample 商標 *shōhyō* trademark	55 67 778, 67 25 412
	924	**HYŌ, tadayo(u), drift about, float**	
漂	85 2678 漂	漂流 *hyōryū* drift, be adrift 漂着 *hyōchaku* drift ashore 漂白剤 *hyōhakuzai* bleach 漂然 *hyōzen* aimless; sudden, unexpected 漂々 *hyōhyō* light, buoyant	247 657 205, 550 651

	925 30 983 鳴	MEI, *na(ku)*, (animals) cry, sing, howl; *na(ru/rasu)*, (intr./tr.) sound, ring	
鳴		共 鳴　*kyōmei*　resonance; sympathy	196
		鳴 動　*meidō*　rumble	231
		鳴 き 声　*nakigoe*　cry, call, chirping (of animals)	746
		海 鳴 り　*uminari*　rumbling/noise of the sea	117

	926 196 5359 鶏	KEI, *niwatori*, chicken, hen, rooster	
鶏		鶏 肉　*keiniku*　chicken, fowl	223
		養 鶏　*yōkei*　poultry raising	402
		鶏 舎　*keisha*　chicken coop, henhouse	791
		鶏 鳴　*keimei*　cockcrow	925
		鶏 頭　*keitō*　cockscomb (flower)	276

	927 30 922 咲	*sa(ku)*, bloom	
咲		咲 き 出 す　*sakidasu*　begin to bloom	53
		咲 き 乱 れ る　*sakimidareru*　bloom in profusion	689
		遅 咲 き　*osozaki*　blooming late	702
		狂 い 咲 き　*kuruizaki*　flowering out of season	883
		返 り 咲 き　*kaerizaki*　second bloom; comeback	442

	928 75 2256 桜	Ō, *sakura*, cherry tree	
桜		桜 花　*ōka*　cherry blossoms	255
		八 重 桜　*yaezakura*　double-petal cherry blossoms	10, 227
		桜 ん ぼ　*sakuranbo*　cherry	
		桜 色　*sakurairo*　pink, cerise	204
		桜 肉　*sakuraniku*　horsemeat	223

	929 38 1215 姿	SHI, *sugata*, form, figure, shape, appearance, posture	
姿		姿 勢　*shisei*　posture, stance	646
		容 姿　*yōshi*　face and figure, appearance	654
		姿 態　*shitai*　figure, pose	387
		姿 見　*sugatami*　full-length mirror	63
		後 ろ 姿　*ushirosugata*　view (of someone) from behind	48

	930 87 2823 妥	DA, peace, contentment	
妥		妥 協　*dakyō*　compromise	234
		妥 結　*daketsu*　compromise, agreement	485
		妥 当　*datō*　proper, appropriate, adequate	77
		妥 協 案　*dakyōan*　compromise plan	234, 106

	931 140 3982 菜	SAI, *na*, vegetable; rape, mustard plant	
菜		野 菜　*yasai*　vegetable	236
		菜 園　*saien*　vegetable garden	447
		菜 食　*saishoku*　vegetarian/herbivorous diet	322
		山 菜　*sansai*　edible wild plant	34
		菜 種　*natane*　rapeseed, coleseed, colza	228

彩	**932**	**SAI**, *irodo(ru)*, color
	59 1590	色 彩　*shikisai*　color, coloration　204 彩 色　*saishiki*　coloring, coloration　204 多 彩　*tasai*　colorful　229 光 彩　*kōsai*　luster, brilliancy　138 水 彩 画　*suisaiga*　a watercolor painting　21, 343

採	**933**	**SAI**, *to(ru)*, take (on), accept, employ; collect
	64 1947	採 用　*saiyō*　adopt; employ　107 採 決　*saiketsu*　voting　356 採 集　*saishū*　collecting (plants/butterflies)　436 採 録　*sairoku*　record (in a book)　538 採 算　*saisan*　a profit　747

就	**934**	**SHŪ**, [**JU**], *tsu(ku)*, take (a seat); engage (in an occupation); *tsu(keru)*, employ
	8 323	就 職　*shūshoku*　find employment　385 就 任　*shūnin*　assumption of office　334 就 業 時 間　*shūgyō jikan*　working hours　279, 42, 43 成 就　*jōju*　accomplish, attain　261

没	**935**	**BOTSU**, sink, go down
	85 2506	没 落　*botsuraku*　downfall, ruin　839 没 入　*botsunyū*　become immersed (in)　52 出 没　*shutsubotsu*　appear and disappear, frequent　53 没 収　*bosshū*　confiscation, forfeiture　757 没 交 渉　*bokkōshō*　unrelated, independent　114, 432

沈	**936**	**CHIN**, *shizu(mu/meru)*, (intr./tr.) sink
	85 2508	沈 没　*chinbotsu*　sinking　935 沈 下　*chinka*　sinking, subsidence, settling　31 沈 静　*chinsei*　stillness, stagnation　663 沈 着　*chinchaku*　composed, calm　657 沈 思　*chinshi*　meditation, contemplation　99

潜	**937**	**SEN**, dive, hide; *mogu(ru)*, dive; crawl into; *hiso(mu)*, lurk, lie hidden
	85 2703	潜 水　*sensui*　dive, submerge　21 潜 水 夫　*sensuifu*　diver　21, 315 潜 在　*senzai*　hidden, latent, potential　268 潜 入　*sennyū*　infiltrate (into)　52

浮	**938**	**FU**, *u(kabu)*, float, rise to the surface; *u(kaberu)*, set afloat; show; *u(ku)*, float, rise to the surface; *u(kareru)*, feel buoyant, be in high spirits
	85 2575	思 い 浮 ぶ　*omoiukabu*　come to mind, occur to　99 浮 か ぬ 顔　*ukanukao*　dejected look　277 浮 世 絵　*ukiyoe*　Japanese woodblock print　252, 345

乳	939 5 266 乳	NYŪ, *chichi, chi*, mother's milk, breast
		牛 乳　*gyūnyū*　(cow's) milk　　　　　　281
		母 乳　*bonyū*　mother's milk　　　　　　112
		乳 がん　*nyūgan*　breast cancer
		乳 首　*chikubi, chichikubi*　nipple　　　148
		乳 母 車　*ubaguruma*　baby carriage　112, 133

孔	940 39 1265 孔	KŌ, hole; Confucius
		気 孔　*kikō*　pore　　　　　　　　　　134
		通/空 気 孔　*tsū/kū-kikō*　air hole　150, 140, 134
		鼻 孔　*bikō*　nostril　　　　　　　　　813
		多 孔　*takō*　porous　　　　　　　　　229
		孔 子　*Kōshi*　Confucius　　　　　　　103

了	941 6 268 了	RYŌ, finish, complete; understand
		終 了　*shūryō*　end, completion, expiration　458
		完 了　*kanryō*　completion; perfect tense　613
		(任 期) 満 了　*(ninki)manryō*　expiration (of a　334, 449, 201
		校 了　*kōryō*　final proofreading　⌊term of office)　115
		了 解　*ryōkai*　understanding; Roger! (on a radio)　474

承	942 4 197 承	SHŌ, *uketamawa(ru)*, hear, be told
		承 知　*shōchi*　consent; be aware of　　214
		承 認　*shōnin*　approval　　　　　　　738
		承 服　*shōfuku*　consent, acceptance　　683
		了 承　*ryōshō*　acknowledgment　⌈generation)　941
		伝 承　*denshō*　hand down (from generation to　434

蒸	943 140 4002 蒸	JŌ, *mu(su)*, steam; be sultry; *mu(rasu)*, steam; *mu(reru)*, be steamed; get hot and stuffy
		(水) 蒸 気　*(sui)jōki*　(water) vapor, steam　21, 134
		蒸 発　*jōhatsu*　evaporate; disappear into thin air　96
		蒸 し 暑 い　*mushiatsui*　hot and humid, sultry　638
		蒸 し 返 す　*mushikaesu*　reheat; repeat, rehash　442

候	944 9 481 候	KŌ, season; weather; *sōrō*, (classical verb suffix)
		天 候　*tenkō*　weather　　　　　　　　141
		気 候　*kikō*　climate　　　　　　　　　134
		測 候 所　*sokkōjo*　meteorological station　610, 153
		候 補 者　*kōhosha*　candidate　　　　889, 164
		居 候　*isōrō*　hanger-on, parasite　　　171

修	945 9 491 修	SHŪ, [SHU], *osa(meru)*, study, master; *osa(maru)*, govern oneself
		修 理　*shūri*　repair　　　　　　　　　143
		修 業　*shūgyō*　pursuit/completion of one's studies　279
		修 正　*shūsei*　revise, correct, retouch　275
		修 行　*shugyō*　training, study　　　　　68

	946	RYŪ, prosperity; high	
隆	170 4999	隆盛 *ryūsei* prosperity	719
		興隆 *kōryū* rise, prosperity, flourishing	368
		隆起 *ryūki* protuberance, rise, elevation	373
	隆	隆々 *ryūryū* prosperous, thriving; muscular	
		法隆寺 *Hōryūji* (temple in Nara)	123, 41

	947	KŌ, *o(riru)*, go down, descend, get off (a bus); *o(rosu)*, let off (a passenger), dismiss; *fu(ru)*, fall (rain/snow)	
降	170 4994	降雨量 *kōryō* (amount of) rainfall	30, 411
		降下 *kōka* descent, fall, landing	31
	降	以降 *ikō* since, from . . . on	46
		飛び降りる *tobioriru* jump down (from)	530

	948	SŌ, *shimo*, frost	
霜	173 5064	霜害 *sōgai* frost damage	518
		霜柱 *shimobashira* ice/frost columns	598
		霜解け *shimodoke* thawing	474
	霜	霜焼け *shimoyake* frostbite ⌜pattern	920
		霜降り *shimofuri* marbled (meat), salt-and-pepper	947

	949	SETSU, *yuki*, snow	
雪	173 5044	雪害 *setsugai* damage from snow	518
		新雪 *shinsetsu* new-fallen snow	174
		初雪 *hatsuyuki* first snow of the year/winter	679
	雪	大雪 *ōyuki* heavy snowfall	26
		雪合戦 *yukigassen* snowball fight	159, 301

	950	MU, *kiri*, fog	
霧	173 5065	五里霧中 *gori-muchū* in a fog, mystified	7, 142, 28
		霧雨 *kirisame* misty rain, drizzle	30
		朝霧 *asagiri* morning mist/fog	469
	霧	夕霧 *yūgiri* evening mist/fog	81
		黒い霧 *kuroi kiri* dark machinations	206

	951	RO, [RŌ], open, public; *tsuyu*, dew	
露	173 5069	露天で *roten de* outdoors, in the open air	141
		露店 *roten* street stall, booth	168
		露出 *roshutsu* (indecent/film) exposure	53
	露	露見 *roken* discovery, detection, exposure	63
		朝露 *asatsuyu* morning dew	469

	952	RAI, *kaminari*, thunder	
雷	173 5049	雷鳴 *raimei* thunder	925
		落雷 *rakurai* thunderbolt, bolt of lightning	839
		雷雨 *raiu* thunderstorm	30
	雷	地雷 *jirai* (land) mine	118
		魚雷 *gyorai* torpedo	290

	953	SHIN, *furu(eru/u)*, tremble, shake	
震	173	地 震 *jishin* earthquake	118
	5055	震 動 *shindō* tremor, vibration	231
		震 度 5 *shindo go* magnitude 5 (on the Japanese	377
		震 央/源 *shin'ō/gen* epicenter ⌊scale of 7)	351, 580
震		身 震 い *miburui* shivering, trembling	59

	954	SHIN, *fu(ruu)*, swing, wield; flourish; *fu(ru)*, wave, shake	
振	64	振 興 *shinkō* advancement, promotion	368
	1920	振 動 *shindō* swing, oscillation, vibration	231
		不 振 *fushin* inactivity, stagnation, slump	94
		振 り 替 え *furikae* transfer	744
振		振 り 返 る *furikaeru* turn one's head, look back	442

	955	NIN, pregnancy	
妊	38	妊 婦 *ninpu* pregnant woman	316
	1197	妊 婦 服 *ninpufuku* maternity dress	316, 683
		不 妊 *funin* sterile, infertile	94
		妊 産 婦 *ninsanpu* expectant and nursing mothers	278, 316
妊			

	956	SHIN, pregnancy	
娠	38	妊 娠 *ninshin* pregnancy	955
	1220	妊 娠 中 絶 *ninshin chūzetsu* abortion	955, 28, 742
娠			

	957	NŌ, *ko(i)*, dark, thick, heavy, strong (coffee)	
濃	85	濃 度 *nōdo* (degree of) concentration	377
	2711	濃 厚 *nōkō* thickness, richness, strength	639
		濃 霧 *nōmu* dense fog	950
濃			

	958	TŌ, [ZU], *mame*, bean, pea; (prefix) miniature	
豆	151	大 豆 *daizu* soybean	26
	4465	小 豆 *azuki* adzuki bean	27
		枝 豆 *edamame* green soybean	870
		コ ー ヒ ー 豆 *kōhīmame* coffee bean	
豆		豆 本 *mamehon* miniature book, pocket edition	25

	959	HŌ, *yuta(ka)*, abundant, rich	
豊	151	豊 富 *hōfu* abundance, wealth	713
	4466	豊 作 *hōsaku* good harvest	360
		豊 漁 *hōryō* good catch (of fish)	699
		豊 年 *hōnen* fruitful year	45
豊		豊 満 *hōman* plump, voluptuous, buxom	201

	960	**TŌ, TO**, *nobo(ru)*, climb	
登	105 3094	登 山 *tozan* mountain climbing	34
		登 場 *tōjō* stage entrance; appearance	154
		登 記 *tōki* registration	371
登		登 録 *tōroku* registration	538
		登 用 *tōyō* appointment; promotion	107

	961	**HAI, *suta(reru/ru)***, become outmoded, go out of fashion, be on the wane	
廃	53 1526	廃 止 *haishi* abolition, abrogation	477
		廃 業 *haigyō* going out of business	279
		退 廃 *taihai* degeneracy, decadence	846
廃		廃 人 *haijin* cripple, invalid	1

	962	**KI**, abandon, throw out, give up	
棄	8 326	廃 棄 物 *haikibutsu* waste (matter)	961, 79
		放 棄 *hōki* give up, renounce, waive	512
		棄 権 *kiken* abstention, nonvoting; renunciation	335
棄		自 棄 *jiki* self-abandonment	62
		破 棄 *haki* destruction; annulment, revocation	665

	963	**TAI**, belt, zone; *obi*, belt, sash; *o(biru)*, wear; be entrusted (with)	
帯	50 1474	包 帯 *hōtai* bandage	804
		地 帯 *chitai* zone, area, region, belt	118
		熱 帯 *nettai* the tropics	645
帯		所 帯 *shotai* household	153

	964	**TAI**, stay, stopping over; *todokō(ru)*, be left undone; fall into arrears, be overdue, be left unpaid	
滞	85 2661	滞 在 *taizai* stay, sojourn	268
		遅 滞 *chitai* delay, procrastination	702
		滞 納 *tainō* delinquency (in payment)	758
滞		沈 滞 *chintai* stagnation, inactivity	936

	965	**JUN**, pure	
純	120 3509	純 毛 *junmō* pure/100 percent wool	287
		純 益 *jun'eki* net profit	716
		純 文 学 *junbungaku* pure literature, belles lettres	111, 109
純		純 日 本 風 *junnihonfū* classical Japanese style	5, 25, 29
		単 純 *tanjun* simple	300

	966	**DON**, *nibu(i)*, dull, thick, slow-witted, sluggish, blunt, dim; *nibu(ru)*, become dull/blunt, weaken	
鈍	167 4830	鈍 感 *donkan* obtuse, thick, insensitive	262
		鈍 重 *donjū* dull-witted, phlegmatic, stolid	227
		鈍 角 *donkaku* obtuse angle	473
鈍		鈍 器 *donki* blunt object (used as a weapon)	527

	967	**MEI**, *mayo(u)*, be perplexed, vacillate; get lost; go astray	
迷	162	迷宮/路 *meikyū/ro* maze, labyrinth	721, 151
	4681	迷信 *meishin* superstition	157
		迷彩 *meisai* camouflage	932
		低迷 *teimei* be low, in a slump (market prices)	561
迷		迷子 *maigo* lost child	103

	968	**JUTSU**, *no(beru)*, state, mention, refer to, explain	
述	162	供述 *kyōjutsu* testimony, deposition	197
	4675	記述 *kijutsu* description	371
		上述 *jōjutsu* above-mentioned	32
		口述 *kōjutsu* oral statement; dictation	54
述		著述家 *chojutsuka* writer, author	859, 165

	969	**WAKU**, *mado(u)*, go astray, be misguided, be tempted	
惑	61	迷惑 *meiwaku* trouble, inconvenience	967
	1710	当惑 *tōwaku* puzzlement, confusion	77
		思惑 *omowaku* opinion, intention, expectation	99
		惑星 *wakusei* planet	730
惑		戸惑い *tomadoi* become disoriented/flurried	152

	970	**IKI**, region, area	
域	32	地域 *chiiki* region, area, zone	118
	1085	区域 *kuiki* boundary, zone, district	183
		領域 *ryōiki* territory, domain	834
		流域 *ryūiki* (river) basin, valley	247
域		聖域 *seiiki* sacred ground	674

	971	**SHŌ**, *tsuguna(u)*, make up for, compensate, indemnify, atone for	
償	9	補償 *hoshō* compensation, indemnification	889
	563	弁償 *benshō* compensation, reimbursement	711
		報償 *hōshō* compensation, remuneration	685
償		無償 *mushō* free of charge, gratis	93

	972	**KO**, *kata(i)*, hard; *kata(maru/meru)*, (intr./tr.) harden	
固	31	固体 *kotai* a solid	61
	1036	固有 *koyū* own, peculiar, characteristic	265
		固定 *kotei* fixed	355
		固執 *koshitsu* hold fast to, persist in, insist on	686
固		強固 *kyōko* firm, solid, strong	217

	973	**KO**, individual; (counter for various objects)	
個	9	個人 *kojin* an individual	1
	489	個体 *kotai* an individual	61
		個性 *kosei* individuality	98
		個別的 *kobetsuteki* individual, separate	267, 210
個		一個 *ikko* 1 piece	2

	974	**KO**, *ka(reru)*, wither; *ka(rasu)*, blight, let wither
枯	75 2238 枯	枯死 *koshi* wither away, die 85 栄枯 *eiko* ups and downs, vicissitudes 723 枯れ木 *kareki* dead/withered tree 22 枯れ葉 *kareha* dead/withered leaf 253 木枯らし *kogarashi* cold winter wind 22
皮	975 107 3109 皮	**HI**, *kawa*, skin, hide, leather, pelt, bark, rind 皮肉 *hiniku* irony 223 皮相 *hisō* superficiality, shallowness 146 毛皮 *kegawa* fur 287 皮細工 *kawazaiku* leatherwork 695, 139 皮切り *kawakiri* beginning, start 39
被	976 145 4225 被	**HI**, *kōmu(ru)*, incur, suffer, receive 被害者 *higaisha* victim 518, 164 被告 (人) *hikoku(nin)* defendant 690, 1 被選挙資格 *hisenkyo shikaku* eligibility 　　　 for election 800, 801, 750, 643 被服 *hifuku* covering, coating 683
彼	977 60 1604 彼	**HI**, he; that; *kare*, he; [*kano*], that 彼岸 *higan* equinoctial week; goal 586 彼ら *karera* they 彼氏 *kareshi* he; boyfriend, lover 566 彼女 *kanojo* she; girlfriend, lover 102
称	978 115 3280 称	**SHŌ**, name, title 名称 *meishō* name, designation 82 愛称 *aishō* term of endearment, pet name 259 尊称 *sonshō* honorific title 704 称号 *shōgō* title, degree 266 相/対 称 *sō/taishō* symmetry 146, 365
飾	979 184 5161 飾	**SHOKU**, *kaza(ru)*, decorate, adorn 修飾 *shūshoku* embellishment; modify (in gram- 飾り付け *kazaritsuke* decoration 　mar) 192 飾り気 *kazarike* affectation, love of display 134 首飾り *kubikazari* necklace, choker 148 着飾る *kikazaru* dress up 657
郎	980 163 4762 郎	**RŌ**, man, husband; (suffix for male given names) 新郎新婦 *shinrō-shinpu* bride and groom 174, 316 郎 等/党 *rōtō/dō* vassals, retainers 569, 495 野郎 *yarō* guy 236 太郎 *Tarō* (male given name) 629 二/次郎 *Jirō* (male given name) 3, 384

	981	RŌ, corridor, hall	
廊	53	廊下　rōka　corridor, hall	31
	1519	回廊　kairō　corridor, gallery	90
		画廊　garō　picture gallery	343
廊			

	982	KŌ, A, No. 1 (in a series); shell, tortoise shell; KAN, high (voice)	
甲	2		
	92	甲鉄　kōtetsu　armor, armor plating	312
		甲状せん　kōjōsen　thyroid gland	626
		甲種　kōshu　Grade A, first class	228
甲		甲高い　kandakai　high-pitched, shrill	190

	983	OTSU, B, No. 2 (in a series); the latter; duplicate; bass (voice); strange; stylish; fine	
乙	5		
	260	甲乙　kō-otsu　A and B; discrimination, gradation	982
		乙女　otome　virgin, maiden	102
乙		乙な味　otsu na aji　delicate flavor	307

	984	HEI, C, No. 3 (in a series)	
丙	1	甲乙丙　kō-otsu-hei　A, B, C; Nos. 1, 2, 3	982, 983
	22	丙午　hinoeuma　(year in the Chinese 60-year cycle; it is said a woman born in such a year [1906, 1966 . . .] will be domineering and will lead her husband to an early grave)	49
丙			

	985	HEI, gara, pattern, design; build; character; e, handle	
柄	75	横柄　ōhei　arrogance	781
	2234	身柄　migara　one's person	59
		人柄　hitogara　character, personality	1
		事柄　kotogara　matters, affairs	80
柄		間柄　aidagara　relation, relationship	43

	986	Ō, o(su), push; o(saeru), restrain, hold in check, suppress	
押	64	押収　ōshū　confiscation	757
	1885	押韻　ōin　rhyme	349
		押し入れ　oshiire　closet, wall-cupboard	52
		後押し　atooshi　push, support, back	48
押		押し付ける　oshitsukeru　press against; force (upon)	192

	987	CHŪ, pull, extract	
抽	64	抽出　chūshutsu　extraction, sampling	53
	1877	抽象　chūshō　abstraction	739
		抽象的　chūshōteki　abstract	739, 210
		抽せん　chūsen　drawing, lottery	
抽		抽せん券　chūsenken　lottery/raffle ticket	506

	988	JIKU, axis, axle, shaft; (picture) scroll	
軸	159	車軸　*shajiku*　axle	133
	4619	地軸　*chijiku*　earth's axis	118
		自転軸 *jitenjiku* axis of rotation	62, 433
軸			

	989	SŌ, *saga(su)*, look/search for	
捜	64	捜査　*sōsa*　investigation ⌜premises	624
	1917	家宅捜査 *kataku sōsa* search of the house/	165, 178, 624
		捜査本部 *sōsa honbu* investigation head-	624, 25, 86
		捜し回る *sagashimawaru* search around for ⌊quarters	90
捜		捜し当てる *sagashiateru* find out, discover, locate	77

	990	U, heaven	
宇	40	宇内　*udai*　the whole world	84
	1280	気宇広大 *kiukōdai* magnanimous	134, 694, 26
		宇都宮 *Utsunomiya* (capital of Tochigi Pre-	
宇		fecture)	188, 721

	991	CHŪ, midair; space, heaven	
宙	40	宇宙　*uchū*　space, the universe	990
	1291	宇宙旅行 *uchū ryokō* space flight	990, 222, 68
		宇宙飛行士 *uchū hikōshi* astronaut	990, 530, 68, 572
		大宇宙 *daiuchū* macrocosm, the universe	26, 990
宙		宙返り *chūgaeri* somersault	442

	992	*todo(ku)*, reach, arrive; *todo(keru)*, report, notify; send, deliver	
届	44		
	1385	欠席届け *kessekitodoke* report of nonattendance	383, 379
		欠勤届け *kekkintodoke* report of absence	383, 559
		届け先 *todokesaki* where to report; receiver's address	50
届		無届け *mutodoke* (absence) without notice	93

	993	TAKU, selection, choice	
択	64	選択　*sentaku*　selection, choice	800
	1845	選択科目 *sentaku kamoku* an elective	
		(subject)	800, 320, 55
		採択　*saitaku*　adoption, selection	933
択		二者択一 *nisha takuitsu* either-or alternative	3, 164, 2

	994	TAKU, *sawa*, swamp, marsh	
沢	85	光沢　*kōtaku*　luster, gloss	138
	2503	ぜい沢 *zeitaku* luxury, extravagance	
		毛沢東 *Mōtakutō* Mao Zedong, Mao Tse-tung	287, 71
沢		金沢　*Kanazawa* (capital of Ishikawa Prefecture)	23

召 18 668 召	**995**	SHŌ, *me(su)*, (honorific) summon; wear; take (a bath/bus)
	召集	*shōshū* convene (the Diet) 436
	応召	*ōshō* be drafted, called up 827
	召し上がる	*meshiagaru* eat, drink, have 32
	お気に召すまま	*O-ki ni Mesu Mama* (As You Like It—Shakespeare) 134

沼 85 2521 沼	**996**	SHŌ, *numa*, swamp, marsh
	沼沢	*shōtaku* marsh, swamp, bog 994
	湖沼	*koshō* lakes and marshes 467
	沼地	*numachi* marshland, swampland 118
	沼田	*numata* marshy rice field 35

昭 72 2114 昭	**997**	SHŌ, bright, clear
	昭和	*Shōwa* (Japanese era, 1926–) 124
	昭和56年	*Shōwa gojūrokunen* 1981 124, 45
	昭和年間	*Shōwa nenkan* the Showa era 124, 45, 43
	昭和元年	*Shōwa gannen* first year of the Showa era (1926) 124, 137, 45

照 86 2785 照	**998**	SHŌ, *te(ru)*, shine; *te(rasu)*, shine on; *te(reru)*, feel embarrassed
	照明	*shōmei* illumination, lighting 18
	対照	*taishō* contrast 365
	参照	*sanshō* reference 710
	東照宮	*Tōshōgū* (shrine in Nikko) 71, 721

焦 172 5029 焦	**999**	SHŌ, fire; impatience; yearning; *ko(gasu)*, scorch, singe; pine for; *ko(geru)*, get scorched; *ko(gareru)*, yearn for; *ase(ru)*, be in a hurry, hasty, impatient
	焦点	*shōten* focal point, focus 169
	焦熱地獄	*shōnetsu jigoku* an inferno 645, 118, 884
	黒焦げ	*kurokoge* charred, burned 206

超 156 4543 超	**1000**	CHŌ, *ko(su/eru)*, cross, go over, exceed
	超過	*chōka* excess 413
	超音速	*chōonsoku* supersonic speed 347, 502
	超大国	*chōtaikoku* a superpower 26, 40
	超満員	*chōman'in* crowded beyond capacity 201, 163
	超人	*chōjin* a superman 1

越 156 4542 越	**1001**	ETSU, *ko(su/eru)*, cross, go over, exceed
	超越	*chōetsu* transcendence 1000
	越権	*ekken* overstepping one's authority 335
	越境	*ekkyō* jumping the border 864
	引っ越す	*hikkosu* move, change residences 216
	勝ち越し	*kachikoshi* a net win, being ahead 509

	1002	SHU, *omomuki*, purport, gist; taste, elegance; appearance	
156 4544		趣味　　*shumi*　interest, liking, taste; hobby	307
		趣向　　*shukō*　plan, idea	199
		趣意　　*shui*　purport, meaning; aim, object	132
趣		情趣　　*jōshu*　mood; artistic effect	209
		野趣　　*yashu*　rural life and beauty, rusticity	236

	1003	YŪ, [YU], *aso(bu)*, play, enjoy oneself, be idle	
162 4726		遊歩道　*yūhodō*　promenade, mall, boardwalk	431, 149
		周遊（券）*shūyū(ken)*　excursion (ticket)	91, 506
		遊説　　*yūzei*　speaking tour, political campaigning	400
遊		遊休　　*yūkyū*　idle, unused	60
		遊び相手　*asobiaite*　playmate	146, 57

	1004	SHI, SE, *hodoko(su)*, give, bestow; carry out, perform, conduct	
70 2085		施設　　*shisetsu*　facilities, institution	577
		施行　　*shikō*　enforce; put in operation	68
		実施　　*jisshi*　carry into effect, enforce, implement	203
施		施政　　*shisei*　administration, governing	483

	1005	SEN, go around, revolve, rotate	
70 2091		旋回　　*senkai*　turning, revolving, circling	90
		周旋　　*shūsen*　good offices, mediation	91
		旋律　　*senritsu*　melody	667
旋		旋風　　*senpū*　whirlwind, cyclone, tornado	29
		あっ旋　*assen*　good offices, mediation	

	1006	KI, *hata*, flag, banner	
70 2093		国旗　　*kokki*　flag (of a country)	40
		校旗　　*kōki*　school banner/flag	115
		半旗　　*hanki*　flag at half-mast	88
旗		星条旗　*seijōki*　the Stars and Stripes (U.S. flag)	730, 564
		旗色　　*hatairo*　the tide of war; things, the situation	204

	1007	RI, an official	
4 183		官吏　　*kanri*　an official	326
		吏員　　*riin*　an official	163
		能吏　　*nōri*　capable official	386
吏		吏党　　*ritō*　party of officials	495

	1008	KŌ, *sara*, anew, again, furthermore; *fu(kasu)*, stay up till late (at night); *fu(keru)*, grow late	
1 42		変更　　*henkō*　alteration, change, modification	257
		更衣室　*kōishitsu*　clothes-changing room	677, 166
		更期年　*kōnenki*　menopause	45, 449
更		更生　　*kōsei*　rebirth, rehabilitation	44

	1009	**KŌ**, *kata(i)*, hard, firm	
硬	112 3193	硬質 *kōshitsu* hard, rigid	176
		硬度 *kōdo* (degree of) hardness	377
		硬化 *kōka* hardening	254
		硬貨 *kōka* coin; hard currency	752
硬		強硬 *kyōkō* firm, unyielding	217

	1010	**KŌ**, *kama(eru)*, build, set up; assume a posture/position; *kama(u)*, mind, care about; meddle in; look after	
構	75 2343	機構 *kikō* mechanism, structure, organization	528
		構成 *kōsei* composition, makeup	261
		構想 *kōsō* conception, plan	147
構		心構え *kokorogamae* mental attitude, readiness	97

	1011	**KŌ**, buy, purchase	
購	154 4522	購入 *kōnyū* purchase	52
		購入者 *kōnyūsha* purchaser, buyer	52, 164
		購買 *kōbai* purchase	241
		購読 *kōdoku* subscription	244
購		購読料 *kōdokuryō* subscription price/fee	244, 319

	1012	**KŌ**, *mizo*, ditch, gutter, groove	
溝	85 2657	下水溝 *gesuikō* drainage ditch, sewage pipe	31, 21
		海溝 *kaikō* an ocean deep, sea trench	117
		日本海溝 *Nippon Kaikō, Nihon Kaikō* Japan Deep/Trench	5, 25, 117
溝			

	1013	**JŌ**, *yuzu(ru)*, transfer, assign; yield, concede	
譲	149 4446	譲歩 *jōho* concession, compromise	431
		割譲 *katsujō* cede (territory)	519
		互譲 *gojō* mutual concession	907
		譲り渡す *yuzuriwatasu* turn over, transfer	378
譲		親譲り *oyayuzuri* inheritance from a parent	175

	1014	**BŌ**, *aba(reru)*, act violently, rage, rampage, run amuck; [BAKU], *aba(ku)*, disclose, expose, bring to light	
暴	72 2157	暴力団 *bōryokudan* gangster syndicate	100, 491
		暴風 *bōfū* high winds, windstorm	29
		乱暴 *ranbō* violence, roughness	689
暴		暴露 *bakuro* expose, bring to light	951

	1015	**BAKU**, explode	
爆	86 2818	爆発 *bakuhatsu* explosion	96
		爆発的 *bakuhatsuteki* explosive	96, 210
		原爆 *genbaku* atomic bomb	136
		被爆者 *hibakusha* bombing victim	976, 164
爆		爆薬 *bakuyaku* explosives	359

	1016	**GEKI**, *u(tsu)*, attack; fire, shoot	
撃	64	攻撃 *kōgeki* attack	819
	1986	反撃 *hangeki* counterattack	324
		爆撃 *bakugeki* bombing raid	1015
擊		撃沈 *gekichin* (attack and) sink	936
		目撃者 *mokugekisha* eyewitness	55, 164

	1017	**GEKI**, *hage(shii)*, violent, fierce, strong, intense	
激	85	過激派 *kagekiha* radicals, extremist faction	413, 912
	2712	感激 *kangeki* deep emotion/gratitude	262
		激情 *gekijō* violent emotion, passion	209
激		激動 *gekidō* violent shaking; excitement, stir	231
		激流 *gekiryū* swift current	247

	1018	**TŌ**, *u(tsu)*, attack	
討	149	検討 *kentō* examination, investigation, study	531
	4316	討論 *tōron* debate, discussion	293
		討議 *tōgi* discussion, deliberation, debate	292
討		討ち死に *uchijini* fall in battle	85
		討ち取る *uchitoru* capture; kill	65

	1019	**TEI**, correcting	
訂	149	訂正 *teisei* correction, revision	275
	4310	校訂 *kōtei* revision	115
		改訂 *kaitei* revision	514
訂		増訂 *zōtei* revised and enlarged (edition)	712

	1020	**DA**, *u(tsu)*, hit, strike	
打	64	打開 *dakai* a break, development, new turn	396
	1829	打算的 *dasanteki* calculating, selfish, mercenary	747, 210
		打楽器 *dagakki* percussion instrument	358, 527
打		打ち合わせ *uchiawase* previous arrangement	159
		打ち消し *uchikeshi* denial; negation	845

	1021	**TŌ**, *na(geru)*, throw	
投	64	投票 *tōhyō* vote	922
	1856	投書 *tōsho* letter to the editor, contribution	131
		投資 *tōshi* investment	750
投		投機 *tōki* speculation	528
		投影 *tōei* projection	854

	1022	**Ō**, Europe	
欧	76	欧州 *Ōshū* Europe	195
	2413	欧州共同体 *Ōshū Kyōdōtai* the European Community	195, 196, 198, 61
		西欧 *Seiō* Western Europe	72
欧		欧米 *Ō-Bei* Europe and America/the U.S.	224

	1023	**SŪ**, pivot	
枢	75 2208	枢軸 *sūjiku* pivot, axis, center	988
		中枢 *chūsū* center	28
		枢要 *sūyō* important	419
枢		枢密 *sūmitsu* state secret	806

	1024	**DAN**, decision, judgment; *kotowa(ru)*, decline, refuse; give notice/warning; prohibit; *ta(tsu)*, cut off	
断	69 2078	決断 *ketsudan* (prompt) decision, resolution	356
		油断 *yudan* inattention, negligence	364
		横断 *ōdan* crossing	781
断		断念 *dannen* abandonment, giving up	579

	1025	**KEI**, *tsu(gu)*, follow; succeed to, inherit	
継	120 3545	後継 *kōkei* succession	48
		継承 *keishō* succession, inheritance	942
		継続 *keizoku* continuance	243
		中継 *chūkei* (radio/TV) relay, hookup	28
継		受け継ぐ *uketsugu* inherit, succeed to	260

	1026	**HAN**, stamp, seal; **BAN**, (paper) size	
判	18 673	判断(力) *handan(ryoku)* judgment	1024, 100
		判決 *hanketsu* a decision, ruling	356
		判事 *hanji* a judge	80
		公判 *kōhan* (public) trial	126
判		判明 *hanmei* become clear, be ascertained	18

	1027	**HAN, BAN**, *tomona(u)*, go with, accompany; entail, be accompanied by, be associated with	
伴	9 396	同伴 *dōhan* keep (someone) company	198
		伴りょ *hanryo* companion, comrade, partner	
伴		相伴う *aitomonau* accompany	146

	1028	**HYŌ**, criticism, comment	
評	149 4339	評論 *hyōron* criticism, critique, commentary	293
		論評 *ronpyō* criticism, comment, review	293
		評価 *hyōka* appraisal	421
		評判 *hyōban* fame, popularity; rumor, gossip	1026
評		書評 *shohyō* book review	131

	1029	**HI**, critique	
批	64 1848	批判 *hihan* critique	1026
		批判的 *hihanteki* critical	1026, 210
		批評 *hihyō* critique, criticism, review	1028
		批評眼 *hihyōgan* critical eye	1028, 848
批		文芸批評 *bungei hihyō* literary criticism	114, 435, 1028

	1030	**NI, two (in documents)**	
弐	1 32 弐	弐万円 *niman'en* 20,000 yen	16, 13

	1031	**BU, MU, military**	
武	1 51 武	武器 *buki* weapon, arms 武力 *buryoku* military force 武道 *budō* military arts 武士 *bushi* samurai, warrior 武者 *musha* warrior	527 100 149 572 164

	1032	**YŪ, *ure(eru)*, grieve, be distressed, be anxious; *ure(e/i)*, grief, distress, anxiety; *u(i)*, unhappy, gloomy**	
憂	1 70 憂	憂国 *yūkoku* patriotism 物憂い *monoui* languid, weary, listless 憂き目 *ukime* grief, misery, hardship 憂い顔 *ureigao* sorrowful face, troubled look	40 79 55 277

	1033	**YŪ, *sugu(reru)*, excel; *yasa(shii)*, gentle, tender, kindhearted**	
優	9 564 優	優勢 *yūsei* predominance, superiority 優勝 *yūshō* victory, championship 優先 *yūsen* priority 優柔不断 *yūjūfudan* indecision, vacillation 774, 94, 1024 女優 *joyū* actress	646 509 50 102

	1034	**HI, *kana(shii)*, sad; *kana(shimu)*, be sad, lament, regret**	
悲	175 5082 悲	悲劇 *higeki* tragedy 悲恋 *hiren* disappointed love 悲鳴 *himei* shriek, scream 悲観 *hikan* pessimism	797 258 925 604

	1035	**HAI, actor**	
俳	9 485 俳	俳優 *haiyū* actor 俳句 *haiku* haiku, 17-syllable Japanese poem in 5–7–5 form 俳人 *haijin* haiku poet	1033 337 1

	1036	**HAI, exclude, reject, expel**	
排	64 1948 排	排気ガス *haikigasu* exhaust gas/fumes 排液 *haieki* drainage (in surgery) 排撃 *haigeki* reject, denounce 排日 *hai-Nichi* anti-Japanese 排他的 *haitateki* exclusive, cliquish	134 472 1016 5 120, 210

	1037	**HAI**, fellow, colleague, companion	
輩	175 5086	先 輩　　*senpai*　one's senior (at school/work) 後 輩　　*kōhai*　one's junior, younger people 年 輩　　*nenpai*　age, elderliness　⌈same age 同 年 輩 の 人 *dōnenpai no hito*　someone of the 輩 出　　*haishutsu*　appear one after another	50 48 45 198, 45, 1 53

	1038	**TOKU**, virtue	
徳	60 1633	道 徳　　*dōtoku*　morality, morals 公 徳　　*kōtoku*　public morality 人 徳　　*jintoku, nintoku*　one's natural virtue 不 徳　　*futoku*　lack of virtue, vice, immorality 徳 川　　*Tokugawa*　(historical surname)	149 126 1 94 33

	1039	**CHŌ**, *ki(ku)*, hear, listen	
聴	128 3716	聴 取　　*chōshu*　listening 聴 衆　　*chōshū*　audience 聴 講　　*chōkō*　attendance at a lecture 公 聴 会　*kōchōkai*　public hearing 聴 覚　　*chōkaku*　sense of hearing	65 792 783 126, 158 605

	1040	**SHI**, *mune*, purport, content, gist; instructions	
旨	21 752	趣 旨　　*shushi*　purport, content, gist 要 旨　　*yōshi*　gist, essential points 本 旨　　*honshi*　main purpose, true aim 論 旨　　*ronshi*　point/drift of an argument	1002 419 25 293

	1041	**SHI**, *yubi*, finger; *sa(su)*, point to	
指	64 1904	指 導　　*shidō*　guidance, leadership 指 令　　*shirei*　order, instruction 指 名　　*shimei*　nomination, designation 指 定 席　*shiteiseki*　reserved seat 人 さ し 指 *hitosashiyubi*　index finger, forefinger	703 831 82 355, 379 1

	1042	**SHI**, *abura*, (animal) fat	
脂	130 3766	油 脂　　*yushi*　oils and fats 脂 身　　*aburami*　fat (of meat) 脂 濃 い *aburakkoi*　greasy, rich (foods)	364 59 957

	1043	**IN**, seal, stamp; *shirushi*, sign, mark	
印	2 102	印 象　　*inshō*　impression 調 印　　*chōin*　signing, signature 印 税　　*inzei*　a royalty (on a book) 印 紙　　*inshi*　revenue stamp 矢 印　　*yajirushi*　(direction) arrow	739 342 399 180 213

	1044	SATSU, *su(ru)*, print	
刷	4	印 刷 *insatsu* printing	1043
	210	印 刷 物 *insatsubutsa* printed matter	1043, 79
		増 刷 *zōsatsu* additional printing, reprinting	712
刷		刷 新 *sasshin* reform	174
		刷 り 直 す *surinaosu* reprint to correct mistakes	423

	1045	HEN, part; *kata-*, one (of two)	
片	91	破 片 *hahen* broken piece, fragment, splinter	665
	2842	断 片 *danpen* fragment, piece, snippet	1024
		木 片 *mokuhen* block/chip of wood, wood shavings	22
片		片 目 *katame* one eye	55
		片 道 *katamichi* one way, each way	149

	1046	HAN, printing block/plate, printing; edition	
版	91	出 版 社 *shuppansha* publishing house	53, 308
	2843	版 権 *hanken* copyright	335
		初 版 *shohan* first edition	679
版		改 訂 版 *kaiteiban* revised edition	514, 1019
		版 画 *hanga* print, woodblock print	343

	1047	HAN, BAN, *ita*, a board	
板	75	甲 板 *kanpan, kōhan* deck (of a ship)	982
	2213	合 板 *gōban, gōhan* plywood	159
		黒 板 *kokuban* blackboard	206
板		床 板 *yukaita* floorboard	826

	1048	HAN, sell	
販	154	販 売 *hanbai* sales, selling	239
	4491	販 売 値 段 *hanbai nedan* selling price	239, 425, 362
		自 動 販 売 機 *jidō hanbaiki* vending ma-	62, 231, 239, 528
		市 販 *shihan* marketing └chine	181
販		販 路 *hanro* market (for goods), outlet	151

	1049	KA, [KE], *kari*, temporary, provisional, tentative, supposing	
仮	9	仮 説 *kasetsu* hypothesis, supposition	400
	382	仮 定 *katei* supposition, assumption, hypothesis	355
		仮 面 *kamen* a mask	274
仮		仮 名 *kamei* fictitious name	82
		仮 病 *kebyō* pretended illness, malingering	380

	1050	KAN, leniency, generosity	
寛	40	寛 大 *kandai* magnanimity, tolerance, leniency	26
	1325	寛 容 *kan'yō* magnanimity, generosity, for- bearance	654
		寛 厚 *kankō* generous, large-hearted	639
寛		寛 厳 *kangen* severity and leniency	822

	1051	KAN, *susu(meru)*, recommend, offer, advise, encourage
勧	19 736	勧告 *kankoku* recommendation, advice ... 690 勧業 *kangyō* encouragement of industry ... 279 勧進 *kanjin* soliciting religious contributions ... 437

	1052	KAN, joy, pleasure
歓	76 2425	歓待 *kantai* hospitality ... 452 歓談 *kandan* pleasant chat ... 593 歓声 *kansei* shout of joy, cheer ... 746 歓楽街 *kanrakugai* amusement center ... 358, 186 歓心を買う *kanshin o kau* curry favor ... 97, 241

	1053	I, *era(i)*, great, eminent, extraordinary, excellent
偉	9 506	偉大 *idai* great, mighty, grand ... 26 偉人 *ijin* great man ... 1 偉才 *isai* man of extraordinary talent ... 551 偉業 *igyō* great achievement ... 279 偉観 *ikan* a spectacular sight ... 604

	1054	I, woof (horizontal thread in weaving); latitude
緯	120 3579	緯度 *ido* latitude ... 377 緯線 *isen* a parallel (of latitude) ... 299 北緯 *hokui* north latitude ... 73 南緯 *nan'i* south latitude ... 74 経緯 *keii* longitude and latitude; the details ... 548

	1055	GEI, *muka(eru)*, go to meet, receive; invite, send for
迎	162 4669	歓迎 *kangei* welcome ... 1052 迎合 *geigō* flattery ... 159 送迎 *sōgei* welcome and sendoff ... 441 出迎え *demukae* meeting (someone) on arrival, reception ... 53

	1056	GYŌ, [KŌ], *ao(gu)*, look up at; look up to, respect; ask for, rely (on); *ō(se)*, what you say, (your/his) wish
仰	9 375	仰視 *gyōshi* look up (at) ... 606 仰天 *gyōten* be astonished, frightened ... 141 信仰 *shinkō* faith, religious conviction ... 157 仰向け *aomuke* facing upward, on one's back, ⌈supine ... 199

	1057	YOKU, *osa(eru)*, hold down/in check, suppress, control
抑	64 1851	抑制 *yokusei* control, restrain, suppress ... 427 抑留 *yokuryū* detention, internment ... 761 抑止 *yokushi* deter, stave off ... 477 抑揚 *yokuyō* rising and falling of tones, intonation ... 631

	1058	RAN, *tamago*, egg (cf. No. 295)		
卵	4	鶏卵	*keiran* (hen's) egg	926
	199	産卵	*sanran* egg-laying, spawning	278
		卵黄	*ran'ō* yolk	780
		卵管	*rankan* Fallopian tube, oviduct	328
卵		卵形	*tamagogata, rankei* egg-shaped, oval	395

	1059	SAKU, rope, cord; search for		
索	24	索引	*sakuin* an index	216
	782	捜索	*sōsaku* search ⌈premises	989
		家宅捜索	*kataku sōsaku* search of the house/ 165,178, 989	
		探索	*tansaku* search, inquiry, investigation	535
索		思索	*shisaku* thinking, speculation, contemplation	99

	1060	RUI, involvement, trouble; accumulation; continually		
累	102	累加/増	*ruika/zō* acceleration, successive in- 709, 712	
	3006	累積	*ruiseki* accumulation, cumulative ⌊crease	656
		累計	*ruikei* (sum) total	340
		係累	*keirui* family encumbrances, dependents	909
累		累進	*ruishin* successive/progressive promotions	437

	1061	I, *koto*, be different		
異	102	異常	*ijō* unusual, abnormal	497
	3008	異質	*ishitsu* heterogeneity	176
		異国	*ikoku* foreign country	40
		異議	*igi* objection	292
異		異教	*ikyō* heathenism, paganism, heresy	245

	1062	YOKU, *tsubasa*, wing		
翼	124	左翼	*sayoku* the left wing, leftist	75
	3680	右翼	*uyoku* the right wing, rightist	76
		両翼	*ryōyoku* both wings	200
翼		比翼の鳥	*hiyoku no tori* happily married couple 798, 285	

	1063	YO, *ama(ru)*, be left over, in excess; *ama(su)*, leave over		
余	9	二十余年	*nijūyonen* more than 20 years	3, 12, 45
	408	余命	*yomei* the rest of one's life	578
		余計	*yokei* too much, unwanted, uncalled-for	340
		余地	*yochi* room, margin	118
余		余波	*yoha* aftereffect	666

	1064	KA, *hima*, free time, leisure		
暇	72	休暇	*kyūka* holiday, vacation, time off	60
	2152	余暇	*yoka* leisure, spare time	1063
		暇つぶし	*himatsubushi* a waste of time, killing time	
		暇取る	*himadoru* take a long time, be delayed	65
暇		暇な時	*hima na toki* leisure time, when one is free	42

	1065	**JO, [JI],** *nozo(ku),* get rid of, exclude	
除	170 4993 除	解除 *kaijo* cancellation 除名 *jomei* remove (someone's) name, expel 除外 *jogai* except, exclude 免除 *menjo* exemption 取り除く *torinozoku* remove, rid	474 82 83 733 65
徐	1066 60 1612 徐	**JO,** slowly 徐々に *jojo ni* slowly, gradually 徐行 *jokō* go/drive slowly 徐歩 *joho* walk slowly, saunter, mosey	 68 431
叙	1067 29 862 叙	**JO,** narrate, describe 叙述 *jojutsu* description, narration 叙景 *jokei* description of scenery 叙情詩 *jojōshi* lyric poem/poetry 叙事詩 *jojishi* epic poem/poetry 自叙伝 *jijoden* autobiography	 968 853 209, 570 80, 570 62, 434
剰	1068 18 698 剰	**JŌ,** surplus 剰余(金) *jōyo(kin)* a surplus (出生)過剰 *(shussei) kajō* surplus, excess (of births) 余剰 *yojō* surplus 剰員 *jōin* superfluous personnel, overstaffing	 1063, 23 53, 44, 413 1063 163
斜	1069 68 2074 斜	**SHA,** *nana(me),* slanting, diagonal, oblique 斜面 *shamen* a slope, slant, incline 斜線 *shasen* slanting line, slash [/] 斜辺 *shahen* oblique side, hypotenuse 斜陽 *shayō* setting sun 斜視 *shashi* squint	 274 299 775 630 606
垂	1070 4 211 垂	**SUI,** *ta(reru/rasu),* (intr./tr.) hang down, dangle, drip 垂直 *suichoku* perpendicular, vertical 垂線 *suisen* a perpendicular (line) 懸垂 *kensui* suspension, dangling; doing chin-ups 虫垂 *chūsui* the appendix 雨垂れ *amadare* raindrops	 423 299 911 873 30
睡	1071 109 3149 睡	**SUI,** sleep 睡眠 *suimin* sleep 睡眠不足 *suimin-busoku* lack of sleep 午睡 *gosui* nap, siesta 熟睡 *jukusui* sound/deep sleep こん睡(状態) *konsui(jōtai)* coma	 849 849, 94, 58 49 687 626, 387

	1072	**TO**, way, road	
162		途中 *tochū* on the way, midway	28
4697		前途 *zento* one's future, prospects	47
		途絶える *todaeru* come to a stop	742
途		帰途 *kito* one's way home ⌈oping country	317
		(開発)途上国 (*kaihatsu*) *tojōkoku* devel-	396, 96, 32, 40

	1073	**TO**, *nu(ru)*, paint	
32		塗料 *toryō* paints, paint and varnish	319
1124		塗布 *tofu* apply (salve)	675
		塗り物 *nurimono* lacquerware	79
塗		塗り立て *nuritate* freshly painted	121
		塗り替える *nurikaeru* repaint, put on a new coating	744

	1074	**KA**, [KE], *hana*, flower, florid, showy, brilliant	
140		華道 *kadō* (Japanese) flower arranging	149
3955		華美 *kabi* splendor, pomp, gorgeousness	401
		中華料理 *chūka ryōri* Chinese food/cooking	28, 319, 143
華		中華人民共和国 *Chūka Jinmin Kyōwakoku*	
		People's Republic of China	28, 1, 177, 196, 124, 40

	1075	**KAKU**, reform; *kawa*, leather	
177		革命 *kakumei* revolution	578
5088		革新 *kakushin* reform	174
		改革 *kaikaku* reform, reorganization	514
革		変革 *henkaku* reform, innovation, revolutionize	257
		皮革 *hikaku* leather	975

	1076	**KA**, *kutsu*, shoe	
177		製靴 *seika* shoemaking	428
5092		革靴 *kawagutsu* leather shoes	1075
		靴下 *kutsushita* socks, stockings	31
靴		靴屋 *kutsuya* shoe store	167
		靴一足 *kutsu issoku* 1 pair of shoes	2, 58

	1077	**SHIN**, *oka(su)*, invade; violate, infringe on; damage	
9		侵略 *shinryaku* aggression, invasion	841
452		侵入 *shinnyū* invasion, raid, trespass	52
		侵害 *shingai* infringement ⌈sion pact	518
侵		不可侵条約 *fukashin jōyaku* nonaggres-	94, 388, 564, 211
		侵食 *shinshoku* erosion, weathering	322

	1078	**SHIN**, *hita(ru)*, be soaked, steeped; *hita(su)*, dip, immerse	
85		浸水 *shinsui* inundation, submersion	21
2572		浸出 *shinshutsu* exuding, oozing out, percolation	53
		浸食 *shinshoku* erosion, corrosion	322
浸		水浸し *mizubitashi* submersion, inundation	21

	1079	SHIN, ne(ru), go to bed, sleep; ne(kasu), put to bed	
寝	40	寝室　　shinshitsu　bedroom	166
	1326	寝台　　shindai　bed	492
		寝具 (類) shingu(rui)　bedclothes, bedding	420, 226
寝		昼寝　　hirune　(daytime) nap, siesta	470
		寝苦しい negurushii　unable to sleep well	545

	1080	SŌ, ha(ku), sweep	
掃	64	(大) 掃除 (ō)sōji　(general) housecleaning	26, 1065
	1945	清掃夫　seisōfu　street sweeper, cleaning man	660, 315
		掃除婦　sōjifu　cleaning lady	1065, 316
掃		掃討　　sōtō　sweeping, clearing, mopping up	1018
		一掃　　issō　sweep away, eradicate, stamp out	2

	1081	KEN, ka(neru), combine, double as; -ka(neru), cannot	
兼	12	兼業　　kengyō　a side business	279
	598	兼任　　kennin　hold 2 posts (simultaneously)	334
		首相兼外相 shushō ken gaishō　prime minister who	
兼		is also foreign minister ⌈tiently for	148, 146, 83
		待ち兼ねる machikaneru　cannot wait, wait impa-	452

	1082	JIN, tazu(neru), search for; ask, inquire	
尋	58	尋問　　jinmon　questioning, interrogation	162
	1585	尋常　　jinjō　normal, ordinary	497
		尋ね人 tazunebito　person being sought, missing	
尋		person	1

	1083	SO, crop tax, tribute	
租	115	租税　　sozei　taxes	399
	3279	地租　　chiso　(obsolete) land tax	118
		租借　　soshaku　lease (land)	766
租		租界　　sokai　(foreign) settlement, concession	454
		租借地　soshakuchi　leased territory	766, 118

	1084	SO, ara(i), coarse, rough	
粗	119	粗末　　somatsu　coarse, plain, crude, rough, rude	305
	3473	粗暴　　sobō　wild, rough, rude, violent	1014
		粗野　　soya　rustic, loutish, vulgar, ill-bred	236
粗		粗悪　　soaku　coarse, crude, base, inferior	304
		粗食　　soshoku　coarse food, plain diet	322

	1085	SO, haba(mu), hamper	
阻	170	阻止　　soshi　obstruct, impede	477
	4984	阻害　　sogai　check, impediment, hindrance	518
		険阻　　kenso　steep, precipitous, rugged	533
阻			

	1086	**GI**, good, all right	
40		便 宜 *bengi* convenience, expediency	330
1290		便 宜 上 *bengijō* for convenience/expediency	330, 32
		時 宜 *jigi* right time/opportunity	42
	宜	適 宜 *tekigi* suitable, appropriate, fitting	415

	1087	**JŌ**, *tatami*, tatami, straw floor-mat; *tata(mu)*, fold up	
102		四 畳 半 *yojōhan* 4½-mat room	6, 88
3010		畳 表 *tatami-omote* woven covering of a tatami	272
		畳 替 え *tatamigae* replacing *tatami-omote*/tatami	744
	畳	畳 屋 *tatamiya* tatami maker/store	167

	1088	**EN**, help, assistance	
64		援 助 *enjo* assistance, aid	623
1961		応 援 *ōen* aid, support, backing, cheering	827
		後 援 *kōen* support, backing	48
		声 援 *seien* shout of encouragement, cheers, rooting	746
	援	援 軍 *engun* reinforcements	438

	1089	**KAN**, *yuru(mu)*, become loose, abate, slacken; *yuru(meru)*, loosen, relieve, relax, slacken; *yuru(i)*, loose; generous; lax; gentle (slope); slow; *yuru(yaka)*, loose, slack; magnanimous; gentle, easy, slow	
120			
3584		緩 和 *kanwa* relieve, ease, lighten	124
	緩	緩 急 *kankyū* fast and slow speed; emergency	303

	1090	**KIN**, *suji*, muscle, tendon; blood vessel; line; reason, logic; plot (of a story); coherence; source (of information)	
118			
3395		筋 肉 *kinniku* muscle	223
		筋 道 *sujimichi* reason, logic, coherence	149
		筋 違 い *sujichigai, sujikai* a cramp; illogical, wrong	814
	筋	筋 書 き *sujigaki* synopsis, outline, plan	131

	1091	*hako*, box	
118		本 箱 *honbako* bookcase	25
3425		貯 金 箱 *chokinbako* savings box, (piggy) bank	762, 23
		重 箱 *jūbako* nested boxes	227
		豚 箱 *butabako* police lockup, jail, hoosegow	796
	箱	箱 根 *Hakone* (resort area near Mt. Fuji)	314

	1092	**HAN**, example, model, pattern; limit	
118		範 例 *hanrei* example	612
3424		師 範 *shihan* teacher, master	409
		規 範 *kihan* norm, criterion	607
	範	広 範 *kōhan* extensive, wide, far-reaching	694

	1093	TAN, red	
丹	4	丹 念 *tannen* application, diligence	579
	163	丹 誠 *tansei* sincerity; efforts, diligence	718
		丹 精 *tansei* exertion, diligence, painstaking care	659
丹		丹 前 *tanzen* man's padded kimono	47

	1094	SHŪ, *fune*, [*funa*], boat	
舟	137	小 舟 *kobune* boat, skiff	27
	3863	舟 遊 び *funaasobi* boating	1003
		舟 歌 *funauta* sailor's song, chantey	392
舟			

	1095	HAKU, ship	
舶	137	船 舶 *senpaku* ship, vessel; shipping	376
	3870	舶 来 *hakurai* imported	69
		舶 来 品 *hakuraihin* imported article/goods	69, 230
舶			

	1096	HAN, carry; all, general	
般	137	一 般 的 *ippanteki* general	2, 210
	3865	一 般 化 *ippanka* generalization, popularization	2, 254
		全 般 *zenpan* the whole	89
般		全 般 的 *zenpanteki* general, overall	89, 210
		先 般 *senpan* recently, some time ago	50

	1097	*sara*, plate, dish, saucer	
皿	108	皿 洗 い *saraarai* washing dishes	692
	3113	サ ラ ダ 一 皿 *sarada hitosara* 1 plate of salad	2
		大 皿 *ōzara* large dish, platter	26
皿		小 皿 *kozara* small plate	27
		受 け 皿 *ukezara* saucer	260

	1098	BAN, (chess/go) board, tray, platter, basin	
盤	108	基 盤 *kiban* basis, foundation	450
	3122	円 盤 *enban* disk; discus	13
		空 飛 ぶ 円 盤 *soratobu enban* flying saucer	140, 530, 13
盤		水 盤 *suiban* basin	21
		終 盤 戦 *shūbansen* end game	458, 301

	1099	BON, Buddhist Festival of the Dead; tray	
盆	12	盆 地 *bonchi* basin, valley	118
	594	盆 景 *bonkei* miniature landscape on a tray	853
		(お) 盆 *(O)Bon* the Bon Festival	
盆		*(o)bon* tray	

	1100	TŌ, *nusu(mu)*, steal	
盗	108	強盗 *gōtō* burglar, robber	217
	3115	盗難(保険) *tōnan (hoken)* theft (insurance)	557, 489, 533
		盗用 *tōyō* embezzlement; surreptitious use, pla-	107
		盗作 *tōsaku* plagiarism ⌊giarism	360
盗		盗品 *tōhin* stolen goods, loot	230

	1101	EN, *shio*, salt	
塩	32	食塩 *shokuen* table salt	322
	1125	塩分 *enbun* salt content, salinity	38
		塩酸 *ensan* hydrochloric acid	516
		塩水 *shiomizu, ensui* salt water, brine	21
塩		塩入れ *shioire* saltshaker	52

	1102	BON, [HAN], common, ordinary	
凡	16	凡人 *bonjin* ordinary person, man of mediocre	
	654	ability	1
		平凡 *heibon* commonplace, mediocre	202
		凡例 *hanrei* introductory remarks	612
凡		凡才 *bonsai* common ability, mediocre talent	551

	1103	HAN, *ho*, sail	
帆	50	出帆 *shuppan* sailing, departure	53
	1469	帆走 *hansō* sailing	429
		帆船 *hansen, hobune* sailing ship, sailboat	376
帆		帆柱 *hobashira* mast	598

	1104	BŌ, *oka(su)*, risk, brave, defy, dare; desecrate	
冒	72	冒険 *bōken* adventure	533
	2117	冒険小説 *bōken shōsetsu* adventure novel	533, 27, 400
		冒頭 *bōtō* beginning, opening, lead	276
		感冒 *kanbō* a cold	262
冒		冒とく *bōtoku* blasphemy, sacrilege, defilement	

	1105	BŌ, cap, hat, headgear	
帽	50	帽子 *bōshi* hat, cap	103
	1483	宇宙帽 *uchūbō* space helmet	990, 991
		赤帽 *akabō* redcap, luggage porter	207
		無帽 *mubō* hatless, bareheaded	93
帽		帽章 *bōshō* badge on a cap	857

	1106	CHŌ, *ha(ru)*, stretch, spread	
張	57	主張 *shuchō* insistence, assertion, contention	155
	1570	出張 *shutchō* business trip	53
		出張所 *shutchōjo* branch office, agency	53, 153
		引っ張る *hipparu* pull, tug at	216
張		見張る *miharu* keep watch, be on the lookout	63

	1107	**CHŌ**, notebook, register; curtain	
帳	50 1478	手帳　*techō*　(pocket) notebook	57
		電話帳　*denwachō*　telephone book/directory	108, 238
		(貯金)通帳　*(chokin) tsūchō*　bankbook, passbook	762, 23, 150
帳		帳面　*chōmen*　notebook, account book	274
		帳消し　*chōkeshi*　cancellation, writing off (debts)	845

	1108	**SHIN**, *no(biru)*, stretch, lengthen, grow; *no(basu)*, stretch out, lengthen, extend	
伸	9 403	伸張　*shinchō*　extend, expand	1106
		二伸　*nishin*　postscript, P.S.	3
伸		伸び伸び　*nobinobi*　at ease, relieved, refreshed	

	1109	**SHIN**, gentleman	
紳	120 3518	紳士　*shinshi*　gentleman	572
		紳士用　*shinshiyō*　men's, for men	572, 107
		紳士服　*shinshifuku*　men's clothing	572, 683
紳		紳士協定　*shinshi kyōtei*　gentleman's agreement	572, 234, 355

	1110	**SHUKU**, *chiji(maru/mu)*, shrink, contract; *chiji(meru)*, shorten, condense; *chiji(rasu/reru)*, make/become curly	
縮	120 3608	伸縮　*shinshuku*　expansion and contraction, flex-	1108
		短縮　*tanshuku*　shortening, reduction ⌊ibility	215
		縮図　*shukuzu*　reduced/scaled-down drawing	339
縮		軍縮　*gunshuku*　arms reduction	438

	1111	**TEI**, imperial court; government office	
廷	54 1546	宮廷　*kyūtei*　imperial court	721
		法廷　*hōtei*　(law) court	123
		開廷　*kaitei*　holding (law) court	396
廷		出廷　*shuttei*　appearance in court	53
		廷臣　*teishin*　court official, courtier	835

	1112	**TEI**, *niwa*, garden	
庭	53 1514	家庭　*katei*　home, family	165
		校庭　*kōtei*　schoolyard, school grounds	115
		庭球　*teikyū*　tennis	726
庭		庭園　*teien*　garden	447
		前庭　*zentei*　front garden	47

	1113	**KAKU**, extend, expand	
拡	64 1876	拡大　*kakudai*　magnification, expansion	26
		拡張　*kakuchō*　extension, expansion	1106
		拡充　*kakujū*　expansion, amplification	828
拡		拡散　*kakusan*　diffusion	767
		拡声機/器　*kakuseiki*　loudspeaker	746, 528, 527

1114	**SEI**, conquer		
60 1603	征服	*seifuku* conquer, subjugate	683
	征服者	*seifukusha* conqueror	683, 164
	出征	*shussei* going to the front, taking the field	53
	遠征	*ensei* (military) expedition; playing tour	446
征	長征	*chōsei* the Long March (in China)	95

1115	**EN**, *no(basu/beru)*, lengthen, prolong, postpone; *no(biru)*, be postponed, delayed, prolonged		
54 1547	延長	*enchō* extension	95
	延期	*enki* postponement, extension	449
	遅延	*chien* delay, being behind time	702
延	引き延ばす	*hikinobasu* draw out, prolong, enlarge	216

1116	**TAN**, birth		
149 4386	誕生	*tanjō* birth	44
	誕生日	*tanjōbi* birthday	44, 5
	誕生祝い	*tanjōiwai* birthday celebration	44, 851
誕	生誕(百年)	*seitan (hyakunen)* (centenary of some-one's) birth	44, 14, 45

1117	**SEKI**, achievements; spinning		
120 3602	成績	*seiseki* performance, results	261
	成績表	*seisekihyō* list of grades, report card	261, 272
	業績	*gyōseki* work, achievements; business per-	279
	功績	*kōseki* meritorious service ⌊formance	818
績	実績	*jisseki* record of performance, actual results	203

1118	**SAI**, debt, loan		
9 531	負債	*fusai* debt, liabilities	510
	国債	*kokusai* national debt, public loan	40
	債券	*saiken* bond, debenture	506
	債権(者)	*saiken(sha)* credit(or)	335, 164
債	債務(者)	*saimu(sha)* debt(or)	235, 164

1119	**KŌ**, empress		
4 181	皇后	*kōgō* empress	297
	皇后陛下	*kōgō-heika* Her Majesty the Empress	297, 589, 31
后	皇太后	*kōtai-gō/kō* the empress dowager	297, 629

1120	**KŌ**, manuscript, draft		
115 3299	原稿(用紙)	*genkō (yōshi)* manuscript (paper)	136, 107, 180
	草稿	*sōkō* rough draft, notes	249
	投稿	*tōkō* contribution (to a periodical)	1021
稿	稿料	*kōryō* fee for a manuscript/article/artwork	319

移	**1121** 115 3282 移	**I**, *utsu(ru)*, move (one's residence), change, be catching; *utsu(su)*, move (one's residence/office), transfer, infect

移動 *idō* moving, migration 231
移転 *iten* move, change of address 433
移 (住) 民 *i(jū)min* emigrant, immigrant 156, 177
移植 *ishoku* transplant 424

崩	**1122** 46 1430 崩	**HŌ**, *kuzu(reru)*, fall to pieces, collapse; *kuzu(su)*, demolish; change, break (a large bill); write (cursive simplified kanji)

崩御 *hōgyo* death of the emperor 708
山崩れ *yamakuzure* landslide 34
荷崩れ *nikuzure* a load falling off (a truck) 391
切り崩す *kirikuzusu* cut through, level (a mountain) 39

裁	**1123** 24 788 裁	**SAI**, *saba(ku)*, pass judgment; *ta(tsu)*, cut out (cloth/leather)

裁判 *saiban* trial, hearing 1026
裁決 *saiketsu* decision, ruling 356
独裁 *dokusai* dictatorship 219
総裁 *sōsai* president, general director 697
洋裁 *yōsai* (Western-style) dressmaking 289

載	**1124** 24 789 載	**SAI**, *no(ru)*, be recorded, appear (in print); *no(seru)*, place on top of; load (luggage); publish, run (an ad)

積載 *sekisai* loading, carrying 656
満載 *mansai* fully loaded 201
記載 *kisai* statement, mention 371
連載 *rensai* a serial 440

栽	**1125** 24 781 栽	**SAI**, planting

盆栽 *bonsai* a bonsai, potted dwarf tree 1099

俗	**1126** 9 453 俗	**ZOKU**, customs, manners; the world, laity; vulgar

俗語 *zokugo* colloquial language 67
俗名 *zokumyō* secular name 82
民俗 *minzoku* folk 177
風俗 *fūzoku* manners, customs; public morals 29
通俗文学 *tsūzoku bungaku* popular literature 150, 111, 109

欲	**1127** 150 4461 欲	**YOKU**, covetousness, desire; *hos(suru)*, desire, want; *ho(shii)*, want

食欲 *shokuyoku* appetite 322
性欲 *seiyoku* sexual desire, sex drive 98
欲望 *yokubō* desire, appetite, craving 673
無欲 *muyoku* free from avarice, unselfish 93

	1128	YOKU, a(biru), be bathed in; a(biseru), pour over, shower
浴	85	入浴 *nyūyoku* bathing, (hot) bath 52
	2568	浴室 *yokushitsu* bathroom 166
		海水浴場 *kaisuiyokujō* (swimming) beach 117, 21, 154
		日光浴 *nikkōyoku* sunbathing 5, 138
浴		浴衣 *yukata* cotton kimono for summer 677

	1129	TEN, expand
展	44	展示 (会) *tenji(kai)* show, exhibition 615, 158
	1396	展望台 *tenbōdai* observation platform 673, 492
		親展 *shinten* confidential 175
		進展 *shinten* development, evolution ⌈country 437
展		発展途上国 *hatten tojōkoku* developing 96, 1072, 32, 40

	1130	DEN, TEN, hall, palace; mister; tono, lord; -dono, Mr.
殿	4	宮殿 *kyūden* palace 721
	242	御殿 *goten* palace 708
		殿下 *denka* His/Your Highness 31
殿		湯殿 *yudono* bathroom 632

	1131	EN, relation, connection; marriage; fate; veranda; fuchi, edge, brink, rim, border
縁	120	絶縁 *zetsuen* (electrical) insulation; break off 742
	3585	因縁 *innen* causality, connection, fate ⌈relations 554
		縁側 *engawa* veranda, porch, balcony 609
縁		額縁 *gakubuchi* (picture) frame 838

	1132	TSUI, fall
墜	32	墜落 *tsuiraku* fall, (airplane) crash 839
	1132	墜死 *tsuishi* fatal fall, fall to one's death 85
		撃墜 *gekitsui* shoot down (a plane) 1016
墜		失墜 *shittsui* loss, fall 311

	1133	SUI, to(geru), accomplish, attain, carry through
遂	162	遂行 *suikō* accomplish, execute, perform 68
	4716	完遂 *kansui* successful execution, completion 613
		(殺人)未遂 (*satsujin*) *misui* attempted
		(murder) 576, 1, 306
遂		やり遂げる *yaritogeru* go through with, carry out

	1134	CHIKU, drive away, pursue, follow
逐	162	放逐 *hōchiku* expulsion, banishment ⌈lation 512
	4696	逐語訳 *chikugoyaku* word-for-word/literal trans- 67, 594
		逐次 *chikuji* one after another, one by one 384
		逐一 *chikuichi* one by one, in detail 2
逐		逐電 *chikuden, chikuten* abscond, make a getaway 108

	1135	KON, *nengo(ro)*, intimacy, friendship	
	61	懇談	*kondan* familiar talk, friendly chat	593
	1781	懇意	*kon'i* intimacy, friendship	132
		懇切	*konsetsu* cordial; exhaustive, detailed	39
		懇願	*kongan* entreaty, earnest appeal	581
		懇親会	*konshinkai* social gathering	175, 158

	1136	KON, opening up farmland, cultivation	
	32	開墾	*kaikon* clearing, reclamation (of land)	396
	1142	開墾地	*kaikonchi* developed/cultivated land	396, 118

	1137	SHO, deal with, treat; sentence, condemn; behave, act	
	34	処分	*shobun* disposal, disposition; punishment	38
	1162	処置	*shochi* disposition, measures, steps	426
		処理	*shori* treat, manage, deal with	143
		対処	*taisho* cope with, tackle	365
		処女	*shojo* virgin	102

	1138	KYO, KO, be due to, based on	
	64	根拠	*konkyo* basis, grounds	314
	1871	拠点	*kyoten* (military) position, base	169
		準拠	*junkyo* be based on, conform to	778
		論拠	*ronkyo* grounds/basis of an argument	293
		証拠	*shōko* evidence	484

	1139	ZEN, *yo(i)*, good	
	12	善悪	*zen'aku* good and evil; quality (whether	304
	606	善良	*zenryō* good, honest, virtuous ⌊good or bad)	321
		善意	*zen'i* good intentions; favorable sense	132
		親善	*shinzen* friendship	175
		改善	*kaizen* improvement, betterment	514

	1140	ZEN, *tsukuro(u)*, repair, mend	
	120	修繕	*shūzen* repair	945
	3612	営繕	*eizen* building and repairs	722

	1141	KICHI, KITSU, good luck	
	32	吉報	*kippō* good news, glad tidings	685
	1053	吉日	*kichinichi* lucky day	5
		不吉	*fukitsu* ill omen, portentous	94
		石部金吉	*ishibe kinkichi* man of strict morals	78, 86, 23
		吉田	*Yoshida* (surname)	35

	1142 149 4359 詰	**KITSU,** *tsu(mu),* be pressed into, closely packed; *tsu(meru),* cram, stuff; shorten; *tsu(maru),* be stopped up, jammed; shrink; be cornered
		詰 問　*kitsumon*　cross-examination, tough ques- 162 ⌐tioning 776
		詰め込む　*tsumekomu*　cram, stuff
		気詰まり　*kizumari*　embarrassment, awkwardness 134

	1143 32 1115 喜	**KI,** *yoroko(bu),* be glad
		喜 劇　*kigeki*　a comedy 797
		歓 喜　*kanki*　joy, delight 1052
		狂 喜　*kyōki*　wild joy, exultation ⌐sorrow 883
		一喜一憂　*ikki-ichiyū*　alternation of joy and 2, 1032
		大喜び　*ōyorokobi*　great joy 26

	1144 75 2377 樹	**JU,** tree, bush
		樹 木　*jumoku*　tree 22
		果 樹　*kaju*　fruit tree 487
		樹 皮　*juhi*　bark (of a tree) 975
		樹 脂　*jushi*　resin 1042
		樹 立　*juritsu*　establish, found 121

	1145 130 3818 膨	**BŌ,** *fuku(reru/ramu),* swell, bulge, rise (dough), expand; sulk, pout
		膨 大　*bōdai*　swelling; large, enormous 26
		青膨れ　*aobukure*　dropsical swelling 208
		膨れっ面　*fukurettsura*　sullen/sulky look 274
		下膨れ　*shimobukure*　full-cheeked, round-faced 31

	1146 130 3736 肢	**SHI,** limbs
		肢 体　*shitai*　limbs; body and limbs 61
		下 肢　*kashi*　lower limbs, legs 31
		上 肢　*jōshi*　upper limbs, arms 32
		四 肢　*shishi*　the limbs, members 6

	1147 207 5415 鼓	**KO,** *tsuzumi,* hand drum
		太 鼓　*taiko*　drum 629
		鼓 手　*koshu*　drummer 57
		鼓 動　*kodō*　(heart) beat 231
		鼓 舞　*kobu*　encouragement, inspiration 810

	1148 190 5255 髪	**HATSU,** *kami,* hair (on the head)
		散 髪　*sanpatsu*　haircut, hairdressing 767
		洗 髪　*senpatsu*　hair washing, a shampoo 692
		間一髪　*kan'ippatsu*　by a hairsbreadth 43, 2
		金 髪　*kinpatsu*　blond 23
		白 髪　*hakuhatsu, shiraga*　white/gray hair 205

	1149	CHŌ, ho(ru), carve, engrave, chisel, sculpt	
彫	4 236	彫像 chōzō carved statue	740
		彫金 chōkin chasing, metal carving	23
		木彫 mokuchō wood carving	22
		木彫り kibori wood carving	22
彫		浮き彫り ukibori relief	938

	1150	RETSU, oto(ru), be inferior	
劣	4 185	劣等 rettō inferiority	569
		劣等感 rettōkan inferiority complex	569, 262
		優劣 yūretsu superiority or inferiority, relative	1033
劣		劣勢 ressei numerical inferiority ⌐merit	646
		劣性 ressei inferior; recessive (gene)	98

	1151	SA, SHA, suna, sand	
砂	112 3181	砂利 jari gravel	329
		土砂降り doshaburi pouring rain, downpour	24, 947
		土砂崩れ doshakuzure washout, landslide	24, 1122
砂		砂浜 sunahama sandy beach	785
		砂時計 sunadokei hourglass	42, 340

	1152	BYŌ, second (of time/arc)	
秒	115 3271	秒針 byōshin second hand (of a clock)	341
		数秒 sūbyō several seconds	225
		1分20秒 ippun nijūbyō 1 minute 20 seconds	38
秒		秒速5メートル byōsoku gomētoru 5 meters per	502
		秒読み byōyomi countdown ⌐second	244

	1153	SHŌ, selection, summary, excerpt	
抄	64 1849	抄録 shōroku excerpt, abstract, summary	538
		抄本 shōhon extract, abridged transcript	25
		抄訳 shōyaku abridged translation	594
抄		詩抄 shishō a selection of poems	570

	1154	MYŌ, strange, odd; a mystery; adroitness, knack	
妙	38 1199	奥妙 ōmyō secret, mystery	476
		妙案 myōan good idea, ingenious plan	106
		妙技 myōgi extraordinary skill	871
妙		妙手 myōshu expert, master, virtuoso	57
		絶妙 zetsumyō miraculous, superb, exquisite	742

	1155	HAI, sakazuki, wine cup (for sakè)	
杯	75 2206	一杯 ippai a glass (of); a drink; full	2
		二杯 nihai 2 glasses (of)	3
		祝杯 shukuhai a toast	851
杯		銀杯 ginpai silver cup	313
		デ杯(戦) Dehai(sen) Davis Cup (tournament)	301

	1156	MAI, (counter for thin, flat objects)	
枚	75	紙 一 枚 *kami ichimai* 1 sheet of paper	180, 2
	2202	何 枚 *nanmai* how many (sheets/plates/stamps)	390
		枚 挙 *maikyo* enumerate, count, list	801
		枚 数 *maisū* number of sheets	225
枚		大 枚 *taimai* a big sum (of money)	26

	1157	SATSU, paper money, slip of paper; *fuda*, chit, card, label	
札	75	千 円 札 *sen'ensatsu* 1,000-yen bill/note	15, 13
	2171	札 束 *satsutaba* bundle/roll of bills	501
		改 札 口 *kaisatsuguchi* wicket, ticket gate	514, 54
		標/表 札 *hyōsatsu* nameplate	923, 272
札		入 札 *nyūsatsu* a bid, tender	52

	1158	SATSU, (counter for books); SAKU, book	
冊	2	十 二 冊 *jūnisatsu* 12 books/volumes	12, 3
	88	別 冊 *bessatsu* separate volume	267
		分 冊 *bunsatsu* individual/separate volumes	38
		冊 子 *sasshi* booklet, brochure, pamphlet	103
冊		短 冊 *tanzaku* strip of fancy paper (for a poem)	215

	1159	HEN, *katayo(ru)*, lean, incline; be one sided, partial	
偏	9	不 偏(不党) *fuhen(futō)* nonpartisan	94, 495
	511	偏 向 *henkō* propensity, leaning, deviation	199
		偏 見 *henken* biased view, prejudice	63
		偏 食 *henshoku* unbalanced diet	322
偏		偏 差 *hensa* deviation, deflection, declination	658

	1160	HEN, far, widespread, general	
遍	162	遍 歴 *henreki* travel, pilgrimage	480
	4718	遍 路 *henro* pilgrim	151
		一 遍 *ippen* once, one time	2
遍			

	1161	BIN, bottle	
瓶	98	花 瓶 *kabin* vase	255
	2984	瓶 詰 *binzume* bottled, in a glass jar	1142
		ビール 瓶 *bīrubin* beer bottle	
		鉄 瓶 *tetsubin* iron kettle	312
瓶		空 き 瓶 *akibin* empty bottle	140

	1162	HEI, *awa(seru)*, put together, unite, combine	
併	9	合 併 *gappei* merger	159
	425	併 合 *heigō* annexation, amalgamation, merger	159
		併 用 *heiyō* use jointly/in combination	107
		併 発 *heihatsu* (medical) complications	96
併		併 記 *heiki* write side by side/on the same page	371

	1163	RIN, principle, code
倫	9 474 倫	倫理 *rinri* ethics, morals — 143 倫理学 *rinrigaku* ethics, moral philosophy 143, 109 人倫 *jinrin* humanity, morality — 1 不倫 *furin* immoral, illicit — 94 絶倫 *zetsurin* peerless, unsurpassed — 742

	1164	RIN, *wa*, wheel, ring, circle; (counter for flowers)
輪	159 4630 輪	車輪 *sharin* wheel — 133 輪番 *rinban* taking turns, in rotation — 185 五輪(大会) *gorin (taikai)* the Olympic Games 7, 26, 158 競輪 *keirin* bicycle race — 852 指輪 *yubiwa* (finger) ring — 1041

	1165	HEI, *nara(bu)*, be lined up; *nara(beru)*, arrange, put side by side; *nara(bi ni)*, and; *nami*, ordinary, average
並	12 589 並	並行 *heikō* parallel — 68 並列 *heiretsu* stand in a row; parataxis — 611 並木 *namiki* row of trees, roadside trees — 22 平年並み *heinennami* as in an average/normal year 202, 45

	1166	FU, general, universal
普	12 605 普	普通 *futsū* usual, ordinary — 150 普(通)選(挙) *fu(tsū) sen(kyo)* general elec- 150, 800, 801 普遍的 *fuhenteki* universal, ubiquitous ⌐tions 1160, 210 普請 *fushin* building, construction — 661 普段 *fudan* usual, ordinary, everyday — 362

	1167	FU, (sheet) music, notes, staff, score; a genealogy; record
譜	149 4437 譜	楽譜 *gakufu* (written) notes, the score — 358 譜面 *fumen* sheet music, score — 274 暗譜 *anpu* learning the notes by heart — 348 年譜 *nenpu* chronological record — 45 系譜 *keifu* genealogical chart, family tree — 908

	1168	REI, RYŌ, *tama*, soul, spirit
霊	173 5056 霊	霊肉 *reiniku* body and soul/spirit — 223 亡霊 *bōrei* soul/spirit of a dead person — 672 聖霊 *seirei* the Holy Spirit — 674 霊園 *reien* cemetery park ⌐tion, man 447 万物の霊長 *banbutsu no reichō* crown of crea- 16, 79, 95

	1169	SHITSU, *shime(ru)*, become damp; *shime(su)*, moisten
湿	85 2631 湿	湿気 *shikke, shikki* moisture, humidity — 134 湿度 *shitsudo* humidity — 377 湿地 *shitchi* damp ground, bog — 118 湿布 *shippu* wet compress, poultice — 675

	1170	KEN, clear, plain obvious
顕	181 5137	露 顕　　　*roken*　discovery, disclosure, exposure　951 顕 著　　　*kencho*　notable, striking, marked　859 顕 花 植 物 *kenka shokubutsu* flowering plant　255, 424, 79
顕		

	1171	KI, *tatto(i)*, *tōto(i)*, valuable, noble; *tatto(bu)*, *tōto(bu)*, value, esteem, respect
貴	154 4504	貴 重　　　*kichō*　valuable, precious　227 貴 重 品　*kichōhin*　valuables　227, 230 貴 族　　　*kizoku*　nobleman, the nobility　221 富 貴　　　*fūki*　riches and honors, wealth and rank　713
貴		

	1172	I, [YUI], leave behind, bequeath
遺	162 4745	遺 伝　　　*iden*　heredity　434 遺 体　　　*itai*　corpse, the remains　61 遺 産　　　*isan*　an inheritance, estate　278 遺 族　　　*izoku*　family of the deceased, survivors　221 遺 言　　　*yuigon*　will, last wishes　66
遺		

	1173	KEN, *tsuka(wasu)*, send; give; *tsuka(u)*, use
遣	162 4732	派 遣　　　　*haken*　dispatch, send (a person)　912 小 遣 い (銭) *kozukai(sen)*　pocket money　27, 648 気 遣 い　　*kizukai*　worry, apprehension　134 心 遣 い　　*kokorozukai*　solicitude, consideration　97
遣		

	1174	TSUI, *o(u)*, drive away; pursue
追	162 4686	追 放　　　*tsuihō*　banishment, purge　512 追 求　　　*tsuikyū*　pursue, follow up　724 追 加　　　*tsuika*　addition, supplement　709 追 い 風　*oikaze*　favorable/tail wind　29 追 い 越 す *oikosu*　overtake, pass　1001
追		

	1175	HAKU, *sema(ru)*, press (someone) for, urge; approach, draw near
迫	162 4676	切 迫　　　*seppaku*　draw near, press, be imminent　39 迫 力　　　*hakuryoku*　force, power, impressiveness　100 迫 害　　　*hakugai*　persecution　518 窮 迫　　　*kyūhaku*　straitened circumstances, poverty　897
迫		

	1176	HAKU, eldest brother (cf. No. 1667); count, earl
伯	9 397	画 伯　　　*gahaku*　great artist, master painter　343 伯 しゃく *hakushaku*　count, earl 伯 母　　　*oba*　aunt (elder sister of a parent)　112 伯 父　　　*oji*　uncle (elder brother of a parent)　113
伯		

	1177	HAKU, *to(maru/meru)*, (intr./tr.) put up (for the night), lodge
泊 85 2527 泊		宿 泊　*shukuhaku*　lodging　　　　　　　　　179 一 泊　*ippaku*　overnight stay　　　　　　　2 泊 り 賃 *tomarichin*　hotel charges　　　　751 泊 り 客 *tomarikyaku*　house guest; (hotel) guest　641

	1178	HAKU, HYŌ, beat (in music)
拍 64 1872 拍		拍 手　*hakushu*　handclapping, applause　　　57 拍 車　*hakusha*　a spur　　　　　　　　133 拍 子　*hyōshi*　time, tempo; chance, the moment　103 拍 子 木 *hyōshigi*　wooden clappers　　103, 22 脈 拍　*myakuhaku*　pulse　　　　　　　913

	1179	TEI, emperor
帝 8 305 帝		帝 国　*teikoku*　empire　　　　　　　　40 帝 国 主 義 *teikoku shugi*　imperialism　40, 155, 291 帝 政　*teisei*　imperial rule　　　　　　483 皇 帝　*kōtei*　emperor　　　　　　　　297 カ ー ル 大 帝 *Kāru Taitei*　Charlemagne　26

	1180	TEI, *shi(meru)*, tie, tighten; *shi(maru)*, be shut; tighten
締 120 3581 締		条 約 の 締 結 *jōyaku no teiketsu*　conclusion of a 　　　　　treaty　　　　654, 211, 485 取 り 締 ま り *torishimari*　control, supervision　65 締 め 切 り *shimekiri*　closing (date), deadline　39 引 き 締 め る *hikishimeru*　tighten, stiffen　216

	1181	HŌ, *tazu(neru)*, *otozu(reru)*, visit
訪 149 4326 訪		訪 問　*hōmon*　visit　　　　　　　　　162 来 訪　*raihō*　visit　　　　　　　　　69 訪 日　*hōnichi*　visit to Japan　　　　　5 訪 客　*hōkyaku*　visitor, guest　　　　641 探 訪　*tanbō*　making inquiries, inquiring into　535

	1182	BŌ, *samata(geru)*, prevent, obstruct, hamper
妨 38 1196 妨		妨 害　*bōgai*　obstruction, disturbance, interference　518

	1183	BŌ, *katawa(ra)*, side
傍 9 520 傍		傍 観　*bōkan*　look on, remain a spectator　604 傍 聴　*bōchō*　hearing, attendance　　1039 傍 系　*bōkei*　collateral (descendant)　　908 傍 証　*bōshō*　supporting evidence, corroboration　484 傍 受　*bōju*　intercept, monitor (a radio message)　260

亭 亭	1184	**TEI**, restaurant, pavilion, arbor	
	8 303	亭主 *teishu* host; innkeeper; husband 料亭 *ryōtei* (Japanese) restaurant	155 319
停 停	1185	**TEI**, stop	
	9 507	停止 *teishi* suspension, stopping 停滞 *teitai* stagnation, accumulation 調停 *chōtei* mediation, arbitration 停留所 *teiryūjo* (bus/streetcar) stop 各駅停車 *kakueki teisha* a local (train)	477 964 342 761, 153 642, 284, 133
轄 轄	1186	**KATSU**, a wedge; control, administration	
	160 4636	管轄 *kankatsu* jurisdiction, competence 管轄官庁 *kankatsu kanchō* the proper au- 所轄 *shokatsu* jurisdiction ⌐thorities 統轄 *tōkatsu* supervision, general control 直轄 *chokkatsu* direct control/jurisdiction	328 328, 326, 763 153 830 423
軒 軒	1187	**KEN**, (counter for buildings); *noki*, eaves	
	159 4611	一軒 *ikken* 1 house 軒数 *kensū* number of houses 軒並 *nokinami* row of houses 軒先 *nokisaki* edge of the eaves; front of the house	2 225 1165 50
汗 汗	1188	**KAN**, *ase*, sweat	
	85 2493	発汗 *hakkan* perspire, sweat 冷汗 *reikan, hiyaase* a cold sweat 汗顔 *kangan* sweating from shame	96 832 277
幹 幹	1189	**KAN**, main part; *miki*, (tree) trunk	
	24 790	幹部 *kanbu* key officers, executives, management 幹事長 *kanjichō* executive secretary, secretary- 根幹 *konkan* basis, root, nucleus ⌐general 語幹 *gokan* stem of a word ⌐train 新幹線 *Shinkansen* New Trunk Line, bullet	86 80, 95 314 67 174, 299
乾 乾	1190	**KAN**, *kawa(ku/kasu)*, (intr./tr.) dry, dry out	
	24 784	乾季 *kanki* the dry season 乾電池 *kandenchi* dry cell, battery 乾物 *kanbutsu* dry provisions, groceries 乾杯 *kanpai* a toast; Cheers!	465 108, 119 79 1155

	1191	MEN, *wata*, cotton	
綿	120	木綿 *momen* cotton	22
	3566	綿布 *menpu* cotton (cloth)	675
		綿織り物 *men'orimono* cotton fabrics, cotton	680, 79
綿		海綿 *kaimen* a sponge ⌐goods	117
		綿密 *menmitsu* minute, close, meticulous	806

	1192	SEN, *izumi*, spring, fountainhead, fountain	
泉	106	温泉 *onsen* hot spring, spa	634
	3099	冷泉 *reisen* cold mineral spring	832
		泉水 *sensui* garden pond, fountain	21
泉		源泉 *gensen* fountainhead, source	580
		平泉 *Hiraizumi* (town in Tohoku)	202

	1193	SEI, [SHŌ], *i*, a well	
井	4	井泉 *seisen* a well	1192
	165	油井 *yusei* oil well	364
		天井 *tenjō* ceiling	141
井		井戸 *ido* a well ⌐Tokyo)	152
		軽井沢 *Karuizawa* (summer resort town NW of 547, 994

	1194	I, *kako(mu/u)*, surround, enclose; lay siege to	
囲	31	範囲 *han'i* extent, scope, range	1092
	1032	周囲 *shūi* circumference, surroundings	91
		包囲 *hōi* encirclement, siege	804
囲		取り囲む *torikakomu* surround, enclose; besiege	65

	1195	SHŪ, arrest, imprison, prisoner	
囚	31	囚人 *shūjin* prisoner, convict	1
	1024	未決囚 *miketsushū* unconvicted prisoner	306, 356
		死刑囚 *shikeishū* criminal sentenced to death	85, 887
囚		女囚 *joshū* female prisoner	102
		免囚 *menshū* released prisoner, ex-convict	733

	1196	KŌ, *tagaya(su)*, till, plow, cultivate	
耕	127	耕地 *kōchi* arable land, cultivated land	118
	3695	耕作 *kōsaku* cultivation, farming	360
		農耕 *nōkō* agriculture, farming	369
耕			

	1197	MŌ, [KŌ], decrease	
耗	127	消耗 *shōmō* consumption, wear and tear	845
	3694	損耗 *sonmō* wear, wastage, loss	350
		心神耗弱(者) *shinshin kō/mō-jaku(sha)* feeble-	
耗		minded (person)	97, 310, 218, 164

	1198	SEKI, (family) register	
	118	戸 籍 *koseki* census registration	152
	3450	本 籍 *honseki* one's domicile, legal residence	25
		除 籍 *joseki* removal from the register	1065
籍		国 籍 *kokuseki* nationality	40
		書 籍 *shoseki* books	131

	1199	SAKU, mix, be in disorder	
	167	錯 覚 *sakkaku* illusion	605
	4880	錯 誤 *sakugo* error	906
		錯 乱 *sakuran* distraction, derangement	689
錯		交 錯 *kōsaku* mixture; intricacy	114
		倒 錯 *tōsaku* perversion	905

	1200	SO, give up, discontinue, set aside	
	64	措 置 *sochi* measures, steps	426
措	1930	報 復 措 置 *hōfuku sochi* retaliatory measures 685, 917, 426	

	1201	HAI, oga(mu), pray, venerate	
	64	参 拝 *sanpai* visit (a shrine/grave)	710
	1884	礼 拝 *reihai* worship, (church) services	620
		拝 見 *haiken* see, have a look at	63
拝		拝 借 *haishaku* borrow	766
		拝 み 倒 す *ogamitoasu* entreat (someone) into consent 905	

	1202	RAN, (newspaper) column; railing	
	75	家 庭 欄 *kateiran* home-life section	165, 1112
	2401	投 書 欄 *tōshoran* letters-to-the-editor column	1021, 131
		欄 外 *rangai* margin (of a page)	83
欄		空 欄 *kūran* blank column/space	140
		欄 干 *rankan* railing, banister	584

	1203	JUN, uruo(su), moisten, wet, water; profit, enrich; uruo(u), become wet; profit, become rich; uru(mu), become wet/blurred/turbid/clouded	
	85		
	2700	浸 潤 *shinjun* permeation, infiltration	1078
		利 潤 *rijun* profits	329
潤		潤 飾/色 *junshoku* embellishment	979, 204

	1204	RYŌ, suzu(shii), cool, refreshing; suzu(mu), cool off, enjoy the evening cool	
	85		
	2598	清 涼 飲 料 *seiryō inryō* carbonated beverage 660, 323, 319	
		涼 味 *ryōmi* the cool, coolness	307
		涼 風 *ryōfū, suzukaze* cool breeze	29
涼		夕 涼 み *yūsuzumi* the evening cool	81

	1205	TŌ, *kō(ru)*, freeze (up); *kogo(eru)*, become frozen/numb	
凍	15 649	冷凍器 *reitōki* refrigerator, freezer	832, 527
		凍結 *tōketsu* freeze (assets)	485
		凍傷 *tōshō* frostbite	633
		凍死 *tōshi* freeze to death	85
凍		凍え死に *kogoejini* freeze to death	85

	1206	HYŌ, *kōri, hi*, ice; *kō(ru)*, freeze (up)	
氷	3 131	氷山 *hyōzan* iceberg	34
		氷河 *hyōga* glacier	389
		流氷 *ryūhyō* floating ice, ice floe	247
		氷点(下) *hyōten(ka)* (below) the freezing point	169, 31
氷		氷結 *hyōketsu* freeze (over)	485

	1207	EI, *naga(i)*, long (time)	
永	3 130	永住 *eijū* permanent residence	156
		永遠 *eien* eternity	446
		永眠 *eimin* eternal sleep, death	849
		永続 *eizoku* permanence, perpetuity	243
永		永田町 *Nagatachō* (area of Tokyo)	35, 182

	1208	EI, *oyo(gu)*, swim	
泳	85 2520	水泳 *suiei* swimming	21
		競泳 *kyōei* swimming race	852
		泳法 *eihō* swimming style/stroke	123
		遠泳 *en'ei* long-distance swim	446
泳		平泳ぎ *hiraoyogi* the breaststroke	202

	1209	EI, *yo(mu)*, compose, write (a poem)	
詠	149 4336	詠歌 *eika* composition of a poem; (Buddhist) chant	392
		詠草 *eisō* draft of a poem	249
詠			

	1210	KYŪ, [KU], *hisa(shii)*, long (time)	
久	4 153	永久 *eikyū* permanence, perpetuity, eternity	1207
		長久 *chōkyū* long continuance, eternity	95
		持久 *jikyū* endurance, persistence	451
		久遠 *kuon* eternity	446
久		久し振り *hisashiburi* (after) a long time	954

	1211	KOKU, *kiza(mu)*, cut fine, chop up; carve, engrave	
刻	18 681	彫刻 *chōkoku* sculpture	1149
		深刻 *shinkoku* grave, serious	536
		時刻 *jikoku* time	42
		一刻 *ikkoku* moment; stubborn	2
刻		夕刻 *yūkoku* evening	81

	1212	**KAKU**, core, nucleus
核	75 2254	核心 *kakushin* core, kernel 97 原子核 *genshikaku* (atomic) nucleus 136, 103 核燃料 *kakunenryō* nuclear fuel 652, 319 核兵器 *kakuheiki* nuclear weapons 784, 527 結核 *kekkaku* tuberculosis 485
核		

	1213	**GAI**, (prefix) the said
該	149 4349	当該官庁 *tōgai kanchō* relevant authorities 77, 326, 763 当該人物 *tōgai jinbutsu* the said person 77, 1, 79 該当 *gaitō* pertain (to), come/fall under 77 該博な知識 *gaihaku na chishiki* profound/vast learning 601, 214, 681
該		

	1214	**SHIN**, *mi(ru)*, diagnose, examine
診	149 4338	診察 *shinsatsu* medical examination 619 検診 *kenshin* medical examination 531 診断 *shindan* diagnosis 1024 打診 *dashin* percussion, tapping; sound out 1020 往診 *ōshin* doctor's visit to a patient, house call 918
診		

	1215	**CHIN**, *mezura(shii)*, rare, unusual
珍	96 2933	珍品 *chinpin* a rarity, curiosity 230 珍談 *chindan* amusing story, anecdote 593 珍味 *chinmi* a delicacy 307 珍重 *chinchō* value highly, prize 227 珍客 *chinkyaku* least-expected/welcome visitor 641
珍		

	1216	**KYŪ**, old, former
旧	2 94	旧式 *kyūshiki* old-type, old-fashioned 525 復旧 *fukkyū* recovery, restoration 917 新旧 *shinkyū* old and new 174 旧悪 *kyūaku* one's past misdeed 304 旧約(聖書) *Kyūyaku (Seisho)* Old Testament 211, 674, 131
旧		

	1217	**JI**, [**NI**], small child, infant
児	10 572	児童 *jidō* child, juvenile 410 育児園 *ikujien* daycare nursery 246, 447 産児制限 *sanji seigen* birth control 278, 427, 847 乳児 *nyūji* (nursing) baby, infant 939 小児科医 *shōnikai* pediatrician 27, 320, 220
児		

	1218	**KAN**, *ochii(ru)*, fall, get, run (into); fall, be reduced; *otoshii-(reru)*, ensnare, entice; capture
陥	170 4990	欠陥 *kekkan* defect, shortcoming 383 陥落 *kanraku* fall, capitulation 839 陥没 *kanbotsu* depression, subsidence, cave-in 935 陥せい *kansei* pitfall, trap, plot
陥		

	1219	KEI, E, *megu(mu)*, bestow a favor, bless	
恵 61 1681 恵		天恵 *tenkei* gift of nature, natural advantage 恩恵 *onkei* benefit, favor 互恵 *gokei* mutual benefit, reciprocity 知恵 *chie* wisdom, sense, brains, intelligence 知恵者 *chiesha* wise/resourceful man	141 555 907 214 214, 164
	1220	TŌ, *ine*, [*ina-*], rice plant	
稲 115 3294 稲		水稲 *suitō* paddy rice 稲作 *inasaku* rice crop 稲荷 *Inari* god of harvests, fox deity 早稲 *wase* (early-ripening variety of rice) 早稲田 *Waseda* (area of Tokyo)	21 360 391 248 248, 35
	1221	SUI, *ho*, ear, head (of grain)	
穂 115 3300 穂		稲穂 *inaho* ear of rice 穂先 *hosaki* tip of an ear/spear/knife/brush 穂波 *honami* waves of grain	1220 50 666
	1222	KIN, fungus, germ, bacteria	
菌 140 3976 菌		細菌 *saikin* bacteria 保菌者 *hokinsha* (germ) carrier 殺菌 *sakkin* sterilization 無菌 *mukin* germ-free, sterilized 抗菌性 *kōkinsei* antibacterial	695 489, 164 576 93 824, 98
	1223	CHIKU, animal raising; domestic animals	
畜 95 2920 畜		家畜 *kachiku* domestic animal, livestock 畜産 *chikusan* stock raising 牧畜業 *bokuchikugyō* stock farming, cattle 畜舎 *chikusha* cattle shed, barn 畜生 *chikushō* beast, brute; Dammit!	165 278 731, 279 791 44
	1224	CHIKU, *takuwa(eru)*, store, save, put aside	
蓄 140 4024 蓄		貯蓄 *chochiku* savings, saving 備蓄 *bichiku* saving for emergencies, storing 蓄積 *chikuseki* accumulation 蓄電池 *chikudenchi* storage battery	762 768 656 108, 119
	1225	GEN, dark, mystery	
玄 95 2918 玄		玄関 *genkan* entranceway 玄関番 *genkanban* doorkeeper, doorman, porter 玄米 *genmai* unpolished/brown rice 玄人 *kurōto* expert, professional, specialist	398 398, 185 224 1

	1226	GEN, *tsuru*, string; bowstring	
弦	57	弦楽器 *gengakki* string instrument, the strings	358, 527
	1568	管弦楽 (団) *kangengaku(dan)* orchestra	328, 358, 491
		正弦曲線 *seigen kyokusen* sine curve	275, 366, 299
	弦	上弦 *jōgen* first quarter (of the moon)	32
		下弦 *kagen* last quarter (of the moon)	31

	1227	GEN, *maboroshi*, illusion, phantom, vision	
幻	52	幻覚 *genkaku* hallucination	605
	1494	幻影 *gen'ei* vision, phantom, illusion	854
		幻想 *gensō* fantasy, illusion	147
	幻	夢幻 *mugen* dreams and phantasms	811

	1228	YŪ, quiet, deep	
幽	2	幽玄 *yūgen* the profound, occult	1225
	112	幽霊 *yūrei* ghost	1168
		幽閉 *yūhei* confinement, imprisonment	397
	幽	幽谷 *yūkoku* deep ravine, narrow valley	653
		幽門 *yūmon* pylorus	161

	1229	YŌ, *osana(i)*, very young; infantile, childish	
幼	52	幼児 *yōji* baby, small child, tot	1217
	1495	幼少 *yōshō* infancy, childhood	144
		幼虫 *yōchū* larva	873
	幼	幼子 *osanago* little child	103
		幼心 *osanagokoro* child's mind/heart	97

	1230	CHI, child	
稚	115	幼稚園 *yōchien* kindergarten	1229, 447
	3292	稚気 *chiki* childlike state of mind	134
		稚児 *chigo* child; child in a Buddhist procession	1217
	稚		

	1231	I, tie, rope	
維	120	維持 *iji* maintenance, support	451
	3552	維持費 *ijihi* upkeep expenses	451, 749
		明治維新 *Meiji Ishin* Meiji Restoration	18, 493, 174
	維		

	1232	JUN, apply correspondingly, imitate, pattern after	
准	15	批准 *hijun* ratify	1029
	648		
	准		

	1233	SUI, *o(su)*, infer, deduce; recommend, propose	
推	64 1950 推	推定 *suitei* presumption, inference	355
		推論 *suiron* reasoning, inference	293
		推理 *suiri* reasoning, inference	143
		類推 *ruisui* (inference by) analogy	226
		推進 *suishin* propulsion, drive	437

	1234	YUI, [I], solely, only, merely	
唯	30 942 唯	唯物論 *yuibutsuron* materialism	79, 293
		唯心論 *yuishinron* spiritualism, idealism	97, 293
		唯理論 *yuiriron* rationalism	143, 293
		唯美主義 *yuibi shugi* estheticism	401, 155, 291
		唯一 *yuiitsu* the only, sole	2

	1235	SHŌ, *wara(u)*, laugh, smile; *e(mu)*, smile	
笑	118 3374 笑	苦笑 *kushō* wry smile, forced laugh	545
		冷笑 *reishō* scornful laugh, sneer	832
		談笑 *danshō* friendly talk, chat	593
		大笑い *ōwarai* loud laughter, hearty laugh	26
		笑顔 *egao* smiling face	277

	1236	KYŪ, *na(ku)*, cry	
泣	85 2532 泣	感泣 *kankyū* be moved to tears	262
		号泣 *gōkyū* wailing, lamentation	266
		泣き声 *nakigoe* tearful voice, sob, whimper	746
		泣き落とす *nakiotosu* obtain (someone's) consent by tears	839
		泣き虫 *nakimushi* crybaby	873

	1237	BŌ, a room; tassel; *fusa*, tassel, tuft, cluster	
房	63 1819 房	暖房 *danbō* heating	635
		独房 *dokubō* solitary (prison) cell	219
		官房長 (官) *kanbōchō(kan)* chief secretary	326, 95
		文房具 *bunbōgu* stationery	111, 420
		女房 *nyōbō* (one's own) wife	102

	1238	REI, *modo(ru)*, go/come back, return; *modo(su)*, give/send back, return, restore; throw up, vomit	
戻	63 1818 戻	取り戻す *torimodosu* regain	65
		払い戻す *haraimodosu* pay back, refund	582
		差し戻す *sashimodosu* send back (to a lower court)	658
		逆戻り *gyakumodori* going backward, retrogression	444

	1239	RUI, *namida*, teardrop	
涙	85 2569 涙	感涙 *kanrui* tears of strong emotion	262
		血涙 *ketsurui* tears of blood, bitter tears	789
		空涙 *soranamida* false/crocodile tears	140
		涙声 *namidagoe* tearful voice	746
		涙ぐましい *namidagumashii* touching, moving	

喫	**1240** 30 961 喫	**KITSU, eat, drink, smoke** 喫茶店 *kissaten* teahouse, café 251, 168 喫煙 *kitsuen* smoking 919 満喫 *mankitsu* eat/drink one's fill, enjoy fully 201 喫する *kissuru* eat, drink, smoke
潔	**1241** 85 2698 潔	**KETSU, pure; *isagiyo(i)*, brave, manly, righteous, pure** 清潔 *seiketsu* clean, neat 660 純潔 *junketsu* pure, chaste 965 潔白 *keppaku* pure, upright, of integrity 205 高潔 *kōketsu* noble, lofty, high-minded 190 不潔 *fuketsu* impure, unclean, filthy 94
息	**1242** 132 3844 息	**SOKU, son; breath; *iki*, breath** 休息 *kyūsoku* a rest, breather 60 消息 *shōsoku* news, information 845 利息 *risoku* interest (on a loan) 329 息切れ *ikigire* shortness of breath 39 息子 *musuko* son 103
憩	**1243** 61 1765 憩	**KEI, *iko(i)*, rest; *iko(u)*, rest** 休憩 *kyūkei* rest, recess 60 休憩所 *kyūkeijo* resting place, lobby 60, 153 休憩時間 *kyūkei jikan* rest period, recess 60, 42, 43 小/少憩 *shōkei* brief recess, a break 27, 144
臭	**1244** 132 3842 臭	**SHŪ, *kusa(i)*, foul-smelling, smelling of** 臭気 *shūki* offensive odor, stink 134 悪臭 *akushū* bad odor, stench 304 俗臭 *zokushū* low taste, vulgarity 1126 古臭い *furukusai* old, outdated; trite, hackneyed 172 かび臭い *kabikusai* musty, moldy
腐	**1245** 53 1532 腐	**FU, *kusa(ru/reru)*, rot, go bad, spoil, turn sour; *kusa(rasu)*, spoil, rot, putrefy, corrode** 豆腐 *tōfu* tofu, bean curd 958 腐食 *fushoku* corrosion 322 腐敗 *fuhai* decomposition, decay; corruption 511 腐心 *fushin* take pains, be intent on 97
嘆	**1246** 30 974 嘆	**TAN, *nage(ku)*, grieve, lament, bemoan; deplore, regret; *nage(kawashii)*, deplorable, regrettable** 感嘆 *kantan* admiration, exclamation 262 嘆願 *tangan* entreaty, petition 581 嘆息 *tansoku* sigh; lament 1242 悲嘆 *hitan* grief, sorrow, lamentation 1034

	1247	**KIN**, *tsutsushi(mu)*, be respectful	
謹	149 4424	謹聴　　*kinchō*　listen attentively	1039
		謹賀新年 *kinga shinnen*　Happy New Year.	756, 174, 45
		謹言　　*kingen*　Sincerely/Respectfully yours,	66
謹		謹んで　*tsutsushinde*　respectfully, humbly	

	1248	**HI**, *ina*, no	
否	1 40	否定　　*hitei*　denial, negation	355
		否認　　*hinin*　denial, repudiation, disavow	738
		否決　　*hiketsu*　rejection, voting down	356
否		賛否　　*sanpi*　approval or disapproval, yes or no	745
		安否　　*anpi*　how (someone) is getting on	105

	1249	**GAN**, *fuku(mu)*, hold in one's mouth; bear in mind; contain, include; *fuku(meru)*, include; give instructions	
含	9 402	含蓄　　*ganchiku*　significance, implication	1224
		包含　　*hōgan*　include, cover, imply	804
含		含有　　*gan'yū*　contain	265

	1250	**GIN**, sing, chant, recite	
吟	30 898	独吟　　*dokugin*　(vocal) solo	219
		詩吟　　*shigin*　recitation of Chinese poems	570
		吟詠　　*gin'ei*　sing, recite; compose a poem	1209
吟		吟味　　*ginmi*　close inquiry, scrutiny	307

	1251	**KIN**, *koto*, koto, Japanese zither	
琴	96 2949	心の琴線 *kokoro no kinsen*　heartstrings	97, 299
		木琴　　*mokkin*　xylophone	22
		風琴　　*fūkin*　organ, harmonium	29
琴		手風琴　*tefūkin*　accordion, concertina	57, 29
		たて琴　*tategoto*　harp, lyre	

	1252	**KYŌ**, *sake(bu)*, shout, cry out	
叫	30 881	絶叫　　*zekkyō*　scream, exclamation	742
		叫び声　*sakebigoe*　a shout, cry, scream	746
叫			

	1253	**TO**, *ha(ku)*, spew, vomit, throw up; express, give vent to	
吐	30 883	吐血　　*toketsu*　vomit blood	789
		吐息　　*toiki*　a sigh	1242
		吐露　　*toro*　express, voice, speak out	951
吐		吐き気　*hakike*　nausea	134
		吐き出す *hakidasu*　vomit, disgorge, spew out	53

	1254	**KO**, *yo(bu)*, call, send for, invite, name	
呼	30 914	点呼 *tenko* roll call	169
		呼応 *koō* act in concert	827
		呼び声 *yobigoe* a call, cry, shout ⌈loudspeaker)	746
呼		呼び出す *yobidasu* page, call (on the telephone/a	53
		呼び戻す *yobimodosu* call back, recall	1238

	1255	**SUI**, *fu(ku)*, blow	
吹	30 901	鼓吹 *kosui* inspire, instill	1147
		吹雪 *fubuki* snowstorm	949
		吹き込む *fukikomu* blow in; record (a song); inspire	776
吹		吹き飛ぶ *fukitobu* be blown away	530
		吹き出物 *fukidemono* skin rash, spots, pimple	53, 79

	1256	**KYŪ**, *su(u)*, suck in, inhale; smoke	
吸	30 885	呼吸 *kokyū* breathing	1254
		吸入 *kyūnyū* inhale	52
		吸引 *kyūin* absorb (by suction)	216
吸		吸収 *kyūshū* absorb	757
		吸い取り紙 *suitorigami* blotting paper	65, 180

	1257	**KYŪ**, *oyo(bu)*, reach, amount to, extend to, match, equal; *oyo(bosu)*, exert; *oyo(bi)*, and, as well as	
及	4 154	普及 *fukyū* spread, come into wide use	1166
		及第点 *kyūdaiten* passing mark/grade	404, 169
		言及 *genkyū* refer to, mention	66
及		言い及ぶ *iioyobu* refer to, touch upon	66

	1258	*atsuka(u)*, handle	
扱	64 1836	取り扱う *toriatsukau* treat, deal with, handle	65
		取り扱い方 *toriatsukaikata* how to handle	65, 70
		取(り)扱(い)注意 *toriatsukai chūi* Handle with	
扱		Care	65, 357, 132
		客扱い *kyakuatsukai* hospitality, service to customers	641

	1259	**ZETSU**, *shita*, tongue	
舌	135 3855	舌戦 *zessen* verbal warfare, war of words	301
		弁舌 *benzetsu* eloquence, tongue, speech ⌈remarks	711
		毒舌 *dokuzetsu* venomous tongue, malicious	522
舌		二枚舌 *nimaijita* forked tongue, duplicity	3, 1156
		舌打ち *shitauchi* clicking one's tongue, tsk, tch	1020

	1260	**KATSU**, tie together, fasten	
括	64 1896	一括 *ikkatsu* lump together, summarize	2
		包括的 *hōkatsuteki* comprehensive, general,	
		sweeping	804, 210
括		総括 *sōkatsu* generalization, summarization	697

	1261	KEN, *kinu*, silk	
120		人絹 *jinken* artificial silk, rayon	1
3543		絹布 *kenpu* silk fabric, silk	675
		絹糸 *kenshi, kinuito* silk thread	242
絹		絹織物 *kinuorimono* silk fabrics	680, 79
		絹針 *kinubari* needle for silk	341

	1262	KŌ, agree to, consent	
77		肯定 *kōtei* affirmation, affirmative	355
2432		首肯 *shukō* assent, consent	148
肯			

	1263	KYŌ, *obiya(kasu)*, *odo(kasu/su)*, threaten	
19		脅迫 *kyōhaku* threat, intimidation	1175
727		脅迫状 *kyōhakujō* threatening letter	1175, 626
脅		脅し文句 *odoshimonku* threatening words	111, 337

	1264	KEN, *kata*, shoulder	
63		肩章 *kenshō* epaulet, shoulder pips	857
1820		比肩 *hiken* rank (with), be comparable (to)	798
		肩書き *katagaki* one's title, degree	131
肩		肩代わり *katagawari* take-over, transfer (of business)	256
		肩身が広い *katami ga hiroi* feel proud	59, 694

	1265	HAI, *se*, back; height; *sei*, height, stature; *somu(ku)*, act contrary (to); *somu(keru)*, avert, turn away	
130			
3754		背景 *haikei* background	853
		背信 *haishin* breach of faith, betrayal, infidelity	157
背		背中 *senaka* the back	28
		背広 *sebiro* business suit	694

	1266	KOTSU, *hone*, bone	
188		骨格 *kokkaku* skeleton, framework	643
5236		頭骨 *tōkotsu* skull	276
		骨子 *kosshi* essential part, main points	103
骨		鉄骨 *tekkotsu* steel frame	312
		骨惜しみ *honeoshimi* avoid effort, spare oneself	765

	1267	KATSU, *sube(ru)*, slide, glide; slip; *name(raka)*, smooth	
85		滑走路 *kassōro* runway	429, 151
2663		潤滑油 *junkatsuyu* lubricating oil	1203, 364
		円滑 *enkatsu* smooth, harmonious, amicable	13
滑		滑り台 *suberidai* (playground) slide	492

	1268	**I, stomach**	
胃	102 3000	胃病 *ibyō* stomach disorder/trouble	380
		胃酸 *isan* stomach acid	516
		胃弱 *ijaku* weak digestion, indigestion, dyspepsia	218
		胃下垂 *ikasui* gastric ptosis	31, 1070
胃		胃がん *igan* stomach cancer	

	1269	**FU, the skin**	
膚	141 4113	皮膚 *hifu* the skin	975
		皮膚病 *hifubyō* skin disease	975, 380
		皮膚移植 *hifu ishoku* skin graft/transplant	975, 1121, 424
膚		完膚なきまで *kanpu-naki made* thoroughly, completely	613

	1270	**CHŌ, intestines, entrails**	
腸	130 3798	胃腸 *ichō* stomach and intestines	1268
		大腸 *daichō* large intestine, colon	26
		腸閉そく *chōheisoku* intestinal obstruction, ileus	397
		腸ねん転 *chōnenten* twist in the intestines, volvulus	433
腸		断腸の思い *danchō no omoi* heartrending grief	1024, 99

	1271	**FUKU, hara, belly; heart, mind**	
腹	130 3800	切腹 *seppuku* hara-kiri	39
		立腹 *rippuku* anger, offense	121
		空腹 *kūfuku* empty belly, hunger	140
		腹巻き *haramaki* belly/stomach band	507
腹		太っ腹 *futoppara* magnanimous; bold, daring	629

	1272	**KAN, kimo, liver; heart, spirit**	
肝	130 3731	肝硬変 *kankōhen* cirrhosis of the liver	1009, 257
		肝油 *kan'yu* cod-liver oil	364
		肝要 *kan'yō* important, vital	419
		肝心 *kanjin* main, vital, essential	97
肝		肝っ玉 *kimottama* pluck, courage, grit	295

	1273	**TAN, gallbladder; courage**	
胆	130 3751	胆石 *tanseki* gallstone	78
		大胆 *daitan* bold, daring	26
		胆力 *tanryoku* courage, mettle	100
胆		落胆 *rakutan* discouragement, disappointment	839

	1274	**TAN, katsu(gu), carry on the shoulder; choose (someone); trick (someone); nina(u), carry on the shoulder; bear, take on**	
担	64 1879	担当 *tantō* being in charge, overseeing	77
		担任 *tannin* charge, responsibility	334
		負担 *futan* burden, load, liability	510
担		担保 *tanpo* a security, guarantee	489

	1275	KŌ, always	
恒	61 1683	恒久 *kōkyū* permanence, perpetuity	1210
		恒星 *kōsei* fixed star, sidereal	730
		恒心 *kōshin* constancy, steadfastness	97
恒		恒例 *kōrei* established practice, custom	612
		恒常 *kōjō* constancy	497

	1276	*kaki*, fence, hedge	
垣	32 1075	石垣 *ishigaki* stone wall	78
		竹垣 *takegaki* bamboo fence	129
		生け垣 *ikegaki* hedge	44
垣		垣根 *kakine* fence, hedge	314
		垣間見る *kaimamiru* peek in, get a glimpse	43, 63

	1277	HAI, lung	
肺	130 3752	肺病 *haibyō* lung/pulmonary disease	380
		肺結核 *haikekkaku* pulmonary tuberculosis	485, 1212
		肺がん *haigan* lung cancer	
肺		肺活量 *haikatsuryō* lung capacity 「heart	237, 411
		肺肝 *haikan* lungs and liver; one's innermost	1272

	1278	NŌ, brain	
脳	130 3774	頭脳 *zunō* brains, intelligence	276
		脳下垂体 *nōka suitai* pituitary gland	31, 1070, 61
		脳卒中 *nōsotchū* cerebral hemorrhage	787, 28
脳		洗脳 *sennō* brainwashing	692
		首脳会談 *shunō kaidan* summit conference	148, 158, 593

	1279	NŌ, *naya(mu)*, be troubled, be distressed, suffer; *naya(masu)*, afflict, beset, worry	
悩	61 1698	苦悩 *kunō* affliction, distress, agony	545
		悩殺 *nōsatsu* enchant, captivate	576
		伸び悩む *nobinayamu* continue stagnant, level off	1108
悩		恋の悩み *koi no nayami* the torments of love	258

	1280	KYŌ, evil, misfortune	
凶	17 663	凶作 *kyōsaku* bad harvest	360
		凶行 *kyōkō* violence, crime, murder	68
		凶悪 *kyōaku* heinous, brutal	304
凶		凶器 *kyōki* murder/lethal weapon	527
		吉凶 *kikkyō* good or ill luck, fortune	1141

	1281	RI, *hana(reru)*, separate, leave; *hana(su)*, separate, keep apart	
離	172 5040	分離 *bunri* separation, secession, segregation	38
		離婚 *rikon* divorce	567
		離反 *rihan* estrangement, alienation, breakaway	324
離		離陸 *ririku* (airplane) takeoff	647
		切り離す *kirihanasu* cut off, sever	39

	1282	ka(ru), cut (hair), clip, mow	
刈	18 666 刈	刈り入れ kariire harvest, reaping 稲刈り inekari rice reaping/harvesting 刈り取る karitoru mow, cut down 刈り込む karikomu cut, trim, prune 芝刈り機 shibakariki lawn mower	52 1220 65 776 250, 528

	1283	KYŌ, mune, [muna], breast, chest	
胸	130 3768 胸	胸像 kyōzō (sculptured) bust 胸部 kyōbu the chest 胸囲 kyōi girth/circumference of the chest 胸中 kyōchū one's bosom, heart, feelings 度胸 dokyō courage, daring, nerve	740 86 1194 28 377

	1284	HŌ, sac, sheath; placenta	
胞	130 3749 胞	細胞 saibō, saihō cell 単細胞 tansaibō 1/single cell 脳細胞 nōsaibō brain cell 胞子 hōshi spore 同胞 dōhō brethren, countrymen	695 300, 695 1278, 695 103 198

	1285	HŌ, da(ku), hug, hold in one's arms; ida(ku), embrace, harbor (feelings); kaka(eru), carry in one's arms; have (dependents); employ, hire	
抱	64 1883 抱	抱負 hōfu aspiration, ambition 介抱 kaihō nursing, care 抱き合う dakiau embrace each other	510 453 159

	1286	ZŌ, kura, storehouse, warehouse, repository	
蔵	140 4042 蔵	冷蔵庫 reizōko refrigerator 蔵書 zōsho collection of books, one's library 貯蔵 chozō storage 蔵相 zōshō minister of finance 大蔵省 Ōkurashō Ministry of Finance	832, 825 131 762 146 26, 145

	1287	ZŌ, internal organs	
臓	130 3828 臓	内臓 naizō internal organs, viscera 臓器 zōki internal organs, viscera 心臓 shinzō the heart 肺臓 haizō the lungs 肝臓 kanzō the liver	84 527 97 1277 1272

	1288	KEN, kashiko(i), wise, intelligent	
賢	154 4517 賢	賢明 kenmei wise, intelligent 先賢 senken wise men of old, ancient sages 賢人 kenjin wise man, sage, the wise 賢母 kenbo wise mother 悪賢い warugashikoi sly, wily, cunning	18 50 1 112 304

	1289	KEN, *kata(i)*, firm, hard, solid	
32 1096	堅実	*kenjitsu* solid, sound, reliable	203
	堅固	*kengo* strong, solid, steadfast	972
	中堅	*chūken* mainstay, backbone, nucleus	28
堅	堅持	*kenji* hold fast to, adhere to	451
	手堅い	*tegatai* firm, solid, dependable	57

	1290	KIN, hard, tight	
120 3560	緊張	*kinchō* tension	1106
	緊迫	*kinpaku* tension	1175
	緊急	*kinkyū* emergency	303
緊	緊縮	*kinshuku* contraction; austerity	1110
	緊密	*kinmitsu* close, tight	806

	1291	RAN, see, look at	
147 4292	展/博覧会	*ten/haku-rankai* an exhibition	1129, 601, 158
	遊覧船	*yūransen* excursion ship, pleasure boat	1003, 376
	観覧	*kanran* viewing, inspection	604
覧	一覧表	*ichiranhyō* table, list	2, 272
	回覧	*kairan* read-and-pass-on circulation	90

	1292	HAN, fullness, luxury; frequency	
120 3596	繁栄	*han'ei* prosperity	723
	繁盛	*hanjō* prosperity; success	719
繁	繁華街	*hankagai* thriving shopping area	1074, 186

	1293	KYO, large, gigantic	
22 758	巨大	*kyodai* huge, gigantic, enormous	26
	巨人	*kyojin* giant	1
	巨漢	*kyokan* very large man, big fellow	556
巨	巨星	*kyosei* giant star; great/prominent man	730
	巨万	*kyoman* millions, immense amount	16

	1294	KYO, distance	
157 4548	距離	*kyori* distance	1281
	短/近距離	*tan/kin-kyori* short distance	215, 445, 1281
	長/遠距離	*chō/en-kyori* long distance	95, 446, 1281
距	中距離競走	*chūkyori kyōsō* medium-distance race	28, 1281, 852, 429

	1295	KYO, *koba(mu)*, refuse, decline	
64 1847	拒否	*kyohi* denial, refusal; rejection, veto	1248
	拒否権	*kyohiken* right of veto	1248, 335
拒	拒絶	*kyozetsu* refusal, rejection, repudiation	742

	1296	**TAI**, womb, uterus	
胎	130 3750	胎盤 *taiban* placenta, afterbirth	1098
		母胎 *botai* mother's womb/uterus	112
		受胎 *jutai* conception	260
胎		胎児 *taiji* embryo, fetus	1217
		胎動 *taidō* fetal movement, quickening	231

	1297	**TAI**, *nama(keru)*, be idle, be lazy, neglect; *okota(ru)*, neglect, be remiss in, default on	
怠	28 851	怠業 *taigyō* work stoppage, slowdown strike	279
		けん怠 *kentai* fatigue, weariness	
怠		怠け者 *namakemono* idler, lazybones	164

	1298	**YŌ**, *koshi*, pelvic region, loins, hips, small of back	
腰	130 3799	腰部 *yōbu* pelvic region, waist, hips, loins	86
		腰布 *koshinuno* loincloth	675
		弱腰 *yowagoshi* without backbone, faint-hearted	218
腰		物腰 *monogoshi* one's manner, demeanor	79
		本腰 *hongoshi* serious, in earnest	25

	1299	**WAN**, *ude*, arm; ability, talent, skill	
腕	130 3786	手腕 *shuwan* ability, capability, skill	57
		腕力 *wanryoku* physical strength	100
		腕前 *udemae* ability, skill	47
腕		腕輪 *udewa* bracelet	1164
		腕時計 *udedokei* wristwatch	42, 340

	1300	**DŌ**, torso, trunk	
胴	130 3767	胴体 *dōtai* the body, torso; fuselage	61
		胴上/揚げ *dōage* hoist (someone) shoulder-high	32, 631
胴		胴回り *dōmawari* one's girth	90

	1301	**DŌ**, *hora*, cave	
洞	85 2546	洞察 *dōsatsu* discernment, insight	619
		空洞 *kūdō* cave, cavity	140
		洞穴 *dōketsu, horaana* cave	899
洞		洞くつ *dōkutsu* cave, grotto	
		秋吉洞 *Akiyoshi-dō* (largest cave in Japan)	462, 1141

	1302	**GA**, *ware, wa*, I, self; my, our	
我	4 200	自我 *jiga* self, ego	62
		我利 *gari* one's own interests, self-interest	329
		無我 *muga* self-effacement, selflessness	93
我		我勝ち *waregachi* each striving to be first	509
		我が国 *wagakuni* our country	40

	1303	**GA, starve**	
餓	184 5171	餓死 *gashi* starve to death	85
	餓		

	1304	**KI, *u(eru)*, starve**	
飢	184 5155	飢餓 *kiga* hunger, starvation 飢きん *kikin* famine 飢死に *uejini* starve to death	1303 85
	飢		

	1305	**KI, *tsukue*, desk**	
机	75 2174	机上 *kijō* desk-top, academic, theoretical, armchair 32 机上の空論 *kijō no kūron* mere academic 　theorizing 32, 140, 293 事務机 *jimuzukue* office desk 80, 235 書き物机 *kakimono-zukue* writing desk 131, 79	
	机		

	1306	***hada*, the skin; disposition, character, temperament**	
肌	130 3726	肌色 *hadairo* flesh-colored	204
		地肌 *jihada* one's skin; surface of the ground	118
		肌着 *hadagi* underwear	657
		肌触り *hadazawari* the touch, feel	874
	肌	肌寒い *hadasamui* chilly	457

	1307	**SŌ, *kura*, storehouse, warehouse, depository**	
倉	9 486	倉庫 *sōko* warehouse	825
		倉荷 *kurani* warehouse goods	391
	倉		

	1308	**SŌ, creation**	
創	18 702	創造 *sōzō* creation	691
		創作 *sōsaku* (literary) creation	360
		創立 *sōritsu* establishment, founding	121
		独創 *dokusō* originality, creativity	219
	創	創価学会 *Sōka Gakkai* (Buddhist sect) 421, 109, 158	

	1309	**FUN, *furu(u)*, be enlivened, rouse up**	
奮	37 1184	興奮 *kōfun* excitement	368
		奮発 *funpatsu* exertion, strenuous effort; splurge	96
		奮起 *funki* rouse oneself (to action), be inspired	373
	奮	奮って *furutte* energetically, willingly	

	1310	DATSU, *uba(u)*, snatch away, take by force; captivate	
奪	37	争 奪(戦) *sōdatsu(sen)* a competition, struggle	302, 301
	1183	略 奪 *ryakudatsu* plunder, pillage, despoliation	841
		強 奪 *gōdatsu* seizure, robbery	217
奪		奪 回/還 *dak-kai/kan* recapture, retaking	90, 866
		奪 い 合 う *ubaiau* scramble, struggle (for)	159

	1311	SEKI, (counter for ships); one (of a pair)	
隻	172	三 隻 *sanseki* 3 ships	4
	5028	数 隻(の 船) *sūseki (no fune)* several (ships)	225, 376
		隻 眼 *sekigan* one-eyed	848
隻		一 隻 眼 *issekigan* discerning eye	2, 848
		隻 手 *sekishu* one-armed	57

	1312	GO, defend, protect	
護	149	弁 護 士 *bengoshi* lawyer, attorney	711, 572
	4447	保 護 *hogo* protection, preservation	489
		援 護 *engo* support, backing, protection	1088
護		護 衛 *goei* guard, escort	815
		護 符 *gofu* amulet, talisman	505

	1313	KAKU, *e(ru)*, obtain, acquire, gain	
獲	94	獲 得 *kakutoku* acquire, gain, win	374
	2912	捕 獲 *hokaku* catch; capture, seizure	890
		漁 獲 *gyokaku* fishing, a catch of fish	699
獲		乱 獲 *rankaku* excessive fishing/hunting	689
		獲 物 *emono* game, a catch, trophy	79

	1314	KAKU, harvest	
穫	115	収 穫 *shūkaku* harvest, harvesting	757
	3309	収 穫 高 *shūkakudaka* the yield, crop	757, 190
		収 穫 期 *shūkakuki* harvest time	757, 449
穫			

	1315	KAN, *wazura(u)*, be ill, suffer (from)	
患	61	患 者 *kanja* a patient	164
	1697	急 患 *kyūkan* person suddenly taken ill	303
		患 部 *kanbu* affected/diseased part	86
患		長 患 い *nagawazurai* long illness	95

	1316	KAN, see	
看	4	看 護 婦 *kangofu* nurse	1312, 316
	222	看 病 *kanbyō* tending the sick, nursing	380
		看 守 *kanshu* (prison) guard	490
看		看 破 *kanpa* see through, detect	665
		看 板 *kanban* sign, signboard	1047

	1317	**SAI**, moyō(su), hold, sponsor; feel	
催	9 533 催	開 催 *kaisai* hold (a meeting) 主 催 *shusai* sponsorship, promotion 催 眠 *saimin* hypnosis 催 涙 ガ ス *sairuigasu* tear gas 催 し 物 *moyōshimono* (program of) entertainments	396 155 849 1239 79

	1318	**SHŌ**, illness, symptoms	
症	104 3039 症	病 症 *byōshō* nature of a disease 症 状/候 *shōjō/kō* symptom 不 眠 症 *fuminshō* insomnia 自 閉 症 *jiheishō* autism 露 出 症 *roshutsushō* exhibitionism	380 626, 944 94, 849 62, 397 951, 53

	1319	**EKI**, [YAKU], epidemic	
疫	104 3028 疫	疫 病 *ekibyō* epidemic, plague 悪 疫 *akueki* plague, pestilence, epidemic 防 疫 *bōeki* prevention of epidemics 検 疫 *ken'eki* quarantine 免 疫 *men'eki* immunity	380 304 513 531 733

	1320	**TSŪ**, ita(mu), feel painful, hurt; be damaged; ita(meru), hurt, damage; cause pain; ita(i), painful	
痛	104 3054 痛	苦 痛 *kutsū* pain 頭 痛 *zutsū* headache 痛 飲 *tsūin* drink heavily, carouse 痛 手 *itade* severe wound; hard blow	545 276 323 57

	1321	**HI**, tsuka(reru), get tired; tsuka(rasu), (tr.) fatigue, tire	
疲	104 3040 疲	疲 労 *hirō* fatigue, weariness 気 疲 れ *kizukare* mental fatigue/exhaustion 疲 れ 果 て る *tsukarehateru* be completely exhausted (お) 疲 れ 様 (o)tsukaresama Thank you (for your tiring work).	233 134 487 403

	1322	**RYŌ**, heal, cure; treat medically	
療	104 3078 療	治 療 *chiryō* medical treatment, therapy 医 療 *iryō* medical treatment 診 療 *shinryō* diagnosis and treatment 施 療 *seryō* free medical treatment ⌈home 療 養 所 *ryōyōsho, ryōyōjo* sanatorium, nursing	493 220 1214 1004 402, 153

	1323	**RYŌ**, hostel, dormitory	
寮	40 1340 寮	学 生 寮 *gakuseiryō* dormitory 社 員 寮 *shainryō* company dormitory 独 身 寮 *dokushinryō* dormitory for bachelors 寮 長 *ryōchō* dormitory director 寮 生 *ryōsei* student living in a dormitory	109, 44 308, 163 219, 59 95 44

僚	1324 9 545 僚	**RYŌ**, an official; companion

官 僚 *kanryō* bureaucrat ⌈bureaucracy 326
官 僚 主 義 *kanryō shugi* bureaucratism, 326, 155, 291
閣 僚 *kakuryō* cabinet member/minister 837
同 僚 *dōryō* colleague, coworker 198
僚 友 *ryōyū* fellow worker, colleague 264

丈	1325 4 151 丈	**JŌ**, (unit of length, about 3 m); *take*, one's height

丈 夫 *jōbu* strong and healthy; strong, durable 315
偉 丈 夫 *ijōfu* great man 1053, 315
気 丈 *kijō* stout-hearted, courageous 134
八 丈 島 *Hachijō-jima* (island south of Tokyo) 10, 286
背 丈 *setake* one's height 1265

壮	1326 90 2837 壮	**SŌ**, manly, strong

壮 大 *sōdai* magnificent, grand, imposing 26
強 壮 *kyōsō* strong, robust, husky 217
壮 健 *sōken* healthy, hale and hearty 893
悲 壮 *hisō* tragic, touching, pathetic 1034
壮 年 *sōnen* prime of manhood/life 45

荘	1327 140 3938 荘	**SŌ**, villa, inn; solemn

別 荘 *bessō* country house, cottage, villa 267
山 荘 *sansō* mountain villa 34
荘 重 *sōchō* solemn, sublime, impressive 227
荘 厳 *sōgon* sublime, grand, majestic 822

装	1328 145 4234 装	**SŌ, SHŌ**, *yosō(u)*, wear; feign, pretend, disguise oneself as

服 装 *fukusō* style of dress, attire 683
変 装 *hensō* disguise 257
装 置 *sōchi* device, apparatus, equipment 426
装 飾 *sōshoku* ornament, decoration 979
武 装 *busō* arms, armament 1031

袋	1329 145 4223 袋	**TAI**, *fukuro*, sack, bag

手 袋 *tebukuro* glove 57
足 袋 *tabi* Japanese socks (worn with kimono) 58
紙 袋 *kamibukuro* paper sack/bag 180
袋 小 路 *fukurokōji* blind alley, cul-de-sac 27, 151
胃 袋 *ibukuro* stomach 1268

裂	1330 145 4233 裂	**RETSU**, *sa(keru/ku)*, (intr./tr.) split, tear, rip

分 裂 *bunretsu* breakup, dissolution, division 38
破 裂 *haretsu* burst, rupture, explode 665
決 裂 *ketsuretsu* (negotiations) break down 356
裂 け 目 *sakeme* a rip, split, crack, fissure 55

	1331	RETSU, violent, intense	
烈	86 2761	烈震 *resshin* violent earthquake	953
		熱烈 *netsuretsu* ardent, fervent, vehement	645
		壮烈 *sōretsu* heroic, brave	1326
		強烈 *kyōretsu* intense, severe	217
烈		痛烈 *tsūretsu* severe, fierce, bitter	1320

	1332	SHŌ, urge, encourage	
奨	37 1181	奨学金 *shōgakukin* a scholarship	109, 23
		奨学生 *shōgakusei* student on a scholarship	109, 44
		勧奨 *kanshō* encouragement, promotion	1051
奨		推奨 *suishō* recommendation, commendation	1233

	1333	TŌ, *hi*, a light, lamp	
灯	86 2745	電灯 *dentō* electric light/lamp	108
		灯火 *tōka* a light, lamplight	20
		街灯 *gaitō* streetlight	186
		船灯 *sentō* ship light	376
灯		灯台 *tōdai* lighthouse	492

	1334	CHŌ, *su(mu)*, become clear; *su(masu)*, make clear; perk (one's ears); look prim/unconcerned/nonchalant	
澄	85 2699	清澄 *seichō* clear, limpid, lucid, serene	660
		澄み切る *sumikiru* become perfectly clear	39
		澄み渡る *sumiwataru* be crystal clear	378
澄		澄まし顔 *sumashigao* unconcerned look	277

	1335	SAI, *wazawa(i)*, misfortune, disaster	
災	47 1448	災難 *sainan* mishap, accident, calamity	557
		災害 *saigai* disaster, accident	518
		火災 *kasai* fire, blaze, conflagration	20
		天災 *tensai* natural disaster/calamity	141
災		震災 *shinsai* earthquake disaster	953

	1336	EN, *honō*, flame	
炎	86 2751	火炎瓶 *kaenbin* firebomb, Molotov cocktail	20, 1161
		炎症 *enshō* inflammation	1318
		肺炎 *haien* pneumonia	1277
		脳炎 *nōen* brain inflammation, encephalitis	1278
炎		中耳炎 *chūjien* inflammation of the middle ear	28, 56

	1337	TAN, *awa(i)*, light, faint, pale; transitory	
淡	85 2602	濃淡 *nōtan* light and shade, shading	957
		淡彩 *tansai* light coloring	932
		冷淡 *reitan* indifferent, apathetic	832
		淡水 *tansui* fresh water	21
淡		淡雪 *awayuki* light snow	949

	1338	METSU, *horo(biru)*, fall to ruin, perish, die out; *horo(bosu)*, ruin, destroy, overthrow, annihilate	
滅	85 2660 滅	破 滅 *hametsu* ruin, downfall, collapse 滅 亡 *metsubō* downfall, destruction 消 滅 *shōmetsu* extinction, disappearance 幻 滅 *genmetsu* disillusionment	665 672 845 1227

	1339	I, authority, dignity, majesty; threat	
威	62 1803 威	権 威 *ken'i* authority 威 勢 *isei* power, influence; high spirits 威 厳 *igen* dignity, stateliness 威 信 *ishin* prestige, dignity 脅 威 *kyōi* menace, threat, danger	335 646 822 157 1263

	1340	REI, encouragement; diligence; *hage(mu)*, be diligent; *hage-(masu)*, encourage, urge on	
励	4 193 励	奨 励 *shōrei* encouragement, promotion 激 励 *gekirei* urging, encouragement 精 励 *seirei* diligence, industriousness 励 行 *reikō* strict enforcement	1332 1017 659 68

	1341	YAKU, misfortune, disaster	
厄	27 816 厄	厄 介 *yakkai* troublesome, burdensome; help, care 厄 介 者 *yakkaimono* a dependent; burden 厄 日 *yakubi* unlucky day; critical day 厄 年 *yakudoshi* unlucky year; critical age 厄 払 い *yakubarai, yakuharai* exorcism	453 453, 164 5 45 582

	1342	ATSU, pressure	
圧	27 818 圧	圧 力 *atsuryoku* pressure 圧 迫 *appaku* pressure, oppression 気 圧 *kiatsu* atmospheric pressure 抑 圧 *yokuatsu* restraint, suppression 圧 倒 的 *attōteki* overwhelming	100 1175 134 1057 905, 210

	1343	KAI, *hai*, ash	
灰	27 820 灰	灰 じ ん *kaijin* ashes 石 灰 *sekkai* (chemical) lime 灰 皿 *haizara* ashtray 火 山 灰 *kazanbai* volcanic ash 灰 色 *haiiro* gray	 78 1097 20, 34 204

	1344	TAN, *sumi*, charcoal	
炭	46 1418 炭	石 炭 *sekitan* coal 木 炭 *mokutan* charcoal 採 炭 *saitan* coal mining 炭 素 *tanso* carbon 炭 酸 *tansan* carbonic acid	78 22 933 271 516

	1345	GAN, *iwa*, rock	
岩	46	岩石 *ganseki* rock	78
	1414	火成岩 *kaseigan* igneous rock	20, 261
		岩塩 *gan'en* rock salt	1101
		岩屋 *iwaya* cave, cavern	167
岩		岩登り *iwanobori* rock climbing	960

	1346	CHŪ, *oki*, open sea	
沖	85	沖積世/期 *chūseki-sei/ki* the alluvial epoch	656, 252, 449
	2505	沖合 *okiai* open sea, offshore	159
沖			

	1347	CHŪ, *naka*, personal relations	
仲	9	仲裁 *chūsai* arbitration	1123
	378	仲介 *chūkai* mediation	453
		伯仲 *hakuchū* be nearly equal, evenly matched	1176
		仲良く *nakayoku* on good terms, like good friends	321
仲		仲人 *nakōdo* go-between, matchmaker	1

	1348	CHŪ, loyalty, faithfulness	
忠	61	忠実 *chūjitsu* faithful, devoted, loyal	203
	1653	忠義 *chūgi* loyalty	291
		忠誠 *chūsei* loyalty, allegiance	718
		忠告 *chūkoku* advice, admonition	690
忠		忠臣蔵 *Chūshingura* (the 47 Ronin story)	835, 1286

	1349	HŌ, *nu(u)*, sew	
縫	120	裁縫 *saihō* sewing	1123
	3582	縫合 *hōgō* a suture, stitch	159
		天衣無縫 *ten'i-muhō* of flawless beauty, ⌈perfect	141, 677, 93
		縫い目 *nuime* seam, stitch	55
縫		仮縫い *karinui* temporary sewing, basting, fitting	1049

	1350	HŌ, *mine*, peak, summit	
峰	46	連峰 *renpō* mountain range	440
	1423	高峰 *kōhō* lofty peak	190
		霊峰 *reihō* sacred mountain	1168
峰			

	1351	*tōge*, mountain pass	
峠	46	峠道 *tōgemichi* road through a mountain pass	149
	1416	峠を越す *tōge o kosu* cross a pass	1001
		十国峠 *Jikkoku Tōge* (pass in Hakone)	12, 40
峠			

	1352	KYŌ, gorge, ravine	
峡 46 1417 峡		山峡 *sankyō* (mountain) gorge 峡谷 *kyōkoku* gorge, ravine, canyon 海峡 *kaikyō* strait, channel, narrows 峡湾 *kyōwan* fjord	34 653 117 670

	1353	KYŌ, *sema(i)*, narrow, small (in area); *seba(maru/meru)*, (intr./tr.) narrow, contract	
狭 94 2882 狭		狭量 *kyōryō* narrow-minded 偏狭 *henkyō* narrow-minded, parochial 狭心症 *kyōshinshō* stricture of the heart, angina 97, 1318 狭苦しい *semakurushii* cramped ⌐pectoris 545	411 1159

	1354	KYŌ, *hasa(mu)*, put between, interpose; *hasa(maru)*, get between, get caught/hemmed/sandwiched between	
挟 64 1915 挟		挟撃 *kyōgeki* pincer attack 挟み撃ち *hasamiuchi* pincer attack 挟み込む *hasamikomu* put between, insert 挟み上げる *hasamiageru* pick up (with chopsticks)	1016 1016 776 32

	1355	KEN, [KON], present, offer	
献 94 2901 献		献金 *kenkin* gift of money, contribution 献血 *kenketsu* blood donation 献上 *kenjō* presentation 文献 *bunken* the literature, documentary records 献立 *kondate* menu; arrangements, plan, program	23 789 32 111 121

	1356	FUKU, *fu(su)*, bend down, lie down/prostrate; *fu(seru)*, cast down (one's eyes), turn over; cover, put over; conceal	
伏 9 377 伏		降伏 *kōfuku* surrender, capitulation 伏兵 *fukuhei* an ambush 潜伏 *senpuku* hide; be dormant, latent 伏線 *fukusen* foreshadowing	947 784 937 299

	1357	KYŪ, *oka*, hill	
丘 4 174 丘		砂丘 *sakyū* sand dune	1151

	1358	GAKU, *take*, mountain, peak	
岳 4 208 岳		山岳 *sangaku* mountains 山岳部 *sangakubu* mountaineering club 岳父 *gakufu* father of one's wife 谷川岳 *Tanigawa-dake* (mountain about 150 km north of Tokyo)	34 34, 86 113 653, 33

匠	**1359** 22 761 匠	**SHŌ, workman, artisan** 巨 匠　　*kyoshō*　(great) master 名 匠　　*meishō*　master craftsman 師 匠　　*shishō*　master, teacher 宗 匠　　*sōshō*　master, teacher 意 匠　　*ishō*　a design	 1293 82 409 616 132
奇	**1360** 37 1176 奇	**KI, strange, curious** 好 奇 心 *kōkishin*　curiosity 奇 妙　　*kimyō*　strange, curious, odd 奇 術　　*kijutsu*　conjuring, sleight of hand 奇 病　　*kibyō*　strange disease 奇 数　　*kisū*　odd number	 104, 97 1154 187 380 225
寄	**1361** 40 1318 寄	**KI,** *yo(ru)*, **approach, draw near; meet; drop in;** *yo(seru)*, **bring near; push aside; gather together; send** 寄 付　　*kifu*　contribution, donation 寄 宿 舎 *kishukusha*　dormitory 寄 生　　*kisei*　parasitism 立 ち 寄 る *tachiyoru*　drop in, stop (at)	 192 179, 791 44 121
崎	**1362** 46 1426 崎	***saki*, cape, promontory, headland, point (of land)** 長 崎　　*Nagasaki*　(city on western coast of Kyushu) 宮 崎　　*Miyazaki*　(city on southern coast of 　　　　　　　　　Kyushu)	 95 721
岬	**1363** 46 1412 岬	***misaki*, promontory, headland, point (of land)** 宗 谷 岬 *Sōya-misaki*　(northern tip of Hokkaido) 知 床 岬 *Shiretoko-misaki*　(eastern tip of 　　　　　　　Hokkaido) 潮 岬　　*Shio-no-misaki*　(southern tip of Kii Pen.) 足 ず り 岬 *Ashizuri-misaki*　(southern tip of Shikoku)	 616, 653 214, 826 468 58
贈	**1364** 154 4525 贈	**ZŌ, [SŌ],** *oku(ru)*, **give, present, bestow** 贈 与 (証 書) *zōyo* (*shōsho*)　gift (certificate) 539, 484, 131 寄 贈　　*kizō, kisō*　presentation, donation, contri- 贈 答　　*zōtō*　exchange of gifts　　　　⌊bution 贈 り 物 *okurimono*　gift, present 贈 り 主 *okurinushi*　sender (of a gift)	 1361 160 79 155
憎	**1365** 61 1757 憎	**ZŌ,** *niku(mu)*, **hate;** *niku(i/rashii)*, **hateful, horrible, repulsive;** *niku(shimi)*, **hatred, animosity** 愛 憎　　*aizō*　love and hate; partiality 憎 悪　　*zōo*　hatred 憎 ま れ っ 子 *nikumarekko*　bad/naughty boy 憎 ま れ 口 *nikumareguchi*　offensive/malicious remarks	 259 304 103 54

1366	**SŌ,** Buddhist priest/monk		
9	僧院	*sōin* temple; monastery	614
536	僧正	*sōjō* Buddhist high priest, bishop	275
	高僧	*kōsō* high/exemplary priest	190
僧	僧服	*sōfuku* priestly robe, monk's habit	683
	小僧	*kozō* young priest; apprentice; boy	27

1367	**SŌ,** layer, level		
44	上層	*jōsō* upper layer/classes/floors	32
1402	多層	*tasō* multilayer	229
	層雲	*sōun* stratus (cloud)	636
層	読者層	*dokushasō* class/level of readers	244, 164
	階層	*kaisō* social stratum, class	588

1368	**ETSU,** joy		
61	喜悦	*kietsu* joy, delight	1143
1696	悦楽	*etsuraku* joy, pleasure, gaiety	358
	法悦	*hōetsu* religious exultation; ecstasy	123
悦	満悦	*man'etsu* delighted, very satisfied	201
	悦に入る	*etsu ni iru* be pleased (with)	52

1369	**ETSU,** inspection, review		
169	閲覧	*etsuran* perusal, inspection, reading	1291
4961	閲覧室	*etsuranshitsu* reading room	1291, 166
	校閲	*kōetsu* revision (of a manuscript)	115
閲	検閲	*ken'etsu* censorship	531
	閲歴	*etsureki* one's career/personal history	480

1370	**DATSU,** omit; escape; *nu(gu),* take off (clothes); *nu(geru),* come off, slip off (footwear/clothing)		
130	脱衣所	*datsuisho, datsuijo* changing/dressing room	677, 153
3775	脱線	*dassen* derailment; digression	299
	離脱	*ridatsu* secession, breakaway	1281
脱	脱税	*datsuzei* tax evasion	399

1371	**EI,** *surudo(i),* sharp		
167	鋭利	*eiri* sharp	329
4864	鋭気	*eiki* spirit, mettle, energy	134
	精鋭	*seiei* elite, choice	659
鋭	新鋭	*shin'ei* fresh, new	174
	鋭角	*eikaku* acute angle	473

1372	**KOKU,** conquer		
24	克服	*kokufuku* conquest, subjugation	683
772	克己	*kokki* self-denial, self-control	370
克	克明	*kokumei* faithful, conscientious	18

	1373	**BŌ**, *isoga(shii)*, busy	
忙	61 1647	多忙 *tabō* busy, hectic 繁忙 *hanbō* (very) busy 忙殺される *bōsatsu sareru* be busily occupied	229 1292 576

	1374	**BŌ**, *wasu(reru)*, forget	
忘	8 291	健忘(症) *kenbō(shō)* forgetfulness 忘恩 *bōon* ingratitude 忘年会 *bōnenkai* year-end party 忘れ物 *wasuremono* article left behind 度/胴忘れ *do/dō-wasure* forget for the moment	893, 1318 555 45, 158 79 377, 1300

	1375	**MŌ**, *mekura*, blindness, blind person; ignorance, ignorant person	
盲	8 297	盲人 *mōjin* blind person, the blind 盲目 *mōmoku* blindness 色盲 *shikimō* color blindness 文盲 *monmō* illiteracy	1 55 204 111

	1376	**MŌ, BŌ**, without reason/authority	
妄	8 288	迷妄 *meimō* illusion, fallacy 妄想 *mōsō* wild fancy, foolish fantasy, delusion 妄信 *mōshin, bōshin* blind belief, overcredulity 被害妄想 *higai mōsō* delusions of persecution, paranoia	967 147 157 976, 518, 147

	1377	**KŌ**, *ara(i)*, rough, wild, violent; *a(reru)*, get rough/stormy, run wild, go to ruin; *a(rasu)*, devastate, lay waste	
荒	140 3941	荒廃 *kōhai* desolation, devastation 荒野 *kōya, areno* wilderness, wasteland 荒れ狂う *arekuruu* rage, run amuck 荒仕事 *arashigoto* heavy work, hard labor	961 236 883 333, 80

	1378	**KŌ**, *awa(teru)*, get flustered, be in a flurry, panic; *awa(tadashii)*, bustling, flurried, confused	
慌	61 1725	慌て者 *awatemono* absentminded person, scatter-brain 大慌て *ōawate* great haste	164 26

	1379	**FUKU**, fortune, blessing; wealth, welfare	
福	113 3256	幸福 *kōfuku* happiness 祝福 *shukufuku* blessing 福音 *fukuin* the Gospel; good news 福引き *fukubiki* lottery, raffle 七福神 *Shichifukujin* the Seven Gods of Good 「Fortune	684 851 347 216 9, 310

	1380	**FUKU**, *haba*, width, breadth, range; influence	
幅	50	振幅 *shinpuku* amplitude	954
	1484	大幅 *ōhaba* broad; large, wholesale, substantial	26
		幅の広い *haba no hiroi* wide, broad	694
幅		横幅 *yokohaba* breadth, width	781
		幅が利く *haba ga kiku* be influential	329

	1381	**HAN**, squad, group	
班	96	首班 *shuhan* head, chief	148
	2935	班長 *hanchō* squad/group leader	95
		救護班 *kyūgohan* relief squad	725, 1312
班		班点 *hanten* spot, speckle, dot	169

	1382	**HAN**, feudal clan/lord	
藩	140	藩主 *hanshu* lord of a feudal clan	155
	4089	藩学 *hangaku* samurai school for clan children	109
		廃藩置県 *haihan-chiken* abolition of clans and	
藩		establishment of prefectures	961, 426, 194

	1383	**SHIN**, hearing, investigation, trial	
審	40	審査 *shinsa* examination, investigation	624
	1341	審議 *shingi* deliberation, consideration	292
		審問 *shinmon* trial, hearing, inquiry	162
審		不審 *fushin* doubt, suspicion	94
		審判 *shinpan* decision, judgment, refereeing	1026

	1384	**RYO**, thought, consideration	
慮	141	考慮 *kōryo* consideration, reflection	541
	4112	遠慮 *enryo* reserve, restraint, hesitation	446
		配慮 *hairyo* consideration, solicitude	515
慮		憂慮 *yūryo* apprehension, concern	1032
		焦慮 *shōryo* impatience; worry	999

	1385	**RYO**, captive	
虜	141	捕虜 *horyo* prisoner of war	890
	4111	捕虜収容所 *horyo shūyōjo* POW camp 890, 757, 654, 153	
虜			

	1386	**YŪ**, *isa(mu)*, be spirited, lively, encouraged	
勇	19	勇気 *yūki* courage	134
	725	武勇 *buyū* bravery, valor	1031
		勇士 *yūshi* brave warrior, hero	572
勇		勇退 *yūtai* retire voluntarily	846
		勇み足 *isamiashi* overeagerness, rashness	58

	1387	YŪ, male; brave; great; *osu, o*, male	
雄	172 5030 雄	英雄 *eiyū* hero	353
		雄弁 *yūben* eloquence	711
		雄大 *yūdai* grand, magnificent	26
		雄鳥 *ondori* rooster, male bird	285
		両雄 *ryōyū* 2 great men (rivals)	200

	1388	SHI, *mesu, me*, female	
雌	77 2435 此隹	雌伏 *shifuku* remain in obscurity, lie low	1356
		雌雄 *shiyū* male and female; victory or defeat	1387
		雌犬 *mesuinu* a bitch	280
		雌牛 *meushi* (female) cow	281
		雌花 *mebana* female flower	255

	1389	SHI, *murasaki*, purple	
紫	120 3534 紫	紫外線 *shigaisen* ultraviolet rays	83, 299
		紫煙 *shien* tobacco smoke, blue cigarette smoke	919
		紫雲 *shiun* auspicious purple clouds	636
		山紫水明 *sanshi-suimei* beautiful scenery	34, 21, 18
		紫色 *murasakiiro* purple	204

	1390	SHI, happiness	
祉	113 3232 祉	福祉 *fukushi* welfare, well-being	1379
		福祉国家 *fukushi kokka* welfare state	1379, 40, 165
		社会福祉 *shakai fukushi* social/public welfare	308, 158, 1379

	1391	YŪ, surplus	
裕	145 4241 裕	余裕 *yoyū* room, margin, leeway; composure	1063
		余裕しゃくしゃく *yoyū-shakushaku* calm and composed	1063
		富裕 *fuyū* wealth, affluence	713
		裕福 *yūfuku* wealth, affluence	1379

	1392	YŌ, *to(keru)*, (intr.) melt, dissolve; *to(kasu/ku)*, (tr.) melt, dissolve	
溶	85 2659 溶	溶解 *yōkai* (intr.) melt, dissolve	474
		溶岩 *yōgan* lava	1345
		溶液 *yōeki* solution	472
		水溶性 *suiyōsei* water-soluble	21, 98

	1393	SEKI, divide, take apart, analyze	
析	75 2194 析	分析 *bunseki* analysis	38
		分析化学 *bunseki kagaku* analytical chemistry	38, 254, 109
		市場分析 *shijō bunseki* market analysis	181, 154, 38
		解析 *kaiseki* analysis	474

	1394	**SETSU**, o(reru), (intr.) break; be folded; yield, compromise; o(ru), (tr.) break; fold, bend; ori, occasion, opportunity	
折	64 1855	右折禁止 *usetsu kinshi* No Right Turn	76, 482, 477
		折半 *seppan* divide into halves	88
		曲折 *kyokusetsu* twists and turns, complications	366
折		折り紙 *origami* paper folding; paper for origami	180

	1395	**SEI**, chika(u), swear, pledge, vow	
誓	149 4369	誓約 *seiyaku* oath, vow, pledge	211
		宣誓 *sensei* oath	625
		祈誓 *kisei* oath, vow	621
誓		誓文 *seimon* written oath	111

	1396	**SEI**, yu(ku), die	
逝	162 4691	逝去 *seikyo* death	414
		急逝 *kyūsei* sudden/untimely death	303
逝			

	1397	**TETSU**, wisdom	
哲	30 931	哲学 *tetsugaku* philosophy	109
		哲学者 *tetsugakusha* philosopher	109, 164
		賢哲 *kentetsu* wise man, sage	1288
		先哲 *sentetsu* wise man of the past, sage of old	50
哲		哲人 *tetsujin* wise man, philosopher	1

	1398	**KEI**, open; say	
啓	30 940	啓発 *keihatsu* enlightenment, edification	96
		啓示 *keiji* revelation	615
		天啓 *tenkei* divine revelation	141
		拝啓 *haikei* Dear Sir:	1201
啓		啓もう *keimō* enlightenment, instruction	

	1399	**ZAN**, (for) a while	
暫	72 2156	暫時 *zanji* (for) a short time	42
		暫定 *zantei* tentative, provisional	355
暫			

	1400	**ZEN**, gradually	
漸	85 2680	漸次 *zenji* gradually, step by step	384
		漸進 *zenshin* gradual progress	437
		漸増 *zenzō* increase gradually	712
漸		漸減 *zengen* decrease gradually, taper off	715

	1401	SEKI, retreat, recede; repel, reject	
斥	4	排斥 *haiseki* rejection, exclusion, boycott	1036
斥	175	排斥運動 *haiseki undō* agitation for expulsion/ exclusion	1036, 439, 231

	1402	SO, *utta(eru)*, sue; complain of; appeal (to)	
訴	149	起訴 *kiso* prosecution, indictment	373
訴	4340	提訴 *teiso* bring before (the court), file (suit)	628
		告訴 *kokuso* complaint, accusation, charges	690
		敗訴 *haiso* losing a suit/case	511
		勝訴 *shōso* winning a suit/case	509

	1403	SHŌ, accuse	
訟	149	訴訟 *soshō* lawsuit, litigation	1402
訟	4320	刑事訴訟 *keiji soshō* criminal suit	887, 80, 1402
		民事訴訟 *minji soshō* civil suit	177, 80, 1402
		離婚訴訟 *rikon soshō* suit for divorce	1281, 567, 1402
		訴訟費用 *soshō hiyō* costs of litigation	1402, 749, 107

	1404	JIN, battle position, camp	
陣	170	陣営 *jin'ei* camp, encampment	722
陣	4992	陣地 *jinchi* (military) position	118
		陣容 *jin'yō* battle array, lineup	654
		退陣 *taijin* decampment, withdrawal	846
		陣痛 *jintsū* labor (pains)	1320

	1405	CHIN, state, explain; show; old	
陳	170	陳列 *chinretsu* display, exhibit	611
陳	5001	陳情 *chinjō* petition, appeal	209
		陳述 *chinjutsu* statement, declaration	968
		陳謝 *chinsha* apology ⌈generation	901
		新陳代謝 *shinchin taisha* metabolism; re-	174, 256, 901

	1406	TŌ, *mune*, [*muna*], ridge of a roof	
棟	75	上棟式 *jōtōshiki* roof-laying ceremony	32, 525
棟	2299	病棟 *byōtō* (hospital) ward	380
		別棟 *betsumune* separate building	267
		棟上げ式 *muneageshiki* roof-laying ceremony	32, 525
		棟木 *munagi* ridgepole, ridge beam	22

	1407	KAI, *kowa(reru)*, get broken, break; *kowa(su)*, break, tear down, destroy, damage	
壊	32	壊滅 *kaimetsu* destruction, annihilation	1338
壊	1147	破壊 *hakai* destruction, wrecking	665
		崩壊 *hōkai* collapse, breakdown, cave-in	1122
		壊血病 *kaiketsubyō* scurvy	789, 380

	1408 61 1782 懐	KAI, pocket; nostalgia; *natsu(kashii)*, dear, fond, longed-for; *natsu(kashimu)*, yearn for; *natsu(ku)*, take kindly (to); *natsu(keru)*, win over; tame; *futokoro*, breast (pocket)
		懐中電灯 *kaichū dentō* flashlight 28, 108, 1333
		述懐 *jukkai* (relating) one's thoughts and remi- 968
		懐柔 *kaijū* conciliation ⌐niscences 774

	1409 61 1654 快	KAI, *kokoroyo(i)*, pleasant, delightful
		快適 *kaiteki* comfortable, pleasant, agreeable 415
		快活 *kaikatsu* cheerful, lighthearted 237
		全快 *zenkai* complete recovery (from illness) 89
		快晴 *kaisei* fine weather, clear skies 662
		快速電車 *kaisoku densha* express train 502, 108, 133

	1410 61 1755 慢	MAN, be lazy, neglect
		我慢 *gaman* exercise patience, tolerate 1302
		自慢 *jiman* pride, boasting, vanity 62
		怠慢 *taiman* negligence, dereliction 1297
		緩慢 *kanman* slow, sluggish 1089
		慢性 *mansei* chronic 98

	1411 85 2683 漫	MAN, aimless, random; involuntarily
		漫画 *manga* cartoon, comic book/strip 343
		漫談 *mandan* chat, idle talk 593
		散漫 *sanman* vague, loose, desultory 767
		漫然 *manzen* random, rambling, discursive 651
		漫才 *manzai* comic (stage) dialogue 551

	1412 40 1335 寧	NEI, peaceful, quiet; rather, preferably
		丁寧 *teinei* polite; careful, meticulous 184
		安寧 *annei* public peace/order 105

	1413 4 152 刃	JIN, *ha*, blade
		白刃 *hakujin* naked blade, drawn sword 205
		刃先 *hasaki* edge (of a blade) 50
		刃物 *hamono* edged tool, cutlery 79
		もろ刃の剣 *moroha no tsurugi* double-edged sword 879

	1414 61 1648 忍	NIN, *shino(bu)*, bear, endure; hide, lie hidden; avoid (being seen); *shino(baseru)*, hide, conceal
		忍苦 *ninku* endurance, stoicism 545
		残忍 *zannin* brutal, ruthless 650
		忍者 *ninja* (feudal) professional spy/assassin 164
		忍び足 *shinobiashi* stealthy steps 58

	1415	**TAI**, *ta(eru)*, endure, bear, withstand; be fit, competent	
耐	126 3690	忍 耐 *nintai* perseverance, patience	1414
		耐 熱 *tainetsu* heatproof, heat-resistant	645
		耐 火 *taika* fireproof, fire-resistant	20
		耐 久 *taikyū* endurance; durability	1210
耐		耐 乏 生 活 *taibō seikatsu* austerity	754, 44, 237

	1416	**JU**, request, need, demand	
需	173 5052	需 要(供 給) *juyō (kyōkyū)* demand (and supply)	419, 197, 346
		需 給 *jukyū* supply and demand	346
		特 需 *tokuju* special procurement (in wartime)	282
需		軍 需 品 *gunjuhin* war matériel	438, 230
		必 需 品 *hitsujuhin* necessary articles, necessities	520, 230

	1417	**JU**, Confucianism	
儒	9 561	儒 教 *jukyō* Confucianism	245
		儒 学 *jugaku* Confucianism	109
		儒 学 者 *jugakusha* Confucian scholar	109, 164
儒		儒 家 *juka* Confucian scholar, Confucianist	165

	1418	**TAN**, correct; end, tip; *hashi*, end, edge; *hata*, side, edge, nearby; *ha*, edge	
端	117 3363	極 端 *kyokutan* extreme, ultra-	336
		異 端 *itan* heresy, heathenism	1061
		道 端 *michibata* roadside, wayside	149
端		端 折 る *hashoru* tuck up; cut short, abridge	1394

	1419	**BI**, minute, slight	
微	60 1631	微 妙 *bimyō* delicate, subtle	1154
		微 笑 *bishō* smile	1235
		微 熱 *binetsu* a slight fever	645
微		微 生 物 *biseibutsu* microorganism, microbe	44, 79
		顕 微 鏡 *kenbikyō* microscope	1170, 863

	1420	**CHŌ**, collect; demand; sign, symptom	
徴	60 1634	徴 候 *chōkō* sign, indication, symptom	944
		象 徴 *shōchō* symbol	739
		特 徴 *tokuchō* distinctive feature	282
徴		徴 兵 *chōhei* conscription, military service; draftee	784
		徴 税 *chōzei* tax collection	399

	1421	**CHŌ**, *ko(rasu/rashimeru)*, chastise, punish, discipline; *ko-(riru)*, learn by experience, be taught a lesson, be sick of	
懲	61 1785	懲 罰 *chōbatsu* disciplinary measure, punishment	886
		懲 役 *chōeki* penal servitude, imprisonment	375
懲		勧 善 懲 悪 *kanzen-chōaku* good over evil, poetic justice	1051, 1139, 304

	1422	TETSU, pierce, go through	
60	徹底的	*tetteiteki* thorough	562, 210
1637	貫徹	*kantetsu* carry through, accomplish	914
	徹夜	*tetsuya* stay up all night	471
徹	冷徹	*reitetsu* coolheaded, levelheaded	832

	1423	TETSU, withdraw, remove	
64	撤回	*tekkai* withdraw, retract, rescind	90
1999	撤去	*tekkyo* withdraw, evacuate, remove	414
	撤退	*tettai* withdraw, pull out, retreat	846
	撤兵	*teppei* withdraw troops, disengage	784
撤	撤廃	*teppai* abolish, do away with, repeal	961

	1424	SŪ, respect, revere; lofty, sublime	
46	崇拝	*sūhai* worship, adoration	1201
1429	祖先崇拝	*sosen sūhai* ancestor worship	622, 50, 1201
	崇敬	*sūkei* veneration, reverence	705
崇	崇高	*sūkō* lofty, sublime, noble	190

	1425	MO, BO, copy, imitate, model	
75	模様	*moyō* pattern, design; appearance; situation	403
2345	模範	*mohan* model, exemplar	1092
	模型	*mokei* (scale) model; a mold	888
	模造	*mozō* imitation	691
模	規模	*kibo* scale, scope	607

	1426	MAKU, membrane	
130	角膜	*kakumaku* cornea	473
3803	鼓膜	*komaku* eardrum	1147
	処女膜	*shojomaku* hymen	1137, 102
	腹膜炎	*fukumakuen* peritonitis	1271, 1336
膜	結膜炎	*ketsumakuen* conjunctivitis, pinkeye	485, 1336

	1427	BAKU, vague, obscure; desert; wide	
85	砂漠	*sabaku* desert	1151
2649	広漠	*kōbaku* vast, boundless	694
	漠然	*bakuzen* vague, hazy, nebulous	651
漠			

	1428	BO, ku(reru), grow dark, come to an end; ku(rasu), live	
140	歳暮	*seibo* end of the year; year-end gift	479
4041	野暮	*yabo* uncouth, rustic, boorish	236
	夕暮れ	*yūgure* evening, twilight	81
暮	一人暮らし	*hitorigurashi* living alone	2, 1

	1429	**BO**, *haka*, a grave	
墓	140	墓地 *bochi* cemetery	118
	4027	墓標 *bohyō* grave marker/post	923
		墓石 *boseki* gravestone	78
墓		墓穴 *boketsu* grave (pit)	899
		墓参り *hakamairi* visit to a grave	710

	1430	**BO**, *tsuno(ru)*, appeal for, invite, raise; grow intense	
募	140	募集 *boshū* recruiting, solicitation	436
	3996	応募 *ōbo* apply for, enlist, enroll	827
		応募者 *ōbosha* applicant, entrant	827, 164
募		募金 *bokin* fund raising	23
		公募 *kōbo* offer for public subscription	126

	1431	**BO**, *shita(u)*, yearn for, love dearly; idolize	
慕	140	慕情 *bojō* longing, love, affection	209
	4040	思慕 *shibo* longing (for), deep attachment (to)	99
		敬慕 *keibo* love and respect	705
慕		恋慕 *renbo* love, affection	258
		追慕 *tsuibo* cherish (someone's) memory, sigh for	1174

	1432	**MAKU**, (stage) curtain; act (of a play); **BAKU**, shogunate	
幕	140	開幕 *kaimaku* commencement of a performance	396
	4026	序幕 *jomaku* opening act, prelude	770
		除幕 *jomaku* unveiling	1065
幕		内幕 *uchimaku, naimaku* behind-the-scenes story	84
		幕府 *Bakufu* Japan's feudal government, shogunate	504

	1433	**TEN**, *so(eru)*, add (to), append; *so(u)*, accompany	
添	85	添加 *tenka* annex, append, affix	709
	2601	添付 *tenpu* attach, append	192
		添乗員 *tenjōin* tour conductor	523, 163
添		付き添い *tsukisoi* attending (someone), escorting	192
		力添え *chikarazoe* help, assistance	100

	1434	**KYŌ**, *uyauya(shii)*, respectful, reverent, deferential	
恭	61	恭順 *kyōjun* fealty, allegiance	769
	1680	恭敬 *kyōkei* reverence, respect	705
		恭賀新年 *kyōga shinnen* Best wishes for a	
恭		happy New Year.	756, 174, 45

	1435	**KŌ**, flood, inundation; vast	
洪	85	洪水 *kōzui* flood, inundation, deluge	21
	2544	洪積層 *kōsekisō* diluvium, diluvial formation	656, 1367
洪			

	1436	**GO**, Wu (dynasty of ancient China)	
呉	12	呉服 *gofuku* drapery, dry goods	683
	583	呉服屋 *gofukuya* draper's shop, dry-goods dealer	683, 167
呉		呉越 *Go-Etsu* Wu and Yue/Yüeh (rival states of China)	1001

	1437	**GO**, pleasure, enjoyment	
娯	38	娯楽 *goraku* amusement, entertainment	358
	1226	娯楽番組 *goraku bangumi* entertainment program	358, 185, 418
娯			

	1438	**GO**, *sato(ru)*, perceive, understand, realize, be enlightened	
悟	61	覚悟 *kakugo* readiness, preparedness, resoluteness	605
	1700	悟り *satori* comprehension, understanding; satori, spiritual awakening	
悟			

	1439	**KŌ**, item, clause, paragraph	
項	48	事項 *jikō* matters, facts; items, particulars	80
	1459	事項索引 *jikō sakuin* subject index	80, 1059, 216
		要項 *yōkō* essential points, gist	419
項		条項 *jōkō* provision, clause	564
		項目 *kōmoku* heading, item	55

	1440	**CHŌ**, *itadaki*, summit, top; *itada(ku)*, be capped with; receive	
頂	181	頂上 *chōjō* summit, peak, top; climax	32
	5118	山頂 *sanchō* summit, mountain top	34
		頂点 *chōten* zenith, peak, climax	169
頂		絶頂 *zetchō* peak, height, climax	742

	1441	**KEI**, *katamu(ku/keru)*, (intr./tr.) lean, incline, tilt	
傾	9	傾向 *keikō* tendency, trend; inclination	199
	534	傾斜 *keisha* inclination, slant, slope	1069
		左傾 *sakei* leftward leanings, radicalization	75
傾		傾聴 *keichō* listen	1039
		傾倒 *keitō* devote oneself (to), be absorbed (in)	905

	1442	**HO**, *ura*, bay, inlet; seashore	
浦	85	浦波 *uranami* wave breaking on the beach, breaker	666
	2571	津々浦々 *tsutsu-uraura* throughout the land, the entire country ⌜folktale⌝	668
浦		浦島太郎 *Urashima Tarō* (character in a	286, 629, 980

	1443	**HO**, shop, store; pavement	
舗	9 552	店舗 *tenpo* shop, store	168
		老舗 *shinise, rōho* long-established store	543
		舗装 *hosō* pave	1328
	舗	舗(装)道(路) *ho(sō)dō(ro)* paved road/ street	1328, 149, 151

	1444	**SHA**, *su(teru)*, throw away; abandon, forsake	
捨	64 1944	取捨 *shusha* adoption or rejection, selection	65
		喜捨 *kisha* charity, almsgiving, donation	1143
		捨て子 *sutego* abandoned child, foundling	103
	捨	見捨てる *misuteru* abandon, desert, forsake	63
		切り捨てる *kirisuteru* cut down; discard, omit	39

	1445	**SHŪ**, *hiro(u)*, pick up, find; **JŪ**, ten (in documents)	
拾	64 1901	拾得物 *shūtokubutsu* an acquisition	374, 79
		収拾 *shūshū* get under control, deal with	757
		(金)拾万円 *(kin)jūman'en* 100,000 yen	23, 16, 13
	拾	拾い物 *hiroimono* something found lying on the ground, a find	79

	1446	**TEKI**, *shizuku*, a drop; *shitata(ru)*, drip, trickle	
滴	85 2674	水滴 *suiteki* drop of water	21
		雨滴 *uteki* raindrop	30
		点滴 *tenteki* falling drop of water/rain; (intravenous) drip	169
	滴	滴下 *tekika* drip, trickle down	31

	1447	**TEKI**, *tsu(mu)*, pick, pluck, nip	
摘	64 1987	摘発 *tekihatsu* exposure, disclosure	96
		摘出 *tekishutsu* pluck out, extract; expose	53
		指摘 *shiteki* point out	1041
	摘	摘要 *tekiyō* summary, synopsis	419
		茶摘み *chatsumi* tea picking	251

	1448	**BAKU**, *shiba(ru)*, tie up, bind	
縛	120 3593	束縛 *sokubaku* restraint, constraint, shackles	501
		捕縛 *hobaku* capture, apprehension, arrest	890
		縛り首 *shibarikubi* (execution by) hanging	148
	縛	金縛り *kanashibari* be bound; be tied down with money	23

	1449	**HAKU**, *usu(i)*, thin (paper), weak (tea), light (color); *usu(maru/ragu/reru)*, thin out, fade; *usu(meru)*, dilute	
薄	140 4075	浅薄 *senpaku* shallow, superficial	649
		薄情 *hakujō* unfeeling, heartless, coldhearted	209
		薄弱 *hakujaku* feebleness	218
	薄	薄明 *hakumei* twilight	18

	1450	BO, record book, ledger, register	
簿 118 3448 簿		簿記 *boki* bookkeeping 帳簿 *chōbo* account book, ledger 家計簿 *kakeibo* housekeeping account book 名簿 *meibo* list of names, roster 会員名簿 *kaiin meibo* list of members	371 1105 165, 340 82 158, 163, 82
	1451	FU, *shi(ku)*, spread, lay, put down	
敷 66 2059 敷		敷設 *fusetsu* laying, construction 屋敷 *yashiki* mansion; residential lot 座敷 *zashiki* a room, reception room 敷金 *shikikin* a deposit, security 敷布 *shikifu* (bed) sheet	577 167 786 23 675
	1452	KŌ, *shi(meru)*, strangle, wring; *shi(maru)*, be wrung out, pressed together; *shibo(ru)*, wring, squeeze, press, milk	
絞 120 3535 絞		絞殺 *kōsatsu* strangle to death; hang 絞首刑 *kōshukei* (execution by) hanging お絞り *oshibori* wet towel (provided in restaurants)	576 148, 887
	1453	KAKU, compare	
較 159 4623 較		比較 *hikaku* comparison 比較的 *hikakuteki* comparatively, relatively 比較文学 *hikaku bungaku* comparative literature ⌐adjective) 比較級 *hikakukyū* the comparative (of an	798 798, 210 798, 111, 109 798, 568
	1454	MON, (family) crest; (textile) pattern	
紋 120 3507 紋		紋章 *monshō* crest, coat of arms 菊の御紋 *kiku no gomon* imperial chrysanthe- 指紋 *shimon* a fingerprint ⌊mum crest 波紋 *hamon* a ripple 紋切り形/型 *monkirigata* conventional pattern	857 475, 708 1041 666 39, 395, 888
	1455	GA, *me*, a sprout, bud	
芽 140 3920 芽		発芽 *hatsuga* germinate, sprout, bud 麦芽 *bakuga* malt 新芽 *shinme* new bud, sprout, shoot 芽生え *mebae* bud, sprout, seedling 木の芽 *ki no me* leaf bud; Japanese pepper bud	96 270 174 44 22
	1456	GA, elegance, gracefulness	
雅 92 2850 雅		優雅 *yūga* elegance, grace, refinement 風雅 *fūga* elegance, refinement, (good) taste 雅趣 *gashu* elegance, tastefulness, artistry 雅楽 *Gagaku* ancient Japanese court music	1033 29 1002 358

	1457	JA, evil, wrong	
92	邪推	*jasui* groundless suspicion, mistrust	1233
2849	邪道	*jadō* evil course, vice; heresy	149
	邪教	*jakyō* heretical religion, heathenism	245
邪	邪宗	*jashū* heretical sect, heathenism	616
	風邪	*kaze* a cold	29

	1458	KI, *sude* (*ni*), already	
138	既成(の)事実	*kisei* (*no*) *jijitsu* accomplished	261, 80, 203
3887	既製服	*kiseifuku* ready-made clothes ⌊fact	428, 683
	既婚	*kikon* married	567
既	既報	*kihō* previous report ⌈history	685
	既往症	*kiōshō* previous illness; medical	918, 1318

	1459	GAI, general, approximate	
75	概算	*gaisan* rough estimate	747
2344	概略	*gairyaku* outline, summary	841
	概括	*gaikatsu* summary, generalization	1260
概	概況	*gaikyō* general situation, outlook	850
	概念	*gainen* concept	579

	1460	GAI, regret, lament, deplore	
61	慨嘆	*gaitan* regret, lament, deplore	1246
1741	感慨	*kangai* deep emotion	262
	感慨無量	*kangai-muryō* filled with deep	
慨		emotion	262, 93, 411

	1461	GAI, shore; end, limit	
85	生涯	*shōgai* a life, one's lifetime	44
2584	生涯教育	*shōgai kyōiku* continuing edu-	
		cation	44, 245, 246
涯	一生涯	*isshōgai* one's (whole) life (long)	2, 44
	天涯	*tengai* horizon; a distant land	141

	1462	KA, good, beautiful	
9	佳人	*kajin* beautiful woman, a beauty	1
429	佳作	*kasaku* a fine piece of work	360
	風光絶佳	*fūkō-zekka* scenic beauty	29, 138, 742
佳	佳境	*kakyō* interesting part, climax (of a story)	864

	1463	FŪ, seal; HŌ, fief	
41	同封	*dōfū* enclose (with a letter)	198
1349	封入	*fūnyū* enclose (with a letter)	52
	封書	*fūsho* sealed letter/document	131
封	開封	*kaifū* open (a letter)	396
	封建制度	*hōken seido* the feudal system	892, 427, 377

	1464	*ka(karu)*, hang; cost, take; *ka(keru)*, hang up; put on top of;
掛	64	spend; multiply; *kakari*, expenses; tax; relation, connection
	1952	腰 掛 け *koshikake*　seat, bench; stepping-stone　1298
掛		掛 け 布 団 *kakebuton*　quilt, bedspread　675, 491
		掛 け 軸 *kakejiku*　hanging scroll　988
		心 掛 け *kokorogake*　intention; attitude; attention　97

	1465	FU, *omomu(ku)*, go, proceed; become
赴	156	赴 任　*funin*　proceed to one's new post　334
	4540	赴 任 地/先 *funin-chi/saki*　one's post, one's place
赴		of appointment　334, 118, 50

	1466	BOKU, simple, plain
朴	75	素 朴　*soboku*　simple, unsophisticated　271
	2176	質 朴　*shitsuboku*　simplehearted, unsophisticated　176
朴		朴 直　*bokuchoku*　simple and honest, ingenuous　423
		朴 とつ *bokutotsu*　ruggedly honest, rudely simple

	1467	MO, *shige(ru)*, grow thick/rank
茂	140	繁 茂　*hanmo*　luxuriant growth　1292
	3915	生 い 茂 る *oishigeru*　grow luxuriantly　44
茂		

	1468	BYŌ, *nae*, [*nawa*], seedling, sapling
苗	140	苗 木　*naegi*　sapling, seedling, young tree　22
	3923	苗 床　*naedoko*　nursery, seedbed　826
苗		苗 代　*nawashiro*　bed for rice seedlings　256
		苗 字　*myōji*　family name, surname　110

	1469	BYŌ, *ega(ku)*, draw, paint, sketch, depict, portray
描	64	描 写　*byōsha*　depiction, portrayal, description　540
	1936	心 理 描 写 *shinri byōsha*　psychological
描		description　97, 143, 540
		素 描　*sobyō*　rough sketch　271
		絵 描 き *ekaki*　painter, artist　345

	1470	*neko*, cat
猫	94	招 き 猫 *manekineko*　porcelain cat beckoning
	2893	customers in stores　455
猫		山 猫　*yamaneko*　wildcat, lynx　34
		山 猫 争 議 *yamaneko sōgi*　wildcat strike　34, 302, 292
		猫 な で 声 *nekonadegoe*　coaxing voice　746

	1471	TEKI, *fue*, flute, whistle	
笛	118 3382	警 笛 *keiteki* alarm whistle; (automobile) horn	706
		汽 笛 *kiteki* steam whistle	135
		霧 笛 *muteki* foghorn	950
笛		口 笛 *kuchibue* a whistle	54
		角 笛 *tsunobue* bugle; huntsman's horn	473

	1472	TŌ, *tsutsu*, pipe, tube	
筒	118 3392	封 筒 *fūtō* envelope	1463
		水 筒 *suitō* canteen, flask	21
		発 煙 筒 *hatsuentō* smoke candle	96, 919
筒		円 筒 *entō* cylinder	13
		竹 筒 *takezutsu* bamboo tube	129

	1473	KA, (single) object; (counter for inanimate objects)	
箇	118 3414	箇 所 *kasho* place, part, passage (in a book)	153
		箇 条 *kajō* article, provision, item	564
		箇 条 書 き *kajōgaki* an itemization	564, 131
箇		一 箇 年 *ikkanen* 1 year	2, 45

	1474	KEI, *kuki*, stalk, stem	
茎	140 3912	地 下 茎 *chikakei* underground stem, rhizome	118, 31
		球 茎 *kyūkei* (tulip) bulb	726
		陰 茎 *inkei* penis	867
茎		歯 茎 *haguki* gums	478

	1475	KEI, path; diameter	
径	60 1602	直 径 *chokkei* diameter	423
		半 径 *hankei* radius	88
		口 径 *kōkei* caliber	54
径		径 路 *keiro* course, route, process	151
		直 情 径 行 *chokujō keikō* straightforwardness	423, 209, 68

	1476	KAI, *aya(shii)*, dubious; suspicious-looking; strange, mysterious; poor, clumsy; *aya(shimu)*, doubt, be sceptical; marvel at, be surprised	
怪	61 1665	怪 物 *kaibutsu* monster, apparition; mystery man	79
怪		奇 怪 *kikai* strange, mysterious; outrageous	1360

	1477	SEI, equal	
斉	210 5423	一 斉 に *issei ni* all at once, all together	2
斉		均 斉 *kinsei* symmetry, good balance	805

	1478	SAI, religious purification; a room	
210 5425		書斎 *shosai* a study, library 斎戒 *saikai* purification 斎戒もく浴 *saikai mokuyoku* ablution, puri- fication	131 876 876, 1128

	1479	JUN, follow, circulate	
60 1625		循環 *junkan* circulation 血液循環 *ketsueki junkan* blood circulation 789, 472, 865 悪循環 *akujunkan* vicious circle	865 304, 865

	1480	KO, lone, alone	
39 1270		孤独 *kodoku* solitary, lonely 孤立 *koritsu* isolation 孤島 *kotō* solitary/desert island 孤客 *kokaku* solitary traveler 孤児(院) *koji(in)* orphan(age)	219 121 286 641 1217, 614

	1481	KO, arc	
57 1567		弧状 *kojō* arc-shaped 円弧 *enko* circular arc 括弧 *kakko* parentheses ( )	626 13 1260

	1482	JŪ, [JU], [SHŌ], *shitaga(u)*, obey, comply with, follow; *shitaga(eru)*, be attended by; conquer	
60 1613		服従 *fukujū* obedience, submission 盲従 *mōjū* blind obedience 従来 *jūrai* up to now, usual, conventional 従業員 *jūgyōin* employee	683 1375 69 279, 163

	1483	JŪ, *tate*, height, length; vertical	
120 3597		縦線 *jūsen* vertical line 放縦 *hōjū* self-indulgent, dissolute, licentious 縦横 *jūō, tateyoko* length and breadth 縦断 *jūdan* vertical section; traverse, travel across	299 512 781 1024

	1484	I, do	
3 138		為政者 *iseisha* statesman, administrator 人為的 *jin'iteki* artificial 行為 *kōi* act, deed, behavior, conduct 無為 *mui* idleness, inaction 為替 *kawase* money order; (foreign) exchange	483, 164 1, 210 68 93 744

偽 9 510 偽	**1485**	**GI**, *itsuwa(ru)*, lie, misrepresent, feign, deceive; *nise*, fake, sham, bogus, counterfeit
	偽造 *gizō* forgery	691
	偽証 *gishō* perjury	484
	真偽 *shingi* true or false, truth	422
	偽物 *nisemono* fake, imitation, counterfeit	79

似 9 376 似	**1486**	**JI**, *ni(ru)*, be similar (to), be like, resemble
	類似 *ruiji* resemblance, similarity	226
	相似 *sōji* resemblance, similarity	146
	似顔 *nigao* likeness, portrait	277
	空似 *sorani* accidental resemblance	140
	似合う *niau* be becoming, suit, go well (with)	159

辛 160 4646 辛	**1487**	**SHIN**, *kara(i)*, hot, spicy, salty; hard, trying
	辛苦 *shinku* hardships, labor, trouble	545
	辛酸 *shinsan* hardships, privations	516
	辛勝 *shinshō* win after a hard fight	509
	辛抱 *shinbō* patience, perseverance	1285
	辛味 *karami* pungent taste, spiciness	307

宰 40 1303 宰	**1488**	**SAI**, manage, rule
	主宰 *shusai* superintendence, presiding over	155
	主宰者 *shusaisha* president, chairman, leader	155, 164
	宰相 *saishō* prime minister, premier	146

壁 32 1148 壁	**1489**	**HEKI**, *kabe*, wall
	障壁 *shōheki* fence, wall, barrier, obstacle	858
	防壁 *bōheki* protective wall, bulwark	513
	岩壁 *ganpeki* rock wall/face	1345
	壁画 *hekiga* fresco, mural	343
	壁紙 *kabegami* wallpaper	180

癖 104 3082 癖	**1490**	**HEKI**, *kuse*, personal habit, quirk, propensity
	性癖 *seiheki* disposition, proclivity	98
	悪癖 *akuheki* bad habit	304
	潔癖 *keppeki* love of cleanliness, fastidiousness	1241
	盗癖 *tōheki* kleptomania	1100
	口癖 *kuchiguse* habit of saying, favorite phrase	54

避 162 4749 避	**1491**	**HI**, *sa(keru)*, avoid
	回避 *kaihi* evasion, avoidance	90
	不可避 *fukahi* unavoidable	94, 388
	避難 *hinan* refuge, evacuation	557
	避妊 *hinin* contraception	955
	避雷針 *hiraishin* lightning rod	952, 341

甘 99 2988 甘	1492	**KAN**, *ama(i)*, sweet; insufficiently salted; indulgent; over-optimistic; *ama(eru)*, coax, wheedle, act spoiled, presume upon (another's) love; *ama(yakasu)*, be indulgent

甘味料 *kanmiryō* sweetener 307, 319
甘美 *kanbi* sweet, dulcet 401
甘言 *kangen* honeyed words, flattery 66

紺 120 3517 紺	1493	**KON**, dark/navy blue

紺色 *kon'iro* dark/navy blue 204
濃紺 *nōkon* deep/dark/navy blue 957
紺屋 *kon'ya*, *kōya* dyer, dyer's shop 167

某 99 2989 某	1494	**BŌ**, a certain

某所 *bōsho* a certain place 153
某氏 *bōshi* a certain person 566
某国 *bōkoku* a certain country 40
某日 *bōjitsu* a certain day, one day 5
何某 *nanibō* a certain person 390

謀 149 4414 謀	1495	**BŌ**, [MU], *haka(ru)*, plan, devise; deceive

陰謀 *inbō* plot, intrigue, conspiracy 867
共謀 *kyōbō* conspiracy, collusion 196
主謀者 *shubōsha* ringleader, mastermind 155, 164
謀略 *bōryaku* strategem, scheme 841
参謀 *sanbō* (general) staff 710

媒 38 1241 媒	1496	**BAI**, go-between

触媒 *shokubai* catalyst 874
触媒作用 *shokubai sayō* catalytic action 874, 360, 107
媒介 *baikai* mediation; matchmaking 453
媒介物 *baikaibutsu* a medium; carrier (of a 453, 79
霊媒 *reibai* (spiritualistic) medium ⌊disease) 1168

搾 64 1975 搾	1497	**SAKU**, *shibo(ru)*, squeeze, press, extract, milk

圧搾 *assaku* pressure, compression 1342
圧搾器 *assakuki* press, compressor 1342, 527
搾乳 *sakunyū* milk (a cow) 939
搾取 *sakushu* exploitation 65
搾り取る *shiboritoru* press, out, extract 65

詐 149 4337 詐	1498	**SA**, lie, deceive

詐称 *sashō* misrepresent oneself 978
詐取 *sashu* fraud, swindle 65

欺	1499 76 2419 欺	**GI**, *azamu(ku)*, deceive, dupe	
		詐欺　*sagi*　fraud	1498
		詐欺師　*sagishi*　swindler	1498, 409

匹	1500 22 756 匹	**HITSU**, compare; alone; *hiki*, (counter for animals)	
		匹敵　*hitteki*　be a match (for), comparable (to)	416
		匹夫　*hippu*　man; man of humble position	315
		犬一匹　*inu ippiki*　1 dog	280, 2

甚	1501 2 111 甚	**JIN**, *hanaha(da/dashii)*, very much, extreme, great, enormous, intense	
		甚大　*jindai*　very great, immense, serious, heavy	26
		激甚　*gekijin*　intense, violent, severe	1017
		幸甚　*kōjin*　very glad, much obliged	684
		甚六　*jinroku*　simpleton, blockhead	8

勘	1502 19 729 勘	**KAN**, perception, intuition, sixth sense	
		勘定　*kanjō*　counting, accounts, bill	355
		割り勘　*warikan*　splitting the bill equally, Dutch	519
		勘弁　*kanben*　pardon, forgive, overlook ⌊treat	711
		勘違い　*kanchigai*　misunderstanding, mistaken idea	814
		勘当　*kandō*　disown, disinherit	77

朱	1503 4 184 朱	**SHU**, scarlet	
		朱色　*shuiro*　scarlet, cinnabar, vermilion	204
		朱印　*shuin*　red seal	1043
		朱肉　*shuniku*　red ink pad	223
		朱筆を加える *shuhitsu o kuwaeru*　correct, retouch	130, 709

珠	1504 96 2936 珠	**SHU**, pearl	
		真珠　*shinju*　pearl	422
		珠玉　*shugyoku*　jewel, gem	295
		珠算　*shuzan*　calculation on the abacus	747
		数珠　*juzu*　rosary	225
		真珠湾　*Shinju-wan*　Pearl Harbor	422, 670

殊	1505 78 2443 殊	**SHU**, *koto (ni)*, especially, in particular	
		特殊　*tokushu*　special, unique	282
		特殊性　*tokushusei*　special characteristics, peculiarity	282, 98
		殊勝　*shushō*　admirable, praiseworthy	509
		殊の外　*koto no hoka*　exceedingly, exceptionally	83

殖	1506 78 2448 殖	SHOKU, *fu(eru)*, grow in number, increase; *fu(yasu)*, increase	
		増殖 *zōshoku* increase, multiply, proliferate	712
		生殖 *seishoku* reproduction, procreation	44
		繁殖 *hanshoku* breeding, reproduction	1292
		養殖 *yōshoku* raising, culture, cultivation	402

迭	1507 162 4672 迭	TETSU, alternation	
		更迭 *kōtetsu* change (in personnel), reshuffle	1008

秩	1508 115 3276 秩	CHITSU, order, sequence	
		秩序 *chitsujo* order, system, regularity	770
		安寧秩序 *annei-chitsujo* peace and order 105, 1412, 770	
		無秩序 *muchitsujo* disorder, chaos, confusion 93, 770	
		秩父 *Chichibu* (resort area NW of Tokyo)	113

伐	1509 9 370 伐	BATSU, attack; cut down	
		征伐 *seibatsu* conquest, subjugation	1114
		討伐 *tōbatsu* subjugation, suppression	1019
		殺伐 *satsubatsu* bloody, savage, warlike, fierce	576
		伐採 *bassai* timber felling, lumbering	933
		乱伐 *ranbatsu* reckless deforestation, overcutting	689

閥	1510 169 4954 閥	BATSU, clique, clan, faction	
		派閥 *habatsu* clique, faction	912
		財閥 *zaibatsu* financial combine	553
		軍閥 *gunbatsu* military clique, the militarists	438
		藩閥 *hanbatsu* clan, clique, faction	1382
		門閥 *monbatsu* lineage; distinguished family	161

闘	1511 169 4973 闘	TŌ, *tataka(u)*, fight, struggle	
		闘争 *tōsō* struggle, conflict; strike	302
		戦闘 *sentō* battle, combat	301
		奮闘 *funtō* hard fighting, strenuous efforts	1309
		春闘 *shuntō* spring (labor) offensive	460
		格闘 *kakutō* hand-to-hand fighting, scuffle	643

頼	1512 181 5129 頼	RAI, *tano(mu)*, ask for, request; entrust (to); *tano(moshii)*, reliable, dependable; promising; *tayo(ru)*, rely, depend (on)	
		依頼 *irai* request; entrust (to); reliance	678
		信頼 *shinrai* reliance, trust, confidence	157
		頼信紙 *raishinshi* telegram form	157, 180

	1513	*se*, shallows; rapids
瀬	85 2735 瀬	浅 瀬 *asase* shoal, shallows, sandbank; ford 649 早 瀬 *hayase* swift current, rapids ⌈(of war) 248 瀬 戸 際 *setogiwa* crucial moment, crisis, brink 152, 618 瀬 戸 物 *setomono* porcelain, china, earthenware 152, 79 瀬 戸 内 海 *Setonaikai* Inland Sea 152, 84, 117

	1514	SO, *uto(mu)*, shun, neglect, treat coldly; *uto(i)*, distant, estranged; know little (of)
疎	103 3021 疎	疎 遠 *soen* estrangement, alienation 446 疎 開 *sokai* evacuation, removal 396 空 疎 *kūso* empty, unsubstantial ⌈standing 140 (意 志 の)疎 通 *(ishi no) sotsū* mutual under- 132, 573, 150

	1515	SO, *ishizue*, cornerstone, foundation (stone)
礎	112 3222 礎	基 礎 *kiso* foundation, basis ⌈groundwork 450 基 礎 工 事 *kiso kōji* foundation work, 450, 139, 80 基 礎 知 識 *kiso chishiki* elementary knowl- 450, 214, 681 礎 石 *soseki* foundation (stone) ⌊edge 78 定 礎 式 *teisoshiki* laying of the cornerstone 355, 525

	1516	GI, *utaga(u)*, be doubtful of, be suspicious of, distrust
疑	21 755 疑	疑 問 *gimon* question, doubt, problem 162 疑 惑 *giwaku* suspicion, distrust, misgivings 969 疑 獄 *gigoku* scandal 884 容 疑 者 *yōgisha* a suspect ⌈wer (session) 654, 164 質 疑 応 答 *shitsugi-ōtō* question and ans- 176, 827, 160

	1517	GI, imitate
擬	64 2026 擬	擬 人 *gijin* personification 1 擬 音 *gion* an imitated sound; sound effects 347 模 擬 *mogi* imitation, simulated 1425 模 擬 試 験 *mogi shiken* mock/trial exam- ination 1425, 526, 532

	1518	GYŌ, *ko(ru)*, grow stiff; be engrossed (in); be fastidious, elaborate (about); *ko(rasu)*, concentrate, strain
凝	15 652 凝	凝 固 *gyōko* solidification, coagulation, freezing 972 凝 結 *gyōketsu* coagulation, curdling, conden- 485 凝 視 *gyōshi* stare at, watch intently ⌊sation 606 凝 り 性 *korishō* fastidiousness, perfectionism 98

	1519	SATSU, *su(reru)*, rub, chafe; become worn; lose one's simplicity; *su(ru)*, rub, file
擦	64 2025 擦	擦 過 傷 *sakkashō* an abrasion, scratch 413, 633 靴 擦 れ *kutsuzure* shoe sore 1076 擦 れ 違 う *surechigau* pass by each other 814 擦 り 傷 *surikizu* an abrasion, scratch 633

撮	1520 64 2001 撮	**SATSU**, pick, pinch; summarize; *to(ru)*, take (a picture) 撮 影　　*satsuei*　photography, filming　　854 撮 影 所　*satsueijo*　movie studio　　854, 153 戸/野 外 撮 影　*ko/ya-gai satsuei*　outdoor photog- 　raphy, outdoor shooting　152, 236, 83, 854 夜 間 撮 影　*yakan satsuei*　night photography　471, 43, 854	

卑	1521 4 221 卑	**HI**, *iya(shimeru/shimu)*, despise, look down on; *iya(shii)*, humble, lowly; base, ignoble, vulgar 男 尊 女 卑　*danson-johi*　predominance of　101, 704, 102 卑 俗　　*hizoku*　vulgar, coarse　⌊men over women 1126 卑 劣 漢　*hiretsukan*　mean bastard, low-down　1150, 556 卑 語　　*higo*　vulgar word/expression　⌊skunk　67	

碑	1522 112 3206 碑	**HI**, tombstone, monument 記 念 碑　*kinenhi*　monument, memorial　371, 579 墓 碑　　*bohi*　tombstone, gravestone　1429 石 碑　　*sekihi*　tombstone, (stone) monument　78 碑 文　　*hibun*　epitaph, inscription　111	

鬼	1523 194 5276 鬼	**KI**, *oni*, ogre, demon, devil; soul of a dead person 鬼 神　　*kijin, kishin, onigami*　fierce god; departed　310 餓 鬼　　*gaki*　hungry ghost; little brat　⌊soul 1303 鬼 才　　*kisai*　genius, man of remarkable talent　551 鬼 ごっこ　*onigokko*　tag; blindman's buff	

塊	1524 32 1122 塊	**KAI**, *katamari*, lump, clod, clump 土 塊　　*dokai*　clod of dirt　24 金 塊　　*kinkai*　gold nugget/bar　23 肉 塊　　*nikkai*　piece of meat　223 塊 根　　*kaikon*　tuberous root　314 塊 状　　*kaijō*　massive　626	

魂	1525 194 5278 魂	**KON**, *tamashii*, soul, spirit 霊 魂　　*reikon*　the soul　1168 商 魂　　*shōkon*　commercial spirit, salesmanship　412 魂 胆　　*kontan*　soul; ulterior motive　1273 負 けじ 魂　*makeji-damashii*　unyielding spirit　510 大 和 魂　*Yamato-damashii*　the Japanese spirit　26, 124	

魅	1526 194 5280 魅	**MI**, charm, enchant, fascinate 魅 力　　*miryoku*　charm, appeal, fascination　100 魅 力 的　*miryokuteki*　fascinating, captivating　100, 210 魅 了　　*miryō*　charm, captivate, hold spellbound　941 魅 惑　　*miwaku*　fascination, charm, lure　969	

	1527	SHŪ, *miniku(i)*, ugly	
醜	164 4798 醜	醜聞 *shūbun* scandal	64
		醜悪 *shūaku* ugly, abominable, scandalous	304
		醜態 *shūtai* unseemly sight; disgraceful behavior	387
		醜女 *shūjo, shikome* ugly woman	102
		美醜 *bishū* beauty or ugliness, appearance	401

	1528	MA, demon, devil, evil spirit	
魔	200 5398 魔	悪魔 *akuma* devil	304
		魔術 *majutsu* black magic, sorcery, witchcraft	187
		魔法 *mahō* magic	123
		魔法瓶 *mahōbin* thermos bottle ⌈turbance 123, 1161	
		邪魔 *jama* encumbrance, interruption, dis-	1457

	1529	MA, *asa*, flax, hemp	
麻	200 5390 麻	大麻 *taima, ōasa* hemp, marijuana	26
		麻薬 *mayaku* narcotics, drugs	359
		麻ひ *mahi* paralysis	
		小児麻ひ *shōni mahi* infantile paralysis, polio 27, 1217	
		麻糸 *asaito* hempen yarn, linen thread	242

	1530	MA, rub, rub off, scrape	
摩	200 5392 摩	摩擦 *masatsu* friction	1519
		冷水摩擦 *reisui masatsu* rubdown with a wet towel	832, 21, 1519
		あん摩 *anma* massage, masseur, masseuse	

	1531	MA, *miga(ku)*, polish, brush	
磨	200 5393 磨	研磨 *kenma* grind, polish; study hard	896
		磨滅 *mametsu* wear, abrasion	1338
		達磨 *daruma* Bodhidharma; quadruple amputee;	448
		歯磨き *hamigaki* toothpaste ⌊prostitute	478
		磨き上げる *migakiageru* polish up	32

	1532	KAN, leisure	
閑	169 4948 閑	閑静 *kansei* quiet, peaceful	663
		森閑 *shinkan* stillness, quiet	128
		安閑 *ankan* idleness	105
		閑散 *kansan* leisure; (market) inactivity	767
		農閑期 *nōkanki* the slack season for farming	369, 449

	1533	KAN, simple, brief	
簡	118 3444 簡	簡単 *kantan* simple, brief	300
		簡略 *kanryaku* simple, concise	841
		簡潔 *kanketsu* concise	1241
		簡素 *kanso* plain and simple	271
		書簡 *shokan* letter, correspondence	131

	1534	**REKI**, *koyomi*, calendar	
暦	27 833	西暦 *seireki* the Western calendar, A.D.	72
		旧暦 *kyūreki* the old (lunar) calendar	1216
		太陽暦 *taiyōreki* the solar calendar	629, 630
		還暦 *kanreki* one's 60th birthday	866
	暦	花暦 *hanagoyomi* floral calendar	255

	1535	**KA**, cake; fruit	
菓	140 3980	(お)菓子 *(o)kashi* candy, confections, pastry	103
		菓子屋 *kashiya* candy store, confectionery shop	103, 167
		和菓子 *wagashi* Japanese-style confection	124, 103
		茶菓 *chaka, saka* tea and cake, refreshments	251
	菓	水菓子 *mizugashi* fruit	21, 103

	1536	**RA**, *hadaka*, naked	
裸	145 4248	裸婦 *rafu* nude woman	316
		裸体画 *rataiga* nude picture	61, 343
		赤裸々 *sekirara* naked; frank, outspoken	207
		裸馬 *hadakauma* unsaddled horse ⌈own body	283
	裸	裸一貫 *hadaka-ikkan* with no property but one's	2, 914

	1537	**KIN**, *eri*, neck; collar, lapel	
襟	145 4267	胸襟 *kyōkin* bosom, heart	1283
		開襟シャツ *kaikin shatsu* open-necked shirt	396
		襟巻き *erimaki* muffler, scarf	507
		襟首 *erikubi* nape, back/scruff of the neck	148
	襟	襟元 *erimoto* the neck	137

	1538	**SŌ**, *su*, nest	
巣	3 141	卵巣 *ransō* ovary ⌈inflammation	1058
		炎症病巣 *enshō byōsō* focus of an	1336, 1318, 380
		古巣 *furusu* old nest, one's old haunt	172
		巣立ち *sudachi* leave the nest, become independent	121
	巣	空き巣 (ねらい) *akisu(nerai)* sneak thief	140

	1539	**DAN**, *tama*, bullet; *hazu(mu)*, bounce; be stimulated; fork out, splurge on; *hi(ku)*, play (piano/guitar)	
弾	57 1575	爆弾 *bakudan* a bomb	1015
		弾薬 *dan'yaku* ammunition	359
		弾丸 *dangan* projectile, bullet, shell	644
	弾	弾力 *danryoku* elasticity	100

	1540	**ZEN**, Zen Buddhism	
禅	113 3255	禅宗 *Zenshū* the Zen sect ⌈sitting)	616
		座禅 *zazen* religious meditation (done while	786
		禅僧 *zensō* Zen priest	1366
		禅寺 *zendera* Zen temple ⌈hensible dialogue	41
	禅	禅問答 *zen mondō* Zen dialogue; incompre-	162, 160

	1541	HŌ, [BU], *tatematsu(ru)*, offer, present; revere	
奉	4	奉納 *hōnō* dedication, offering	758
	212	奉献 *hōken* dedication, consecration	1355
		信奉 *shinpō* belief, faith	157
奉		奉仕 *hōshi* attendance; service	333
		奉公 *hōkō* public duty; domestic service	126

	1542	HŌ, salary	
俸	9	俸給 *hōkyū* salary, pay	346
	480	年俸 *nenpō* annual salary	45
		号俸 *gōhō* pay level, salary class ⌜allowance	266
俸		年功加俸 *nenkō kahō* long-service pension/	45, 818, 709
		減俸 *genpō* salary reduction, pay cut	715

	1543	BŌ, stick, pole	
棒	75	鉄棒 *tetsubō* iron bar; the horizontal bar (in gym-	312
	2302	心棒 *shinbō* axle, shaft ⌊nastics)	97
		棒立ち *bōdachi* standing bolt upright	121
棒		相棒 *aibō* pal; accomplice	146
		棒暗記 *bōanki* indiscriminate memorization	348, 371

	1544	SŌ, *kana(deru)*, play (a musical instrument)	
奏	37	演奏会 *ensōkai* concert, recital	344, 158
	1178	前奏 *zensō* prelude	47
		独奏 *dokusō* a solo (performance)	219
奏		二重奏 *nijūsō* duet	3, 227
		伴奏 *bansō* accompaniment	1027

	1545	TAI, calm, peace	
泰	85	泰然自若 *taizen jijaku* imperturbability	651, 62, 544
	2526	安泰 *antai* tranquility; security	105
		泰平 *taihei* peace, tranquility	202
泰		泰西 *taisei* Occident, the West ⌜painting	72
		泰西名画 *taisei meiga* a famous Western	72, 82, 343

	1546	SHITSU, *urushi*, lacquer	
漆	85	漆器 *shikki* lacquerware	527
	2679	漆黒 *shikkoku* jet-black, pitch-black	206
		乾漆像 *kanshitsuzō* dry-lacquered image (of	1190, 740
漆		漆くい *shikkui* mortar, plaster ⌊Buddha)	
		漆塗り *urushinuri* lacquered, japanned	1073

	1547	JI, *itsuku(shimu)*, love, treat with affection	
慈	12	慈善 *jizen* charity, philanthropy	1139
	612	慈悲 *jihi* mercy, benevolence, pity	1034
		慈恵 *jikei* charity	1219
慈		慈愛 *jiai* affection, kindness, love	259
		慈雨 *jiu* beneficial/welcome rain	30

	1548	JI, magnetism; porcelain	
磁	112	磁気　　*jiki*　magnetism, magnetic	134
	3209	磁石　　*jishaku*　magnet	78
		電磁石　*denjishaku*　electromagnet	108, 78
磁		磁場　　*jiba, jijō*　magnetic field	154
		磁器　　*jiki*　porcelain	527

	1549	JI, more and more, luxuriant	
滋	85	滋養　　*jiyō*　nourishment, nutrition	402
	2626	滋養分　*jiyōbun*　nutritious element, nutriment	402, 38
滋		滋賀県　*Shiga-ken*　Shiga Prefecture	756, 194

	1550	JU, *kotobuki*, congratulations; longevity	
寿	4	寿命　　*jumyō*　lifespan, life	578
	194	天寿　　*tenju*　one's natural span of life	141
		長寿　　*chōju*　longevity	95
寿		喜寿　　*kiju*　one's 77th birthday ⌈vinegared rice	1143
		寿司　　*sushi*　raw fish and other delicacies with	842

	1551	CHŪ, *i(ru)*, cast (metal)	
鋳	167	鋳造　　*chūzō*　casting; minting, coinage	691
	4865	鋳鉄　　*chūtetsu*　cast iron	312
		改鋳　　*kaichū*　recoinage; recasting	514
鋳		鋳型　　*igata*　a mold, cast	888
		鋳物　　*imono*　an article of cast metal, a casting	79

	1552	MEI, inscription, signature, name; precept, motto	
銘	167	銘記　　*meiki*　bear in mind	371
	4852	感銘　　*kanmei*　deep impression	262
		銘柄　　*meigara*　a brand (name)	985
銘		座右銘　*zayūmei*　motto	786, 76
		碑銘　　*himei*　inscription; epitaph	1522

	1553	KO, *yato(u)*, employ; charter	
雇	63	終身雇用制　*shūshin koyōsei*　lifetime employment	
	1826	system	458, 59, 107, 427
		解雇　　*kaiko*　dismiss, fire	474
雇		雇い人　*yatoinin*　employee; servant	1
		雇い主　*yatoinushi*　employer	155

	1554	KO, *kaeri(miru)*, look back; take into consideration	
顧	181	回顧　　*kaiko*　recollection, retrospect	90
	5141	回顧録　*kaikoroku*　reminiscences, memoirs	90, 538
		顧慮　　*koryo*　regard, consideration	1384
顧		顧問　　*komon*　adviser	162
		顧客　　*kokaku, kokyaku*　customer	641

	1555	**SEN**, *ōgi*, fan, folding fan	
扇	63 1823	扇子 *sensu* folding fan	103
		扇風機 *senpūki* electric fan	29, 528
		扇形 *senkei, ōgigata* fan shape, sector, segment	395
扇		扇動 *sendō* incitement, instigation, agitation	231
		舞扇 *maiōgi* dancer's fan	810

	1556	**HI**, *tobira*, door; title page	
扉	63 1825	開扉 *kaihi* opening of the door	396
		門扉 *monpi* the doors of a gate	161
扉			

	1557	**SOKU**, *unaga(su)*, urge, prompt, spur on	
促	9 444	促進 *sokushin* promotion, acceleration	437
		催促 *saisoku* press, urge, demand	1317
促		促成 *sokusei* artificially accelerate, force (growth)	261

	1558	**YŌ**, *odo(ru)*, dance; *odo(ri)*, a dance, dancing	
踊	157 4565	舞踊 *buyō* a dance, dancing	810
		盆踊り *Bon odori* Bon Festival dance	1099
		踊り子 *odoriko* dancer, dancing girl	103
踊		踊り場 *odoriba* dance hall/floor; (stairway) landing	154
		踊り狂う *odorikuruu* dance ecstatically	883

	1559	**TŌ**, *fu(mu)*, step on; *fu(maeru)*, stand on, be based on	
踏	157 4571	舞踏会 *butōkai* ball, dance party	810, 158
		雑踏 *zattō* hustle and bustle, (traffic) congestion	575
		踏査 *tōsa* survey, field investigation	624
踏		踏切 *fumikiri* railroad crossing	39
		足踏み *ashibumi* step, stamp, mark time	58

	1560	**YAKU**, *odo(ru)*, jump, leap, hop	
躍	157 4595	飛躍 *hiyaku* a leap; activity; rapid progress	530
		活躍 *katsuyaku* active, action	237
		暗躍 *an'yaku* behind-the-scenes maneuvering	348
躍		躍進 *yakushin* advance by leaps and bounds	437
		躍動 *yakudō* lively motion	231

	1561	**TAKU**, wash, rinse	
濯	85 2718	洗濯 *sentaku* washing, the wash, laundry	692
		洗濯機 *sentakuki* washing machine, washer	692, 528
濯		洗濯物 *sentakumono* the wash, laundry	692, 79

兆 15 637 兆	1562	**CHŌ**, sign, indication; trillion; *kiza(shi)*, sign, symptoms; *kiza(su)*, show signs; sprout, germinate
	兆候	*chōkō* sign, indication　　　　　　　　　　　　944
	前兆	*zenchō* omen, portent, foreshadowing　　　　47
	吉兆	*kitchō* good omen/sign　　　　　　　　　　1141
	億兆	*okuchō* the multitude, the people　　　　　382

跳 157 4562 跳	1563	**CHŌ**, *to(bu)*, *ha(neru)*, leap, spring up, jump, bounce
	跳躍	*chōyaku* spring, jump, leap　　　　　　　　1560
	跳び上がる	*tobiagaru* jump up　　　　　　　　　　　　32
	跳ね上がる	*haneagaru* jump up　　　　　　　⌈high jump　32
	走り高跳び	*hashiri-takatobi* the (running)　　　429, 190
	飛び跳ねる	*tobihaneru* jump up and down　　　　　　530

挑 64 1898 挑	1564	**CHŌ**, *ido(mu)*, challenge
	挑戦	*chōsen* challenge　　　　　　　　　　　　301
	挑戦者	*chōsensha* challenger　　　　　　　　301, 164
	挑発	*chōhatsu* arouse, excite, provoke　　　　　96
	挑発的	*chōhatsuteki* provocative, suggestive　　96, 210

眺 109 3138 眺	1565	**CHŌ**, *naga(meru)*, look at, watch, gaze at
	眺望	*chōbō* a view (from a window)　　　　　　673

逃 162 4682 逃	1566	**TŌ**, *ni(geru)*, run away, escape, flee; *noga(reru)*, escape; *ni(gasu)*, *noga(su)*, let go, set free; let escape
	逃走	*tōsō* escape, flight, desertion　　　　　　429
	逃亡	*tōbō* escape, flight, desertion　　　　　　672
	逃げ出す	*nigedasu* break into a run, run off/away　　53
	見逃す	*minogasu* overlook　　　　　　　　　　　63

桃 75 2255 桃	1567	**TŌ**, *momo*, peach
	桃源郷/境	*Tōgenkyō* Shangri-la, paradise　　580, 855, 864
	桃色	*momoiro* pink　　　　　　　　⌊on earth　204
	桃の節句	*Momo no Sekku* Doll Festival (March 3)
	桃山時代	⌈period (1573–1615) 464, 337 *Momoyama jidai* Momoyama 34, 42, 256

践 157 4558 践	1568	**SEN**, step, step up; realize, put into practice
	実践	*jissen* practice　　　　　　　　　　　　203
	実践的	*jissenteki* practical　　　　　　　　203, 210
	実践理性批判	*Jissen Risei Hihan* (Critique of 　Practical Reason—Kant) 203, 143, 98, 1029, 1026

	1569	SEKI, *ato*, mark, traces, vestiges, remains, ruins	
跡	157	遺跡 *iseki* remains, ruins, relics	1172
	4560	史跡 *shiseki* historic site/relics	332
		足跡 *ashiato, sokuseki* footprint	58
		傷跡 *kizuato* a scar	633
跡		跡継ぎ *atotsugi* successor, heir	1025

	1570	SHA, forgive	
赦	155	大赦 *taisha* (general) amnesty	26
	4536	恩赦 *onsha* an amnesty, general pardon	555
		赦免 *shamen* pardon, clemency	733
		特赦 *tokusha* an amnesty	282
赦		容赦 *yōsha* pardon, forgiveness, mercy	654

	1571	SEN, fine, slender	
繊	120	繊維 *sen'i* fiber, textiles	1231
	3607	繊維工業 *sen'i kōgyō* textile industry	1231, 139, 279
		合成繊維 *gōsei sen'i* synthetic fiber	159, 261, 1231
		化繊 *kasen* synthetic fiber	254
繊		繊細 *sensai* delicate, fine, subtle	695

	1572	KYO, [KO], empty	
虚	141	虚無主義 *kyomu shugi* nihilism	93, 155, 291
	4109	虚栄(心) *kyoei(shin)* vanity	723, 97
		虚弱 *kyojaku* weak, feeble, frail	218
		虚偽 *kyogi* false, untrue	1485
虚		虚空 *kokū* empty space, the air	140

	1573	GI, *tawamu(reru)*, play, sport; jest; flirt	
戯	4	遊戯 *yūgi* amusement	1003
	246	戯曲 *gikyoku* drama, play	366
		前戯 *zengi* (sexual) foreplay	47
		戯画 *giga* a caricature	343
戯		悪戯 *akugi, itazura* mischief, prank; lewdness	304

	1574	GYAKU, *shiita(geru)*, oppress, tyrannize	
虐	141	虐待 *gyakutai* treat cruelly, mistreat	452
	4106	暴虐 *bōgyaku* tyrannical, cruel	1014
		虐殺 *gyakusatsu* massacre, slaughter, butchery	576
		残虐 *zangyaku* cruel, brutal, inhuman	650
虐		自虐的 *jigyakuteki* self-torturing	62, 210

	1575	SHŪ, *oso(u)*, attack, assail; succeed to, inherit	
襲	212	来襲 *raishū* attack, assault, invasion	69
	5443	空襲 *kūshū* air raid	140
		夜襲 *yashū* night attack	471
		世襲 *seshū* hereditary	252
襲		因襲 *inshū* long-established custom, convention	554

1576 祥

SHŌ, happiness; good omen

113
3246

不 祥 事	*fushōji*	scandal	94, 80
発 祥	*hasshō*	origin	96
発 祥 地	*hasshōchi*	birthplace, cradle	96, 118
吉 祥	*kisshō*	good omen	⌈dess⌉ 1141
吉 祥 天	*Kichijōten, Kisshōten*	(Buddhist god-	1141, 141

祥

1577 詳

SHŌ, *kuwa(shii)*, detailed, full; familiar with (something)

149
4357

詳 細	*shōsai*	details, particulars	695
不 詳	*fushō*	unknown, unidentified	94
未 詳	*mishō*	unknown, unidentified	306
詳 報	*shōhō*	full/detailed report	685
詳 述	*shōjutsu*	detailed explanation, full account	968

詳

1578 黙

MOKU, *dama(ru)*, become silent, say nothing

86
2796

沈 黙	*chinmoku*	silence	936
黙 認	*mokunin*	tacit approval	738
黙 殺	*mokusatsu*	take no notice of, ignore	576
黙 秘 権	*mokuhiken*	right against self-incrim-	
		ination	807, 335

黙

1579 猛

MŌ, strong, fierce

94
2895

猛 烈	*mōretsu*	fierce, violent, strong	1331
猛 打	*mōda*	hard hit, heavy blow	1020
猛 暑	*mōsho*	fierce heat	638
猛 犬	*mōken*	vicious dog	280
猛 者	*mosa*	man of courage, stalwart veteran	164

猛

1580 猟

RYŌ, hunting

94
2894

猟 師	*ryōshi*	hunter	409
密 猟 者	*mitsuryōsha*	poacher	806, 164
猟 犬	*ryōken*	hunting dog	280
猟 銃	*ryōjū*	hunting gun, shotgun	829
禁 猟	*kinryō*	prohibition on hunting	482

猟

1581 狩

SHU, *ka(ri)*, hunting; *ka(ru)*, hunt

94
2883

狩 猟(期)	*shuryō(ki)*	hunting (season)	1580, 449
狩 り 小 屋	*karigoya*	hunting cabin	27, 167
狩 人	*karyūdo*	hunter	1
潮 干 狩 り	*shiohigari*	shell gathering (at low tide)	468, 584
み か ん 狩 り	*mikangari*	picking mandarin oranges	

狩

1582 獣

JŪ, *kemono*, animal, beast

94
2909

野 獣	*yajū*	wild animal	236
猛 獣	*mōjū*	vicious animal, ferocious beast	1579
怪 獣	*kaijū*	monster	⌈wildlife sanctuary 1476
鳥 獣 保 護 区 域	*chōjū hogo kuiki*	285, 489, 1312, 183, 970
獣 区	*jūi*	veterinarian	220

獣

	1583	YŪ, delay; still, still more
94		猶予 *yūyo* postponement, deferment 393
2897		猶予なく *yūyonaku* without delay, promptly 393
猶		執行猶予 *shikkō yūyo* suspended sentence, probation 686, 68, 393

	1584	EN, *saru*, monkey
94		野猿 *yaen* wild monkey 236
2905		類人猿 *ruijin'en* anthropoid ape ⌈matters 226, 1
		猿知恵 *sarujie* cleverness in managing petty 214, 1219
猿		犬猿の仲 *ken'en no naka* hating each other, like cats and dogs 280, 1347

	1585	KŌ, scales, weigh
60		均衡 *kinkō* balance, equilibrium 805
1641		平衡 *heikō* balance, equilibrium 202
		平衡感覚 *heikō kankaku* sense of equi- librium 202, 262, 605
衡		度量衡 *doryōkō* weights and measures 377, 411

	1586	KAN, *ka(eru)*, substitute; *ka(waru)*, be replaced
64		交換 *kōkan* exchange, substitution 114
1964		転換 *tenkan* conversion, switchover; diversion 433
		変換 *henkan* change, conversion 257
		換算(率) *kansan(ritsu)* conversion, exchange (rate) 747, 788
換		乗り換える *norikaeru* transfer, change (trains) 523

	1587	KAN, call
30		召喚 *shōkan* summons, subpoena ⌈witness) 995
958		(証人)喚問 *(shōnin) kanmon* summons (of a 484, 1, 162
		喚起 *kanki* evoke, awaken, call forth 373
		叫喚 *kyōkan* shout, outcry, scream ⌈lam 1252
喚		あ鼻叫喚 *abi-kyōkan* (2 Buddhist hells); bed- 813, 1252

	1588	YŪ, dissolve, melt
193		融合 *yūgō* fusion 159
5274		融通 *yūzū* accommodation, loan; versatility 150
		金融 *kin'yū* money, finance 23
		金融機関 *kin'yū kikan* financial institution 23, 528, 398
融		融資 *yūshi* financing, loan 750

	1589	KAKU, *heda(teru)*, separate, interpose; estrange; *heda(taru)*, be distant, apart; become estranged
170		間隔 *kankaku* space, spacing, interval 43
5016		隔離 *kakuri* isolation, quarantine 1281
		遠隔 *enkaku* distant, remote, outlying 446
隔		横隔膜 *ōkakumaku* the diaphragm 781, 1426

	1590	TEI, offer, present, exhibit	
呈	30	進呈 *shintei* give, present	437
	895	贈呈 *zōtei* present, donate	1364
		献呈本 *kenteibon* presentation copy	1355, 25
	呈	謹呈 *kintei* With the compliments of the author	1247
		露呈 *rotei* exposure, disclosure	951

	1591	ZE, right, correct, just	
是	72	是非 *zehi* right and wrong; by all means	498
	2120	是正 *zesei* correct, rectify	275
		是認 *zenin* approval, sanction	738
	是	是々非々 *zeze-hihi* being fair and unbiased	498

	1592	TEI, *tsutsumi*, bank, embankment, dike	
堤	32	堤防 *teibō* embankment, dike, levee	513
	1108	防波堤 *bōhatei* breakwater	513, 666
	堤		

	1593	*mata*, again; also, moreover	
又	29	又聞き *matagiki* hearsay, secondhand information	64
	855	又貸し *matagashi* sublease	748
		又々 *matamata* once again	
	又	又は *mata wa* or, either . . . or . . .	

	1594	SŌ, *futa*, pair, both	
双	29	双方 *sōhō* both parties/sides	70
	859	双生児 *sōseiji* twins	44, 1217
		双眼鏡 *sōgankyō* binoculars	848, 863
	双	双肩 *sōken* one's shoulders	1264
		双子 *futago* twins	103

	1595	DO, *tsuto(meru)*, exert oneself, make efforts, strive	
努	19	努力 *doryoku* effort, endeavor	100
	717	努力家 *doryokuka* hard worker	100, 165
	努		

	1596	DO, *oko(ru)*, *ika(ru)*, get angry	
怒	61	怒気 *doki* (fit of) anger	134
	1664	激怒 *gekido* wild rage, wrath, fury ⌈infuriated	1017
		怒髪天を突く *dohatsu ten o tsuku* be	1148, 141, 898
	怒	怒号 *dogō* angry roar	266
		喜怒 *kido* joy and anger, emotion	1143

悠	**1597**	**YŪ**, distant; leisure		
	61	悠然	*yūzen* calm, perfect composure	651
	1701	悠長	*yūchō* leisurely, slow, easygoing	95
		悠々	*yūyū* calm, composed, leisurely	
悠		悠揚	*yūyō* composed, calm, serene	631
		悠久	*yūkyū* eternity, perpetuity	1210

愉	**1598**	**YU**, joy, pleasure		
	61	愉快	*yukai* pleasant, merry, cheerful	1409
	1726	不愉快	*fuyukai* unpleasant, disagreeable	94, 1409
愉		愉楽	*yuraku* pleasure, joy	358

諭	**1599**	**YU**, *sato(su)*, admonish, remonstrate, warn, counsel		
	149	教諭	*kyōyu* teacher, instructor	245
	4411	説諭	*setsuyu* admonition, reproof, caution	400
諭		諭旨	*yushi* official suggestion (to a subordinate)	1040

癒	**1600**	**YU**, heal, cure		
	104	癒着	*yuchaku* heal up, adhere, knit together	657
	3081	治癒	*chiyu* healing, cure, recovery	493
癒		平癒	*heiyu* recovery	202

愁	**1601**	**SHŪ**, *ure(i)*, grief, sorrow, distress; anxiety, cares; *ure(eru)*, grieve, be distressed; fear, be apprehensive		
	61			
	1729	郷愁	*kyōshū* homesickness, nostalgia	855
		旅愁	*ryoshū* loneliness on a journey	222
愁		憂愁	*yūshū* melancholy, grief, gloom	1032
		ご愁傷様	*goshūshō-sama* My heartfelt sympathy.	633, 403

恐	**1602**	**KYŌ**, *oso(reru)*, fear, be afraid of; *oso(roshii)*, terrible, frightful, awful		
	61			
	1685	恐縮	*kyōshuku* be very grateful; be sorry	1110
		恐慌	*kyōkō* panic	1378
恐		恐妻家	*kyōsaika* henpecked husband	671, 165
		空恐ろしい	*soraosoroshii* have a vague fear	140

築	**1603**	**CHIKU**, *kizu(ku)*, build, erect		
	118	建築	*kenchiku* architecture, construction	892
	3435	建築家	*kenchikuka* architect	892, 165
		新築	*shinchiku* new construction	174
築		改築	*kaichiku* rebuilding, reconstruction	514
		築山	*tsukiyama* mound, artificial hill	34

鉱	1604	**KŌ**, ore		
	167	鉱石	*kōseki* ore, mineral, crystal	78
	4843	鉱物	*kōbutsu* mineral	79
		鉄鉱	*tekkō* iron ore	312
鉱		鉱山	*kōzan* a mine	34
		鉱業	*kōgyō* mining	279

銅	1605	**DŌ**, copper		
	167	銅山	*dōzan* copper mine	34
	4853	銅版画	*dōhanga* copper print	1046, 343
		銅像	*dōzō* bronze statue	740
銅		青銅	*seidō* bronze	208
		銅メダル	*dōmedaru* bronze medal	

鉛	1606	**EN**, *namari*, lead		
	167	鉛筆	*enpitsu* pencil	130
	4842	黒鉛	*kokuen* graphite	206
		鉛版	*enban* stereotype, printing plate	1046
鉛		鉛毒	*endoku* lead poisoning	522
		鉛色	*namariiro* lead color/gray	204

沿	1607	**EN**, *so(u)*, stand along (a street), run parallel (to)		
	85	沿岸	*engan* coast, shore	586
	2525	沿海	*enkai* coastal waters, coast	117
		沿線	*ensen* along the (train) line	299
沿		沿革	*enkaku* history, development	1075
		川沿い	*kawazoi* along the river	33

鋼	1608	**KŌ**, *hagane*, steel		
	167	鋼鉄	*kōtetsu* steel	312
	4883	特殊鋼	*tokushukō* special steel	282, 1505
		鋼板	*kōhan, kōban* steel plate	1047
鋼		製鋼所	*seikōjo* steel plant	428, 153
		製鋼業	*seikōgyō* steel industry	428, 279

綱	1609	**KŌ**, *tsuna*, rope, cord		
	120	綱領	*kōryō* plan, program, platform	834
	3561	綱紀	*kōki* official discipline, public order	372
		手綱	*tazuna* bridle, reins	57
綱		綱渡り	*tsunawatari* tightrope walking	378
		横綱	*yokozuna* sumo grand champion	781

剛	1610	**GŌ**, strength, hardness		
	2	外柔内剛	*gaijū-naigō* gentle-looking but sturdy	83, 774, 84
	114	剛健	*gōken* strong and sturdy, virile	893
		剛勇	*gōyū* valor, bravery	1386
剛		金剛石	*kongōseki* diamond	23, 78

	1611	SAKU, *kezu(ru)*, whittle down, sharpen (a pencil); delete; curtail	
削	18 690 削	削除 *sakujo* deletion, elimination	1065
		削減 *sakugen* reduction, cutback	715
		添削 *tensaku* correction (of a composition)	1433
		鉛筆削り *enpitsukezuri* pencil sharpener	1606, 130

	1612	MŌ, *ami*, net	
網	120 3563 網	漁網 *gyomō* fishing net	699
		交通網 *kōtsūmō* traffic network	114, 150
		支店網 *shitenmō* network of branch offices	318, 168
		金網 *kanaami* wire mesh/netting	23
		網袋 *amibukuro* net (shopping) bag	1329

	1613	KŌ, pit, hole	
坑	32 1063 坑	炭坑 *tankō* coalpit, coal mine	1344
		坑夫 *kōfu* coal miner	315
		坑道 *kōdō* (mine) shaft, level, gallery	149
		坑内事故 *kōnai jiko* mine accident	84, 80, 173
		廃坑 *haikō* abandoned mine	961

	1614	JŌ, redundant, superfluous	
冗	14 625 冗	冗談 *jōdan* a joke	593
		冗語 *jōgo* redundancy	67
		冗員 *jōin* superfluous member/personnel, over-	163
		冗長 *jōchō* redundant, verbose ⌊staffing	95
		冗漫 *jōman* wordy, verbose, rambling	1411

	1615	KAN, *kanmuri*, crown	
冠	14 627 冠	王冠 *ōkan* (royal) crown; bottle cap	294
		金冠 *kinkan* gold crown	23
		栄冠 *eikan* crown (of victory), laurels	723
		弱冠 *jakkan* 20 years of age; youth	218
		草冠 *kusakanmuri* Radical No. 140 [艹]	249

	1616	A, rank next, come after, sub-; Asia	
亜	1 43 亜	亜熱帯 *anettai* subtropical zones, subtropics	645, 963
		亜鉛 *aen* zinc	1606
		亜麻 *ama* flax	1529
		亜流 *aryū* follower, epigone	247
		東亜 *Tōa* East Asia	71

	1617	I, officer	
尉	4 231 尉	尉官 *ikan* officer below the rank of major	326
		大尉 *taii* captain	26
		中尉 *chūi* lieutenant	28
		少尉 *shōi* second lieutenant	144
		准尉 *jun'i* warrant officer	1232

	1618	**I**, *nagusa(meru)*, comfort, console, cheer up; amuse, divert; *nagusa(mu)*, be diverted; banter; make a plaything of
慰	61 1758 慰	慰問 *imon* consolation, sympathy 162 慰安 *ian* comfort, recreation, amusement 105 慰霊祭 *ireisai* a memorial service 1168, 617 慰謝料 *isharyō* consolation money, solatium 901, 319
	1619	**JIN**, [NI], virtue, benevolence, humanity, charity
仁	9 349 仁	仁義 *jingi* humanity and justice 291 仁愛 *jin'ai* benevolence, charity, philanthropy 259 仁術 *jinjutsu* benevolent act; the healing art 187 仁徳 *jintoku* benevolence, goodness 1038 仁王 (門) *Niō(mon)* Deva (gate) 294, 161
	1620	**NI**, *ama*, nun
尼	44 1378 尼	尼僧 *nisō* nun 1366 尼寺 *amadera* convent 41
	1621	**DEI**, *doro*, mud
泥	85 2533 泥	泥炭 *deitan* peat 1344 雲泥の差 *undei no sa* enormous difference 636, 658 泥沼 *doronuma* bog, quagmire 996 泥棒 *dorobō* thief, robber, burglar, burglary 1543
	1622	**KATSU**, *kawa(ku)*, be thirsty
渇	85 2596 渇	飢渇 *kikatsu* hunger and thirst 1304 渇望 *katsubō* craving, longing, thirst 673 枯渇 *kokatsu* run dry, become depleted 974 渇水 *kassui* water shortage 21 渇きを覚える *kawaki o oboeru* feel thirsty 605
	1623	**KATSU**, woolen/quilted clothing
褐	145 4254 褐	褐色 *kasshoku* brown 204 茶褐色 *chakasshoku* brown, chestnut brown 251, 204 赤褐色 *sekkasshoku* reddish brown 207, 204 黒褐色 *kokkasshoku* dark/blackish brown 206, 204
	1624	**KEI**, *kaka(geru)*, put up (a sign), hoist (a flag); publish, print
掲	64 1934 掲	掲揚 *keiyō* hoist, raise, fly (a flag) 631 掲示 *keiji* notice, bulletin 615 掲示板 *keijiban* bulletin board 615, 1047 掲載 *keisai* publish, print, carry, mention 1124 前掲 *zenkei* shown above, aforementioned 47

濁	1625	**DAKU**, *nigo(ru)*, become muddy/turbid; *nigo(su)*, make turbid
85 2710 濁		混濁　*kondaku*　turbidity, muddiness　799 清濁　*seidaku*　purity and impurity, good and evil　660 濁流　*dakuryū*　muddy river, turbid waters　247 濁音　*dakuon*　voiced sound; cardiac dullness　347

潟	1626	*kata*, beach, lagoon, inlet
85 2695 潟		干潟　*higata*　dry beach, beach at ebb tide　584 新潟県　*Niigata-ken*　Niigata Prefecture　174, 194

巧	1627	**KŌ**, *taku(mi)*, skill, dexterity, ingenuity
48 1453 巧		技巧　*gikō*　art, craftsmanship, technical skill　871 巧妙　*kōmyō*　skilled, clever, ingenious　1154 巧者　*kōsha*　skilled, adroit, clever　164 精巧　*seikō*　elaborate, exquisite, sophisticated　659 老巧　*rōkō*　experienced, seasoned, veteran　543

朽	1628	**KYŪ**, *ku(chiru)*, rot, decay
75 2175 朽		不朽　*fukyū*　immortal, undying　⌈masterpiece 94 不朽の名作　*fukyū no meisaku*　immortal　94, 82, 360 腐朽　*fukyū*　deteriorate, rot away, molder　1245 老朽　*rōkyū*　senescence, advanced age　543 朽ち葉　*kuchiba*　decayed/dead leaves　253

誇	1629	**KO**, *hoko(ru)*, boast of, be proud of
149 4354 誇		誇張　*kochō*　exaggeration, overstatement　1106 誇大妄想(狂)　*kodai mōsō(kyō)*　delusions of 　　grandeur, megalomania　26, 1376, 147, 883 誇示　*koji*　display, flaunt　615 勝ち誇る　*kachihokoru*　exult in one's triumph　509

麗	1630	**REI**, *uruwa(shii)*, beautiful, pretty
198 5381 麗		美麗　*birei*　beautiful, pretty　401 華麗　*karei*　glory, splendor, magnificence　1074 麗人　*reijin*　beautiful woman　1 端麗　*tanrei*　grace, elegance, beauty　⌈flourishes 1418 美辞麗句　*biji-reiku* speech full of rhetorical　401, 688, 337

薦	1631	**SEN**, *susu(meru)*, recommend; advise; offer, present
140 4067 薦		推薦　*suisen*　recommendation　1233 推薦状　*suisenjō*　letter of recommendation　1233, 626 他薦　*tasen*　recommendation (by another)　120 自薦　*jisen*　self-recommendation　62

	1632	KEI, rejoice, be happy over; congratulate	
慶	53	慶賀 *keiga* congratulation	756
	1539	慶祝 *keishuku* congratulation; celebration	851
		慶事 *keiji* happy event, matter for congratulation	80
慶		慶応 *Keiō* (Japanese era, 1865–68) ⌈China	827
		国慶節 *Kokkeisetsu* Anniv. of Founding of P.R.	40, 464

	1633	HA, supremacy, domination, hegemony	
覇	146	覇権 *haken* hegemony	335
	4281	覇者 *hasha* supreme ruler; champion, titleholder	164
		制覇 *seiha* conquest, domination; championship	427
覇		覇気 *haki* ambition, aspirations	134
		連覇 *renpa* successive championships	440

	1634	FUKU, ō(u), cover; conceal; kutsugae(ru), be overturned; kutsugae(su), overturn, overthrow	
覆	146		
	4279	覆面 *fukumen* mask	274
		転覆 *tenpuku* overturn, topple	433
覆		覆水盆に返らず *fukusui bon ni kaerazu* What's done is done.	21, 1099, 442

	1635	RI, ha(ku), put on, wear (shoes/pants)	
履	44	履歴書 *rirekisho* curriculum vitae	480, 131
	1404	履行 *rikō* perform, fulfill, implement	68
		草履 *zōri* (toe-strap) sandals	249
履		履き物 *hakimono* footwear	79
		履き古し *hakifurushi* worn-out shoes/socks	172

	1636	TAKU, entrust (to), leave in the care (of)	
託	149	委託 *itaku* trust, charge, commission	466
	4315	信託 *shintaku* trust	157
		託児所 *takujisho* day nursery	1217, 153
託		託宣 *takusen* oracle, revelation from God	625
		結託 *kettaku* conspiracy, collusion	485

	1637	ZOKU, belong (to)	
属	44	所属 *shozoku* belong, be assigned (to)	153
	1400	付属 *fuzoku* attached, affiliated, incidental	192
		金属 *kinzoku* metal	23
属		専属 *senzoku* belong exclusively (to)	600
		従属 *jūzoku* subordination, dependence	1482

	1638	SHOKU, request, entrust, commission	
嘱	30	嘱託 *shokutaku* part-time worker	1636
	989	委嘱 *ishoku* commission, charge, request	466
		嘱望 *shokubō* expect much of	673
嘱			

	1639	GŪ, (married) couple; even number; doll; chance, accidental	
偶	9	偶然 *gūzen* chance, accident	651
	508	偶発 *gūhatsu* chance occurrence	96
		偶像 *gūzō* image, statue, idol	740
偶		配偶者 *haigūsha* spouse	515, 164
		偶数 *gūsū* even number	225

	1640	GŪ, *sumi*, corner, nook	
隅	170	一隅 *ichigū* corner, nook	2
	5009	片隅 *katasumi* corner, nook	1045
		四隅 *yosumi* the 4 corners	6
隅		隅々 *sumizumi* every nook and cranny, all over	
		隅田川 *Sumida-gawa* Sumida River	35, 33

	1641	GŪ, treat, deal with; entertain, receive; meet	
遇	162	待遇 *taigū* treatment; service; pay	452
	4715	優遇 *yūgū* cordial reception, hospitality	1033
		冷遇 *reigū* cold reception, inhospitality	832
遇		境遇 *kyōgū* one's circumstances	864
		奇遇 *kigū* chance meeting	1360

	1642	GU, *oro(ka)*, foolish, stupid	
愚	61	愚劣 *guretsu* stupidity, foolishness, nonsense	1150
	1730	愚鈍 *gudon* stupid, dim-witted	966
		愚問 *gumon* stupid question	162
愚		愚連隊 *gurentai* gang of hoodlums	440, 795

	1643	SŌ, *a(u)*, meet, see, come across, encounter	
遭	162	遭難 *sōnan* disaster, accident, mishap	557
	4736	遭難者 *sōnansha* victim	557, 164
		遭難信号 *sōnan shingō* distress signal, SOS	557, 157, 266
遭		遭遇 *sōgū* encounter	1641
		災難に遭う *sainan ni au* meet with disaster	1335, 557

	1644	SŌ, tub, tank, vat	
槽	75	水槽 *suisō* water tank, cistern	21
	2351	浴槽 *yokusō* bathtub	1128
槽			

	1645	SHŌ, clear; crystal	
晶	72	結晶 *kesshō* crystal, crystallization	485
	2137	愛の結晶 *ai no kesshō* fruit of love, child	259, 485
		晶化 *shōka* crystallization	254
晶		水晶 *suishō* (rock) crystal, quartz	21
		紫水晶 *murasaki suishō* amethyst	1389, 21

	1646	SHŌ, *tona(eru)*, chant; cry; advocate, espouse	
唱	30	合唱(団) *gasshō(dan)* chorus	159, 491
	941	独唱 *dokushō* vocal solo	219
		唱歌 *shōka* singing	392
唱		主/首唱 *shushō* advocacy, promotion	155, 148
		提唱 *teishō* advocate	628

	1647	YŌ, song; Noh chanting; *uta(u)*, sing	
謡	149	民謡 *min'yō* folk song	177
	4410	童謡 *dōyō* children's song	410
		歌謡 *kayō* song	392
謡		歌謡曲 *kayōkyoku* popular song	392, 366
		謡曲 *yōkyoku* Noh song	366

	1648	YŌ, *yu(reru/ragu/rugu)*, shake, sway, vibrate, roll, pitch, joggle; *yu(ru/suru/suburu/saburu)*, shake, rock, joggle	
揺	64	動揺 *dōyō* shaking; unrest, tumult	231
	1965	揺(す)り起こす *yu(su)riokosu* awaken by shaking	373
揺		揺り返し *yurikaeshi* aftershock	442

	1649	KAN, can	
缶	121	缶詰 *kanzume* canned goods	1142
	3634	製缶工場 *seikan kōjō* cannery, canning factory	
			428, 139, 154
缶		缶切り *kankiri* can opener	39
		空き缶 *akikan* empty can	140

	1650	TŌ, porcelain, pottery	
陶	170	陶器 *tōki* china, ceramics, pottery	527
	5003	陶磁器 *tōjiki* ceramics, china and porcelain	1548, 527
		陶芸 *tōgei* ceramic art	435
陶		陶工 *tōkō* potter	139

	1651	SŌ, *sa(su)*, insert	
挿	64	挿入 *sōnyū* insertion	52
	1916	挿話 *sōwa* episode, little story	238
		挿し木 *sashiki* a cutting	22
挿		挿絵 *sashie* an illustration	345

	1652	KI, shake, brandish; direct, command; scatter	
揮	64	指揮 *shiki* command, direct, conduct	1041
	1960	指揮者 *shikisha* (orchestra) conductor	1041, 164
		指揮官 *shikikan* commander	1041, 326
揮		発揮 *hakki* exhibit, display, manifest	96
		揮発 *kihatsu* volatilization	96

輝 輝	1653 42 1371	**KI**, *kagaya(ku)*, shine, gleam, sparkle, be brilliant 光輝 *kōki* brilliance, brightness; glory 輝度 *kido* (degree of) brightness 光り輝く *hikarikagayaku* shine, beam, glisten 輝かしい *kagayakashii* bright, brilliant	138 377 138

繰 繰	1654 120 3619	*ku(ru)*, reel, wind; spin (thread); turn (pages); consult (a reference book), look up; count 繰り返す *kurikaesu* repeat 繰り言 *kurigoto* same old story, complaint 繰り延べ *kurinobe* postponement, deferment 繰り上げる *kuriageru* advance, move up (a date)	442 66 1115 32

操 操	1655 64 2015	**SŌ**, *ayatsu(ru)*, manipulate, operate; *misao*, chastity; constancy, fidelity, honor 操縦 *sōjū* control, operate, manipulate (遠隔)操作 (*enkaku*) *sōsa* (remote) control 446, 1589, 360 体操 *taisō* gymnastics, exercises 節操 *sessō* fidelity, integrity; chastity	1483 61 464

燥 燥	1656 86 2810	**SŌ**, dry 乾燥 *kansō* dry (up/out) 乾燥器 *kansōki* (clothes) dryer 無味乾燥 *mumi-kansō* dry, uninteresting 焦燥 *shōsō* impatience, nervous restlessness	1190 1190, 527 93, 307, 1190 999

藻 藻	1657 140 4098	**SŌ**, *mo*, water plant 藻類 *sōrui* water plants 海藻 *kaisō* saltwater plant, seaweed 藻草 *mogusa* water plant	226 117 249

暁 暁	1658 72 2139	**GYŌ**, *akatsuki*, dawn, daybreak 暁天 *gyōten* dawn, daybreak 暁星 *gyōsei* morning stars; Venus 今暁 *kongyō* early this morning 通暁 *tsūgyō* thorough knowledge, mastery 暁には *akatsuki niwa* in the event, in case (of)	141 730 51 150

奔 奔	1659 37 1175	**HON**, run 奔走 *honsō* running about, efforts 奔放 *honpō* wild, extravagant, uninhibited 狂奔 *kyōhon* rush madly about 奔馬 *honba* galloping/runaway horse 出奔 *shuppon* abscond; elope	429 512 883 283 53

	1660	FUN, *fu(ku)*, emit, spout, spew forth	
噴	30 995	噴火　*funka*　(volcanic) eruption 噴水　*funsui*　jet of water; fountain 噴出　*funshutsu*　eruption, gushing, spouting 噴射　*funsha*　jet, spray, injection 噴霧器　*funmuki*　sprayer, vaporizer	20 21 53 900 950, 527
	噴		

	1661	FUN, *ikidō(ru)*, resent, be enraged, be indignant	
憤	61 1773	憤慨　*fungai*　indignation, resentment 公憤　*kōfun*　public/righteous indignation 義憤　*gifun*　righteous indignation 憤然と　*funzen to*　indignantly 発憤　*happun*　be stimulated, roused	1460 126 291 651 96
	憤		

	1662	FUN, burial mound, tomb	
墳	32 1141	墳墓　*funbo*　grave, tomb 古墳　*kofun*　ancient burial mound, old tomb 前方後円墳　*zenpō-kōen fun*　ancient burial mound 　　　(square at the head and rounded at the 　　　foot)	1429 172 47, 70, 48, 13
	墳		

	1663	KAN, keep watch over	
監	108 3121	監視　*kanshi*　keeping watch, supervision, sur- 監査　*kansa*　inspection; auditing　⌊veillance 総監　*sōkan*　inspector/superintendent general 監禁　*kankin*　imprison, confine 監獄　*kangoku*　prison	606 624 697 482 884
	監		

	1664	KAN, model, pattern, example; mirror	
鑑	167 4924	鑑定　*kantei*　appraisal, expert opinion 鑑賞　*kanshō*　admiration, enjoyment 鑑別　*kanbetsu*　discrimination, differentiation 年鑑　*nenkan*　yearbook, almanac 印鑑　*inkan*　one's seal, seal impression	355 500 267 45 1043
	鑑		

	1665	KAN, warship	
艦	137 3881	軍艦　*gunkan*　warship 戦艦　*senkan*　battleship 航空母艦　*kōkū bokan*　aircraft carrier 潜水艦　*sensuikan*　submarine 艦隊　*kantai*　fleet, squadron	438 301 823, 140, 112 937, 21 795
	艦		

	1666	TEI, small boat	
艇	137 3875	艦艇　*kantei*　naval vessels 舟艇　*shūtei*　boat, craft 巡視艇　*junshitei*　patrol boat 艇庫　*teiko*　boathouse 艇身　*teishin*　a boat length	1665 1094 777, 606 825 59
	艇		

叔 叔	**1667** 29 861	SHUKU, younger sibling of a parent (cf. No. 1176)

叔母 *oba, shukubo* aunt 112
叔父 *oji, shukufu* uncle 113

淑 淑	**1668** 85 2592	SHUKU, graceful; polite; pure

淑女 *shukujo* lady, gentlewoman 102
淑徳 *shukutoku* feminine virtues 1038
私淑 *shishuku* look up to as one's model 125

寂 寂	**1669** 40 1315	JAKU, [SEKI], *sabi(shii)*, lonely; *sabi(reru)*, decline in prosperity; *sabi*, elegant simplicity

静寂 *seijaku* stillness, silence 663
閑寂 *kanjaku* quietness, tranquility 1532
寂然 *sekizen, jakunen* lonesome, desolate 651
寂りょう *sekiryō* loneliness, desolation

督 督	**1670** 109 3147	TOKU, lead, command; superintend, supervise

監督 *kantoku* supervision, direction; (movie) 1663
督励 *tokurei* encourage, urge ⌊director 1340
督促 *tokusoku* urge, press, dun 1557
総督 *sōtoku* governor-general ⌈house, heirship 697
家督相続 *katoku sōzoku* succession to a 165, 146, 243

豪 豪	**1671** 8 329	GŌ, strength, power; splendor, magnificence

豪華 *gōka* splendor, gorgeousness, pomp 1074
豪壮 *gōsō* magnificent, grand 1326
富豪 *fugō* man of great wealth, multimillionaire 713
豪族 *gōzoku* powerful/influential family 221
豪雨 *gōu* heavy rainfall, torrential downpour 30

享 享	**1672** 8 293	KYŌ, enjoy; receive

享楽 *kyōraku* enjoyment ⌈donism 358
享楽主義 *kyōraku shugi* epicureanism, he- 358, 155, 291
享受 *kyōju* enjoy, have, be given 260
享有 *kyōyū* enjoyment, possession ⌈of 75 265
享年75歳 *kyōnen nanajūgosai* dead at the age 45, 479

郭 郭	**1673** 163 4765	KAKU, enclosure, quarters; red-light district

輪郭 *rinkaku* contours, outline 1164
外郭 *gaikaku* outer wall (of a castle); perimeter 83
外郭団体 *gaikaku dantai* auxiliary organiza- 83, 491, 61
城郭 *jōkaku* castle, fortress; castle walls ⌊tion 720
郭公 *kakkō* (Japanese) cuckoo 126

	1674	**JUKU**, private school	
塾	32	私塾 *shijuku* private class at a teacher's home	125
	1133	学習塾 *gakushūjuku* (private) cram school	109, 591
塾		塾生 *jukusei* student of a *juku*	44

	1675	**AI**, *awa(re)*, sorrowful, piteous; *awa(remu)*, pity, sympathize	
哀	8	哀愁 *aishū* sadness, sorrow, grief	1601
	304	悲哀 *hiai* sorrow, grief, misery	1034
		哀話 *aiwa* sad story, pathetic tale	238
哀		哀歌 *aika* doleful song, elegy, lament ⌈emotions	392
		喜怒哀楽 *kido-airaku* joy and pathos, 1143, 1596, 358	

	1676	**SUI**, *otoro(eru)*, grow weak, decline, wane	
衰	8	老衰 *rōsui* feebleness of old age, senility	543
	312	衰弱 *suijaku* weakening, debility	218
		衰微 *suibi* decline, wane	1419
衰		衰亡 *suibō* decline and fall, ruin, downfall	672
		盛衰 *seisui* rise and fall, vicissitudes	719

	1677	**CHŪ**, heart, mind, inside	
衷	2	衷心 *chūshin* one's inmost heart/feelings	97
	110	衷情 *chūjō* one's inmost feelings	209
		苦衷 *kuchū* anguish, predicament	545
衷		和洋折衷 *wayō setchū* blending of Japanese	
		and Western styles 124, 289, 1394	

	1678	**SŌ**, *mo*, mourning	
喪	2	喪失 *sōshitsu* loss	311
	117	喪服 *mofuku* mourning clothes	683
		喪章 *moshō* mourning badge/band	857
喪		喪主 *moshu* chief mourner	155
		喪中 *mochū* period of mourning	28

	1679	**TAKU**, table, desk; high	
卓	25	食卓 *shokutaku* dining table	322
	802	卓球 *takkyū* table tennis, ping-pong	726
		電卓 *dentaku* (desk-top) calculator	108
卓		卓上 *takujō* table-top, desk-top	32
		卓越 *takuetsu* be superior, excel, surpass	1001

	1680	**TŌ**, *ita(mu)*, grieve over, mourn, lament	
悼	61	追悼 *tsuitō* mourning	1174
	1706	追悼会/式 *tsuitō-kai/shiki* memorial services 1174, 158, 525	
		哀悼 *aitō* condolence, mourning, grief	1675
悼		悼辞 *tōji* message of condolence, funeral address	688

貞 25 803 貞	**1681**	**TEI**, chastity, constancy, righteousness	
	貞淑	*teishuku* chastity, feminine modesty	1668
	貞節	*teisetsu* fidelity, chastity	464
	貞操	*teisō* chastity, female honor, virginity	1655
	貞潔	*teiketsu* chaste and pure	1241
	不貞	*futei* unchastity, infidelity	94

香 186 5188 香	**1682**	**KŌ**, [**KYŌ**], *kao(ri)*, *ka*, fragrance, aroma; *kao(ru)*, smell sweet	
	香気	*kōki* fragrance, aroma, sweet smell	134
	香料	*kōryō* spices; perfume	319
	線香	*senkō* stick of incense	299
	色香	*iroka* color and scent; (feminine) beauty	204

秀 115 3263 秀	**1683**	**SHŪ**, *hii(deru)*, excel, surpass	
	優秀	*yūshū* excellent, superior	1033
	秀逸	*shūitsu* superb, masterly	734
	秀麗	*shūrei* graceful, beautiful, handsome	1630
	秀才	*shūsai* talented man, bright boy/girl ⌜painter	551
	けい秀画家	*keishū gaka* accomplished woman	343, 165

誘 149 4371 誘	**1684**	**YŪ**, *saso(u)*, invite; induce; lure, entice	
	誘惑	*yūwaku* temptation, seduction	969
	勧誘	*kan'yū* invitation, canvassing, solicitation	1051
	誘因	*yūin* enticement, inducement	554
	誘発	*yūhatsu* induce, give rise to	96
	誘い水	*sasoimizu* pump priming	21

透 162 4699 透	**1685**	**TŌ** *su(ku)*, be transparent; leave a gap; *su(kasu)*, look through; leave a space; *su(keru)*, shine through	
	透明	*tōmei* transparent ⌜voyance	18
	透視	*tōshi* seeing through; fluoroscopy; clair-	606
	浸透	*shintō* permeation, osmosis, infiltration	1078
	透き通る	*sukitōru* be transparent	150

携 64 1977 携	**1686**	**KEI**, *tazusa(eru)*, carry (in one's hand), have with one; *tazusa(waru)*, participate (in)	
	携帯	*keitai* carrying, bring with; portable	963
	必携	*hikkei* handbook, manual; indispensable	520
	提携	*teikei* cooperation, tie-up	628
	連携	*renkei* cooperation, league, concert	440

謙 149 4422 謙	**1687**	**KEN**, modesty, humility	
	謙虚	*kenkyo* modest, humble	1572
	謙譲	*kenjō* modest, humble ⌜of modesty	1013
	謙譲の美徳	*kenjō no bitoku* the virtue	1013, 401, 1038
	恭謙	*kyōken* modesty, humility, deference	1434
	謙そん	*kenson* modesty, humility	

	1688	**KEN, [GEN],** *kira(u),* dislike, hate	
嫌	38 1250	嫌悪　*ken'o*　hatred, dislike, loathing	304
		嫌疑　*kengi*　suspicion	1516
		機嫌　*kigen*　mood, humor	528
嫌		大嫌い　*daikirai*　hate, strong aversion	26
		毛嫌い　*kegirai*　antipathy, prejudice	287

	1689	**REN,** pure; honest; low price	
廉	53 1530	清廉　*seiren*　integrity, uprightness	660
		清廉潔白　*seiren-keppaku*　spotless integrity 660, 1241, 205	
廉		廉売　*renbai*　bargain sale	239
		廉価　*renka*　low price	421

	1690	**CHI,** *haji,* shame, disgrace; *ha(jiru),* feel shame; *ha(jirau),* be shy; *ha(zukashii),* shy, ashamed	
恥	128 3704	無恥　*muchi*　shameless, brazen	93
		破廉恥　*harenchi*　shameless, disgraceful	665, 1689
恥		恥毛　*chimō*　pubic hair	287
		恥知らず　*hajishirazu*　shameless person	214

	1691	**KAN,** daring, bold	
敢	66 2054	勇敢　*yūkan*　brave, daring, courageous	1386
		果敢　*kakan*　resolute, determined, bold, daring	487
		敢然　*kanzen*　bold, fearless	651
敢		敢闘　*kantō*　fight courageously	1511
		敢行　*kankō*　take decisive action, dare; carry out	68

	1692	**SETSU,** act in place of; take	
摂	64 1976	摂取　*sesshu*　take in, ingest	65
		摂生　*sessei*　taking care of one's health	44
		摂政　*sesshō*　regency, regent	483
摂		摂理　*setsuri*　providence	143
		摂氏20度　*sesshi nijūdo*　20 degrees centigrade	566, 377

	1693	**JŪ,** *shibu(i),* astringent, puckery; glum; quiet and tasteful; *shibu,* astringent juice (of unripe persimmons); *shibu(ru),* hesitate, be reluctant	
渋	85 2600		
		渋滞　*jūtai*　delay, retardation	964
渋		渋面　*jūmen, shibuzura*　sour face, scowl	274
		渋味　*shibumi*　puckery taste; severe elegance	307

	1694	**RUI,** parapet, rampart; base (in baseball)	
塁	102 3009	堅塁　*kenrui*　fortress, stronghold	1289
		敵塁　*tekirui*　enemy's fortress/position	416
		塁審　*ruishin*　base umpire	1383
塁		本塁打　*honruida*　home run	25, 1020
		満塁　*manrui*　bases loaded	201

	1695	SHUKU, quietly, softly, solemnly	
肅	2 115 肅	静 肅　seishuku　stillness, quiet, hush 厳 肅　genshuku　solemnity, austerity, gravity 自 肅　jishuku　self-discipline, self-control 肅 清　shukusei　(political) purge ⌈party 肅 党　shukutō　purge disloyal elements from a	663 822 62 660 495
庸	1696 53 1520 庸	YŌ, mediocre, ordinary 中 庸　chūyō　middle path, golden mean 凡 庸　bon'yō　mediocre, run-of-the-mill 登 庸　tōyō　appointment, promotion	 28 1102 960
唐	1697 53 1516 唐	TŌ, Tang, T'ang (Chinese dynasty); Kara, China, Cathay 唐 突　tōtotsu　abrupt 毛 唐(人)　ketō(jin)　hairy barbarian, foreigner 遣 唐 使　kentōshi　Japanese envoy to Tang China 唐 様　karayō　Chinese style	 898 287, 1 1173, 331 403
糖	1698 119 3485 糖	TŌ, sugar 砂 糖　satō　sugar 製 糖　seitō　sugar manufacturing 糖 分　tōbun　sugar content 糖 質　tōshitsu　sugariness, saccharinity 血 糖　kettō　blood sugar	 1151 428 38 176 789
粧	1699 119 3475 粧	SHŌ, adorn (one's person) 化 粧　keshō　makeup 化 粧 品　keshōhin　cosmetics 化 粧 室　keshōshitsu　dressing room; lavatory 化 粧 箱　keshōbako　a vanity, dressing case 薄 化 粧　usugeshō　light makeup	 254 254, 230 254, 166 254, 1091 1449, 254
粒	1700 119 3471 粒	RYŪ, tsubu, a grain 粒 状　ryūjō　granular, granulated 粒 子　ryūshi　(atomic) particle; grain (in film) 素 粒 子　soryūshi　elementary/subatomic particle 米 粒　kometsubu　grain of rice 雨 粒　amatsubu　raindrop	 626 103 271, 103 224 30
粉	1701 119 3469 粉	FUN, kona, ko, flour, powder 粉 末　funmatsu　powder 製 粉 所　seifunjo　flour mill 粉 飾　funshoku　makeup; embellishment 粉 ミ ル ク　konamiruku　powdered milk メ リ ケ ン 粉　merikenko　wheat flour	 305 428, 153 979

	1702	FUN, *magi(reru)*, be mistaken (for), be hardly distinguishable; get mixed, disappear (among); be diverted; *magi(rasu/rawasu)*, divert, distract; conceal; evade; *magi(rawashii)*, ambiguous, liable to be confused	
紛	120 3506		
	紛	紛争 *funsō* dispute, strife 紛失 *funshitsu* loss, be missing	302 311

	1703	KYŪ, twist (rope); ask, inquire into	
糾	120 3498	糾弾 *kyūdan* impeach, censure 糾明 *kyūmei* study, inquiry, investigation 糾問 *kyūmon* close examination, grilling	1539 18 162
	糾	紛糾 *funkyū* complication, entanglement 糾合 *kyūgō* rally, muster	1702 159

	1704	RYŌ, [RŌ], *kate*, food, provisions	
糧	119 3490	食糧 *shokuryō* food, foodstuffs 糧食 *ryōshoku* provisions, food supplies 兵糧 *hyōrō* (military) provisions	322 322 784
	糧	日々の糧 *hibi no kate* one's daily bread 心の糧 *kokoro no kate* food for thought	5 97

	1705	BOKU, *sumi*, India ink, ink stick	
墨	203 5404	水墨画 *suibokuga* India-ink painting 白墨 *hakuboku* chalk 墨守 *bokushu* adherence (to tradition)	21, 343 205 490
	墨	墨絵 *sumie* India-ink drawing 入れ墨 *irezumi* tattooing; a tattoo	345 52

	1706	SEN, *shi(meru)*, occupy, hold; *urana(u)*, tell fortunes	
占	25 799	占有 *sen'yū* occupancy, possession 占領 *senryō* occupation, capture 独占 *dokusen* monopoly	265 834 219
	占	買い占め *kaishime* cornering (the market) 星占い *hoshiuranai* astrology; horoscope	241 730

	1707	NEN, *neba(ru)*, be sticky; stick to it, persevere	
粘	119 3472	粘着(力) *nenchaku(ryoku)* adhesion, viscosity 粘土 *nendo* clay 粘液 *nen'eki* mucus 粘膜 *nenmaku* mucous membrane	657, 100 24 472 1426
	粘	粘り強い *nebarizuyoi* tenacious, persistent	217

	1708	SUI, purity, essence; elite, choice; elegant, fashionable, chic; considerateness	
粋	119 3467	純粋 *junsui* pure, genuine 粋人 *suijin* man of refined tastes, man about town 精粋 *seisui* pure, selfless	965 1 659
	粋	粋狂 *suikyō* whimsical, capricious	883

酔 164 4781 酔	1709	**SUI**, *yo(u)*, get drunk, be intoxicated; feel sick	
		麻酔 *masui* anesthesia; narcosis	1529
		泥酔 *deisui* get dead drunk	1621
		心酔 *shinsui* be fascinated (with), ardently admire	97
		酔っ払い *yopparai* a drunk	582
		船粋い *funayoi* seasickness	376

砕 112 3179 砕	1710	**SAI**, *kuda(keru)*, break, be smashed; condescend, get familiar; *kuda(ku)*, break, smash, pulverize	
		紛砕 *funsai* pulverize, shatter, crush	701
		砕石 *saiseki* rubble, broken stone ⌈most efforts	78
		紛骨砕身 *funkotsu-saishin* make one's ut- 1701, 1266, 59	
		玉砕 *gyokusai* death for honor	295

酷 164 4788 酷	1711	**KOKU**, severe, harsh, cruel	
		残酷 *zankoku* cruel	650
		冷酷 *reikoku* heartless, cruel	832
		酷評 *kokuhyō* sharp/harsh criticism	1028
		酷使 *kokushi* work (someone) hard	331
		酷暑 *kokusho* intense heat, swelter	638

披 64 1874 披	1712	**HI**, open	
		披露 *hirō* announcement	951
		結婚披露宴 *kekkon hirōen* wedding reception	
		485, 567, 951, 640	
		披歴 *hireki* express (one's opinion)	480
		披見 *hiken* open and read (a letter)	63

抜 64 1854 抜	1713	**BATSU**, *nu(ku)*, pull out; remove; leave out; outdistance, surpass; *nu(keru)*, come/fall out; be omitted; be gone; escape; *nu(karu)*, make a blunder; *nu(kasu)*, omit, skip over	
		抜群 *batsugun* preeminent, outstanding	794
		選抜 *senbatsu* selection, picking out	800
		骨抜き *honenuki* unboned; emasculated, toothless	1266

握 64 1963 握	1714	**AKU**, *nigi(ru)*, grasp, grip, take hold of	
		握手 *akushu* shake hands	57
		掌握 *shōaku* hold, seize, grasp	499
		一握り *hitonigiri* handful	2
		握り飯 *nigirimeshi* rice ball	325
		握り締める *nigirishimeru* grasp tightly, clench	1180

擁 64 2013 擁	1715	**YŌ**, embrace	
		抱擁 *hōyō* embrace	1285
		擁護 *yōgo* protect, defend	1312
		擁立 *yōritsu* support, back	121

	1716	CHITSU, plug up, obstruct; nitrogen	
窒	116 3325	窒息 *chissoku* suffocation, asphyxiation	1242
		窒息死 *chissokushi* death from suffocation	1242, 85
室		窒素 *chisso* nitrogen	271

	1717	SETSU, steal	
窃	116 3320	窃盗 *settō* theft, thief	1100
		窃盗罪 *settōzai* theft, larceny	1100, 885
		窃盗犯 *settōhan* thief	1100, 882
窃		窃取 *sesshu* steal	65
		ひょう窃 *hyōsetsu* plagiarism	

	1718	KŌ, *hika(eru)*, hold back, refrain from; note down; wait	
控	64 1941	控除 *kōjo* deduct, subtract ⌈court)	1065
		控訴 *kōso* (intermediate) appeal (to a higher	1402
		手控え *tebikae* note, memo; holding off/back	57
控		控え室 *hikaeshitsu* anteroom, lobby	166
		控え目 *hikaeme* moderate, reserved	55

	1719	KŌ, [KU], *mitsu(gu)*, pay tribute; support (financially)	
貢	48 1458	貢献 *kōken* contribution, services	1355
		年貢 *nengu* annual tribute	45
貢		貢ぎ(物) *mitsugi(mono)* tribute	79

	1720	GŌ, beat, torture	
拷	64 1895	拷問 *gōmon* torture	162
		拷問具 *gōmongu* instrument of torture	162, 420
拷			

	1721	FU, help	
扶	64 1850	扶養 *fuyō* support (a family) ⌈(someone)	402
		扶養義務 *fuyō gimu* duty of supporting	402, 291, 235
		扶養料 *fuyōryō* sustenance allowance, alimony	402, 319
扶		扶助 *fujo* aid, support, relief	623
		扶持 *fuchi* rice ration allotted to a samurai	451

	1722	HAN, carry, transport	
搬	64 1973	運搬 *unpan* transport, conveyance, delivery	439
		搬送 *hansō* convey, carry	441
		搬入 *hannyū* carry/send in	52
搬		搬出 *hanshutsu* carry/take out	53

肥 130 3740 肥	**1723**	**HI**, *koe, ko(yashi)*, manure, dung, night soil; *ko(yasu)*, fertilize; *ko(eru)*, grow fat; grow fertile; have fastidious taste	
		肥料 *hiryō* manure, fertilizer	319
		肥満 *himan* corpulence, fatness, obesity	201
		肥大 *hidai* fleshiness, corpulence	26

把 64 1846 把	**1724**	**HA**, take, grasp; bundle	
		把握 *haaku* grasp, comprehend	1714
		把持 *haji* hold on to, grasp	451
		一把 *ichiwa* 1 bundle	2
		三把 *sanba* 3 bundles	4
		十把 *jippa* 10 bundles	12

惨 61 1713 惨	**1725**	**SAN, ZAN**, *miji(me)*, piteous, wretched, miserable	
		悲惨 *hisan* misery, distress, tragedy	1034
		惨事 *sanji* disaster, tragic accident	80
		惨状 *sanjō* miserable state, disastrous scene	626
		惨敗 *sanpai, zanpai* crushing defeat	511
		惨死 *zanshi* tragic/violent death	85

尽 44 1380 尽	**1726**	**JIN**, *tsu(kusu)*, exhaust, use up; render (service), make efforts; *tsu(kiru)*, be exhausted, be used up, run out, end; *tsu(kasu)*, exhaust, use up, run out of	
		尽力 *jinryoku* efforts, exertions; assistance	100
		無尽蔵 *mujinzō* inexhaustible supply	93, 1286
		論じ尽くす *ronjitsukusu* discuss fully/exhaustively	293

款 76 2418 款	**1727**	**KAN**, article, section; goodwill, friendship	
		借款 *shakkan* (international) loan	766
		長期借款 *chōki shakkan* long-term loan	95, 449, 766
		定款 *teikan* articles of association/incorporation	355
		約款 *yakkan* agreement, provision, clause	211
		落款 *rakkan* signature (and seal)	839

殻 79 2456 殻	**1728**	**KAKU**, *kara*, husk, hull, shell	
		地殻 *chikaku* the earth's crust	118
		地殻変動 *chikaku hendō* movement of the earth's crust	118, 257, 231
		貝殻 *kaigara* seashell	240
		卵の殻 *tamago no kara* eggshell	1058

穀 79 2461 穀	**1729**	**KOKU**, grain, cereals	
		穀物 *kokumotsu* grain	79
		穀類 *kokurui* grains ⌈2 millets, beans)	226
		五穀 *gokoku* the 5 grains (rice, wheat and barley,	7
		穀倉 *kokusō* granary, grain elevator	1307
		脱穀機 *dakkokuki* threshing machine, thresher	1370, 528

	1730	ICHI, one (in documents)	
壱 32 1059 壱		金壱万円 *kin ichiman'en*　10,000 yen	23, 16, 13

	1731	KETSU, excel	
傑 9 517 傑		傑出　*kesshutsu*　excel, be eminent 傑作　*kessaku*　masterpiece 傑物　*ketsubutsu*　great man, outstanding figure 豪傑　*gōketsu*　hero, great man 豪傑笑い　*gōketsu warai*　broad/hearty laugh	53 360 79 1671 1671, 1235

	1732	SHUN, *matata(ku)*, wink, blink, twinkle	
瞬 109 3159 瞬		瞬間　*shunkan*　instant, moment 瞬時　*shunji*　moment, instant 一瞬　*isshun*　instant; for an instant 瞬刻　*shunkoku*　instant, moment	43 42 2 1211

	1733	KAI, *ku(iru)*, regret, rue; *ku(yamu)*, regret, rue; lament, mourn over; offer condolences; *kuya(shii)*, vexatious, vexing	
悔 61 1682 悔		後悔　*kōkai*　regret 悔悟　*kaigo*　repentance, remorse 悔み(状)　*kuyami(jō)*　(letter of) condolence	48 1438 626

	1734	BAI, *ume*, ume, Japanese plum/apricot (tree)	
梅 75 2258 梅		梅雨　*baiu, tsuyu*　the rainy season 紅梅　*kōbai*　ume with red/pink blossoms 梅見　*umemi*　ume-blossom viewing 梅酒　*umeshu*　ume brandy 梅干し　*umeboshi*　pickled ume	30 820 63 517 584

	1735	BIN, agile, alert	
敏 66 2047 敏		敏速　*binsoku*　promptness, alacrity 敏感　*binkan*　sensitive 鋭敏　*eibin*　sharp, keen, acute 機敏　*kibin*　smart, astute, alert 敏腕　*binwan*　able, capable	502 262 1371 528 1299

	1736	BU, *anado(ru)*, despise	
侮 9 421 侮		軽侮　*keibu*　scorn, contempt 侮言　*bugen*　an insult 侮べつ　*bubetsu*　scorn, contempt	547 66

	1737	**SHIN**, *kuchibiru*, lip	
唇	161	口 唇	*kōshin* lips	54
	4654	紅 唇	*kōshin* red lips	820
		唇 音	*shin'on* a labial (sound)	347
唇		上 唇	*uwa-kuchibiru, jōshin* upper lip	32
		下 唇	*shita-kuchibiru, kashin* lower lip	31

	1738	**JOKU**, *hazukashi(meru)*, humiliate, disgrace	
辱	161	侮 辱	*bujoku* insult	1736
	4655	恥 辱	*chijoku* disgrace, dishonor	1690
		汚 辱	*ojoku* disgrace, dishonor	693
辱		雪 辱	*setsujoku* vindication; revenge	949

	1739	**WAI**, *makana(u)*, provide board; supply, furnish; pay, finance	
賄	154	贈 賄	*zōwai* giving a bribe, bribery	1364
	4507	収 賄	*shūwai* accepting a bribe, bribery	757
		賄 ろ	*wairo* a bribe	
賄		賄 い 付 き	*makanaitsuki* with meals	192

	1740	**ZUI**, marrow	
髄	188	骨 髄	*kotsuzui* bone marrow	1266
	5242	せ き 髄	*sekizui* spinal cord	
		脳 髄	*nōzui* brain	1278
髄		真/神/心 髄	*shinzui* essence, quintessence, soul	422, 310, 97
		精 髄	*seizui* essence, quintessence, soul	659

	1741	**ZUI**, follow	
随	170	追 随	*tsuizui* follow (someone)	1174
	5004	随 意	*zuii* voluntary, optional	132
		随 筆	*zuihitsu* essay, miscellaneous writings	130
随		付 随 現 象	*fuzui genshō* concomitant phe-	192, 298, 739
		随 一	*zuiichi* most, greatest, first ⌊nomenon	2

	1742	**DA**, fall	
堕	32	堕 落	*daraku* depravity, corruption	839
	1092	堕 胎	*datai* abortion	1296
堕				

	1743	**DA**, lazy, inactive	
惰	61	怠 惰	*taida* laziness, idleness, sloth	1297
	1727	惰 性	*dasei* inertia; force of habit	98
		惰 気	*daki* inactivity, dullness	134
惰		惰 眠	*damin* idle slumber, lethargy	849

	1744	**SA**, help		
佐	9 392	補佐	*hosa* aid; assistant, adviser ⌐the navy)	889
		少佐	*shōsa* major; lieutenant commander (in	144
		大佐	*taisa* colonel; captain (in the navy)	26
	佐	佐官	*sakan* field officer	326
		土佐	*Tosa* (city and region in Shikoku)	24

	1745	**SEI**, *muko*, son-in-law; bridegroom		
婿	38 1239	花婿	*hanamuko* bridegroom	255
		婿養子	*mukoyōshi* son-in-law taken into the family	402, 103
	婿	婿選び	*mukoerabi* looking for a husband for one's daughter	800

	1746	**SEI, SHŌ**, surname, family name		
姓	38 1203	姓名	*seimei* (one's full) name	82
		同姓	*dōsei* same surname; namesakes	198
		改姓	*kaisei* change one's surname	514
	姓	旧姓	*kyūsei* one's former/maiden name	1216
		百姓	*hyakushō* farmer	14

	1747	**JO, NYO**, equal, like, as, as if		
如	38 1189	突如	*totsujo* suddenly, unexpectedly	898
		躍如	*yakujo* vivid, lifelike	1560
		欠如	*ketsujo* lack, deficiency	383
	如	如実	*nyojitsu* true to life, realistic	203
		如何	*ikaga* how	390

	1748	**IN**, marriage		
姻	38 1214	婚姻	*kon'in* marriage, matrimony	567
		婚姻法	*kon'inhō* the Marriage Law	567, 123
	姻	姻族	*inzoku* relatives by marriage	221

	1749	**KA**, marry (a man); blame; *totsu(gu)*, get married; *yome*, bride, young wife, daughter-in-law		
嫁	38 1249	転嫁	*tenka* remarriage; impute (blame)	433
		花嫁	*hanayome* bride	255
	嫁	嫁入り	*yomeiri* marriage, wedding (of a woman)	52

	1750	**KA**, *kase(gu)*, work, earn (a living)		
稼	115 3301	稼働	*kadō* operation, work	232
		稼業	*kagyō* one's trade/occupation	279
		出稼ぎ	*dekasegi* work away from home	53
	稼	時間稼ぎ	*jikankasegi* playing/stalling for time	42, 43
		稼ぎ手	*kasegite* breadwinner; hard worker	57

	1751	*tsuka*, mound, hillock	
塚	32 1120 塚	貝塚 *kaizuka* heap of shells あり塚 *arizuka* anthill 一里塚 *ichirizuka* milepost, milestone	240 2, 142

	1752	*musume*, daughter; girl	
娘	38 1225 娘	孫娘 *magomusume* granddaughter 娘婿 *musumemuko* son-in-law 娘盛り *musumezakari* (a girl in) the prime of youth 娘心 *musumegokoro* girlish mind/innocence 田舎娘 *inakamusume* country girl	910 1745 719 97 35, 791

	1753	RŌ, waves; wander	
浪	85 2570 浪	波浪 *harō* waves, high seas 浮浪 *furō* vagrancy, vagabondage 流浪 *rurō* vagrancy, wandering 浪人 *rōnin* lordless samurai; unaffiliated person 浪費 *rōhi* waste, squander	666 938 247 1 749

	1754	RŌ, *hoga(raka)*, clear, bright, cheerful	
朗	130 3762 朗	明朗 *meirō* bright, clear, cheerful 朗々 *rōrō* clear, sonorous 朗詠 *rōei* recite (a Japanese/Chinese poem) 朗読 *rōdoku* read aloud, recite 朗報 *rōhō* good news, glad tidings	18 1209 244 685

	1755	KON, *ura(mu)*, bear ill will/a grudge against, feel resentment/reproachful; *ura(meshii)*, reproachful, rueful, have a grudge, feel bitter (against)	
恨	61 1677 恨	遺恨 *ikon* grudge, rancor, malice, enmity 悔恨 *kaikon* remorse, contrition 痛恨 *tsūkon* great sorrow, bitter regret	1172 1733 1320

	1756	HI, (married) princess	
妃	38 1188 妃	王妃 *ōhi* queen, empress 皇太子妃 *kōtaishihi* the crown princess 妃殿下 *hidenka* Her Imperial Highness	294 297, 629, 103 1130, 31

	1757	*hime*, princess	
姫	38 1216 姫	姫君 *himegimi* princess 舞姫 *maihime* dancing girl, dancer 歌姫 *utahime* songstress 姫路 *Himeji* (city with a famous castle, about 100 km west of Osaka)	793 810 392 151

	1758	RYŪ, *tatsu*, dragon	
竜	212 5440 竜	飛竜 *hiryū* flying dragon	530
		竜宮 *ryūgū* Palace of the Dragon King	721
		恐竜 *kyōryū* dinosaur	1602
		竜骨 *ryūkotsu* keel	1266
		竜巻 *tatsumaki* tornado	507

	1759	*taki*, waterfall	
滝	85 2655 滝	滝口 *takiguchi* top/crest of a waterfall	54
		滝つぼ *takitsubo* bottom/basin of a waterfall	
		滝登り *takinobori* (salmon) climbing a waterfall	960
		華厳の滝 *Kegon no Taki* (waterfall near Nikko)	1074, 822

	1760	JŌ, *nawa*, rope	
縄	120 3617 縄	縄文 *jōmon* (ancient Japanese) straw-rope pattern	111
		自縄自縛に陥る *jijō-jibaku ni ochiiru* fall in one's own trap	62, 1448, 1218
		縄張 *nawabari* rope off; one's domain	1106
		縄跳び *nawatobi* skipping/jumping rope	1563

	1761	SHI, *ukaga(u)*, visit, call at; ask, inquire	
伺	9 395 伺	伺候 *shikō* wait upon, attend; make a courtesy call	944
		奉伺 *hōshi* attend, serve	1541
		暑中伺い *shochū ukagai* hot-season greeting	638, 28
		進退伺い *shintai ukagai* informal resignation	437, 846

	1762	SHI, *ka(u)*, raise, keep (animals)	
飼	184 5163 飼	飼育 *shiiku* raising, breeding	246
		飼料 *shiryō* feed, fodder	319
		飼い主 *kainushi* (pet) owner, master	155
		羊飼い *hitsujikai* shepherd	288
		飼い犬 *kaiinu* pet dog	280

	1763	HŌ, *a(kiru)*, get (sick and) tired of; *a(kasu)*, cloy, satiate, surfeit; tire, bore, make (someone) fed up	
飽	184 5162 飽	飽食 *hōshoku* gluttony, engorgement	322
		飽和 *hōwa* saturation	124
		見飽きる *miakiru* get tired of seeing	63
		...に飽かして *...ni akashite* regardless of ...	

	1764	HŌ, gun, cannon	
砲	112 3185 砲	大砲 *taihō* cannon	26
		鉄砲 *teppō* gun	312
		砲撃 *hōgeki* shelling, bombardment	1016
		砲兵 *hōhei* artillery, artilleryman, gunner	784
		(十字)砲火 (*jūji*) *hōka* (cross) fire	12, 110, 20

	1765	HŌ, *awa*, bubble, foam, froth, suds	
泡	85 2523	気泡 *kihō* (air) bubble	134
		水泡 *suihō* foam, bubble	21
		発泡 *happō* foaming	96
泡		泡立つ *awadatsu* bubble, foam, lather up	121
		泡を食う *awa o kuu* be flurried, lose one's head	322

	1766	SHO, all; illegitimate child	
庶	53 1522	庶務 *shomu* general affairs	235
		庶務課 *shomuka* general affairs section	235, 488
		庶民 *shomin* the (common) people	⌈cratic 177
庶		庶民的 *shominteki* popular, common, demo-	177, 210
		庶子 *shoshi* illegitimate child	103

	1767	SHA, *saegi(ru)*, interrupt, obstruct, block	
遮	162 4737	遮断 *shadan* interception, isolation, cutoff	1024
		遮断機 *shadanki* railroad-crossing gate	1024, 528
		遮断器 *shadanki* circuit breaker	1024, 527
遮			

	1768	SHŌ, sunken rock	
礁	112 3220	暗礁 *anshō* sunken rock, unseen reef, snag	348
		岩礁 *ganshō* (shore) reef	1345
		環礁 *kanshō* atoll	865
礁		さんご礁 *sangoshō* coral reef	
		離礁 *rishō* get (a ship) off the rocks, refloat	1281

	1769	SHI, *haka(ru)*, consult, confer, solicit advice	
諮	149 4404	諮問 *shimon* question, inquiry	162
		諮問機関 *shimon kikan* advisory body	162, 528, 398
諮			

	1770	DAKU, consent, agree to	
諾	149 4383	承諾 *shōdaku* consent, agreement	942
		許諾 *kyodaku* consent, approval, permission	737
		受諾 *judaku* acceptance (of an offer)	260
諾		内諾 *naidaku* informal consent	84
		諾否 *dakuhi* acceptance or refusal, definite reply	1248

	1771	TOKU, shelter, hide	
匿	22 764	匿名 *tokumei* anonymity; pseudonym	82
		隠匿 *intoku* conceal, stash away, cover up	868
		隠匿者 *intokusha* hoarder, concealer	868, 164
匿		隠匿物資 *intoku busshi* secret cache of goods	868, 79, 750

	1772	SHŌ, collision
衝	60 1638	衝撃 *shōgeki* shock ⌜collision 1016 (正面)衝突 (*shōmen*) *shōtotsu* (head-on) 275, 274, 898 緩衝地帯 *kanshō chitai* buffer zone 1089, 118, 963 折衝 *sesshō* negotiations 1394 衝動(行為) *shōdō* (*kōi*) (acting on) impulse 231, 68, 1484
衝		

	1773	KUN, merit
勲	86 2794	勲功 *kunkō* distinguished service, merits 818 勲章 *kunshō* order, decoration, medal 857 勲一等 *kun ittō* First Order of Merit ⌜deeds 2, 569 殊勲 *shukun* distinguished service, meritorious 1505 偉勲 *ikun* brilliant exploit, great achievement 1053
勲		

	1774	KUN, *kao(ru)*, be fragrant, smell good
薫	140 4073	薫香 *kunkō* incense; fragrance 1682 薫風 *kunpū* balmy breeze 29 薫陶 *kuntō* discipline, training; education 1650 風薫る五月 *kaze kaoru gogatsu* the balmy month of May 29, 7, 17
薫		

	1775	HŌ, fragrance; (honorific prefix); *kanba(shii)*, sweet-smelling; favorable, fair
芳	140 3907	芳香 *hōkō* fragrance, perfume, aroma 1682 芳名 *hōmei* good name/reputation; your name 82 (来客)芳名録 (*raikyaku*) *hōmeiroku* 69, 641, 82, 538 芳紀 *hōki* age (of a young lady) ⌞visitors' book 372
芳		

	1776	HŌ, *nara(u)*, imitate, follow
倣	9 466	模倣 *mohō* imitation 1425 先例に倣う *senrei ni narau* follow precedent 50, 612
倣		

	1777	SHŌ, *nobo(ru)*, rise, be promoted
昇	72 2109	上昇 *jōshō* rise, ascent; upward trend 32 昇進 *shōshin* promotion, advancement 437 昇格 *shōkaku* promotion to a higher status, up- 643 昇給 *shōkyū* pay raise ⌞grading 346 昇級 *shōkyū* promotion to a higher grade 568
昇		

	1778	KYŌ, *odoro(ku)*, be surprised, astonished; be frightened; *odoro(kasu)*, surprise, astonish; frighten
驚	187 5229	驚嘆 *kyōtan* admiration, wonder 1246 驚異 *kyōi* wonder, miracle, marvel 1061 驚がく *kyōgaku* astonishment; alarm, consternation
驚		

1779 騰 TŌ, copy

130 / 3824 / 騰

騰写	tōsha	copy, duplication	540
騰写器	tōshaki	mimeograph machine	540, 527
騰写版	tōshaban	mimeograph	540, 1046
騰本	tōhon	transcript, copy	25

1780 騰 TŌ, rise (in prices)

130 / 3834 / 騰

(物価)騰貴	(bukka) tōki	rise (in prices)	79, 421, 1171
暴騰	bōtō	sudden/sharp rise	1014
高騰	kōtō	sudden rise, jump (in prices)	190

1781 幣 HEI, Shinto zigzag paper offerings; money

50 / 1490 / 幣

紙幣	shihei	paper money	180
貨幣	kahei	money; coin, coinage	752
貨幣価値	kahei kachi	the value of money/	752, 421, 425
造幣局	Zōheikyoku	Mint Bureau　currency	691, 170
幣制	heisei	monetary system	427

1782 弊 HEI, evil, abuse, vice; (humble prefix) our

55 / 1551 / 弊

弊害	heigai	an evil, ill effect	518
疲弊	hihei	impoverishment, exhaustion	1321
旧弊	kyūhei	an old evil; old-fashioned	1216
弊社	heisha	our company, we	308

1783 却 KYAKU, pull back, withdraw

26 / 808 / 却

却下	kyakka	reject, dismiss	31
返却	henkyaku	return, repay	442
退却	taikyaku	retreat	846
売却	baikyaku	sale, disposal by sale	239
忘却	bōkyaku	forget, lose sight of	1374

1784 脚 KYAKU, [KYA], ashi, leg

130 / 3773 / 脚

橋脚	kyōkyaku	bridge pier	597
失脚	shikkyaku	lose one's position/standing	311
脚注	kyakuchū	footnote	357
脚本	kyakuhon	play, script	25
脚色	kyakushoku	dramatization, stage/film adaptation	204

1785 慎 SHIN, tsutsushi(mu), be discreet, careful; restrain oneself, refrain from

61 / 1742 / 慎

謹慎	kinshin	good behavior; house arrest	1247
慎重	shinchō	cautious	227
慎み深い	tsutsushimibukai	discreet, cautious	536

	1786	CHIN, *shizu(meru)*, calm, quell; *shizu(maru)*, calm down
鎮	167 4903	鎮静剤 *chinseizai* a sedative　　　　　　　　663, 550
		鎮痛剤 *chintsūzai* pain-killer　　　　　　　1320, 550
		鎮圧　 *chin'atsu* suppression, quelling　　　　1342
鎮		鎮魂曲/歌 *chinkon-kyoku/ka* requiem　1525, 366, 392
		鎮守　 *chinju* local/tutelary deity　　　　　　490

	1787	KI, wheel track, rut, railway, orbit
軌	159 4610	軌道　 *kidō* railroad track; orbit　　　　　　149
		狭軌鉄道 *kyōki tetsudō* narrow-gauge　1353, 312, 149
		常軌　 *jōki* normal course of action ⌐railway　497
軌		軌範　 *kihan* model, example　　　　　　　1092
		軌跡　 *kiseki* (geometrical) locus　　　　　1569

	1788	NAN, *yawa(rakai/raka)*, soft
軟	159 4614	柔軟　 *jūnan* soft, pliable　　　　　　　　774
		軟化　 *nanka* become soft; relent　　　　　254
		軟弱　 *nanjaku* weak, weak-kneed　　　　　218
軟		軟骨　 *nankotsu* cartilage　　　　　　　1266
		軟着陸 *nanchakuriku* soft landing　　　657, 647

	1789	YŌ, *kama*, kiln
窯	116 3336	窯業　 *yōgyō* ceramic industry, ceramics　　279
		窯元　 *kamamoto* place where pottery is made　137
窯		

	1790	RO, furnace, hearth
炉	86 2750	暖炉　 *danro* fireplace　　　　　　　　　635
		溶鉱炉 *yōkōro* smelting/blast furnace　1392, 1604
		原子炉 *genshiro* atomic reactor　　　　136, 103
炉		核反応炉 *kaku hannōro* nuclear reactor　1212, 324, 827
		増殖炉 *zōshokuro* breeder reactor　　　712, 1506

	1791	SUI, *ta(ku)*, burn, light a fire; boil, cook
炊	86 2752	炊事　 *suiji* cooking　　　　　　　　　　80
		自炊　 *jisui* do one's own cooking　　　　　62
		炊飯器 *suihanki* rice cooker　　　　　325, 527
炊		雑炊　 *zōsui* porridge of rice and vegetables　575
		炊き出し *takidashi* emergency group cooking　53

	1792	FUTSU, *wa(ku)*, boil, seethe; *wa(kasu)*, (bring to a) boil
沸	85 2524	沸騰　 *futtō* boiling; excitement, agitation　　1780
		沸(騰)点 *fut(tō)ten* boiling point　　　1780, 169
		沸き立つ *wakitatsu* boil up, seethe　　　　121
沸		湯沸かし(器) *yuwakashi(ki)* hot-water heater　632, 527

漬	1793 85 2676 漬	tsu(keru), soak, immerse; pickle, preserve; tsu(karu), soak, steep, be submersed; be well seasoned 漬物　tsukemono　pickled vegetables　79 漬物石　tsukemonoishi　weight stone (used in making pickles)　79, 78 塩漬　shiozuke　food preserved with salt　1101	

汁	1794 85 2485 汁	JŪ, shiru, juice, sap; soup, broth, gravy （天然）果汁　(tennen) kajū　(natural) fruit juice 141, 651, 487 肉汁　nikujū　meat juices, gravy　223 墨汁　bokujū　India ink　1705 汁粉　shiruko　adzuki-bean soup with rice cake　1701 みそ汁　misoshiru　miso soup	

煮	1795 86 2771 煮	SHA, ni(eru/ru), (intr./tr.) boil, cook 煮沸　shafutsu　boiling　1792 雑煮　zōni　rice-cake soup with vegetables　575 生煮え　namanie　half-cooked, underdone　44 煮返す　nikaesu　reboil, cook over again　442 業を煮やす　gō o niyasu　become exasperated　279	

弔	1796 2 80 弔	CHŌ, tomura(u), mourn, condole 弔意　chōi　condolence, sympathy　132 弔辞　chōji　words/message of condolence　688 弔電　chōden　telegram of condolence　108 弔問　chōmon　visit of condolence　162 慶弔　keichō　congratulations and condolences　1632	

忌	1797 49 1463 忌	KI, i(mu), hate, loathe; avoid, shun; i(mawashii), abominable, disgusting, scandalous; ominous 忌中　kichū　in mourning　28 忌避　kihi　evasion, shirking; (legal) challenge　1491 忌み言葉　imikotoba　word taboo by superstition　66, 253	

迅	1798 162 4664 迅	JIN, fast 迅速　jinsoku　quick, rapid, speedy　502 迅雷　jinrai　thunderclap　952 奮迅　funjin　roused to powerful action　1309	

殉	1799 78 2444 殉	JUN, follow into death; lay down one's life 殉教者　junkyōsha　martyr　245, 164 殉難　junnan　martyrdom　557 殉職　junshoku　die in the line of duty　385 殉国　junkoku　dying for one's country　40 殉死　junshi　kill oneself on the death of one's lord　85	

	1800	**KŌ**, seize, arrest; adhere to	
拘	64	拘束　*kōsoku* restriction, restraint	501
	1881	拘留　*kōryū* detention, custody	761
		拘置　*kōchi* keep in detention, confine, hold	426
拘		拘置所　*kōchisho* house of detention, prison	426, 153
		拘泥　*kōdei* adhere (to), be a stickler (for)	1621

	1801	**SETSU**, unskillful, clumsy	
拙	64	拙劣　*setsuretsu* clumsy, bungling, unskillful	1150
	1880	稚拙　*chisetsu* artless, crude, naïve	1230
		拙策　*sessaku* poor policy, imprudent measure	880
拙		拙速　*sessoku* not elaborate but fast, rough-and-	502
		巧拙　*kōsetsu* skill, dexterity ⌊ready	1627

	1802	**KUTSU**, bend; yield	
屈	44	屈曲　*kukkyoku* crookedness; refraction; curvature	366
	1386	不屈　*fukutsu* indomitability, dauntlessness	94
		屈辱　*kutsujoku* humiliation, indignity	1738
屈		卑屈　*hikutsu* lack of moral courage, servility	1521
		退屈　*taikutsu* tedious, monotonous, boring	846

	1803	**KUTSU**, *ho(ru)*, dig	
掘	64	採掘　*saikutsu* mining, digging	933
	1943	発掘　*hakkutsu* excavation; exhumation	96
		掘り出し物 *horidashimono* treasure trove; lucky	53, 79
掘		掘り返す　*horikaesu* dig up ⌊find; bargain	442
		掘り抜く　*horinuku* dig through, bore	1713

	1804	*hori*, moat; canal; ditch	
堀	32	堀割　*horiwari* canal, waterway	519
	1095	堀江　*horie* canal	821
		堀川　*horikawa* canal	33
堀		内堀　*uchibori* inner moat	84
		外堀　*sotobori* outer moat	83

	1805	**HEI**, wall, fence	
塀	32	板塀　*itabei* board fence	1047
	1131	石塀　*ishibei* stone fence	78
		土塀　*dobei* mud/earthen wall	24
塀			

	1806	**RŌ**, *mo(ru/reru)*, leak, slip from; *mo(rasu)*, let leak, divulge	
漏	85	漏電　*rōden* electric leakage, short circuit	108
	2682	脱漏　*datsurō* be omitted, left out	1370
		遺漏なく *irōnaku* without omission, exhaustively	1172
漏		雨漏り　*amamori* leak in the roof	30
		聞き漏らす *kikimorasu* fail to hear, miss (a word)	64

	1807	**ZOKU**, rebel; robber	
賊	154 4508 賊	盗賊 *tōzoku* thief, burglar, robber 海賊 *kaizoku* pirate 山賊 *sanzoku* mountain robber, bandit 賊軍 *zokugun* rebel army, rebels 国賊 *kokuzoku* traitor	1100 117 34 438 40

	1808	**FU**, tribute; payment, installment; prose poem	
賦	154 4513 賦	月賦 *geppu* monthly installment 賦税 *fuzei* taxation 賦課 *fuka* levy, assessment 賦役 *fueki* compulsory labor, corvée 天賦 *tenpu* inherent nature; inborn, natural	17 399 488 375 141

	1809	**KA**, calamity, misfortune	
禍	113 3254 禍	禍根 *kakon* root of evil, source of calamity 災禍 *saika* accident, disaster 戦禍 *senka* the ravages of war, war damage 禍福 *kafuku* fortune and misfortune 舌禍 *zekka* unfortunate slip of the tongue	314 1335 301 1379 1259

	1810	**KA**, *uzu*, swirl, vortex, whirlpool, eddy	
渦	85 2629 渦	渦流 *karyū* eddy, whirlpool 渦中 *kachū* maelstrom, vortex 戦渦 *senka* the confusion of war 渦巻き *uzumaki* eddy, vortex, whirlpool; spiral	247 28 301 507

	1811	**RI**, diarrhea	
痢	104 3049 痢	下痢 *geri* diarrhea 赤痢 *sekiri* dysentery 疫痢 *ekiri* children's dysentery, infant diarrhea	31 207 1319

	1812	**SHITSU**, illness, disease; fast	
疾	104 3041 疾	疾患 *shikkan* disease, ailment 悪疾 *akushitsu* malignant disease 廃疾 *haishitsu* disablement, disability 疾走 *shissō* run at full speed 疾風 *shippū* strong wind, gale	1315 304 961 429 29

	1813	**CHI**, foolish	
痴	104 3061 痴	白痴 *hakuchi* idiocy, idiot 痴漢 *chikan* molester of women, masher 痴情 *chijō* foolish passion, blind love; jealousy 音痴 *onchi* tone-deaf 愚痴 *guchi* idle complaint, grumbling	205 556 209 347 1642

	1814	FU, kowa(i), frightening, scary, dreadful; eerie, weird
怖	61 1662 怖	恐怖 *kyōfu* fear, terror 1602 恐怖政治 *kyōfu seiji* reign of terror 1602, 483, 493 恐怖症 *kyōfushō* phobia, morbid dread 1602, 1318 高所恐怖症 *kōsho kyōfushō* acro- phobia 190, 153, 1602, 1318
憾	1815 61 1778 憾	KAN, regret 遺憾 *ikan* regrettable 1172
錬	1816 167 4881 錬	REN, forge, temper (iron); polish, refine; train, drill 精錬所 *seirensho* refinery 659, 153 錬金術 *renkinjutsu* alchemy 23, 187 錬成 *rensei* training 261 修錬 *shūren* training, discipline 945
鍛	1817 167 4895 鍛	TAN, kita(eru), forge, temper; train, drill, discipline 鍛工 *tankō* metalworker, smith 139 鍛錬 *tanren* temper, anneal; train, harden 1816 鍛え上げる *kitaeageru* become highly trained 32
錠	1818 167 4874 錠	JŌ, lock, padlock; pill, tablet 錠前 *jōmae* a lock 47 組み合わせ錠 *kumiawasejō* combination lock 418, 159 手錠 *tejō* handcuffs 57 錠剤 *jōzai* tablet, pill 550 一錠 *ichijō* 1 tablet/pill 2
鎖	1819 167 4901 鎖	SA, close, shut; kusari, chain 封鎖 *fūsa* blockade 1463 閉鎖 *heisa* closing, shutdown, lockout 397 鎖国 *sakoku* national isolation 40 連鎖反応 *rensa hannō* chain reaction 440, 324, 827 金鎖 *kingusari* gold chain 23
鉢	1820 167 4840 鉢	HACHI, [HATSU], bowl, pot; brainpan, crown 火鉢 *hibachi* hibachi, charcoal brazier 20 植木鉢 *uekibachi* flowerpot 424, 22 衣鉢 *ihatsu* the mantle, secrets (of one's master) 677 すり鉢 *suribachi* (conical) earthenware mortar 鉢巻き *hachimaki* cloth tied around one's head 507

	1821	SHŌ, *kane*, bell	
鐘	167 4917 鐘	晩鐘　*banshō*　evening bell 警鐘　*keishō*　alarm bell 半鐘　*hanshō*　fire bell 鐘乳洞　*shōnyūdō*　stalactite cave	736 706 88 939, 1301
鈴	1822 167 4837 鈴	REI, RIN, *suzu*, bell 電鈴　*denrei*　electric bell 呼び鈴　*yobirin*　doorbell, (hotel) service bell 風鈴　*fūrin*　wind-bell 鈴虫　*suzumushi*　"bell-ring" insect 鈴木　*Suzuki*　(surname)	 108 1254 29 873 22
零	1823 173 5048 零	REI, zero 零点　*reiten*　(a score of) zero 零時　*reiji*　12 o'clock 零度　*reido*　zero (degrees), the freezing point 零下　*reika*　below zero, subzero 零細　*reisai*　small, trifling	 169 42 377 31 695
霧	1824 173 5045 霧	FUN, fog 雰囲気　*fun'iki*　atmosphere, ambience	 1194, 134
棺	1825 75 2298 棺	KAN, coffin 棺おけ　*kan'oke*　coffin 石棺　*sekkan*　stone coffin, sarcophagus 納棺　*nōkan*　place (a body) in the coffin 出棺　*shukkan*　start of a funeral procession	 78 758 53
埋	1826 32 1084 埋	MAI, *u(maru)*, be buried (under), filled up; *u(meru)*, bury, fill up; *u(moreru)*, be buried; sink into obscurity 埋葬　*maisō*　burial, interment 埋没　*maibotsu*　be buried; fall into oblivion 埋蔵　*maizō*　buried stores, underground reserves 埋め立て　*umetate*　land reclamation	 812 935 1286 121
彰	1827 59 1593 彰	SHŌ, clear 顕彰　*kenshō*　manifest, exhibit, exalt 表彰　*hyōshō*　official commendation 表彰状　*hyōshōjō*　certificate of commendation, citation	 1170 272 272, 626

培 培	1828	**BAI**, *tsuchika(u)*, cultivate, foster
	32 1091	栽 培　　*saibai*　cultivation, culture, growing　　　1125 培 養　　*baiyō*　cultivation, culture　　　402 培 養 液 *baiyōeki*　culture fluid/solution　　　402, 472 純 粋 培 養 *junsui baiyō*　pure culture　　965, 1708, 402
賠 賠	1829	**BAI**, indemnify
	154 4512	賠 償　　*baishō*　reparation, indemnification　　　971 賠 償 金 *baishōkin*　indemnities, reparations, 　　　damages　　　971, 23 損 害 賠 償 *songai baishō*　compensation for 　　　damages　　　350, 518, 971
剖 剖	1830	**BŌ**, divide
	18 693	解 剖　　*kaibō*　dissection, postmortem, autopsy　　474 解 剖 学 *kaibōgaku*　anatomy　　　474, 109 生 体 解 剖 *seitai kaibō*　vivisection　　44, 61, 474
賜 賜	1831	**SHI**, *tamawa(ru)*, grant, bestow, confer
	154 4514	下 賜　　*kashi*　imperial grant, donation　　　31 恩 賜　　*onshi*　imperial gift　　　555 賜 暇　　*shika*　leave of absence, furlough　　　1064
据 据	1832	*su(eru)*, set, place, put into position; *su(waru)*, sit, be set
	64 1935	据 え 付 ける *suetsukeru*　set into position, install　192 据 え 置 く *sueoku*　leave as is, let stand　　　426 腹 を 据 え る *hara o sueru*　decide, make up one's 　　　mind　　　1271
拓 拓	1833	**TAKU**, open, clear, break up (land)
	64 1873	開 拓　　*kaitaku*　reclamation, clearing　　　396 開 拓 者 *kaitakusha*　settler, pioneer　　　396, 164 拓 殖　　*takushoku*　colonization, settlement　　1506 干 拓　　*kantaku*　land reclamation by drainage　　584 拓 本　　*takuhon*　a rubbing (of an inscription)　　25
碁 碁	1834	**GO**, (the board game) go
	112 3202	囲 碁　　*igo*　(the game of) go　　　1194 碁 石　　*goishi*　go stone　　　78 碁 盤　　*goban*　go board　　　⌈board layout　1098 碁 盤 の 目 *goban no me*　go-board grid, checker- 1098, 55 碁 会 所 *gokaisho, gokaijo*　go club　　158, 153

	1835	**KI**, go; shogi, Japanese chess	
棋	75 2294 棋	将 棋 *shōgi* shogi, Japanese chess 将棋盤 *shōgiban* shogi board 棋 譜 *kifu* record of a game of go/shogi 棋 士 *kishi* (professional) go/shogi player 将 棋 倒 し *shōgidaoshi* fall down (like dominoes)	627 627, 1098 1167 572 627, 905
嬢	1836 38 1257 嬢	**JŌ**, daughter; young lady お 嬢 さん *ojōsan* (your) daughter; young lady (御)令 嬢 *(go)reijō* (your) daughter; young lady 愛 嬢 *aijō* one's dear/favorite daughter	708, 831 259
醸	1837 164 4804 醸	**JŌ**, *kamo(su)*, brew; bring about, give rise to 醸 造 所 *jōzōsho* brewery, distillery 醸 成 *jōsei* brew; cause, bring about	691, 153 261
塑	1838 32 1121 塑	**SO**, modeling, molding 塑 像 *sozō* modeling, molding 可 塑 性 *kasosei* plasticity 彫 塑 *chōso* carving and (clay) modeling, plastic arts	740 388, 98 1149
壇	1839 32 1146 壇	**DAN**, [**TAN**], rostrum, dais, podium 演 壇 *endan* (speaker's) platform, rostrum 祭 壇 *saidan* altar 文 壇 *bundan* the literary world 花 壇 *kadan* flower bed ⌈execution 土 壇 場 *dotanba* last/critical moment; place of	344 617 111 255 24, 154
塔	1840 32 1109 塔	**TŌ**, tower 監 視 塔 *kanshitō* watchtower 管 制 塔 *kanseitō* control tower 広 告 塔 *kōkokutō* poster column, advertising 象 げ の 塔 *zōge no tō* ivory tower ⌊pillar 五 重 の 塔 *gojū no tō* 5-story pagoda	1663, 606 328, 427 694, 690 739 7, 227
楼	1841 75 2322 楼	**RŌ**, tower, turret, lookout 鐘 楼 *shōrō* bell tower, belfry 楼 閣 *rōkaku* many-storied building, castle 楼 門 *rōmon* 2-story gate 摩 天 楼 *matenrō* skyscraper	1821 837 161 1530, 141

	1842	SEN, stopper, cork, plug, spigot	
栓	75 2247	消火栓 *shōkasen* fire hydrant	845, 20
		給水栓 *kyūsuisen* water tap, hydrant	346, 21
		水道栓 *suidōsen* hydrant, tap	21, 149
		ガス栓 *gasusen* gas tap	
栓		栓抜き *sennuki* bottle opener	1713

	1843	FU, attach; accompany (cf. No. 192)	
附	170 4983	附属 *fuzoku* belonging to, accessory	1637
		寄附 *kifu* contribution, donation	1361
		附近 *fukin* neighborhood, vicinity	445
		附録 *furoku* supplement, appendix	538
附		附随 *fuzui* accompany, be entailed by	1741

	1844	RYŌ, *misasagi*, imperial tomb, mausoleum	
陵	170 4998	丘陵 *kyūryō* hill	1357
		丘陵地帯 *kyūryō chitai* hilly area	1357, 118, 963
		御陵 *goryō* tomb of the emperor/empress	708
陵			

	1845	SHUN, excellence, genius	
俊	9 448	俊秀 *shunshū* person of outstanding talent	1683
		俊英 *shun'ei* talent, gifted person	353
		俊才 *shunsai* genius, outstanding talent	551
		俊傑 *shunketsu* great man	1731
俊		俊敏 *shunbin* keen, quick-witted	1735

	1846	SA, *sosonoka(su)*, tempt, entice; incite, abet	
唆	30 925	示唆 *shisa* suggestion	615
		教唆 *kyōsa* instigation, incitement	245
唆			

	1847	HIN, occur repeatedly	
頻	181 5128	頻度 *hindo* frequency, rate of occurrence	377
		頻発 *hinpatsu* frequency, frequent occurrence	96
		頻繁 *hinpan* frequency, rapid succession	1292
頻		頻々と *hinpin to* frequent, in rapid succession	

	1848	GAN, stubborn, obstinate	
頑	181 5122	頑固 *ganko* stubborn, obstinate	972
		頑迷 *ganmei* bigoted, obstinate	967
		頑強 *gankyō* stubborn, obstinate, unyielding	217
		頑健 *ganken* strong and robust, in excellent health	893
元頁		頑張る *ganbaru* persist in, stick to it, hang in there	1106

	1849	HAN, [BON], *wazura(u)*, worry about; be ill, suffer from; *wazura(wasu)*, trouble, bother, annoy	
煩	86 2782 煩	煩雑 *hanzatsu* complicated, troublesome	575
		煩忙 *hanbō* busy, pressed with business	1373
		煩悩 *bonnō* evil passions, carnal desires	1279
		煩わしい *wazurawashii* troublesome, tangled	

	1850	HAN, divide, distribute	
頒	181 5119 頒	頒布 *hanpu* distribute, circulate	675

	1851	KA, alone, widowed; few, small	
寡	40 1337 寡	多寡 *taka* quantity, number, amount	229
		寡婦 *kafu* widow	316
		寡聞 *kabun* little knowledge, ill-informed	64
		寡黙 *kamoku* taciturn, reticent	1578
		寡占 *kasen* oligopoly	1706

	1852	HIN, guest	
賓	40 1339 賓	賓客 *hinkaku, hinkyaku* honored guest, visitor	641
		貴賓 *kihin* distinguished guest, guest of honor	1171
		主賓 *shuhin* guest of honor	155
		来賓 *raihin* guest, visitor	69
		迎賓館 *geihinkan* reception hall, guest mansion 1055, 327	

	1853	SHŌ, further; value, respect	
尚	42 1361 尚	高尚 *kōshō* lofty, noble, refined	190
		尚武 *shōbu* militaristic, martial	1031
		尚早 *shōsō* premature, too early ⌈ripe	248
		時機尚早 *jiki-shōsō* too soon, time is not 42, 528, 248	
		和尚 *oshō* Buddhist priest	124

	1854	SHŌ, *yoi*, early evening	
宵	40 1307 宵	春宵 *shunshō* spring evening	460
		徹宵 *tesshō* all night long ⌈ning	1422
		宵越し *yoigoshi* (left over) from the previous eve-	1001
		宵っ張り *yoippari* staying up till late; night owl	1106
		宵の口 *yoi no kuchi* early evening	54

	1855	SHŌ, saltpeter	
硝	112 3192 硝	硝酸 *shōsan* nitric acid	516
		硝石 *shōseki* saltpeter	78
		硝煙 *shōen* gunpowder smoke	919

	1856	**RYŪ**, sulfur	
硫	112	硫 酸　*ryūsan*　sulfuric acid	516
	3191	硫 化 水 素　*ryūka suiso*　hydrogen sulfide	254, 21, 271
硫		硫 黄　*iō*　sulfur	780

	1857	**BŌ**, (animal) fat	
肪	130	脂 肪　*shibō*　fat	1042
	3734	皮 下 脂 肪　*hika shibō*　subcutaneous fat	975, 31, 1042
		脂 肪 ぶ と り　*shibōbutori*　fat, obese	1042
肪		脂 肪 層　*shibōsō*　layer of fat 「table fat	1042, 1367
		植 物 性 脂 肪　*shokubutsusei shibō*　vege-	424, 79, 98, 1042

	1858	**BŌ**, [BO'], priest's residence; Buddhist priest; boy	
坊	32	坊 主　*bōzu*　Buddhist priest, bonze	155
	1062	朝 寝 坊　*asanebō*　a late riser	469, 1079
		け ち ん 坊　*kechinbō*　stingy person, tightwad	
坊		赤 ん 坊　*akanbō*　baby	207
		坊 ち ゃ ん　*botchan*　(your) son, young master, boy	

	1859	**BŌ**, *tsumu(gu)*, spin, make yarn	
紡	120	紡 績　*bōseki*　spinning	1117
	3505	紡 績 工 場　*bōseki kōjō*　spinning mill	1117, 139, 154
		紡 織　*bōshoku*　spinning and weaving	680
紡		混 紡　*konbō*　mixed/blended spinning	799

	1860	**RA**, silk gauze, thin silk	
羅	122	羅 列　*raretsu*　enumerate, cite	611
	3654	羅 針　*rashin*　compass needle	341
		羅 針 盤　*rashinban*　compass	341, 1098
羅		網 羅　*mōra*　be all-inclusive, comprehensive	1612
		一 張 羅　*itchōra*　one's best/only clothes	2, 1106

	1861	**HI**, end, discontinue, stop; leave, withdraw	
罷	122	罷 免　*himen*　dismissal (from one's post)	733
	3649	罷 業　*higyō*　strike, walkout	279
罷			

	1862	*tsu(ru)*, fish, angle; decoy, allure, take in	
釣	167	釣 り 道 具　*tsuridōgu*　fishing tackle	149, 420
	4820	釣 り 針　*tsuribari*　fishhook	341
		釣 り 堀　*tsuribori*　fishing pond	1804
釣		釣 り 合 い　*tsuriai*　balance, equilibrium, proportion	159
		釣 り 銭　*tsurisen*　(make) change	648

	1863	SHAKU, pour (wine), serve at table	
酌	164 4778 酌	媒酌 *baishaku* matchmaking	1496
		媒酌人 *baishakunin* matchmaker, go-between	1496, 1
		晩酌 *banshaku* evening drink	736
		独酌 *dokushaku* drinking alone	219
		しん酌 *shinshaku* take into consideration	

	1864	SHŪ, reward, compensation	
酬	164 4785 酬	報酬 *hōshū* remuneration	685
		無報酬 *muhōshū* without remuneration, free of charge	93, 685
		応酬 *ōshū* reply, response, retort	827

	1865	RAKU, whey	
酪	164 4786 酪	酪農(場) *rakunō(jō)* dairy, dairy farm	369, 154
		酪製品 *rakuseihin* dairy products	428, 230
		酪農家 *rakunōka* dairy farmer, dairyman	369, 165

	1866	KŌ, fermentation; yeast	
酵	164 4787 酵	酵母 *kōbo* yeast	112
		酵母菌 *kōbokin* yeast fungus	112, 1222
		酵素 *kōso* enzyme	271
		発酵 *hakkō* fermentation	96

	1867	SAKU, *su*, vinegar	
酢	164 4783 酢	酢酸 *sakusan* acetic acid	516
		酢漬け *suzuke* pickling in vinegar	1793
		酢の物 *su no mono* vinegared dish	79
		甘酢 *amazu* sweet vinegar	1492

	1868	BI, *o*, tail	
尾	44 1383 尾	末尾 *matsubi* the end	305
		首尾 *shubi* beginning and end; result, outcome	148
		尾行 *bikō* shadow, tail (someone)	68
		尾灯 *bitō* taillight	1333
		徹頭徹尾 *tettō-tetsubi* thoroughly	1422, 276

	1869	NYŌ, urine	
尿	44 1382 尿	尿素 *nyōso* urea	271
		尿酸 *nyōsan* uric acid	516
		排尿 *hainyō* urination	1036
		夜尿症 *yanyōshō* nocturnal enuresis, bed-	471, 1318
		糖尿病 *tōnyōbyō* diabetes ⌊wetting	1698, 380

	1870	**HITSU, HI,** flow, secrete	
泌	85 2522	分泌 *bunpitsu, bunpi* secretion	38
		内分泌 *naibunpi* internal secretion	84, 38
		分泌物 *bunpibutsu* a secretion	38, 79
		泌尿器 *hinyōki* urinary organs	1869, 527
泌		泌尿器科 *hinyōkika* urology	1869, 527, 320

	1871	**RYŪ,** *yanagi,* willow tree	
柳	75 2233	川柳 *senryū* humorous 17-syllable Japanese poem	33
		花柳界 *karyūkai* demimonde, red-light district	255, 454
		柳び *ryūbi* beautiful eyebrows	
		枝垂れ柳 *shidare yanagi* weeping willow	870, 1070
柳		柳腰 *yanagi-goshi* slender graceful hips	1298

	1872	*sugi,* Japanese cedar	
杉	75 2190	杉並木 *suginamiki* avenue of *sugi* trees	1165, 22
		杉並区 *Suginami-ku* Suginami Ward (Tokyo)	1165, 183
杉			

	1873	**SŌ,** *kuwa,* mulberry tree	
桑	29 864	桑門 *sōmon* Buddhist priest/monk	161
		桑園 *sōen* mulberry farm/orchard	447
		桑田 *sōden* mulberry orchard	35
		桑畑 *kuwabatake* mulberry field	「God! 36
桑		桑原桑原 *kuwabara-kuwabara* Heaven forbid! Thank 136	

	1874	**KON,** elder brother; later; insect	
昆	72 2106	昆虫 *konchū* insect	873
		昆虫学 *konchūgaku* entomology	873, 109
		昆虫採集 *konchū saishū* insect collecting	873, 933, 436
		昆布 *konbu, kobu* sea tangle, tang, kelp	675
昆		昆布茶 *kobucha* tang tea	675, 251

	1875	**JA, DA,** *hebi,* snake	
蛇	142 4130	蛇の目 *janome* bull's-eye design (on oilpaper umbrella) 55	
		蛇腹 *jabara* accordion-like folds, bellows; cornice 1271	
		蛇行 *dakō* meander, zigzag, fishtail	68
		蛇足 *dasoku* superfluous (like legs on a snake)	58
蛇		長蛇の列 *chōda no retsu* long queue/line of people 95, 611	

	1876	*ka,* mosquito	
蚊	142 4123	蚊帳/屋 *kaya* mosquito net	1107, 167
		蚊取り線香 *katori senkō* mosquito-repellent incense	65, 299, 1682
蚊		蚊柱 *kabashira* column of swarming mosquitoes	598

1877

蚕

蚕

SAN, *kaiko*, silkworm

1	養 蚕	*yōsan* sericulture, silkworm raising	402
57	蚕糸	*sanshi* silk thread/yarn	242
	蚕食	*sanshoku* encroachment, inroads	322

1878

蛍

蛍

KEI, *hotaru*, firefly, glowworm

142	蛍光灯	*keikōtō* fluorescent lamp	138, 1333
4176	蛍光塗料	*keikō-toryō* fluorescent paint	138, 1073, 319
	蛍雪の功	*keisetsu no kō* the fruits of diligent study	949, 818
	蛍狩り	*hotarugari* firefly catching	1581

1879

蛮

蛮

BAN, barbarian

8	(野)蛮人	*(ya)banjin* barbarian, savage	236, 1
322	南蛮	*nanban* southern barbarian, European (hist.)	74
	蛮風	*banpū* barbarous ways/customs	29
	蛮行	*bankō* act of barbarity, brutality	68
	蛮勇	*ban'yū* recklessness; brute force	1386

1880

駄

駄

DA, pack horse; footwear; of poor quality

187	駄賃	*dachin* reward, recompense, tip	751
5198	駄菓子	*dagashi* cheap candy	1535, 103
	駄作	*dasaku* poor work, worthless stuff	360
	無駄	*muda* futile, useless, in vain	93
	下駄	*geta* geta, Japanese wooden clogs	31

1881

騎

騎

KI, horse riding; (counter for horsemen)

187	騎手	*kishu* rider, jockey	57
5222	騎士	*kishi* rider, horseman	572
	騎兵	*kihei* cavalry soldier	784
	騎馬	*kiba* on horseback, mounted ⌈fight	283
	一騎打ち	*ikkiuchi* single combat, man-to-man	2, 1020

1882

駆

駆

KU, *ka(keru)*, gallop; run, rush; *ka(ru)*, drive, spur on

187	先駆	*senku* forerunner, pioneer	50
5200	駆逐	*kuchiku* drive away, expel, get rid of	1134
	駆除	*kujo* exterminate	1065
	駆け回る	*kakemawaru* run around	90
	駆け足	*kakeashi* running, galloping	58

1883

篤

篤

TOKU, serious; cordial

118	危篤	*kitoku* critically ill	534
3434	篤行	*tokkō* good deed, act of charity	68
	篤志家	*tokushika* benefactor, volunteer	573, 165
	篤農家	*tokunōka* exemplary farmer ⌈studies	369, 165
	篤学	*tokugaku* love of learning, diligence in	109

	1884	**KEI**, valley	
	85	渓 谷　*keikoku*　ravine, gorge, valley	653
	2581	渓 流　*keiryū*　mountain stream, torrent	247
渓		雪 渓　*sekkei*　snowy valley/ravine	949
		渓 間　*keikan*　ravine; in the valley	43

	1885	**SHŌ**, *mikotonori*, imperial edict	
	149	大 詔　*taishō*　imperial rescript	26
	4333	詔 書　*shōsho*　imperial edict/rescript	131
詔			

	1886	**CHOKU**, imperial decree	
	19	勅 語　*chokugo*　imperial message, speech from the throne	67
	725	勅 命　*chokumei*　imperial order/commission	578
勅		詔 勅　*shōchoku*　imperial proclamation	1885
		勅 使　*chokushi*　imperial messenger/envoy	331

	1887	**JI**, imperial seal	
	1	国 璽　*kokuji*　great seal, seal of state	40
	71	御 璽　*gyoji*　imperial/privy seal	708
璽		玉 璽　*gyokuji*　imperial seal	295
		璽 書　*jisho*　document with the imperial seal	131

	1888	**BOKU, I** (in masculine speech); manservant	
	9	従 僕　*jūboku*　servant, attendant	1482
	544	家 僕　*kaboku*　manservant	165
僕		僕 ら　*bokura*　we (in masculine speech)	

	1889	**BOKU**, hit, strike	
	64	打 撲 傷　*dabokushō*　bruise, contusion	1020, 633
	1993	撲 滅　*bokumetsu*　eradication, extermination	1338
撲		相 撲　*sumō*　sumo wrestling	146
		相 撲 取 り　*sumōtori*　sumo wrestler 「bout	146, 65
		大 相 撲　*ōzumō*　grand sumo tournament; exciting	26, 146

	1890	**HYŌ**, *tawara*, straw bag/sack	
	9	土 俵　*dohyō*　sandbag; sumo ring	24
	467	米 俵　*komedawara*　straw rice-sack; bag of / for rice	224
俵		炭 俵　*sumidawara*　sack for charcoal	1344
		一 俵　*ippyō*　1 bag/sack	2

	1891	**SEN**, hermit; wizard	
仙 9 359 仙		仙 人　　*sennin*　mountain wizard; hermit, settler 仙 女　　*sennyo*　fairy, nymph 酒 仙　　*shusen*　heavy drinker 水 仙　　*suisen*　narcissus 仙 台　　*Sendai*　(city in Tohoku)	1 102 517 21 492

	1892	**TOTSU**, protruding, convex	
凸 2 90 凸		凸 レ ン ズ *totsurenzu*　convex lens 凸 面　　*totsumen*　convex (surface) 両 凸　　*ryōtotsu*　biconvex 凸 版 (印 刷)(*insatsu*)　letterpress, relief 　　　　　printing　　1046, 1043, 1044	 274 200

	1893	**Ō**, indentation, hollowed out, sunken in, concave	
凹 17 664 凹		凹 凸　　*ōtotsu*　uneven, jagged, rough 凹 面 鏡　*ōmenkyō*　concave mirror 凹 レ ン ズ *ōrenzu*　concave lens	1892 274, 863

	1894	**SUN**, (unit of length, about 3 cm)	
寸 41 1348 寸		寸 法　　*sunpō*　measurements; plan 寸 評　　*sunpyō*　brief comment 寸 暇　　*sunka*　a moment's leisure, spare moments 寸 前　　*sunzen*　immediately/right before 寸 断　　*sundan*　cut/tear to pieces	123 1028 1064 47 1024

	1895	**SHAKU**, (unit of length, about 30 cm); measure, length	
尺 44 1377 尺		尺 貫 法 *shakkanhō*　old Japanese system of weights 　　　　　and measures　　914, 123 巻 き 尺 *makijaku*　tape measure, surveying tape 縮 尺　　*shukushaku*　reduced scale (map) 尺 八　　*shakuhachi*　Japanese end-blown bamboo flute	 507 1110 10

	1896	*tsubo*, (unit of area, about 3.3 m²)	
坪 32 1072 坪		坪 数　　*tsubosū*　number of *tsubo*, area 延 べ 坪(数)*nobetsubo*(*sū*)　total area (of all floors) 建 坪　　*tatetsubo*　floor space/area 坪 二 万 円 *tsubo niman'en*　20,000 yen per *tsubo* 坪 当 た り *tsuboatari*　per *tsubo*	225 1115, 225 892 3, 16, 13 77

	1897	**KIN**, (unit of weight, about 600 g)	
斤 69 2076 斤		一 斤　　*ikkin*　1 *kin* 斤 量　　*kinryō*　weight	2 411

	1898	SHŌ, *masu*, (unit of volume, 1.8 liters)	
升	4	一 升　*isshō*　1 *shō*	2
	160	一 升 瓶　*isshōbin*　1.8-liter bottle	2, 1161
	升		

	1899	TO, (unit of volume, 18 liters)	
斗	68	一 斗　*itto*　1 *to*	2
	2073	斗酒　*toshu*　kegs of sakè	517
	斗	北 斗 (七) 星　*hokuto(shichi)sei*　the Big Dipper	73, 9, 730

	1900	RIN, (old unit of currency, 1/1,000 yen); (unit of length, about 0.3 mm)	
厘	27	二 銭 五 厘　*nisen gorin*　2 *sen* 5 *rin*, 2.5 *sen*	3, 648, 7
	823	一 分 一 厘　*ichibu ichirin*　1 *bu* 1 *rin*, 1.1 *bu*; some, little, slight	2, 38
	厘	厘 毛　*rinmō*　a trifle; unimportant, insignificant	287

1. INDEX by Radicals

慨	1460	折	1394	揺	1648	**—70—**		様	403
慎	1785	投	1021	揚	631			構	1010
態	387	扱	1138	提	628	方	70	木	22	概	1459
慢	1410	拍	1178	搬	1722	放	512	札	1157	模	1425
慣	915	拓	1833	搾	1497	施	1004	机	1305	槽	1644
憎	1365	披	1712	摂	1692	旅	222	朽	1628	標	923
慰	1618	拡	1113	携	1686	族	221	朴	1466	権	335
憩	1243	抽	987	損	350	旋	1005	材	552	横	781
憤	1661	抵	560	撃	1016	旗	1006	杉	1872	樹	1144
憾	1815	担	1274	摘	1447			村	191	橋	597
憶	381	拙	1801	撲	1889	**—72—**		析	1393	機	528
懇	1135	拘	1800	撤	1423	日	5	枚	1156	欄	1202
懐	1408	招	455	撮	1520	早	248	杯	1155		
懲	1421	抱	1285	擁	1715	昆	1874	枢	1023	**—76—**	
懸	911	拝	1201	操	1655	易	759	林	127	欠	383
		押	986	擦	1519	昔	764	枝	870	欧	1022
—62—		拷	1720	擬	1517	昇	1777	松	696	款	1727
成	261	括	1260			明	18	板	1047	欺	1499
戒	876	挑	1564	**—65—**		昭	997	柳	1871	歌	392
威	1339	拾	1445	支	318	冒	1104	柄	985	歓	1052
戦	301	挙	801			映	352	査	624		
		持	451	**—66—**		昨	361	柱	598	**—77—**	
—63—		指	1041	故	173	是	1591	架	755	止	477
戸	152	挟	1354	政	483	星	730	枯	974	肯	1262
戻	1238	挿	1651	敏	1735	春	460	栄	723	歩	431
房	1237	捜	989	救	725	時	42	染	779	歳	479
肩	1264	捕	890	教	245	晶	1645	相	146	雌	1388
所	153	振	954	敢	1691	暑	638	栓	1842	整	503
扇	1555	措	1200	敬	705	晩	1658	核	1212		
扉	1556	揭	1624	散	767	替	744	桃	1567	**—78—**	
雇	1553	据	1832	数	225	量	411	桜	928	列	611
		描	1469	敷	1451	景	853	株	741	死	85
—64—		控	1718	敵	416	晴	662	梅	1734	殊	1505
手	57	掘	1803			晚	736	格	643	殉	1799
払	582	捨	1444	**—67—**		最	263	校	115	残	650
打	1020	掃	1080	文	111	暇	1064	根	314	殖	1506
扱	1258	授	602	対	365	暖	635	械	529		
択	993	採	933			暗	348	棋	1835	**—79—**	
把	1724	排	1036	**—68—**		暫	1399	棺	1825	段	362
拒	1295	探	535	斗	1899	暴	1014	棟	1406	殺	576
批	1029	推	1233	斜	1069	曇	637	森	128	殻	1728
抄	1153	接	486			曜	19	棒	1543	穀	1729
扶	1721	掛	1464	**—69—**		題	354	植	424		
抑	1057	揮	1652	斤	1897			検	531	**—80—**	
抗	824	援	1088	断	1024	**—74—**		極	336	母	112
技	871	握	1714	新	174	月	17	楼	1841	毎	116
抜	1713	換	1586					楽	358	毒	522

貫 914	洞 1301	溝 1012	燥 1656	—95—	疎 1514
—81—	派 912	溶 1392	爆 1015	玄 1225	—104—
比 798	浄 664	滅 1338	—87—	畜 1223	疫 1319
皆 587	浅 649	滞 964	妥 930	—96—	症 1318
—82—	洋 289	漢 556	受 260	王 294	疲 1321
毛 287	洗 692	滑 1267	愛 259	玉 295	疾 1812
—83—	活 237	滴 1446	—88—	珍 1215	病 380
氏 566	海 117	潰 1793	父 113	班 1381	痢 1811
—84—	浜 785	漂 924	—90—	珠 1504	痛 1320
気 134	浴 1128	漆 1546	壮 1326	望 673	痴 1813
—85—	涙 1239	漸 1400	状 626	球 726	療 1322
水 21	浪 1753	漏 1806	将 627	理 143	癒 1600
汁 1794	浦 1442	漫 1411	—91—	現 298	癖 1490
池 119	浸 1078	漁 699	片 1045	琴 1251	—105—
江 821	酒 517	演 344	版 1046	聖 674	発 96
汗 1188	消 845	渇 1626	—92—	環 865	登 960
汚 693	浮 938	潔 1241	邪 1457	—98—	—106—
沢 994	流 247	澄 1334	雅 1456	瓶 1161	白 205
沖 1346	渓 1884	潤 1203	—93—	—99—	的 210
没 935	涯 1461	潮 468	牛 281	甘 1492	泉 1192
汽 135	渉 432	潜 937	牧 731	某 1494	皇 297
沈 936	淑 1668	濁 1625	物 79	—100—	—107—
決 356	渇 1622	濃 957	牲 282	生 44	皮 975
況 850	済 549	激 1017	特 282	—101—	—108—
泳 1208	涼 1204	濯 1561	犠 728	用 107	皿 1097
沼 996	液 472	瀬 1513	—94—	—102—	盗 1100
泌 1870	洪 1693	—86—	犬 280	田 35	盛 719
泡 1765	添 1433	火 20	犯 882	町 182	盟 717
沸 1792	淡 1337	灯 1333	狂 883	男 101	監 1663
沿 1607	混 799	炉 1790	狭 1353	界 454	盤 1098
泰 1545	清 660	炎 1336	狩 1581	胃 1268	—109—
泊 1177	深 536	炊 1791	独 219	思 99	目 55
治 493	滋 1549	畑 36	猫 1470	留 761	具 420
波 666	湾 670	烈 1331	猟 1580	累 1060	眠 849
河 389	湖 467	然 651	猛 1579	略 841	眺 1565
注 357	渦 1810	煮 1795	猶 1583	異 1061	眼 848
泣 1236	港 669	焼 920	献 1355	畏 1694	督 1670
泥 1621	湿 1169	無 93	猿 1584	畳 1087	睡 1071
油 364	測 610	煩 1849	獄 884	—103—	瞬 1732
法 123	湯 632	煙 919	獣 1582		—110—
津 668	温 634	照 998	獲 1313		
洪 1435	渡 378	勲 1773			
	満 201	熟 687			
	滅 715	黙 1578			
	漠 1427	熱 645			
	滝 1759	燃 652			
	源 580				

矛	773	季	465	筒	1472	紳	1109	買	241	肉	223
柔	774	委	466	策	880	組	418	署	860	肌	1306
務	235	和	124	答	160	終	458	罪	885	有	265
		秒	1152	筋	1090	細	695	置	426	肝	1272
—111—		科	320	等	569	経	548	罰	886	肪	1857
矢	213	秋	462	筆	130	絡	840	罷	1861	肢	1146
知	214	秩	1508	節	464	紫	1389	羅	1860	肥	1723
短	215	租	1083	箇	1473	絞	1452			服	683
		称	978	算	747	統	830	**—123—**		胞	1284
—112—		秘	807	管	328	絵	345	羊	288	胎	1296
石	78	移	1121	範	1092	給	346	美	401	胆	1273
砕	1710	程	417	箱	1091	絶	742	差	658	肺	1277
研	896	税	399	篤	1883	結	485	着	657	背	1265
砂	1151	稚	1230	築	1603	絹	1261	群	794	朗	1754
砲	1764	稲	1220	簡	1533	続	243	義	291	脈	913
破	665	種	228	簿	1450	継	1025	養	402	脂	1042
硫	1856	稿	1120	籍	1198	維	1231			胴	1300
硝	1855	穂	1221			緒	862	**—124—**		胸	1283
硬	1009	稼	1750	**—119—**		緊	1290	羽	590	豚	796
碑	1522	穏	869	米	224	綱	1609	翌	592	脚	1784
碁	1834	積	656	粋	1708	網	1612	習	591	脳	1278
磁	1548	穫	1314	料	319	緑	537	翼	1062	脱	1370
確	603			粉	1701	練	743	翻	596	期	449
礁	1768	**—116—**		粒	1700	綿	1191			腕	1299
礎	1515	穴	899	粘	1707	総	697	**—125—**		勝	509
		究	895	粗	1084	緯	1054	老	543	朝	469
—113—		突	898	粧	1699	線	299	考	541	腸	1270
示	615	空	140	精	659	締	1180	者	164	腰	1298
礼	620	窃	1717	糖	1698	縫	1349			腹	1271
社	308	窒	1716	糧	1704	編	682	**—126—**		膜	1426
祉	1390	窓	698			緩	1089	耐	1415	膨	1145
祈	621	窯	1789	**—120—**		縁	1131			膳	1779
祖	622	窮	897	糸	242	縛	1448	**—127—**		臓	1287
祝	851			級	568	繁	1292	耗	1197	騰	1780
神	310	**—117—**		紀	372	縦	1483	耕	1196		
祥	1576	立	121	糾	1703	績	1117			**—131—**	
祭	617	産	278	約	211	繊	1571	**—128—**		臣	835
視	606	童	410	紅	820	縮	1110	耳	56	臨	836
禁	482	端	1418	紡	1859	繕	1140	取	65		
禍	1809	競	852	紛	1702	織	680	恥	1690	**—132—**	
禅	1540			紋	1454	縄	1760	聴	1039	自	62
福	1379	**—118—**		納	758	繰	1654	職	385	臭	1244
		竹	129	純	965					息	1242
—115—		笑	1235	紙	180	**—121—**		**—129—**			
秀	1683	笛	1471	素	271	缶	1649	書	131	**—133—**	
利	329	符	505	紹	456					至	902
私	125	第	404	紺	1493	**—122—**		**—130—**		到	904

魔 1528

—201—

黄 780

—203—

黒 206
墨 1705

—207—

鼓 1147

—209—

鼻 813

—210—

斉 1477
剤 550
斎 1478

—211—

歯 478
齢 833

—212—

竜 1758
襲 1575

2. INDEX by Stroke Count

— 1 —

一　2
乙　983

— 2 —

丁　184
九　11
七　9
了　941
二　3
人　1
入　52
八　10
刀　37
力　100
十　12
又　1593

— 3 —

与　539
万　16
三　4
下　31
丈　1325
刃　1413
久　1210
及　1257
丸　644
千　15
才　551
亡　672
凡　1102
上　32
口　54
土　24
士　572
夕　81
大　26
女　102
子　103
寸　1894
小　27
山　34
川　33
工　139
己　370

干　584
弓　212

— 4 —

五　907
五　7
天　141
不　94
弔　1796
中　28
内　84
升　1898
午　49
丹　1093
夫　315
井　1193
少　144
予　393
元　137
六　8
介　453
仁　1619
化　254
仏　583
今　51
分　38
公　126
円　13
冗　1614
凶　1280
刈　1282
切　39
匹　1500
区　183
厄　1341
反　324
友　264
双　1594
収　757
太　629
孔　940
尺　1895
幻　1227
引　216
心　97
戸　152
手　57

支　318
文　111
斗　1899
斤　1897
方　70
日　5
月　17
木　22
欠　383
止　477
比　798
毛　287
氏　566
水　21
火　20
父　113
片　1045
牛　281
犬　280
王　294

— 5 —

丙　984
可　388
民　177
平　202
正　275
央　351
冊　1158
由　363
凸　1892
史　332
甲　982
申　309
旧　1216
世　252
本　25
出　53
必　520
永　1207
氷　1206
半　88
乏　754
丘　1357
斥　1401
包　804
末　305

失　311
未　306
市　181
主　155
以　46
仙　1891
令　831
他　120
仕　333
付　192
代　256
写　540
凹　1893
召　995
加　709
句　337
北　73
巨　1293
古　172
占　1706
圧　1342
弁　711
台　492
兄　406
司　842
右　76
号　266
囚　1195
四　6
去　414
冬　459
処　1137
外　83
尼　1620
巧　1627
功　818
左　75
布　675
刊　585
幼　1229
庁　763
広　694
払　582
打　1020
札　1157
母　112
汁　1794

犯　882
玄　1225
玉　295
甘　1492
生　44
用　107
田　35
白　205
皮　975
皿　1097
目　55
矛　773
矢　213
石　78
示　615
礼　620
穴　899
立　121
込　776
辺　775

— 6 —

弐　1030
百　14
両　200
再　782
州　195
色　204
向　199
印　1043
曲　366
后　1119
吏　1007
朱　1503
劣　1150
争　302
危　534
年　45
多　229
妄　1376
充　828
交　114
件　732
伐　1509
企　481
任　334
仰　1056

伏　1356
仲　1347
伝　434
休　60
会　158
仮　1049
合　159
全　89
伴　1027
先　50
共　196
同　198
兆　1562
次　384
刑　887
旬　338
旨　1040
匠　1359
灰　1343
叫　1252
吐　1253
吸　1256
因　554
団　491
回　90
吉　1141
寺　41
在　268
地　118
声　746
各　642
名　82
妃　1756
如　1747
好　104
存　269
宅　178
宇　990
字　110
守　490
安　105
光　138
当　77
尽　1726
尾　1868
帆　1103
式　525

忙	1373	寿	1550	志	573	決	356	岳	1358	姓	1746
成	261	系	908	均	805	妥	930	刷	1044	妹	408
扱	1258	束	501	壳	239	状	626	垂	1070	妻	671
早	248	卵	1058	条	564	狂	883	東	71	姉	407
机	1305	我	1302	妨	1182	町	182	乳	939	始	494
朽	1628	兵	784	妊	955	男	101	事	80	学	109
朴	1466	来	69	妙	1154	社	308	享	1672	宜	1086
列	611	奉	1541	完	613	秀	1683	卒	787	宙	991
死	85	忘	1374	肖	844	利	329	京	189	宝	296
毎	116	似	1486	尿	1869	私	125	育	246	宗	616
気	134	佐	1744	局	170	究	895	盲	1375	官	326
池	119	伺	1761	岐	872	肝	1272	夜	471	定	355
江	821	伯	1176	災	1335	臣	835	侮	1736	実	203
汗	1188	位	122	攻	819	乱	689	価	421	尚	1853
汚	693	含	1249	忌	1797	良	321	舎	791	届	992
灯	1333	伸	1108	改	514	即	463	念	579	屈	1802
壮	1326	住	156	希	676	芝	250	併	1162	居	171
竹	129	体	61	序	770	芳	1775	依	678	岬	1363
米	224	低	561	床	826	芸	435	侍	571	岸	586
糸	242	作	360	応	827	花	255	例	612	岩	1345
缶	1649	余	1063	廷	1111	初	679	佳	1462	府	504
羊	288	何	390	形	395	見	63	命	578	底	562
耳	56	児	1217	役	375	角	473	供	197	店	168
羽	590	呉	1436	忍	1414	言	66	使	331	延	1115
老	543	弟	405	快	1409	谷	653	免	733	弦	1226
考	541	冷	832	戒	876	豆	958	典	367	径	1475
肉	223	判	1026	戻	1238	迎	1055	周	91	征	1114
肌	1306	別	267	択	993	貝	240	券	506	彼	977
有	265	努	1595	把	1724	赤	207	刻	1211	往	918
自	62	助	623	批	1029	走	429	刺	881	忠	1348
至	902	労	233	抄	1153	足	58	制	427	怖	1814
舌	1259	医	220	扶	1721	身	59	効	816	怪	1476
舟	1094	克	1372	抑	1057	車	133	協	234	性	98
虫	873	孝	542	抗	824	辛	1487	直	423	房	1237
血	789	却	1783	技	871	返	442	卓	1679	肩	1264
行	68	呈	1590	抜	1713	近	445	卸	707	所	153
衣	677	吟	1250	折	1394	邦	808	参	710	拒	1295
西	72	君	793	投	1021	里	142	叔	1667	拠	1138
迅	1798	告	690	対	365	防	513	味	307	拍	1178
巡	777	吹	1255	材	552	麦	270	呼	1254	拓	1833
—7—		囲	1194	杉	1872	**—8—**		固	972	披	1712
否	1248	困	558	村	191	画	343	国	40	拡	1113
更	1008	図	339	沢	994	武	1031	坪	1896	抽	987
亜	1616	壱	1730	沖	1346	果	487	幸	684	抵	560
求	724	坂	443	没	935	表	272	並	1165	担	1274
励	1340	坊	1858	汽	135	承	942	奔	1659	拙	1801
		坑	1613	沈	936			奇	1360	拘	1800

招 455	的 210	卑 1521	峠 1351	浄 664	虐 1574
抱 1285	具 420	看 1316	峡 1352	浅 649	要 419
拝 1201	知 214	乗 523	炭 1344	洋 289	訂 1019
押 986	祉 1390	重 227	巻 507	洗 692	計 340
放 512	祈 621	亭 1184	度 377	活 237	負 510
昆 1874	季 465	哀 1675	建 892	海 117	則 608
易 759	委 466	帝 1179	弧 1481	畑 36	赴 1465
昔 764	和 124	変 257	律 667	牲 729	軌 1787
昇 1777	突 898	促 1557	待 452	狭 1353	迷 967
明 18	空 140	俊 1845	後 48	狩 1581	逃 1566
析 1393	者 164	係 909	怒 1596	独 219	送 441
枚 1156	取 65	便 330	急 303	珍 1215	退 846
杯 1155	肪 1857	侵 1077	恨 1755	某 1494	逆 444
枢 1023	肢 1146	俗 1126	悔 1733	界 454	追 1174
林 127	肥 1723	信 157	恒 1275	胃 1268	郊 817
枝 870	服 683	保 489	威 1339	思 99	郎 980
松 696	到 904	盆 1099	拷 1720	疫 1319	限 847
板 1047	茎 1474	前 47	括 1260	発 96	面 274
柳 1871	茂 1467	冠 1615	挑 1564	泉 1192	革 1075
欧 1022	芽 1455	軍 438	拾 1445	皇 297	音 347
肯 1262	苗 1468	削 1611	持 451	柔 774	風 29
歩 431	若 544	勅 1886	指 1041	砕 1710	飛 530
毒 522	英 353	勇 1386	挟 1354	研 896	食 322
況 850	苦 545	南 74	故 173	砂 1151	首 148
泳 1208	迭 1507	貞 1681	政 483	祖 622	香 1682
沼 996	述 968	点 169	施 1004	祝 851	
泌 1870	迫 1175	厘 1900	昭 997	神 310	—10—
泡 1765	邸 563	厚 639	冒 1104	秒 1152	蚕 1877
沿 1607	金 23	怠 1297	映 352	科 320	夏 461
泊 1177	長 95	叙 1067	昨 361	秋 462	師 409
治 493	門 161	咲 927	是 1591	級 568	剛 1610
波 666	附 1843	品 230	星 730	紀 372	粛 1695
河 389	阻 1085	垣 1276	春 460	糾 1703	勉 735
注 357	雨 30	型 888	柄 985	約 211	島 286
泣 1236	青 208	城 720	査 624	紅 820	衰 1676
泥 1621	非 498	契 565	柱 598	美 401	恋 258
油 364	斉 1477	奏 1544	架 755	耐 1415	倣 1776
法 123		姻 1748	枯 974	胞 1284	俵 1890
炉 1790	—9—	姿 929	栄 723	胎 1296	倫 1163
炎 1336	昼 470	孤 1480	染 779	胆 1273	倹 878
炊 1791	衷 1677	室 166	相 146	肺 1277	俸 1542
沸 1792	甚 1501	宣 625	段 362	背 1265	候 944
受 260	幽 1228	客 641	皆 587	臭 1244	倍 87
版 1046	為 1484	封 1463	津 668	荘 1327	俳 1035
邪 1457	単 300	専 600	洪 1435	草 249	倉 1307
牧 731	盾 772	県 194	洞 1301	茶 251	倒 905
物 79	省 145	屋 167	派 912	荒 1377	

値	425	帰	317	特	282	蚊	1876	側	609	情	209
個	973	徐	1066	畜	1223	被	976	偽	1485	措	1200
借	766	従	1482	班	1381	託	1636	偏	1159	掲	1624
修	945	徒	430	珠	1504	討	1018	健	893	据	1832
益	716	恭	1434	瓶	1161	訓	771	傘	790	描	1469
兼	1081	恵	1219	留	.761	記	371	貧	753	控	1718
准	1232	恩	555	症	1318	財	553	剰	1068	掘	1803
凍	1205	恐	1602	疲	1321	起	373	副	714	捨	1444
弱	218	悦	1368	疾	1812	射	900	勘	1502	掃	1080
剖	1830	悩	1279	病	380	軒	1187	動	231	授	602
剣	879	悟	1438	眠	849	唇	1737	乾	1190	採	933
脅	1263	扇	1555	砲	1764	辱	1738	啓	1398	排	1036
匿	1771	拳	801	破	665	逝	1396	唱	1646	探	535
栽	1125	挿	1651	祥	1576	逐	1134	唯	1234	推	1233
索	1059	捜	989	秩	1508	途	1072	域	970	接	486
真	422	捕	890	租	1083	透	1685	培	1828	掛	1464
原	136	振	954	称	978	速	502	堀	1804	教	245
能	386	敏	1735	秘	807	造	691	執	686	斜	1069
桑	1873	救	725	竜	1758	連	440	基	450	断	1024
唆	1846	旅	222	窃	1717	通	150	婚	567	族	221
員	163	時	42	笑	1235	郡	193	婦	316	旋	1005
哲	1397	栓	1842	粋	1708	酌	1863	寂	1669	械	529
純	965	核	1212	料	319	配	515	密	806	殻	1728
埋	1826	桃	1567	粉	1701	針	341	宿	179	貫	914
姫	1757	桜	928	紡	1859	陛	589	寄	1361	渓	1884
娠	956	株	741	紛	1702	陥	1218	常	497	涯	1461
娘	1752	梅	1734	紋	1454	院	614	堂	496	渉	432
娯	1437	格	643	納	758	陣	1404	崎	1362	淑	1668
孫	910	校	115	紙	180	除	1065	崇	1424	渇	1622
宰	1488	根	314	素	271	降	947	崩	1122	済	549
宴	640	殊	1505	差	658	隻	1311	帳	1107	涼	1204
害	518	殉	1799	耗	1197	飢	1304	康	894	液	472
宵	1854	残	650	耕	1196	馬	283	廊	981	渋	1693
案	106	殺	576	恥	1690	骨	1266	庸	1696	添	1433
容	654	泰	1545	書	131	高	190	庶	1766	淡	1337
宮	721	浜	785	朗	1754	鬼	1523	張	1106	混	799
家	165	浴	1128	脈	913	剤	550	強	217	清	660
党	495	涙	1239	脂	1042			弾	1539	深	536
展	1129	浪	1753	胴	1300	**—11—**		彩	932	猫	1470
峰	1350	浦	1442	胸	1283	悪	304	術	187	猟	1580
貢	1719	浸	1078	息	1242	巣	1538	得	374	猛	1579
帯	963	酒	517	致	903	尉	1617	御	708	望	673
庫	825	消	845	般	1096	彫	1149	患	1315	球	726
席	379	浮	938	航	823	率	788	悠	1597	理	143
庭	1i12	流	247	既	1458	商	412	悼	1680	現	298
座	786	烈	1331	華	1074	停	1185	惜	765	累	1060
唐	1697	将	627	荷	391	偶	1639	惨	1725	略	841

異	1061	訟	1403	奥	476	惰	1743	無	93	詞	843
盗	1100	許	737	蛮	1879	扉	1556	猶	1583	詠	1209
盛	719	設	577	就	934	雇	1553	琴	1251	詐	1498
眺	1565	訪	1181	棄	962	揮	1652	塁	1694	診	1214
眼	848	訳	594	偉	1053	援	1088	畳	1087	評	1028
務	235	欲	1127	備	768	握	1714	疎	1514	訴	1402
祭	617	販	1048	傍	1183	換	1586	痢	1811	証	484
視	606	責	655	普	1166	揺	1648	痛	1320	象	739
禅	1540	貫	752	善	1139	揚	631	登	960	費	749
移	1121	敗	511	尊	704	提	628	短	215	貿	760
窒	1716	赦	1570	創	1308	敢	1691	硫	1856	賀	756
窓	698	軟	1788	割	519	敬	705	硝	1855	貯	762
産	278	転	433	勤	559	散	767	硬	1009	貸	748
笛	1471	逮	891	博	601	晶	1645	程	417	越	1001
符	505	週	92	裁	1123	暑	638	税	399	超	1000
粒	1700	逸	734	喚	1587	晩	1658	童	410	貴	1171
粘	1707	郭	1673	喫	1240	替	744	筒	1472	距	1294
粗	1084	郷	855	営	722	量	411	策	880	軸	988
紹	456	部	86	圏	508	景	853	答	160	軽	547
紺	1493	郵	524	堕	1742	晴	662	筋	1090	遇	1641
紳	1109	都	188	堅	1289	晩	736	等	569	遂	1133
組	418	進	437	堤	1592	最	263	筆	130	遍	1160
終	458	酔	1709	塔	1840	棋	1835	粧	1699	達	448
細	695	釈	595	場	154	棺	1825	絡	840	遅	702
経	548	野	236	報	685	棟	1406	紫	1389	過	413
絶	742	釣	1862	喜	1143	森	128	絞	1452	道	149
翌	592	問	162	塚	1751	棒	1543	統	830	運	439
習	591	閉	397	塀	1805	植	424	絵	345	遊	1003
豚	796	陵	1844	婿	1745	検	531	給	346	酢	1867
脚	1784	隆	946	媒	1496	款	1727	結	485	番	185
脳	1278	険	533	富	713	欺	1499	買	241	鈍	966
脱	1370	陳	1405	寒	457	殖	1506	着	657	間	43
舶	1095	陶	1650	掌	499	滋	1549	群	794	閑	1532
船	376	陸	647	属	1637	湾	670	期	449	開	396
第	404	陰	867	順	769	湖	467	腕	1299	随	1741
菌	1222	雪	949	項	1439	渦	1810	勝	509	隅	1640
菓	1535	章	857	帽	1105	港	669	朝	469	隊	795
菊	475	頂	1440	幅	1380	湿	1169	募	1430	階	588
菜	931	魚	290	幾	877	測	610	葬	812	陽	630
著	859	鳥	285	廃	961	湯	632	落	839	雄	1387
葉	253	麻	1529	尋	1082	温	634	衆	792	焦	999
虚	1572	黄	780	循	1479	渡	378	裂	1330	集	436
蛇	1875	黒	206	街	186	満	201	装	1328	雰	1824
蛍	1878	斎	1478	復	917	減	715	裕	1391	雲	636
袋	1329			惑	969	然	651	補	889	悲	1034
票	922	—12—		慌	1378	煮	1795	覚	605	飯	325
規	607	喪	1678	愉	1598	焼	920	詔	1885	飲	323

3. INDEX by Readings

— A —

A	亜	1616
aba(ku)	暴	1014
aba(reru)	暴	1014
a(biru)	浴	1128
a(biseru)	浴	1128
abu(nai)	危	534
abura	油	364
	脂	1042
a(garu)	上	32
	挙	801
	揚	631
a(geru)	上	32
	挙	801
	揚	631
AI	哀	1675
	愛	259
ai-	相	146
aida	間	43
aji	味	307
aji(wau)	味	307
aka	赤	207
aka(i)	赤	207
aka(rameru)		
	赤	207
aka(ramu)	明	18
	赤	207
a(kari)	明	18
aka(rui)	明	18
aka(rumu)	明	18
a(kasu)	明	18
	飽	1763
akatsuki	暁	1658
a(keru)	明	18
	空	140
	開	396
aki	秋	462
akina(u)	商	412
aki(raka)	明	18
a(kiru)	飽	1763
AKU	悪	304
	握	1714
a(ku)	明	18
	空	140
	開	396
a(kuru)	明	18

ama	尼	1620
	天	141
	雨	30
ama(eru)	甘	1492
ama(i)	甘	1492
ama(ru)	余	1063
ama(su)	余	1063
ama(yakasu)		
	甘	1492
ame	天	141
	雨	30
ami	網	1612
a(mu)	編	682
AN	安	105
	案	106
	暗	348
	行	68
ana	穴	899
anado(ru)	侮	1736
ane	姉	407
ani	兄	406
ao	青	208
ao(gu)	仰	1056
ao(i)	青	208
ara(i)	粗	1084
	荒	1377
araso(u)	争	302
a(rasu)	荒	1377
ara(ta)	新	174
arata(maru)	改	514
arata(meru)	改	514
ara(u)	洗	692
arawa(reru)	表	272
	現	298
arawa(su)	表	272
	現	298
	著	859
a(reru)	荒	1377
a(ru)	在	268
	有	265
aru(ku)	歩	431
asa	朝	469
	麻	1529
asa(i)	浅	649
ase	汗	1188
ase(ru)	焦	999
ashi	脚	1784

	足	58
aso(bu)	遊	1003
ata(eru)	与	539
atai	価	421
	値	425
atama	頭	276
atara(shii)	新	174
ata(ri)	辺	775
a(taru)	当	77
atata(ka)	暖	635
	温	634
atata(kai)	暖	635
	温	634
atata(maru)	暖	635
	温	634
atata(meru)	暖	635
	温	634
a(teru)	充	828
	当	77
ato	後	48
	跡	1569
ATSU	圧	1342
atsu(i)	厚	639
	暑	638
	熱	645
atsuka(u)	扱	1258
atsu(maru)	集	436
atsu(meru)	集	436
a(u)	会	158
	合	159
	遭	1643
awa	泡	1765
awa(i)	淡	1337
awa(re)	哀	1675
awa(remu)	哀	1675
a(waseru)	合	159
	併	1162
a(wasu)	合	159
awa(tadashii)		
	慌	1378
awa(teru)	慌	1378
ayama(chi)	過	413
ayama(ru)	誤	906
	謝	901
ayama(tsu)	過	413
aya(shii)	怪	1476
aya(shimu)	怪	1476

ayatsu(ru)	操	1655
aya(ui)	危	534
ayu(mu)	歩	431
aza	字	110
azamu(ku)	欺	1499
aza(yaka)	鮮	701
azu(karu)	預	394
azu(keru)	預	394

— B —

BA	馬	283
ba	場	154
BACHI	罰	886
BAI	倍	87
	売	239
	培	1828
	媒	1496
	梅	1734
	買	241
	賠	1829
ba(kasu)	化	254
ba(keru)	化	254
BAKU	博	601
	暴	1014
	爆	1015
	縛	1448
	幕	1432
	麦	270
BAN	万	16
	蛮	1879
	伴	1027
	晩	736
	板	1047
	盤	1098
	番	185
	判	1026
BATSU	末	305
	伐	1509
	抜	1713
	罰	886
	閥	1510
-be	辺	775
BEI	米	224
BEN	勉	735
	便	330
	弁	711

Reading	Kanji	No.
beni	紅	820
BETSU	別	267
BI	備	768
	尾	1868
	微	1419
	美	401
	鼻	813
BIN	便	330
	貧	753
	敏	1735
	瓶	1161
BO	模	1425
	母	112
	簿	1450
	募	1430
	墓	1429
	慕	1431
	暮	1428
BO'	坊	1858
BŌ	乏	754
	亡	672
	妄	1376
	忘	1374
	傍	1183
	剖	1830
	坊	1858
	妨	1182
	帽	1105
	忙	1373
	房	1237
	冒	1104
	暴	1014
	棒	1543
	望	673
	某	1494
	紡	1859
	肪	1857
	膨	1145
	謀	1495
	貿	760
	防	513
BOKU	僕	1888
	撲	1889
	木	22
	朴	1466
	牧	731
	目	55
	墨	1705
BON	盆	1099
	凡	1102
	煩	1849
BOTSU	没	935
BU	不	94
	武	1031
	奉	1541
	侮	1736
	分	38
	歩	431
	無	93
	舞	810
	部	86
BUN	分	38
	文	111
	聞	64
buta	豚	796
BUTSU	仏	583
	物	79
BYAKU	白	205
BYŌ	平	202
	描	1469
	病	380
	秒	1152
	苗	1468

—C—

Reading	Kanji	No.
CHA	茶	251
CHAKU	着	657
CHI	値	425
	地	118
	池	119
	治	493
	痴	1813
	知	214
	稚	1230
	置	426
	恥	1690
	致	903
	質	176
	遅	702
chi	千	15
	乳	939
	血	789
chichi	乳	939
	父	113
chiga(eru)	違	814
chiga(u)	違	814
chigi(ru)	契	565
chii(sai)	小	27
chiji(maru)	縮	1110
chiji(meru)	縮	1110
chiji(mu)	縮	1110
chiji(rasu)	縮	1110
chiji(reru)	縮	1110
chika(i)	近	445
chikara	力	100
chika(u)	誓	1395
CHIKU	畜	1223
	竹	129
	築	1603
	蓄	1224
	逐	1134
CHIN	沈	936
	珍	1215
	賃	751
	鎮	1786
	陳	1405
chi(rakaru)	散	767
chi(rakasu)	散	767
chi(rasu)	散	767
chi(ru)	散	767
CHITSU	秩	1508
	窒	1716
CHO	緒	862
	著	859
	貯	762
CHŌ	丁	184
	弔	1796
	重	227
	彫	1149
	兆	1562
	帳	1107
	庁	763
	張	1106
	徴	1420
	懲	1421
	挑	1564
	澄	1334
	潮	468
	町	182
	眺	1565
	聴	1039
	朝	469
	腸	1270
	調	342
	跳	1563
	長	95
	頂	1440
	鳥	285
	超	1000
CHOKU	勅	1886
	直	423
CHŪ	昼	470
	中	28
	夷	1677
	仲	1347
	宙	991
	忠	1348
	抽	987
	柱	598
	沖	1346
	注	357
	虫	873
	鋳	1551
	駐	599

—D—

Reading	Kanji	No.
DA	堕	1742
	惰	1743
	打	1020
	妥	930
	蛇	1875
	駄	1880
DAI	内	84
	代	256
	弟	405
	台	492
	大	26
	題	354
	第	404
DAKU	濁	1625
	諾	1770
da(ku)	抱	1285
dama(ru)	黙	1578
DAN	団	491
	壇	1839
	弾	1539
	断	1024

	暖	635	EI	永	1207		布	675	fuku(reru)	膨	1145
	段	362		営	722		府	504	fukuro	袋	1329
	男	101		影	854		腐	1245	fu(maeru)	踏	1559
	談	593		衛	815		怖	1814	fumi	文	111
da(su)	出	53		映	352		扶	1721	fu(mu)	踏	1559
DATSU	奪	1310		栄	723		敷	1451	FUN	分	38
	脱	1370		泳	1208		浮	938		噴	1660
DE	弟	405		英	353		父	113		墳	1662
DEI	泥	1621		詠	1209		符	505		奮	1309
DEN	殿	1130		鋭	1371		膚	1269		憤	1661
	伝	434	EKI	益	716		譜	1167		粉	1701
	田	35		役	375		負	510		紛	1702
	電	108		易	759		賦	1808		雰	1824
de(ru)	出	53		液	472		赴	1465	funa	舟	1094
DO	土	24		疫	1319		附	1843		船	376
	度	377		駅	284		風	29	fune	舟	1094
	努	1595	e(mu)	笑	1235		歩	431		船	376
	怒	1596	EN	円	13	FŪ	夫	315	fu(reru)	触	874
DŌ	働	232		園	447		富	713	fu(ru)	振	954
	同	198		塩	1101		封	1463		降	947
	動	231		宴	640		風	29	furu(eru)	震	953
	導	703		延	1115	fuchi	縁	1131	furu(i)	古	172
	堂	496		援	1088	fuda	札	1157	furu(su)	古	172
	洞	1301		沿	1607	fude	筆	130	furu(u)	奮	1309
	童	410		演	344	fue	笛	1471		震	953
	胴	1300		炎	1336	fu(eru)	増	712	fu(ruu)	振	954
	道	149		煙	919		殖	1506	fusa	房	1237
	銅	1605		猿	1584	fuka(i)	深	536	fuse(gu)	防	513
DOKU	毒	522		縁	1131	fuka(maru)	深	536	fuse(ru)	伏	1356
	独	219		遠	446	fuka(meru)	深	536	fushi	節	464
	読	244		鉛	1606	fu(kasu)	更	1008	fu(su)	伏	1356
DON	曇	637	era(bu)	選	800	fu(keru)	更	1008	futa	二	3
	鈍	966	era(i)	偉	1053		老	543		双	1594
-dono	殿	1130	eri	襟	1537	FUKU	伏	1356	futata(bi)	再	782
doro	泥	1621	e(ru)	得	374		副	714	futa(tsu)	二	3
				獲	1313		幅	1380	futo(i)	太	629
—E—			ETSU	悦	1368		復	917	futokoro	懐	1408
E	会	158		越	1001		福	1379	futo(ru)	太	629
	依	678		閲	1369		服	683	FUTSU	払	582
	回	90					腹	1271		沸	1792
	恵	1219	**—F—**				複	916	fu(yasu)	増	712
	絵	345	FU	不	94		覆	1634		殖	1506
e	江	821		夫	315	fu(ku)	吹	1255	fuyu	冬	459
	柄	985		付	192		噴	1660			
-e	重	227		普	1166	fuku(meru)	含	1249	**—G—**		
eda	枝	870		婦	316	fuku(mu)	含	1249	GA	画	343
ega(ku)	描	1469		富	713	fuku(ramu)	膨	1145		我	1302

	雅	1456
	芽	1455
	賀	756
	餓	1303
GA'	合	159
GAI	外	83
	害	518
	街	186
	慨	1460
	概	1459
	涯	1461
	該	1213
GAKU	岳	1358
	学	109
	楽	358
	額	838
GAN	丸	644
	願	581
	元	137
	含	1249
	岸	586
	岩	1345
	眼	848
	頑	1848
	顔	277
gara	柄	985
GATSU	月	17
GE	下	31
	夏	461
	外	83
	華	1074
	解	474
GEI	芸	435
	迎	1055
	鯨	700
GEKI	劇	797
	撃	1016
	激	1017
GEN	厳	822
	元	137
	原	136
	嫌	1688
	幻	1227
	弦	1226
	減	715
	源	580
	玄	1225
	現	298
	眼	848
	言	66
	限	847
	験	532
GETSU	月	17
GI	戯	1573
	偽	1485
	儀	727
	疑	1516
	宜	1086
	技	871
	擬	1517
	欺	1499
	犠	728
	義	291
	議	292
GIN	吟	1250
	銀	313
GO	互	907
	五	7
	午	49
	呉	1436
	娯	1437
	後	48
	御	708
	悟	1438
	碁	1834
	期	449
	誤	906
	語	67
	護	1312
GŌ	剛	1610
	業	279
	豪	1671
	合	159
	号	266
	強	217
	拷	1720
	郷	855
GOKU	極	336
	獄	884
GON	厳	822
	勤	559
	権	335
	言	66
GU	愚	1642
	具	420
GŪ	偶	1639
	宮	721
	遇	1641
	隅	1640
GUN	軍	438
	群	794
	郡	193
GYAKU	虐	1574
	逆	444
GYO	御	708
	漁	699
	魚	290
GYŌ	業	279
	仰	1056
	凝	1518
	形	395
	暁	1658
	行	68
GYOKU	玉	295
GYŪ	牛	281

—H—

HA	把	1724
	波	666
	派	912
	破	665
	覇	1633
HA'	法	123
ha	刃	1413
	端	1418
	羽	590
	葉	253
	歯	478
haba	幅	1380
haba(mu)	阻	1085
habu(ku)	省	145
HACHI	八	10
	鉢	1820
hada	肌	1306
hadaka	裸	1536
ha(e)	栄	723
ha(eru)	映	352
	栄	723
	生	44
hagane	鋼	1608
hage(masu)	励	1340
hage(mu)	励	1340
hage(shii)	激	1017
haha	母	112
HAI	俳	1035
	廃	961
	拝	1201
	排	1036
	杯	1155
	肺	1277
	背	1265
	敗	511
	配	515
	輩	1037
hai	灰	1343
hai(ru)	入	52
haji	恥	1690
haji(maru)	始	494
haji(me)	初	679
haji(meru)	始	494
haji(mete)	初	679
ha(jirau)	恥	1690
ha(jiru)	恥	1690
haka	墓	1429
haka(rau)	計	340
haka(ru)	図	339
	量	411
	測	610
	計	340
	諮	1769
	謀	1495
hako	箱	1091
hako(bu)	運	439
HAKU	伯	1176
	博	601
	拍	1178
	泊	1177
	白	205
	舶	1095
	薄	1449
	迫	1175
ha(ku)	吐	1253
	履	1635
	掃	1080
hama	浜	785
HAN	半	88
	伴	1027
	凡	1102

	火	20		掘	1803	ichi	市	181	i(ru)	入	52

	火	20		掘	1803
	穂	1221	hoshi	星	730
HŌ	包	804	ho(shii)	欲	1127
	奉	1541	hoso(i)	細	695
	褒	803	hoso(ru)	細	695
	倣	1776	hos(suru)	欲	1127
	俸	1542	ho(su)	干	584
	報	685	hotaru	蛍	1878
	宝	296	hotoke	仏	583
	封	1463	HOTSU	発	96
	峰	1350	HYAKU	百	14
	崩	1122	HYŌ	表	272
	抱	1285		氷	1206
	方	70		兵	784
	放	512		俵	1890
	泡	1765		拍	1178
	法	123		標	923
	砲	1764		漂	924
	縫	1349		票	922
	胞	1284		評	1028
	芳	1775			
	訪	1181	**— I —**		
	豊	959	I	為	1484
	邦	808		尉	1617
	飽	1763		以	46
hodo	程	417		位	122
hodoko(su)	施	1004		依	678
hoga(raka)	朗	1754		偉	1053
				医	220
hoka	外	83		唯	1234
hoko	矛	773		囲	1194
hoko(ru)	誇	1629		慰	1618
HOKU	北	73		威	1339
homare	誉	802		易	759
ho(meru)	褒	803		胃	1268
hōmu(ru)	葬	812		異	1061
HON	本	25		委	466
	反	324		移	1121
	奔	1659		維	1231
	翻	596		緯	1054
hone	骨	1266		衣	677
honō	炎	1336		違	814
hora	洞	1301		遺	1172
hori	堀	1804		意	132
horo(biru)	滅	1338	i	井	1193
horo(bosu)	滅	1338	ICHI	一	2
ho(ru)	彫	1149		壱	1730

ichi	市	181	i(ru)	入	52
ichijiru(shii)				居	171
	著	859		要	419
ida(ku)	抱	1285		射	900
ido(mu)	挑	1564		鋳	1551
ie	家	165	isagiyo(i)	潔	1241
ika(ru)	怒	1596	isa(mu)	勇	1386
i(kasu)	生	44	ishi	石	78
ike	池	119	ishizue	礎	1515
i(keru)	生	44	isoga(shii)	忙	1373
IKI	域	970	iso(gu)	急	303
iki	息	1242	ita	板	1047
ikidō(ru)	憤	1661	itadaki	頂	1440
ikio(i)	勢	646	itada(ku)	頂	1440
i(kiru)	生	44	ita(i)	痛	1320
iko(i)	憩	1243	ita(meru)	傷	633
iko(u)	憩	1243		痛	1320
IKU	育	246	ita(mu)	傷	633
i(ku)	行	68		悼	1680
iku-	幾	877		痛	1320
ikusa	戦	301	ita(ru)	至	902
ima	今	51	ita(su)	致	903
imashi(meru)			ito	糸	242
	戒	876	itona(mu)	営	722
i(mawashii)	忌	1797	ITSU	一	2
imōto	妹	408		逸	734
i(mu)	忌	1797	itsu	五	7
IN	印	1043	itsuku(shimu)		
	員	163		慈	1547
	因	554	itsu(tsu)	五	7
	姻	1748	itsuwa(ru)	偽	1485
	引	216	i(u)	言	66
	陰	867	iwa	岩	1345
	院	614	iwa(u)	祝	851
	隠	868	iya(shii)	卑	1521
	音	347	iya(shimeru)		
	韻	349		卑	1521
	飲	323	iya(shimu)	卑	1521
ina	否	1248	izumi	泉	1192
ina-	稲	1220	**— J —**		
ine	稲	1220	JA	邪	1457
inochi	命	578		蛇	1875
ino(ru)	祈	621	JAKU	弱	218
inu	犬	280		寂	1669
i(reru)	入	52		着	657
iro	色	204		若	544
irodo(ru)	彩	932			

ka(karu)	懸	911		乾	1190	kane	金	23	katamari	塊	1524

ka(karu) 懸 911
　　　　掛 1464
　　　　架 755
ka(keru) 懸 911
　　　　掛 1464
　　　　架 755
　　　　欠 383
　　　　駆 1882
kaki 垣 1276
kako(mu) 囲 1194
kako(u) 囲 1194
KAKU 画 343
　　　各 642
　　　客 641
　　　拡 1113
　　　核 1212
　　　格 643
　　　殻 1728
　　　獲 1313
　　　確 603
　　　穫 1314
　　　覚 605
　　　角 473
　　　較 1453
　　　郭 1673
　　　閣 837
　　　隔 1589
　　　革 1075
ka(ku) 欠 383
　　　書 131
kaku(reru) 隠 868
kaku(su) 隠 868
kama 窯 1789
kama(eru) 構 1010
kama(u) 構 1010
kamba(shii) 芳 1775
kami 上 32
　　　神 310
　　　紙 180
　　　髪 1148
kaminari 雷 952
kamo(su) 醸 1837
KAN 甲 982
　　　看 1316
　　　冠 1615
　　　勘 1502
　　　勧 1051

　　　乾 1190
　　　幹 1189
　　　喚 1587
　　　完 613
　　　官 326
　　　寒 457
　　　寛 1050
　　　巻 507
　　　干 584
　　　刊 585
　　　患 1315
　　　感 262
　　　慣 915
　　　憾 1815
　　　換 1586
　　　敢 1691
　　　棺 1825
　　　款 1727
　　　歓 1052
　　　貫 914
　　　汗 1188
　　　漢 556
　　　環 865
　　　甘 1492
　　　監 1663
　　　管 328
　　　簡 1533
　　　緩 1089
　　　缶 1649
　　　肝 1272
　　　艦 1665
　　　観 604
　　　還 866
　　　鑑 1664
　　　閑 1532
　　　間 43
　　　関 398
　　　陥 1218
　　　館 327
kan 神 310
kana 金 23
kana(deru) 奏 1544
kanara(zu) 必 520
kana(shii) 悲 1034
kana(shimu)
　　　悲 1034
kanba(shii) 芳 1775

kane 金 23
　　　鐘 1821
ka(neru) 兼 1081
kanga(eru) 考 541
kanmuri 冠 1615
kano 彼 977
kao 顔 277
kao(ri) 香 1682
kao(ru) 薫 1774
　　　香 1682
kara 殻 1728
　　　空 140
Kara 唐 1697
karada 体 61
kara(i) 辛 1487
kara(maru) 絡 840
kara(mu) 絡 840
ka(rasu) 枯 974
kare 彼 977
ka(reru) 枯 974
kari 仮 1049
ka(ri) 狩 1581
ka(riru) 借 766
karo(yaka) 軽 547
ka(ru) 刈 1282
　　　狩 1581
　　　駆 1882
karu(i) 軽 547
kasa 傘 790
kasa(naru) 重 227
kasa(neru) 重 227
kase(gu) 稼 1750
kashiko(i) 賢 1288
kashira 頭 276
ka(su) 貸 748
kata 型 888
　　　形 395
　　　肩 1264
　　　方 70
　　　渇 1626
kata- 片 1045
katachi 形 395
kata(i) 固 972
　　　堅 1289
　　　硬 1009
　　　難 557
kataki 敵 416

katamari 塊 1524
kata(maru) 固 972
kata(meru) 固 972
katamu(keru)
　　　傾 1441
katamu(ku) 傾 1441
katana 刀 37
kata(rau) 語 67
kata(ru) 語 67
katawa(ra) 傍 1183
katayo(ru) 偏 1159
kate 糧 1704
KATSU 割 519
　　　括 1260
　　　活 237
　　　渇 1622
　　　褐 1623
　　　轄 1186
ka(tsu) 勝 509
katsu(gu) 担 1274
ka(u) 交 114
　　　買 241
　　　飼 1762
kawa 側 609
　　　川 33
　　　河 389
　　　皮 975
　　　革 1075
kawa(kasu) 乾 1190
kawa(ku) 乾 1190
　　　渇 1622
ka(waru) 変 257
　　　代 256
　　　換 1586
　　　替 744
ka(wasu) 交 114
kayo(u) 通 150
kaza- 風 29
kaza(ru) 飾 979
kaze 風 29
kazo(eru) 数 225
kazu 数 225
KE 化 254
　　　仮 1049
　　　家 165
　　　懸 911

	枯	974		構	1010	kokoroyo(i)	快	1409	koro(su)	殺	576
	湖	467		肯	1262	kokorozashi	志	573		凝	1518
	虚	1572		江	821	kokoroza(su)	志	573	kō(ru)	氷	1206
	誇	1629		洪	1435		志	573		凍	1205
	顧	1554		港	669	KOKU	刻	1211	koshi	腰	1298
	鼓	1147		溝	1012		克	1372	ko(su)	越	1001
ko	子	103		皇	297		告	690		超	1000
	木	22		硬	1009		国	40	kota(e)	答	160
	黄	780		紅	820		穀	1729	kota(eru)	答	160
	粉	1701		絞	1452		谷	653	koto	事	80
ko-	小	27		綱	1609		酷	1711		殊	1505
KŌ	更	1008		考	541		黒	206		琴	1251
	甲	982		耗	1197		石	78	koto-	異	1755
	向	199		耕	1196	koma(ka)	細	695	-koto	言	66
	后	1119		航	823	koma(kai)	細	695	kotobuki	寿	1550
	交	114		荒	1377	koma(ru)	困	558	kotowa(ru)	断	1024
	仰	1056		行	68	kome	米	224	KOTSU	骨	1266
	候	944		講	783	ko(meru)	込	776	ko(u)	恋	258
	公	126		購	1011	ko(mu)	込	776		請	661
	興	368		郊	817	kōmu(ru)	被	976	kowa-	声	746
	効	816		酵	1866	KON	今	51	kowa(i)	怖	1814
	孝	542		鉱	1604		困	558	kowa(reru)	壊	1407
	厚	639		鋼	1608		墾	1136	kowa(su)	壊	1407
	口	54		降	947		婚	567	ko(yashi)	肥	1723
	坑	1613		香	1682		建	892	ko(yasu)	肥	1723
	幸	684		高	190		恨	1755	koyomi	暦	1534
	好	104		黄	780		懇	1135	KU	九	11
	孔	940	kō	神	310		昆	1874		久	1210
	光	138	koba(mu)	拒	1295		根	314		供	197
	工	139	koe	声	746		混	799		句	337
	巧	1627		肥	1723		献	1355		区	183
	功	818	ko(eru)	肥	1723		紺	1493		口	54
	攻	819		越	1001		金	23		宮	721
	貢	1719		超	1000		魂	1525		工	139
	項	1439	ko(garu)	焦	999	kona	粉	1701		功	818
	広	694	ko(gasu)	焦	999	kono(mu)	好	104		貢	1719
	康	894	ko(geru)	焦	999	ko(rashimeru)				庫	825
	後	48	kogo(eru)	凍	1205		懲	1421		紅	820
	衡	1585	koi	恋	258	ko(rasu)	凝	1518		苦	545
	恒	1275	ko(i)	濃	957		懲	1421		駆	1882
	慌	1378	koi(shii)	恋	258	kōri	氷	1206	KŪ	空	140
	抗	824	kokono	九	11	ko(riru)	懲	1421	kuba(ru)	配	515
	拘	1800	kokono(tsu)			koro(bu)	転	433	kubi	首	148
	控	1718		九	11	koro(garu)	転	433	kuchi	口	54
	格	643	kokoro	心	97	koro(gasu)	転	433	kuchibiru	唇	1737
	校	115	kokoro(miru)			koro(geru)	転	433	ku(chiru)	朽	1628
	稿	1120		試	526	koromo	衣	677	kuda	管	328

kuda(keru)	砕	1710		掘	1803		橋	597		町	182
kuda(ku)	砕	1710	kutsu	靴	1076		況	850	mado	窓	698
kuda(ru)	下	31					狂	883	mado(u)	惑	969
kuda(saru)	下	31	kutsugae(ru)	覆	1634		狭	1353	mae	前	47
kuda(su)	下	31					競	852	ma(garu)	曲	366
ku(iru)	悔	1733	kutsugae(su)				経	548	ma(geru)	曲	366
kujira	鯨	700		覆	1634		胸	1283	magi(rasu)	紛	1702
kuki	茎	1474	ku(u)	食	322		郷	855	magi(rawashii)		
kumi	組	418	kuwa	桑	1873		鏡	863		紛	1702
kumo	雲	636	kuwada(teru)				響	856	magi(rawasu)		
kumo(ru)	曇	637		企	481		香	1682		紛	1702
ku(mu)	組	418	kuwa(eru)	加	709		驚	1778	magi(reru)	紛	1702
KUN	君	793	kuwa(shii)	詳	1577	KYOKU	曲	366	mago	孫	910
	勲	1773	kuwa(waru)	加	709		局	170	MAI	埋	1826
	薫	1774	ku(yamu)	悔	1733		極	336		妹	408
	訓	771	kuya(shii)	悔	1733	KYŪ	旧	1216		枚	1156
kuni	国	40	kuzu(reru)	崩	1122		求	724		毎	116
kura	倉	1307	kuzu(su)	崩	1122		九	11		米	224
	蔵	1286	KYA	脚	1784		久	1210	mai	舞	810
kura(beru)	比	798	KYAKU	却	1783		及	1257	mai(ru)	参	710
kurai	位	122		客	641		丘	1357	maji(eru)	交	114
kura(i)	暗	348		脚	1784		休	60	ma(jiru)	交	114
ku(rasu)	暮	1428	KYO	巨	1293		吸	1256		混	799
ku(rau)	食	322		去	414		宮	721	maji(waru)	交	114
kurenai	紅	820		居	171		弓	212	makana(u)	賄	1739
ku(reru)	暮	1428		拒	1295		急	303	maka(seru)	任	334
kuro	黒	206		拠	1138		救	725	maka(su)	任	334
kuro(i)	黒	206		挙	801		朽	1628	ma(kasu)	負	510
ku(ru)	来	69		虚	1572		泣	1236	ma(keru)	負	510
	繰	1654		許	737		球	726	maki	巻	507
kuruma	車	133		距	1294		究	895		牧	731
kuru(oshii)	狂	883	KYŌ	享	1672		窮	897	makoto	誠	718
kuru(shii)	苦	545		京	189		級	568	MAKU	膜	1426
kuru(shimeru)				供	197		糾	1703		幕	1432
	苦	545		共	196		給	346	ma(ku)	巻	507
kuru(shimu)				興	368				mame	豆	958
	苦	545		凶	1280	—M—			mamo(ru)	守	490
kuru(u)	狂	883		脅	1263				MAN	万	16
kusa	草	249		協	234	MA	麻	1529		慢	1410
kusa(i)	臭	1244		兄	406		摩	1530		満	201
kusa(rasu)	腐	1245		叫	1252		磨	1531		漫	1411
kusa(reru)	腐	1245		境	864		魔	1528	mana(bu)	学	109
kusari	鎖	1819		峡	1352	ma	目	55	manako	眼	848
kusa(ru)	腐	1245		強	217		間	43	mane(ku)	招	455
kuse	癖	1490		恭	1434		真	422	manuka(reru)		
kusuri	薬	359		恐	1602		馬	283		免	733
KUTSU	屈	1802		挟	1354	maboroshi	幻	1227	maru	丸	644
				教	245	machi	街	186			

maru(i)	丸	644	METSU	滅	1338	mizo	溝	1012		基	450
	円	13	mezura(shii)			mizu	水	21	motoi	基	450
maru(meru)	丸	644		珍	1215	mizuka(ra)	自	62	moto(meru)	求	724
masa(ni)	正	275	MI	未	306	mizuumi	湖	467	MOTSU	物	79
masa(ru)	勝	509		味	307	MO	模	1425	mo(tsu)	持	451
masu	升	1898		魅	1526		茂	1467	motto(mo)	最	263
ma(su)	増	712	mi	三	4	mo	喪	1678	mo(yasu)	燃	652
mata	又	1593		実	203		藻	1657	moyō(su)	催	1317
matata(ku)	瞬	1732		身	59	MŌ	亡	672	MU	武	1031
mato	的	210	michi	道	149		妄	1376		無	93
MATSU	末	305	michibi(ku)	導	703		盲	1375		矛	773
matsu	松	696	mi(chiru)	満	201		毛	287		務	235
ma(tsu)	待	452	mida(reru)	乱	689		猛	1579		夢	811
matsu(ri)	祭	617	mida(su)	乱	689		望	673		謀	1495
matsurigoto	政	483	midori	緑	537		網	1612		霧	950
matsu(ru)	祭	617	mi(eru)	見	63		耗	1197	mu	六	8
matta(ku)	全	89	miga(ku)	磨	1531	mochi(iru)	用	107	mugi	麦	270
ma(u)	舞	810	migi	右	76	modo(ru)	戻	1238	mui	六	8
mawa(ri)	周	91	mijika(i)	短	215	modo(su)	戻	1238	muka(eru)	迎	1055
mawa(ru)	回	90	miji(me)	惨	1725	mo(eru)	燃	652	mukashi	昔	764
mawa(su)	回	90	miki	幹	1189	mogu(ru)	潜	937	mu(kau)	向	199
mayo(u)	迷	967	mikotonori	詔	1885	mō(keru)	設	577	mu(keru)	向	199
ma(zaru)	交	114	mimi	耳	56	MOKU	木	22	muko	婿	1745
	混	799	MIN	民	177		黙	1578	mu(kō)	向	199
ma(zeru)	交	114		眠	849		目	55	mu(ku)	向	199
	混	799	mina	皆	587	momo	桃	1567	muku(iru)	報	685
mazu(shii)	貧	753	minami	南	74	MON	文	111	muna	棟	1406
me	目	55	minamoto	源	580		紋	1454		胸	1283
	芽	1455	minato	港	669		門	161	mune	旨	1040
	女	102	mine	峰	1350		問	162		棟	1406
me-	雌	1388	miniku(i)	醜	1527		聞	64		胸	1283
megu(mu)	恵	1219	mino(ru)	実	203	mono	物	79	mura	村	191
megu(ru)	巡	777	mi(ru)	見	63		者	164		群	794
MEI	命	578		診	1214	moppa(ra)	専	600	murasaki	紫	1389
	鳴	925	misaki	岬	1363	mo(rasu)	漏	1806	mu(rasu)	蒸	943
	名	82	misao	操	1655	mo(reru)	漏	1806	mu(re)	群	794
	明	18	misasagi	陵	1844	mori	守	490	mu(reru)	群	794
	盟	717	mise	店	168		森	128		蒸	943
	迷	967	mi(seru)	見	63	mo(ru)	漏	1806	muro	室	166
	銘	1552	mi(tasu)	満	201		盛	719	mushi	虫	873
mekura	盲	1375	mito(meru)	認	738	mo(shikuwa)			mu(su)	蒸	943
MEN	免	733	MITSU	密	806		若	544	musu(bu)	結	485
	綿	1191	mi(tsu)	三	4	mo(su)	燃	652	musume	娘	1752
	面	274	mitsu(gu)	貢	1719	mō(su)	申	309	mu(tsu)	六	8
meshi	飯	325	mit(tsu)	三	4	moto	下	31	mut(tsu)	六	8
mesu	雌	1388	miya	宮	721		本	25	muzuka(shii)		
me(su)	召	995	miyako	都	188		元	137		難	557

		柔	774	oka(su)	侵 1077	oroshi	卸 707	oyo(bi)	及 1257

	利	329		量	411	sa(geru)	下	31		削	1611
	里	142		涼	1204		提	628		索	1059
	離	1281		漁	699	sagu(ru)	探	535		搾	1497
RICHI	律	667		猟	1580	SAI	再	782		昨	361
RIKI	力	100		療	1322		才	551		策	880
RIKU	陸	647		料	319		債	1118		酢	1867
RIN	倫	1163		糧	1704		催	1317		錯	1199
	厘	1900		良	321		切	39	sa(ku)	割	519
	林	127		陵	1844		裁	1125		咲	927
	臨	836		霊	1168		裁	1123		裂	1330
	輪	1164		領	834		載	1124	sakura	桜	928
	鈴	1822	RYOKU	力	100		妻	671	sama	様	403
	隣	809		緑	537		宰	1488	sa(masu)	冷	832
RITSU	率	788	RYŪ	柳	1871		災	1335		覚	605
	律	667		流	247		彩	932	samata(geru)		
	立	121		留	761		採	933		妨	1182
RO	炉	1790		硫	1856		最	263	sa(meru)	冷	832
	路	151		立	121		歳	479		覚	605
	露	951		粒	1700		殺	576	samu(i)	寒	457
RŌ	労	233		隆	946		済	549	samurai	侍	571
	廊	981		竜	1758		砕	1710	SAN	三	4
	楼	1841					祭	617		蚕	1877
	浪	1753	—S—				細	695		傘	790
	漏	1806	SA	再	782		菜	931		参	710
	糧	1704		佐	1744		西	72		山	34
	老	543		作	360		財	553		惨	1725
	朗	1754		唆	1846		際	618		散	767
	郎	980		左	75		斎	1478		産	278
	露	951		査	624	saiwa(i)	幸	684		算	747
ROKU	六	8		砂	1151	saka	坂	443		賛	745
	緑	537		差	658		酒	517		酸	516
	録	538		茶	251	saka(eru)	栄	723	sara	皿	1097
RON	論	293		詐	1498	sakai	境	864		更	1008
RU	流	247		鎖	1819	saka(n)	盛	719	saru	猿	1584
	留	761	SA'	早	248	sakana	魚	290	sa(ru)	去	414
RUI	涙	1239	saba(ku)	裁	1123	saka(rau)	逆	444	sasa(eru)	支	318
	累	1060	sabi	寂	1669	saka(ru)	盛	719	sa(saru)	刺	881
	塁	1694	sabi(reru)	寂	1669	sakazuki	杯	1155	saso(u)	誘	1684
	類	226	sabi(shii)	寂	1669	sake	酒	517	sa(su)	刺	881
RYAKU	略	841	sachi	幸	684	sake(bu)	叫	1252		指	1041
RYO	旅	222	sada(ka)	定	355	sa(keru)	裂	1330		挿	1651
	虜	1385	sada(maru)	定	355		避	1491		差	658
	慮	1384	sada(meru)	定	355	saki	先	50	sato	里	142
RYŌ	両	200	saegi(ru)	遮	1767		崎	1362	sato(ru)	悟	1438
	了	941	sa(garu)	下	31	SAKU	冊	1158	sato(su)	諭	1599
	僚	1324	saga(su)	捜	989		作	360	SATSU	冊	1158
	寮	1323		探	535					刷	1044

	察 619		逝 1396		遷 921	士 572
	撮 1520		青 208		選 800	姉 407
	擦 1519		静 663		銭 648	始 494
	札 1157		斉 1477	se(ru)	競 852	姿 929
	殺 576	sei	背 1265	SETSU	切 39	子 103
sawa	沢 994	SEKI	斥 1401		折 1394	指 1041
sawa(gu)	騒 875		夕 81		拙 1801	支 318
sawa(ru)	触 874		寂 1669		接 486	施 1004
	障 858		席 379		摂 1692	枝 870
sazu(karu)	授 602		惜 765		殺 576	止 477
sazu(keru)	授 602		昔 764		窃 1717	雌 1388
SE	世 252		析 1393		節 464	死 85
	施 1004		石 78		設 577	氏 566
se	瀬 1513		積 656		説 400	思 99
	背 1265		籍 1198		雪 949	矢 213
seba(maru)	狭 1353		績 1117	SHA	舎 791	示 615
seba(meru)	狭 1353		責 655		写 540	祉 1390
SECHI	節 464		赤 207		捨 1444	視 606
SEI	正 275		跡 1569		斜 1069	私 125
	世 252		隻 1311		煮 1795	糸 242
	井 1193	seki	関 398		砂 1151	紙 180
	省 145	sema(i)	狭 1353		社 308	紫 1389
	制 427	sema(ru)	迫 1175		者 164	肢 1146
	勢 646	se(meru)	攻 819		謝 901	脂 1042
	声 746		責 655		赦 1570	自 62
	姓 1746	SEN	千 15		射 900	至 902
	婿 1745		仙 1891		車 133	詞 843
	征 1114		宣 625		遮 1767	詩 570
	性 98		先 50	SHAKU	借 766	試 526
	情 209		占 1706		尺 1895	誌 574
	成 261		専 600		昔 764	諮 1769
	政 483		川 33		石 78	資 750
	星 730		戦 301		酌 1863	賜 1831
	晴 662		扇 1555		釈 595	飼 1762
	歳 479		旋 1005	SHI	史 332	歯 478
	整 503		染 779		師 409	shiawa(se) 幸 684
	清 660		栓 1842		市 181	shiba 芝 250
	牲 729		浅 649		仕 333	shiba(ru) 縛 1448
	聖 674		洗 692		伺 1761	shibo(ru) 搾 1497
	生 44		潜 937		使 331	絞 1452
	盛 719		泉 1192		次 384	shibu 渋 1693
	精 659		線 299		刺 881	shibu(i) 渋 1693
	製 428		繊 1571		旨 1040	shibu(ru) 渋 1693
	西 72		船 376		司 842	SHICHI 七 9
	誠 718		薦 1631		四 6	質 176
	誓 1395		鮮 701		志 573	shige(ru) 茂 1467
	請 661		践 1568			shi(iru) 強 217

	趣	1002			阻	1085		則	608	su(giru)	過	413
	首	148	SŌ		喪	1678		足	58	su(gosu)	過	413
SHŪ	州	195			巣	1538		速	502	sugu(reru)	優	1033
	衆	792			争	302	so(maru)	染	779	SUI	出	53
	就	934			倉	1307	so(meru)	染	779		垂	1070
	修	945			僧	1366	-so(meru)	初	679		衰	1676
	周	91			創	1308	somu(keru)	背	1265		吹	1255
	収	757			双	1594	somu(ku)	背	1265		推	1233
	囚	1195			桑	1873	SON	尊	704		水	21
	執	686			奏	1544		存	269		炊	1791
	宗	616			宗	616		孫	910		睡	1071
	愁	1601			層	1367		損	350		穂	1221
	拾	1445			想	147		村	191		粋	1708
	祝	851			挿	1651	sona(eru)	供	197		遂	1133
	秀	1683			捜	989		備	768		酔	1709
	秋	462			掃	1080	sona(waru)	備	768	su(i)	酸	516
	終	458			操	1655	sono	園	447	suji	筋	1090
	習	591			早	248	sora	空	140	su(kasu)	透	1685
	臭	1244			相	146	so(rasu)	反	324	suke	助	623
	舟	1094			槽	1644	sōrō	候	944	su(keru)	透	1685
	衆	792			燥	1656	so(ru)	反	324	suko(shi)	少	144
	週	92			壮	1326	soso(gu)	注	357	suko(yaka)	健	893
	酬	1864			窓	698	sosonoka(su)			su(ku)	好	104
	醜	1527			総	697		唆	1846		透	1685
	集	436			荘	1327	soto	外	83	suku(nai)	少	144
	襲	1575			草	249	SOTSU	卒	787	suku(u)	救	725
SHUKU	粛	1695			葬	812		率	788	su(masu)	済	549
	叔	1667			藻	1657	so(u)	沿	1607		澄	1334
	宿	179			装	1328		添	1433	su(mau)	住	156
	淑	1668			贈	1364	SU	主	155	sumi	炭	1344
	縮	1110			走	429		子	103		隅	1640
	祝	851			送	441		守	490		墨	1705
SHUN	俊	1845			遭	1643		数	225	sumi(yaka)	速	502
	春	460			霜	948		素	271	su(mu)	住	156
	瞬	1732			騒	875	su	州	195		済	549
SHUTSU	出	53	soda(teru)	育	246		巣	1538		澄	1334
SO	塑	1838	soda(tsu)	育	246		酢	1867	SUN	寸	1894
	想	147	so(eru)	添	1433	SŪ	崇	1424	suna	砂	1151
	措	1200	soko	底	562		数	225	su(reru)	擦	1519
	疎	1514	soko(nau)	損	350		枢	1023	su(ru)	刷	1044
	礎	1515	soko(neru)	損	350	sube(ru)	滑	1267		擦	1519
	祖	622	SOKU	束	501	su(beru)	統	830	surudo(i)	鋭	1371
	租	1083		促	1557	sude(ni)	既	1458	susu(meru)	勧	1051
	粗	1084		側	609	sue	末	305		薦	1631
	素	271		測	610	su(eru)	据	1832		進	437
	組	418		息	1242	sugata	姿	929	susu(mu)	進	437
	訴	1402		即	463	sugi	杉	1872	suta(reru)	廃	961

	鉄	312		踏	1559		共	196	tsudo(u)	集	436

tsumu(gu)	紡	1859				uruwa(shii)	麗	1630	wa(katsu)	分	38
tsuna	綱	1609	ugo(kasu)	動	231	ushi	牛	281	wake	訳	594
tsune	常	497	ugo(ku)	動	231	ushina(u)	失	311	wa(keru)	分	38
tsuno	角	473	u(i)	憂	1032	ushi(ro)	後	48	WAKU	惑	969
tsuno(ru)	募	1430	ui	初	679	usu(i)	薄	1449	wa(ku)	沸	1792
tsura	面	274	uji	氏	566	usu(maru)	薄	1449	WAN	湾	670
tsura(naru)	連	440	u(kaberu)	浮	938	usu(meru)	薄	1449		腕	1299
tsura(neru)	連	440	u(kabu)	浮	938	usu(ragu)	薄	1449	warabe	童	410
tsuranu(ku)	貫	914	ukaga(u)	伺	1761	usu(reru)	薄	1449	wara(u)	笑	1235
tsu(reru)	連	440	u(kareru)	浮	938	uta	歌	392	ware	我	1302
tsuru	弦	1226	u(karu)	受	260	utaga(u)	疑	1516	wa(reru)	割	519
tsu(ru)	釣	1862	u(keru)	受	260	utai	謡	1647	wari	割	519
tsurugi	剣	879		請	661	uta(u)	歌	392	wa(ru)	割	519
tsuta(eru)	伝	434	uketamawa(ru)				謡	1647	waru(i)	悪	304
tsuta(u)	伝	434		承	942	uto(i)	疎	1514	wasu(reru)	忘	1374
tsuta(waru)	伝	434	u(ku)	浮	938	uto(mu)	疎	1514	wata	綿	1191
tsuto(maru)	勤	559	uma	馬	283	u(tsu)	打	1020	watakushi	私	125
tsuto(meru)	努	1595	u(mareru)	生	44		撃	1016	wata(ru)	渡	378
	勤	559		産	278		討	1018	wata(su)	渡	378
	務	235	u(maru)	埋	1826	utsuku(shii)			waza	業	279
tsutsu	筒	1472	ume	梅	1734		美	401		技	871
tsutsumi	堤	1592	u(meru)	埋	1826	utsu(ru)	写	540	wazawa(i)	災	1335
tsutsu(mu)	包	804	umi	海	117		映	352	wazura(u)	患	1315
tsutsushi(mu)			u(moreru)	埋	1826		移	1121		煩	1849
	慎	1785	u(mu)	生	44	utsu(su)	写	540	wazura(wasu)		
	謹	1247		産	278		映	352		煩	1849
tsuyo(i)	強	217	UN	運	439		移	1121			
tsuyo(maru)				雲	636	utsuwa	器	527	—Y—		
	強	217	unaga(su)	促	1557	utta(eru)	訴	1402	YA	夜	471
tsuyo(meru)	強	217	uo	魚	290	uwa-	上	32		野	236
tsuyu	露	951	ura	裏	273	u(waru)	植	424	ya	八	10
tsuzu(keru)	続	243		浦	1442	uyama(u)	敬	705		屋	167
tsuzu(ku)	続	243	ura(meshii)	恨	1755	uyauya(shii)				矢	213
tsuzumi	鼓	1147	ura(mu)	恨	1755		恭	1434		家	165
			urana(u)	占	1706	uzu	渦	1810	yabu(reru)	破	665
—U—			ure(eru)	憂	1032					敗	511
U	右	76	ure(i)	憂	1032	—W—			yabu(ru)	破	665
	宇	990		愁	1601	WA	和	124	yado	宿	179
	羽	590	ure(ru)	売	239		話	238	yado(ru)	宿	179
	有	265	u(reru)	熟	687	wa	我	1302	yado(su)	宿	179
	雨	30		売	239		輪	1164	ya(keru)	焼	920
uba(u)	奪	1310	u(ru)	得	374	WAI	賄	1739	YAKU	益	716
ubu	産	278	uru(mu)	潤	1203	waka(i)	若	544		厄	1341
uchi	内	84	uruo(su)	潤	1203	wa(kareru)	分	38		役	375
ude	腕	1299	uruo(u)	潤	1203	waka(reru)	別	267		疫	1319
ue	上	32	urushi	漆	1546	wa(karu)	分	38		約	211
u(eru)	植	424				wa(kasu)	沸	1792		薬	359

— Z —

——————— SUPPLEMENT ———————

The 45 characters which follow, together with the 1,900 characters in the main Kanji List, constitute the 1,945 basic Jōyō Kanji (Characters for Daily Use) recommended by the Japanese Language Council in 1981. The sequence of these 45 characters and the arrangement of the entries follow those in the Kanji List, except that here the stroke count is indicated by the number at the lower right-hand corner of the large character in brush form. The 45 kanji are indexed on page 392.

	1901	*se*, (unit of area, about 1 are); *une*, ridge (between furrows); rib (in fabric)
畝 *10*	8 311	
	畝	畝 間　　*unema*　space between ridges, furrow　　43 畝 織　　*uneori*　rep, ribbed fabric　　680
	1902	*monme*, (unit of weight, about 3.75 g)
匁 *4*	4 159	
	匁	
	1903	SHAKU, (unit of volume, about 18 ml)
勺 *3*	20 740	
	勺	

	1904	SUI, *tsumu*, spindle	
錘	167	紡錘　　*bōsui*　spindle	1859
	4872	錘状　　*suijō*　spindle-shaped	626
16	錘		

	1905	SEN, pig iron	
銑	167	銑鉄　　*sentetsu*　pig iron	312
	4850		
14	銑		

	1906	SAN, crosspiece, frame, bolt (of a door)	
桟	75	桟橋　　*sanbashi*　wharf, jetty	597
	2252	*sankyō*　wharf; bridge	
		桟道　　*sandō*　plank bridge	149
10	桟		

	1907	*waku*, frame, framework; limit, confines	
枠	75	窓枠　　*madowaku*　window frame	698
	2205	枠内　　*wakunai*　within the limits	84
		枠組　　*wakugumi*　frame, framework; framing	418
8	枠		

	1908	*tana*, shelf	
棚	75	本棚　　*hondana*　bookshelf	25
	2300	戸棚　　*todana*　cupboard	152
		棚上げ　　*tanaage*　put on the shelf, shelve	32
		大陸棚　　*tairikudana*　continental shelf	26, 647
12	棚	棚卸　　*tanaoroshi*　inventory, stock taking	707

	1909	*imo*, potato	
芋	140	じゃが芋　*jagaimo*　(white) potato	
	3896	焼き芋　*yakiimo*　baked sweet potato	920
		里芋　　*satoimo*　taro	142
6	芋	芋掘り　*imohori*　digging sweet potatoes	1803

	1910	SHIN, *takigi*, firewood	
薪	140	薪水　　*shinsui*　firewood and water	21
	4069	薪炭　　*shintan*　firewood and charcoal, fuel	1344
16	薪		

繭 18	1911 140 4087 繭	**KEN**, *mayu*, cocoon
		繭糸 *kenshi* cocoon and (silk) thread; silk thread 242
		繭玉 *mayudama* (type of New Year's decoration) 295

壞 16	1912 32 1143 壞	**JŌ**, soil
		土壤 *dojō* soil 24

堪 12	1913 32 1112 堪	**KAN**, *ta(eru)*, endure
		堪忍 *kannin* patience, forbearance; forgiveness 1414
		堪弁 *kanben* pardon, forgive 711
		堪え忍ぶ *taeshinobu* bear patiently 1414
		堪えかねる *taekaneru* cannot bear

抹 8	1914 64 1870 抹	**MATSU**, erase, expunge
		抹殺 *massatsu* expunge; deny; ignore 576
		抹消 *masshō* erase, cross out 845
		一抹 *ichimatsu* a tinge of 2

搭 12	1915 64 1959 塔	**TŌ**, ride
		搭乗 *tōjō* board, get on 523
		搭乗券 *tōjōken* boarding pass 523, 506
		搭載 *tōsai* load, embark 1124

拐 8	1916 64 1865 拐	**KAI**, kidnap
		誘拐 *yūkai* kidnap 1684
		拐帯 *kaitai* abscond with money 963

嗣 13	1917 30 969 嗣	**SHI**, heir
		嗣子 *shishi* heir 103
		後嗣 *kōshi* heir 48

嚇 17 嚇	1918 30 1008	KAKU, threat 威嚇　*ikaku*　threat, menace	1339
喝 11 喝	1919 30 953	KATSU, scold 恐喝　*kyōkatsu*　threaten, blackmail 喝破　*kappa*　declare, proclaim	1602 665
謁 15 謁	1920 149 4382	ETSU, audience (with someone) 謁見　*ekken*　have an audience (with) 拝謁　*haietsu*　have an audience (with) 謁する　*essuru*　have an audience (with)	63 1201
朕 10 朕	1921 130 3757	CHIN, (imperial) we	
脹 12 脹	1922 130 3782	CHŌ, swell 膨脹　*bōchō*　expansion	1145
爵 17 爵	1923 87 2830	SHAKU, peerage, court rank 男爵　*danshaku*　baron 公爵　*kōshaku*　prince, duke 伯爵　*hakushaku*　count, earl 爵位　*shakui*　peerage, court rank 授爵　*jushaku*　elevate to the peerage, create a peer	101 126 1176 122 602
侯 9 侯	1924 9 443	KŌ, marquis 王侯　*ōkō*　royalty 諸侯　*shokō*　feudal lords 侯爵　*kōshaku*　marquis	294 861 1923

矯 17 矯	1925 111 3175	KYŌ, *ta(meru)*, straighten; correct
		矯正　*kyōsei*　correct, reform　275
		矯激　*kyōgeki*　radical, extreme　1017
		奇矯　*kikyō*　eccentric conduct　1360
		矯め直す *tamenaosu*　set up again, correct, reform, cure　423
且 5 且	1926 1 23	*ka(tsu)*, and
		且つ又 *katsumata*　and　1593
但 7 但	1927 9 394	*tada(shi)*, but, however, provided
		但し書き *tadashigaki*　proviso　131
偵 11 偵	1928 9 502	TEI, spy
		探偵　*tantei*　detective　535
		探偵小説 *tantei shōsetsu*　detective story, whodunit　535, 27, 400
		探察　*teisatsu*　reconnaissance　619
		内偵　*naitei*　scouting; private inquiry　84
曹 11 曹	1929 72 2134	SŌ, friend
		法曹　*hōsō*　the legal profession; lawyer　123
		法曹界 *hōsōkai*　legal circles, the bench and bar　123, 454
翁 10 翁	1930 12 596	Ō, old man
		老翁　*rōō*　old man　543
婆 11 婆	1931 38 1234	BA, old woman
		老婆　*rōba*　old woman　543
		産婆　*sanba*　midwife　278
		お転婆 *otenba*　tomboy　433
		塔婆　*tōba*　wooden grave tablet　1840

	1932	CHAKU, legitimate	
嫡 14	38 1253 嫡	嫡(出)子 *chaku(shutsu)shi* legitimate child 嫡嗣 *chakushi* legitimate heir 嫡流 *chakuryū* lineage of the eldest son 嫡男 *chakunan* eldest son, heir, legitimate son 嫡孫 *chakuson* eldest son of one's son and heir	53, 103 1917 247 101 910
奴 5	1933 38 1186 奴	DO, servant, slave, fellow 守銭奴 *shusendo* miser 農奴 *nōdo* serf 売国奴 *baikokudo* traitor	490, 648 369 239, 40
隷 16	1934 171 5026 隷	REI, servant 奴隷 *dorei* slave 隷従 *reijū* slavery 隷属 *reizoku* be subordinate (to) 隷書 *reisho* (ancient squared style of kanji)	1933 1482 1637 131
帥 9	1935 2 109 帥	SUI, leading troops 元帥 *gensui* field marshal 総帥 *sōsui* commander in chief 統帥 *tōsui* supreme/high command	137 697 830
屯 4	1936 5 264 屯	TON, barracks 駐屯 *chūton* be stationed 駐屯地 *chūtonchi* military post	599 599, 118
逓 10	1937 162 4695 逓	TEI, in turn; send 逓信 *teishin* communications 逓送 *teisō* convey, send by mail, forward 逓減 *teigen* successive diminution 逓増 *teizō* gradual increase	157 441 715 712
遵 15	1938 162 4742 遵	JUN, follow, obey 遵守 *junshu* obey, comply with 遵奉 *junpō* observe, adhere to, abide by 遵法 *junpō* law abiding; work-to-rule (tactics)	490 1541 123

劾 8	1939 19 721 劾	GAI, criminal investigation
		弾劾　*dangai*　impeachment　　　　1539

殴 8	1940 79 2451 殴	Ō, *nagu(ru)*, beat, hit, strike
		殴打　*ōda*　assault (and battery)　　1020
		殴り殺す *nagurikorosu* beat to death, strike dead　576
		殴り付ける *naguritsukeru* strike, beat, thrash　192
		殴り込み *nagurikomi* an attack, raid　776
		ぶん殴る *bunnaguru* give a good whaling/thrashing

虞 13	1941 141 4110 虞	*osore*, fear, danger, risk

痘 12	1942 104 3053 痘	TŌ, smallpox
		種痘　*shutō*　vaccination　　　　228
		痘苗　*tōbyō*　vaccine　　　　　1468
		天然痘 *tennentō* smallpox　141, 651
		水痘　*suitō*　chickenpox　　　　21

陪 11	1943 170 5002 陪	BAI, follow, accompany, attend on
		陪審　*baishin*　jury　　　　　1383
		陪席　*baiseki*　sitting as an associate (judge)　379
		陪食　*baishoku*　dining with a superior　322

濫 18	1944 85 2724 濫	RAN, overflow
		濫用　*ranyō*　abuse, misuse, misappropriation　107
		濫費　*ranpi*　waste, extravagance　749
		濫作　*ransaku*　overproduction　360
		濫伐　*ranbatsu*　reckless deforestation　1509
		濫獲　*rankaku*　overfishing, overhunting　1313

畔 10	1945 102 3002 畔	HAN, rice-paddy ridge, levee
		湖畔　*kohan*　lakeshore　　　　467
		河畔　*kahan*　riverside　　　　389

Table 12. THE 214 HISTORICAL RADICALS
(arranged by stroke count)

1	一	丨	丶	丶	丿	㇏	一	乙	乚	乚	亅
	1	2	(2)	3	4	(4)	(4)	5	(5)	(5)	6

2	二	亠	人	亻	𠆢	儿	入	八	⺉	丷	冂	刀
	7	8	9	(9)	(9)	10	11	12	(12)	(12)	13	(13)

冖	冫	几	凵	刀	刂	力	勹	匕	匚	匚	匸	十
14	15	16	17	18	(18)	19	20	21	22	(22)	23	24

十	卄	卜	卜	卜	卩	厂	厶	又	辶	阝	阝
(24)	(24)	25	(25)	(25)	26	27	28	29	(162)	(163)	(170)

3	口	囗	土	士	土	士	夂	夂	夊	夕	大	六
	30	31	32	(32)	(32)	33	34	(34)	35	36	37	(37)

女	子	宀	寸	小	⺌	尢	尸	屮	山	川	巛	工
38	39	40	41	42	(42)	43	44	45	46	47	(47)	48

己	巾	干	幺	广	廴	廾	弋	弓	ヨ	⺕	彡	彳
49	50	51	52	53	54	55	56	57	58	(58)	59	60

忄	扌	氵	爿	犭	⺿	辶	阝	阝
(61)	(64)	(85)	(90)	(94)	(140)	(162)	(163)	(170)

4	心	小	忄	戈	戈	戶	戶	手	扌	支	攴	攵
	61	(61)	(61)	62	(62)	63	(63)	64	(64)	65	66	(66)

文	斗	斤	方	无	旡	日	曰	月	木	欠	止	歹
67	68	69	70	71	(71)	72	73	74	75	76	77	78

歹	殳	毋	母	比	毛	氏	气	水	氵	米	火	灬
(78)	79	80	(80)	81	82	83	84	85	(85)	(85)	86	(86)

爪	爫	父	爻	爿	丬	片	牙	牛	牜	犬	犭	王
87	(87)	88	89	90	(90)	91	92	93	(93)	94	(94)	(96)

疋	礻	内	耂	月	⺾
(103)	(113)	(114)	(125)	(130)	(140)

5	无	母	比	水	牙	玄	玉	王	瓜	瓦	甘	生
	(71)	(80)	(81)	(85)	(92)	95	96	(96)	97	98	99	100

用	田	疋	疋	疒	癶	白	皮	皿	目	矛	矢	石
101	102	103	(103)	104	105	106	107	108	109	110	111	112